Mindfulness Giving

This accessible book offers a unique, evidence-based perspective on the art and science of giving. It combines concepts from psychology, neuroscience, and social science theory with stories from interviewees on their experiences as a giver and receiver.

This book offers a holistic overview of the reciprocal aspects of giving, strategies for selecting a recipient of a gift in a never-ending sea of need, and a guide to developing one's personal philosophy, boundary, and plan on giving. As people seek to reconnect and find meaning, this book offers a venue for exploration. Covering topics such as empowering children to give, the financial considerations of giving, compassion fatigue, and how to set healthy boundaries, this book helps readers think about unique ways of giving. Through the use of action plans and worksheets, readers are encouraged to consider their own place in giving, empower themselves as a change agent, and recognize the positive social power and ripple effect of giving.

Mindfulness Giving is valuable reading for students of positive psychology, social and health psychology, social work, and sociology, as well as professionals and coaches working in self-improvement and self-care.

Maria Cuddy-Casey, PhD, has always had a passion for serving the community and chose a field in psychology to help others. She is a licensed clinical psychologist and professor at Immaculata University where she has taught for over 25 years. Her clinical work focuses on children through to young adults, and she specializes in underserved populations.

Mindfulness Giving
Harnessing the Art and Science of Positive Psychology

Maria Cuddy-Casey PhD

NEW YORK AND LONDON

Designed cover image: Svetlana Krivenceva via Getty Images

First published 2025
by Routledge
605 Third Avenue, New York, NY 10158

and by Routledge
4 Park Square, Milton Park, Abingdon, Oxon, OX14 4RN

Routledge is an imprint of the Taylor & Francis Group, an informa business

© 2025 Maria Cuddy-Casey

The right of Maria Cuddy-Casey to be identified as author of this work
has been asserted in accordance with sections 77 and 78 of the Copyright,
Designs and Patents Act 1988.

All rights reserved. No part of this book may be reprinted or reproduced
or utilised in any form or by any electronic, mechanical, or other means,
now known or hereafter invented, including photocopying and recording,
or in any information storage or retrieval system, without permission in
writing from the publishers.

Trademark notice: Product or corporate names may be trademarks or
registered trademarks, and are used only for identification and explanation
without intent to infringe.

ISBN: 978-1-032-57215-4 (hbk)
ISBN: 978-1-032-57214-7 (pbk)
ISBN: 978-1-003-43835-9 (ebk)

DOI: 10.4324/9781003438359

Typeset in Galliard
by codeMantra

Contents

Acknowledgments		*xi*
Preface		*xiii*

1 Introduction and Giving Defined   1
Introduction: Purpose and Approach 1
Giving Defined 5
Terms 5
Learning about Giving 10

2 Theories on Why We Give   22
Introduction 22
Biological Theory: Evolution Theory 22
  Darwin's Survival of the Fittest 22
Individual Growth and Wellness: Humanistic
  Theories 24
  Maslow's Hierarchy of Needs 25
  Erik Erickson's Psychosocial Development 27
  Positive Psychology 29
  Health Psychology: Mindfulness Theory 33
Environment: Behavioral Theories 39
  Skinner's Operant Conditioning 39
  Pavlov's Classical Conditioning 41
  Social Learning Theory 42
Human Tendencies: Social Psychology 45
  Norm of Reciprocity 46
  Social Exchange Theory 48

vi *Contents*

3 Who, What, Where, How, and Why to Giving   55
Introduction 55
How Much We Give: Global Statistics 56
Motivation for Giving 58
Who to Give To? 67
What to Give? 72
   1. The NICU Helping Hands
      Angel Gown®Program: https://
      nicuhelpinghands.org/programs/
      angel-gown-program/ 76
   2. Emma and Evan Foundation: https://
      www.evefoundation.org/angel-gowns 77
   3. Sweet Grace Ministries: https://
      sweetgraceministries.com/ 78
Where to Give? 87
How to Give 88

**4 Evaluating Where We Give: Nonprofit
Organizations**   101
Introduction 101
Rehearsed or Fake Viral Clips 101
*Crowdfunding: Giving through Online
   Platforms 103*
What Are Nonprofit Organizations? 107
How to Evaluate Nonprofit Organizations 108
Giving to the Church 126

5 Benefits to Giving   132
Introduction 132
Benefits to the Receiver 132
Benefits to the Giver 137
   Psychological Benefits to the Giver 138
    Negative Psychological Effects to Giving 142
Neurobiological Benefits to the Giver 144

Contents vii

6 Gratitude and Being a Recipient 153
Introduction 153
What Is Gratitude? 154
Is It Better to Give or Receive? 156
Benefits to Gratitude 157
Showing Gratitude 159
Barriers to Gratitude 160
Ways to Cultivate Gratitude 164
  Session One 169
  Session Two 169
  Session Three 169
  Session Four 170
  Session Five 170
Influencing Gratitude in Children 173

7 Ill Effects of Giving and the Need for Creating Boundaries 180
Introduction 180
Ill Effects of Giving 181
  Negative Experiences with Giving 181
  Burnout, Secondary Trauma, Compassion
    Fatigue, and Giving Fatigue 195
Creating Boundaries 211
  How Have You Already Given? 211
  Review Your Entries Above and Answer the
    Following Questions to Extract Possible
    Themes: 213
  Lessons Learned 214
  What Are Boundaries? 214
  Why Are Boundaries Important to Set and
    Maintain? 218
  Setting Boundaries 220
  Setting Boundaries/Budget for Giving 225
  Mindfulness Theory Analysis 231

viii *Contents*

8 Developing Your Plan/Creating a Ripple: What Will Be Your Story? 239

Introduction 239
Exploring and Setting Your Intention 239
Who to Give To? 241
What to Give? 243
Where to Give? 245
When to Give? 246
How to Give? 246
Goal: Set an Intention 250
Create a Giving Plan 250
Ripple Effect 252
Creating a Legacy 256
    Giving to Heal and in Remembrance 256
    Create Your Own Legacy 261

9 Empowering Children in Their Giving 271

Introduction 271
Brief Overview of Child Development 271
Research on Children and Giving 272
    Influences on Children's Giving 276
    Children's Happiness in Giving 277
Research on Adolescents and Giving 279
Children's Influence on Parents 281
Teaching Giving through Stories 282
Ideas to Cultivate Giving in Children and Their Families 285
Give Items In-Kind 286
Collections 289
Volunteering Time 290
Mindful Consumerism 293
Give Social Support 293

Contents ix

**10 Cultivating Giving: Ideas for Advancement
Personnel and Those That Fundraise** 298
Introduction 298
Theory and Research on Social Influences
  Affecting Fundraising 298
  Mental Budget 300
  What Is Important to the Donor? 302
  Donor Demographics 304
  Words Matter! 307
  Inspiring Donors/Dial Up Giving and
    Preventing Donor Fatigue 311
  Balancing Donor Retention with Donor
    Fatigue 313
  The Power of a "Thank You" 315

Index *325*

Acknowledgments

My deepest gratitude to the many people who have given me support and encouragement throughout this process. It is truly your beautiful example of giving that motivated me to create this writing. I am fortunate to be surrounded by family, friends, colleagues, and community members that value giving. You all make it easy for me to believe in the power of this loving act.

I am indebted to my interviewees for their willingness to take the time to share with us their experiences with giving. This was not an easy emotional process for them as they often recalled deeply moving memories. I too felt moved by their experiences. These interviewees trusted me with their stories and offered them to us for consideration as we journey through the material of this book. I am grateful for their rich material that really helped bring the material to life.

I owe special acknowledgment to my family. My parents and grandparents being my first models of giving behavior. I remember vivid examples throughout my childhood of their giving. My mother is the most giving person I know. I have seen her literally take a vest she was wearing off to give to someone that complimented it.

My children, now adults, offered encouragement and support. You two are always my motivation to contribute to a better world. To my husband, your support is beyond measure. As with everything I do in life, you are my pillar. I value your honest feedback and constant belief in me.

To the reader. I am grateful that you chose this book to read. That means you too are drawn to giving, and together we can continue to make positive change in this world. Never underestimate your positive influence!

Preface

Thank you for deciding to read my book on mindfulness giving. This book, while focused on theory, application, and research from positive psychology includes other theories as well. The material is conceptualized from the lens of social science, but also from my perspective as a psychologist, professor, parent, and community member. While these angles serve to provide a wide overview, the material is not all inclusive. Even though the material comes from the field of psychology and personal experiences from my interviewees, it is offered, no doubt, though my own filter, thereby creating a potential bias. Not all material will be viewed the same by all readers, and there will be material unintentionally left out. As an educated, upper middle-class, Caucasian, Christian, heterosexual American women, I have experiences and perspectives that are not necessarily shared by others. These perspectives may at times be from an advantage point, unintentionally influenced by my own privilege. While certainly not wealthy, I am fortunate to be able to budget time and money for giving. However, it is a core principle of this book that we all have something to give. The reader will find throughout these chapters, examples of free and minimal time commitment ways to give. We are all beautifully diverse, which further offers eclecticism with giving. You will likely think of unique need areas and ways to give depending on your own geographical region, culture, and experiences. I encourage you to reflect on your own views and ideas so that your giving is true to your boundaries and resources. Allow giving to be your own personal reflection, your gift to our collective community.

1 Introduction and Giving Defined

Introduction: Purpose and Approach

Giving has always been a significant part of who I am. I remember early childhood experiences shaping my empathetic nature, resulting in discovering giving as a method for tangibly making a difference in the lives of others. My 25 years as a clinical psychologist have been spent working and consulting in nonprofit organizations while overlapping with my academic role as a professor at a private university. Throughout my personal and professional life, I have been involved in fundraising campaigns, writing grants, and volunteering on numerous community service projects; all with the goal of making a difference in another's life. In preparation for this book, I interviewed people willing to share their perspectives and stories on giving. Teaching various theories and research to undergraduate and graduate students has also prepared me for this writing. My teaching style is to ground theoretical concepts and scientific research with pertinent applications. I believe giving is our most relevant application to the expression of humanity. This book, therefore, is designed as a series of academic lectures on the topic of giving, grounded in theory, research, and stories. The writing is applied in that the reader is encouraged to think about the concepts and work through them to hone their view on giving.

While my personal experiences and professional expertise on human emotion and behavior afford me a unique perspective on giving, I in no way want to replace the many other resources on this topic. Instead, I encourage the reader to expand their reading across the vast topics found in other sources such as stories from large donors, ways to select just the right gift, how to give efficiently, etc. This book, being different from others, serves to help

DOI: 10.4324/9781003438359-1

2 Introduction and Giving Defined

the reader become aware of the emotions and behaviors associated with giving (science), the effects of giving (well-being), and the development of boundaries around giving as well as creating a plan for giving (mindfulness). Giving involves a plethora of human elements, thereby the need for the overview of existing theories and research. Giving also requires awareness, boundaries, and planning, aspects applicable to the field of positive psychology. I cannot imagine being able to make this a comprehensive all-inclusive summary on giving. Instead, like any good lecture, I hope that this writing sparks interest and inquisitiveness so that the reader continues their research and thinking on this topic. I also hope to offer a healthy dose of scientific inquiry so that we can evaluate concepts for their efficacy. For these reasons, this book was written to aid the reader to be a more thoughtful and effective giver, to enable the reader to give with enhanced wellness through empowerment, planning, and choice, and to add a ripple of good in a world most needing.

Giving is the cornerstone of a community. When we give, we evidence a desire for a collective. Today, the need for giving and kindness is especially necessary to combat shared experiences such as loss and isolation from COVID-19, fluctuations in the economy, civil discord fueled by political divides, an abundancy of injustices and inequities, and the inclination for us to escape it all via technology. These events and avoidances move us farther and farther from interpersonal connectedness. Giving can serve as a method to tangibly bond with others; it is an indicator of humanity. Each act of giving is an opportunity to tangibly let others be "seen" and valued. It is also an opportunity for us to feel good in the process.

This book serves to highlight concepts from social science theory and positive psychology research as it pertains to giving while interspersing stories from interviewees on their experiences as a giver and receiver. Excerpts from interviews with people of various ages, locations, and backgrounds are woven throughout the book. Strategies for giving are also included along with a guide for the reader to develop personal boundaries around giving and a giving plan. The reader is encouraged to research needs and provided ways to differentiate among these needs. The goal is for the reader to consider their own place in giving, empower them as a change agent, and recognize the positive social power and rippling effects

Introduction and Giving Defined 3

of giving. This undertaking will provide the reader with the "art" and "science" of giving.

This book is designed with three distinct components, aimed at enhancing mindfulness to giving. The first section provides the science of giving by reviewing the existing knowledge from theory and research (Chapters 1–4), well-being as the effect of giving (Chapters 5 and 6), and mindfulness giving in creating a plan (Chapters 7–10).

1 Knowledge (Science): Positive psychology, biological science, and other psychological theories are reviewed. This first section of the book serves to summarize what is known about the who, what, where, why, and how of giving. Knowledge includes many aspects such as statistics on need and giving behaviors, ways to increase support for a cause, and stories of giving. Utilizing many areas of social science helps enhance the understanding of this multifaceted concept. While a variety of research and theory are covered, ultimately, the lens in which the material is offered is through that of positive psychology. This body of psychology strives to enhance well-being. Chapters devoted specially to the knowledge of giving are as follows:

   Chapter 1 Introduction: Purpose, approach, and terms defined.
   Chapter 2 Theories and research on why we give.
   Chapter 3 The who, what, where, and how of giving with stories from interviewees.
   Chapter 4 Evaluating where to give.

2 Effect (Well-being): Material in this section covers the benefits to giving and receiving; psychologically, emotionally, and neurochemically.

   Chapter 5 Benefits to the giver and receiver.
   Chapter 6 Gratitude and being a recipient.

3 Plan (Mindfulness): The final section of the book is devoted to theory, research, techniques, and examples for wellness and balance in being a giver. This material guides the reader in developing appropriate boundaries, developing a plan, creating a legacy, empowering children to be givers, and strategies for fundraising. True to positive psychological and mindfulness thinking, insight is an essential part to our decision making.

4 Introduction and Giving Defined

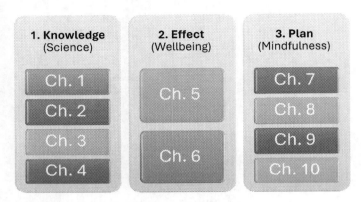

Figure 1.1 Chapter Organization.

With so many pressing needs in the world, a balanced approach will enable us to give without depletion. Having a plan on giving and awareness of the ill effects if boundaries are not created and maintained will enable the reader to make decisions consistent with their goals. Awareness of our giving involves our thoughts and feelings, both of which could make us act (or not act). Without careful mindfulness, our giving may become impulse and not congruent with our goals and available resources. Mindful giving is being aware of others but also thyself. Balance occurs when we are aware of the needs of the recipient but give in proportion to our own plan and resources. The need to create and maintain boundaries to giving, so that ill effects of giving are prevented, is achieved through prospective approaches.

Chapter 7 Creating boundaries to giving.
Chapter 8 Developing a plan for giving; creating a ripple.
Chapter 9 Empowering children as givers.
Chapter 10 Cultivating giving through development and fundraising.

Figure 1.1 provides a visual of the chapter organization of this book.

The intent of the book is to offer scientific and theoretical grounding to explain giving in hopes of helping people be mindful givers so that they may experience all the benefits and joy in

Introduction and Giving Defined 5

giving. Giving is often something done without much forethought and analysis. Many interviewees commented that they had never thought before about some of the questions posed. The intentions with this book were to make the giving process intentional and explicit. Knowing more about our patterns and motivations to give will likely lead to more satisfaction in the process and effectiveness.

Giving Defined

In this book, giving is referred to as sharing one's money, time, possessions, or expertise. Giving can be planned or spontaneous: random, targeted, and even anonymous. Although all forms of giving share underlying commonalities, giving to someone in need is the focus of this book as opposed to exchanging gifts during holidays.

As a psychologist, I see the driving forces to human behavior as being impacted by one's previous experiences and their current environment. These two forces are often covered separately in a variety of theories and research findings. Social learning theory emphasizes the impact of the environment on one's behavior whereas our current thoughts, feelings, and emotions are best viewed through the lens of positive psychology theory. Since our minds are directly influenced by our body and vice versa, an overview of neurobiological research is also warranted. These theories and their research findings will be reviewed throughout the book to support what is known about giving behavior. Chapter 2 provides a deeper dive into these various contributors.

The psychology of giving starts with awareness and empathy. How we were raised, what we were exposed to, and the role models we had, all impact our views on giving. Likewise, our actions can create a "ripple effect" in that we serve as a model to others. We will return to these concepts throughout the book. Chapter 1 provides an overview of terms used in giving as well as a broad overview of the many social influences on our giving.

Terms

When you think about the word "giving," what comes to mind? Major donors? Charity? A special gift you received? Giving can be

6 *Introduction and Giving Defined*

defined in many ways. We all have ideas, images, and recollections about giving, some positive and perhaps some negative. The word likely sparks a very personal association. I encourage you to dig deep into your experiences and formulate your own definition. Think for a moment of all the terms that came to your mind. Some may have included charity, donations, and philanthropy. "Charity" is often referred to as an act that fulfills an immediate need, whereas "philanthropy" is used to describe a long-term plan for giving. The word "donations" conjures up a variety of images and can consist of practically anything! Typically, when we think of the word "donation," we think monetary gifts, but there are also gifts of time, work, and "in-kind" consisting of items. As author Steve Goodier (1999) wrote: "The point is, none of us can ever run out of something worthwhile to give." If the word "giving" had a human face, it would likely be that of Mother Theresa. While she herself had little, she is well known for her lifetime devotion to serving the poor. Her compassion for all was perhaps the biggest gift she imparted to those she fed, nursed when sick, and served. In a biography about her, Kathryn Spink (2011) wrote that Mother Theresa was one of the greatest humanitarians of the 21st century.

Additional terms emerge when considering the concept of giving that warrant some discussion here. "Empathy" is an important concept as it involves putting oneself into the frame of reference of another; to be "in their shoes" so to speak. Empathy is a skill that can be honed and explicitly taught. Empathy involves thinking about another's circumstance (Lim & DeSteno, 2016). However, empathy alone does not spark action. Storytellers, song writers, and various other artists are likely to be rather empathic – able to put themselves in other's frame of reference to tell the story vividly and compellingly. It is why we feel the artist is speaking directly to or about us. Artists of this caliber often have a tremendous ability to think introspectively and abstractly about an experience they have not directly had. Through study and observation, they can understand one's frame of reference. Empathy enables us to be attuned with the world of others. As such, it is a necessary first step to giving – to be aware of the need. An example of empathy is when we see a homeless person and wonder how they are being fed, how they will be sheltered. Empathy is not sympathy but can certainly lead to one sympathizing for another. Sympathy is when one feels bad for another's situation; it results in feelings of pity.

Introduction and Giving Defined 7

Social science research shows that those that rate high in empathy give more than those rated less empathic (Aronson et al., 2023). C. Daniel Batson (1991) wrote specifically about empathy and its influence on giving in the "empathy-altruism hypothesis." This hypothesis states that when we observe someone in need and feel empathy, we are likely to help regardless of benefit to us, even with a cost involved. However, if we witness a need and do not feel empathy, we may still help if it is in our self-interest to do so, and some type of gain is to be had. One of the goals of this book is to increase awareness and empathy, and thereby action. Throughout the book, a plethora of needs are discussed. Usually, we learn the act of giving through observation (Bandura social learning theory, discussed in Chapter 2). But explicit teachings are especially valuable as some environments do not offer many models for giving. By teaching giving and empathy directly, people can readily recognize needs and the potential opportunities to give. Once honed, giving and empathy become fluid. Once insight to a need occurs and empathy is activated, one can be empowered to know what to do; give.

To act, one needs a sense of compassion (Lim & DeSteno, 2016). Compassion involves an emotional response aimed at reducing the suffering of another. It is something observed and usually learned with or without stated instruction. Observation is a powerful teacher, the core of social learning theory. Once one engages in an act of giving, they are further fueled by emotional and biochemical reinforcers (explored in Chapter 5). Our giving actions can become reinforced and serve as a model for others' behavior.

People who have experienced significant adversity in life have been shown to have high empathy which leads to compassion for others (Lim & DeSteno, 2016). It seems that people who have experienced hardship are made aware of the challenges that exist in life through their own experiences. They no longer have the "privilege" of being unaware. The word "privileged" is a term sorely misunderstood and even politicized. People get highly insulted at the mere suggestion that they have privilege. To clear the record for our purposes, "privilege" is a social science term used to describe a benefit one receives without having to earn it. It does not mean one does **not** deserve the benefit; it just means they did not have to prove their worthiness. A component of privilege is the

8   *Introduction and Giving Defined*

luxury of not having the awareness of a need, such as never having to worry about where one's next meal is coming from or how their family will be fed. Having security and safety in life allows many of us to not realize or to forget what it is like for others to not have the same resources and opportunities. Privilege has a strong association to the concept of giving; it can hinder one's awareness of need. Being aware of one's own privilege will increase empathy and awareness. To that end, think for a moment about an aspect of your life in which you are privileged. Do you have safe shelter and regular meals? Imagine the barriers that exist for those that do not have this same foundation. Understanding one's privilege is a prequel to empathy. Without it, we tend to think others have the same advantages, opportunities, and resources. Some of the resistance to giving is the idea that people should do for themselves. "God helps those that help themselves" is the phrase that echoes in our collective minds. Digging deeper, many think that giving is not necessary as the individual in need **should** do for themselves, "they should work harder… longer hours… have more jobs." Privilege is evident in this way of thinking as it assumes one is physically and mentally capable of working, that one has the transportation to commute to and from work, that one has safe and reliable childcare for their dependents, that the hourly pay rate is a livable rate, that one has the marketable skills, hope, and grit to navigate the job market. There is a time and place in which we all have a degree of privilege and a time and place in which we do not. Privilege can be bestowed on you due to your age, gender, race, role, etc. For example, consider how different people may be viewed differently by a salesperson while shopping for a car. There are biases and assumptions that make one customer appear better than another. Does the age of the customer hinder or help how they are viewed? As a middle aged, Caucasian mother/grandmother-looking woman in the United States, I have some assumed privilege. It is likely that I am viewed as a "viable" customer, assumed to be someone with a job, and credit history. These assumptions may be true or not true. But the likelihood that I will be served first and be deemed a preferred customer is an example of privilege. It is not something I earned or had to prove.

Now, consider driving down the road and you are stopped by a police officer. What are your initial thoughts? Mine are "What did I do wrong?", "Was I speeding?", "Did I run through a red traffic

Introduction and Giving Defined 9

light/stop sign?" Perhaps a bit further down my line of thinking, as a female, is... "Am I safe to stop?" For the most part in the United States, I have privilege given my age, gender, and ethnicity. This is not something I feel is fair and often protest; I speak out against my own privilege. While it limits my advantage (unearned anyway), I do so to create awareness and empathy. Now, consider an African American young adult male. What might his initial thoughts be? Note this experience is felt long before the interaction with the police officer begins. It is a life script that has been playing out for marginalized individuals, such as people of color in the United States, throughout their life. That young man has likely been told by his loved ones to keep his hands visible, preferably placing his hands on the steering wheel and to be respectful. His first thoughts are likely of fear as he does not have the privilege in the United States of the assumption that he would be perceived as innocent. Again, not fair by a long shot, but a reality. If you are struggling in reading this material or find yourself disputing it, I implore you to reflect on the privilege you do have and how others may not have the same. This process is very important in enhancing one's ability to be aware, to create empathy, to feel for others, and then to maybe act in a manner of kindness. There is a plethora of examples on the internet of everyday experiences of people without privilege being denied services, such as being followed around a store, and even charged more to purchase items. The television show *What Would You Do?* secretly records people's reactions to being placed in reality-based scenarios. There are episodes specific to people being privileged over another, witnessing others being treated unfairly. Often, most people do not get involved, a phenomenon known as "bystander effect." Privilege, our failure to explore our privilege, and our human tendency to not act, hinders our giving and negatively impacts our sense of community.

"Generosity" is a term echoed throughout these chapters. Rosalyn Diprose (2002) described generosity by emphasizing not the outcome, but the intent of the giver. The deliberation to make a difference for others using our resources and power is generous. Generosity is viewed as a method to advance society and involves a social interaction where the giver is open to the existence of others. Across the world, communities have generously given to others. In the United States, one source for tracking generosity is through *Giving USA* (https://givingusa.org/). Giving USA

10 Introduction and Giving Defined

is run by Indiana University through the Lilly Family School of Philanthropy. They have been reporting on philanthropic giving throughout the United States since 1956. They produce an annual report on the sources and uses of charitable giving in the United States. This is an enormous undertaking as givers comprise of approximately 53 million US households, 16 million corporations, over a million estates, and approximately 82,000 foundations. Recipients of gifts are also researched and include about 1.1 million charities and over 300,000 religious organizations. The most recent summary report indicated that giving had increased significantly in 2020 and 2021 but decreased in 2022 (https://philanthropy.iupui.edu/).

Generosity and altruism are often used interchangeably but do differ. For example, generosity is often used to describe a kind act, whereas altruism is an act of giving that comes at a cost to the giver.

Learning about Giving

Our earliest and most salient learning environment is our family. Early childhood experiences model social behaviors. This learning continues every day from the environments in which we live. Social learning theory, covered in the next chapter, maintains that we learn how to behave by observing others and copying them (Aronson et al., 2023). In addition to family influence, our environment provides a plethora of social learning models and messaging on giving. Social influences are all around us in various forms of media: social media, movies, music, art, etc. Social media hosts an abundance of giving campaigns and challenges, e.g., the ice bucket challenge promoting awareness and funds for Lou Gehrig's Disease (ALS), a progressive nervous system disease. Social media has become a place for posting personal pleas for giving such as the story of Carson King. While at a football game on September 19, 2019, he held up a sign requesting beer money with his Venmo details (https://www.cnn.com/2019/09/22/us/carson-king-busch-beer-venmo-trnd/index.html). The picture went viral and resulted in close to 3 million dollars being raised, including matching funds from Busch beer. After the initial flood of support came in totaling $1,600.00, King announced that he would give the donations to the Stead Family Children's Hospital, located just behind the sporting arena where he sat. These online

Introduction and Giving Defined 11

trends can create traction as the capacity for viewers is limitless! This phenomenon is known as "going viral"; the creation of a contagion effect. The challenge is figuring out **what** content creates this traction as the answers remain a bit of a scientific mystery. Certainly, celebrities and internet "influencers," by virtue of their popularity and following, have a tremendous amount of social capital. Other social influences, such as movies, can offer powerful examples of giving.

The Jimmy Lustig Family Foundation (https://jimmylustig. org/best-movies-about-philanthropy/) lists movies deemed inspirational for giving and gratitude. The list includes some of my very favorites like *The Blind Side*, *The Pursuit of Happiness*, and *Patch Adams*. *The Blind Side* starring Sandra Bullock and Tim McGraw is based on a true story about a wealthy Caucasian family who adopts a 17-year-old African American male from the projects (an impoverished housing community). The two protagonists, the adoptive mother (Leigh Anne Tuohy) and the oversized teen (Michael Oher), are opposites when it comes to their ethnicity, gender, age, and social economic status. As Leigh Anne aggressively ensures Michael's needs are met, the teen adds meaning to the family. The story depicts Michael receiving, for the first time, regular meals, clothing that fits and is weather-appropriate, a safe place to live and a family to love. News broke on August 14, 2023, that the subject of this real-life story, an NFL tackle, filed a lawsuit claiming that the Tuohy family never adopted him but instead had him sign conservator's papers giving them financial ownership over Michael. In September 2023, a judge overturned the conservatorship. Even with this court ruling, the true intent behind taking in this young man is not known as both sides have a different account. Ironically, the movie suggests that the family had an ulterior motive, to ensure that their Alabama Ole Miss football team would have a winning season. This example implores the question "Does having an ulterior motive diminish an act of giving?" Through a variety of concepts such as intention and boundaries, this question is explored throughout the book.

More recently, *A Man Called Otto* (Forster, 2022), starring the iconic Tom Hanks, is about an elderly man who loses his wife and will to live. A generous neighbor named Marisol befriends Otto. Marisol gives her time and love to Otto. She gives and gives, even as Otto rejects her attempts to connect. Eventually, Otto feels a

12   Introduction and Giving Defined

sense of belonging and newfound purpose in life, thanks to Marisol's grace. Marisol eventually wins Otto over with her kind persistence and delicious food. So not to ruin the ending for readers who have yet to see this "must-see" movie, more acts of giving are present, such as the quarter Otto carries with him because that was given to him by his wife when they first met. This coin was a token of the love they shared. The symbolism of his deceased wife is powerfully depicted as Otto carried the quarter in his pocket every day. He kept it secured at night in a ceramic bowl at bedside. Imagine a gift of a quarter having so much value! It is the symbolism that carries the worth of a gift. The meaning behind a gift is what many value far greater than the object itself.

What we view through media has a drastic impact on how we feel and our world view. Social learning theory maintains that we learn through models and exposure. We have a choice over these influences, so choose wisely! Fill up on influences that align with your purpose. Choose shows or movies that empower and uplift your sense of humanity.

One of my earliest examples of media addressing the area of giving was the 1993 classic movie by Rubin, *My Life*, starring Michael Keaton and Nicole Kidman. Spoiler alert: Keaton plays the role of a father who finds out that he has kidney cancer. Panicked that he will not live to rear his unborn son, he makes video-recorded messages of life lessons he wants to impart to his son. Through these videos, he teaches his son to shave and to drive. One of the messages he recorded was that of giving; he incites his son to "be generous." This scene resonated with me, even though I was not yet a parent. Periodically, I would think about that one line in the movie and would ask myself: "What life lessons would I want my children to receive?" Many come to mind; however, the main one would be to give. Give within boundaries; give to others when able; give to yourself. Perhaps this book is a reminder to my two adult children to continue to develop their generous hearts, but to do so with balance and mindfulness.

A more modern example of shows on giving is a series called *The Good Place*, created by Michael Schur. This comedy is about the main character, Eleanor (played by Kristen Bell), mistakenly accepted into a town that depicts heaven. Only she knows that she does not belong. Through episodes of light comedic plot, deep philosophical undertones on the topic of what is "good" and how

Introduction and Giving Defined 13

much good does one need to do to earn a place in heaven is unraveled. Watching an episode, one is likely to ponder thoughts, such as "Have I done enough to be considered 'good'?" "Have I earned a spot in heaven?" These questions, and more, are contemplated throughout our development. As we enter mid-adulthood, we tend to be driven for generativity. Generativity is the need to give back, to leave a legacy. Erik Erickson, a German American psychoanalyst, and well-known developmental theorist, proposed eight psychosocial "crises" we negotiate as we develop. This theory is discussed in more detail in Chapter 2. The goal is to not sail through these stages unscathed but to negotiate each stage with relative success. Each level is a continuum with healthy outcomes on one end and unhealthy on the other. If one successfully works through a stage, a virtue is acquired. The generativity stage occurs between the ages of 40 and 65 years. This seventh stage of development has generativity at one end of the continuum and stagnation at the other end. During this stage, adults strive to leave a legacy; to create something that outlasts themselves. Legacies can be seen in monetary gifts funding buildings in their name, but also in less tangible acts such as mentoring. Ideas for creating your own legacy are noted in Chapter 8.

As a professor and psychologist, I like to think that I have left an influence on my students and individuals I have treated in my therapy practice. As a mother, I hope that my legacy is solidified in the lives of both of my children, both of whom I know carry ideals, experiences, and views that I have helped shape. Yet another way in which my legacy is created and how I have explicitly been generative is to establish my planned giving through my will. These ideas and more regarding how to give and develop a plan for giving will be addressed in Chapter 8. But for further application of Erickson's generative versus stagnation stage, I offer an excerpt from an article I wrote regarding my planned giving to my local theater, *People's Light Theater* (*PLT*). In addition to being a regular donor, I am also a "legacy donor" in that I have included PLT in my will. To bring awareness to this valuable form of giving, I wrote the following:

Our family has been attending shows at PLT for well over 20 years. Leaving one show in particular, my then 10-year-old son stated: "I have so many good memories here." This

14 *Introduction and Giving Defined*

statement encapsulated the feeling for the entire family. As a parent, we always left PLT with the feeling that we just did something really enriching for our family. Through the magnificent set designs and the relevant plots, we have experienced the full range of emotions. The theater has allowed us to have a lived and shared experience both validating and hopeful. It is abundantly clear that we have always enjoyed the shows and have our favorites. But for PLT to be able to resonate with our children through these same story lines is quite special.

The environment at PLT is welcoming, extending to the outside community. The sharing of their talent to school programs, underserved communities, and adaptive performances are just a few examples of how PLT ensures that all are welcome, that all are part of the "story." My son, having dealt with bullying for years, found a safe and caring home at PLT. He enjoyed years of theater school and camps where he had exceptional instructors. These gifted instructors, like Aubie, Nadira, Susan, Teri, Wendy, and Tabitha, empowered their students to not only be who they are, but to express themselves through writing, movement, and acting! Our son was immersed in the art and the accepting culture, allowing him to be his authentic self. For this welcoming community to embrace our son and empower him as they have, they have earned our unwavering devotion and gratitude.

Our family is far from wealthy but felt compelled to support the "legacy" of PLT programming so that others can be enriched just as our family continues to be. The Legacy Circle allows us to select any amount or percentage of funds to leave to PLT in our Will, thereby allowing us to leave our "legacy" too. We chose to be part of the PLT Legacy Circle to show our gratitude to all that PLT has done for our family and the community. When we considered organizations to leave in our Will, we thought of organizations that have been truly influential in our lives, and PLT easily rose to the top of the list. I hope everyone reading this will consider supporting PLT in a similar way.

(PLT Donor Spotlight, Fall 2022)

My generative work is not finished; it is an area I continue to develop. How and when one fully realizes this stage is individually determined. When thinking about leaving a legacy, pondering if

Introduction and Giving Defined 15

we have done enough, it is easy for us to think of giving as meeting a quota. We may run the risk of thinking in terms of quantity over quality. I want to discourage that way of thinking and instead encourage you to develop your own philosophy and plan. These areas will be explicitly covered in Chapter 8. For now, as we focus on the topic of generativity, I can assure you that you will at some time be contemplating whether you have given enough. You will wonder if you did all you could, whether you have a legacy to leave, and if your life had meaning. I encourage you to not wait until your final years of life to ask these questions, leaving little time to act. Instead, ask these hard questions now and adjust accordingly. Part of this reflective analysis is to recognize what you have done, who you have helped, and when you have given. A balanced and fair assessment can be just the insight you need to successfully negotiate Erickson's eighth and final stage of development, integrity versus despair. It is during this stage, starting around age 65, that people look over their lives and are either satisfied with how they spent their time (integrity) or regretful (despair). Why wait until later years, seize the opportunity to frequently engage in a life review. I recommend reviewing yearly. I suggest using the promise of a new year to be a time of reflecting on one's legacy. Another option would be to conduct a life review on one's birthday. Regardless of when, be sure to establish a review on a regular basis.

Returning to media influences, the stories we read can vividly fulfill our need for human connection and offer experiences outside ourselves. A compelling book I came across a few years ago by Laura Schroff and Alex Tresniowski (2012) is *An Invisible Thread*. The book is based on a true story about a boy Laura met who was basically raising himself. His mother was addicted to drugs and was negligent. A relationship between Laura and the boy, Maurice, formed and many acts of giving unfolded. Perhaps the most poignant giving example was when Maurice asked Laura not for money to buy lunch at school but for her to pack him a brown bag lunch. At first, Laura did not realize the symbolism involved. Maurice explained that he always wanted to be like the kids in the lunchroom with brown bags for he saw them as the ones with someone at home that cared to see that they were fed. Sometimes a gift seems so small but has incredibly meaningful significance. I think about a gift I received from a fellow undergraduate back in my college days. She and I sat in the same spot of a large auditorium during

16   *Introduction and Giving Defined*

lecture hall and became friends. We would talk before class, never during it! We even got coffee after class once or twice. One day she handed me an oval stone pin and thanked me for being kind to her, for not judging her, as she shared with me stories of her struggles overcoming substance abuse. I had no idea until that moment how much our brief conversations meant to her. I viewed her as nothing but brave and always admired her grit in overcoming this obstacle while doing something rather hard – attending college. The symbolism in that pin is beyond words and a reminder for me to focus on the person, they are more than their struggles.

Another story on giving is a classic, *The Giving Tree*. This children's story is about an apple tree and a boy. The tree gives relentlessly to the boy, but as the boy ages, he spends less and less time with the tree. The boy eventually only goes to the tree to take. We will return to this story in Chapter 7 when we discuss setting boundaries to giving. This story is interpreted from many perspectives, some optimistically in that the tree is God giving with grace whereas others are more pessimistic interpreting the dynamic as parental selfless giving to an unappreciative child. How do you interpret this story? Has it shaped your views on giving?

A book by Peter Singer (2009) is on global giving to the poor, *The Life You Can Save*, is available as a free download at https://www.thelifeyoucansave.org/mp3-book-downloads/. The audiobook is narrated by a variety of celebrities such as Kristen Bell (yes, the actress in *The Good Place*, and many other works), Michael Schur (the creator of *The Good Place*), and Paul Simon to name a few. This resource offers an overview of the best charities fighting poverty across the world. Singer proclaimed that there is only so much money one needs to sustain their life, the rest should be given away.

Art and music also serve as powerful environmental influences. Poems encapsulate depth to our emotions; TED talks offer condensed views and research findings on generosity; and webinars offer a vast array of advice on whether to give or not to give. Art offers visual depictions of giving with beautiful depictions such as open and receiving hands. The theater offers live experiences. Songs are part of our social influence as well. A variety of genres have songs that speak in some fashion or another about giving. Some musical artists like Bono, Taylor Swift, and Dolly Parton capitalized on their popularity and fanbase, bringing awareness

Introduction and Giving Defined 17

to needs across the world or to those right next door. Taylor Swift's 2012 song, *Ronan*, was co-written by Maya Thompson, the mother who blogged the journey of her son's neuroblastoma treatment. Ronan died three days before his fourth birthday, after undergoing eight months of aggressive treatment. To honor Ronan's legacy, Swift donated the profits of the song to cancer charities. Some songs are directly about giving such as the classic 1984 Band Aid song *Do They Know Its Christmas?* This song is centered on the theme of the enormous suffering and need in Africia. The chilling line "Well tonight thank God it's them instead of you" is sung by many loudly and vehemently, perhaps without truly listening to the meaning. It is hard to disagree that we are grateful to not be the one struggling in destitute. If we "hear" these lyrics, would we be singing along or would we be taken aback by our guilt for survival... our privilege? As the song continues... "You ain't gotta feel guilt just selfless... Give a little help to the helpless." The choir urges listeners to "feed the world." Yes, we can have survivor's guilt when we become aware of need. This could be one reason people avoid breaking through their privileged mindset. It is certainly an uncomfortable feeling. It is so emotionally painful that people may try to avoid it at all cost.

The "Just World Hypothesis" (Aronson et al., 2023) is known in social psychology research as a human tendency for us to erroneously believe that people get what they deserve. This cognitive bias is rooted in our need to claim order in the world. Randomness and devastation strike our core of vulnerability. Image if we were consciously aware of the many horrible things that could happen to us at any given moment. We would be paralyzed with fear. Instead, we shake off news reports, acts of violence, environmental and human-made catastrophes, and even the poor and less advantaged by thinking that there must have been something that "they" did or did not do to put them in this situation. Therefore, their experience is "different than mine" and "I can have control over it happening to me." While at times, this may be logical, many times it is erroneous. It is a way for us to "get our head around" an overwhelming situation that we cannot control. We falsely impose control in a chaotic world. I offer here and throughout this book the idea that giving is something we can do to promote some level of control in the world. It is an act that can cause positive permutations beyond measure.

18   *Introduction and Giving Defined*

Think of the homeless as an example of how many view their existence. Imagine having no shelter; no idea when your next meal will be. Imagine not having a safe place to sleep. Perhaps family was once there for you, but you exhausted their generosity – maybe due to drug addiction or mental illness. There are many reasons people end up homeless. No one wakes up one day and says, "today is the day I will become addicted to drugs." What drives one individual to be more susceptible to becoming addicted over another involves many factors, including genetics, life experiences, coping mechanism, supports, etc. Given the "right" amount of these factors any one of us could be living a different life. Any one of us could be susceptible to addiction, homelessness, poverty, and crises. In my psychology classes, from social psychology to statistics, I tell my students that the human condition is multifaceted. Anyone that tells you they know the one reason for large-scale society concerns is thinking too linearly, they are missing the variety of factors that interplay in often complex ways to create such unfavorable conditions. Therefore, the solutions are not simplistic either. Change is dependent on attacking multiple variables, often at a systemic level.

An interviewee offered a story about coming upon a homeless man in a restaurant:

I went with my young daughters. The place was packed. A homeless man was there. He was filthy and was struggling to get his coat on. No one got up to help him. I got up and helped him with his jacket. I waited to go to the bathroom to wash my hands so I would not offend him.

In explaining the story, she added: "Sometimes when our bodies don't work as they used to, we all need a little help." Reading this excerpt, it is probably not surprising to read that no one initially came to this man's aid. Would this have been the case if the individual in the restaurant was not homeless? If the individual was an elderly man? How about an elderly woman? Notice how our biases come to light as we think about slight alterations in the scenarios. To work on being aware of biases, I encourage my students to change the pronoun or the descriptor of a person, then ask themselves if they would respond in the same way. I use this technique often to detect my own biases to help me act fairly and

Introduction and Giving Defined 19

consistently. Most importantly, is continual internal work toward humanistic thinking, seeing everyone as having value and purpose. The interviewee, noting that she wanted to wash her hands, withheld that urge to do so until the man could not see her go to the bathroom. This interviewee had thoughts and concerns about the cleanliness perhaps due to real or perceived threat yet waited so not to shame or embarrass the homeless man. That was an act of goodwill. The act of helping the man is a clear example of giving as the interviewee treated him with humanity, she "saw" him as a person. He was not invisible.

With all the many concepts and terms covered so far, I summarize giving as an act of humanity. It is something we say or do that lets another know that they matter, they are seen, and they have value. I maintain that giving to any degree betters society. I will add to this in later chapters to explain how giving can create positive ripple effects. Chapter 5 covers the benefits of giving. To the receiver, a gift can be life changing, but the positive effects do not end there. The giver experiences many positive results to their mental and physical health. With all the potential benefits to giving, one might think I am advocating for endless giving. This is not the case. Instead, I aim to increase awareness around giving and the variety of needs that exist. I encourage mindfulness giving through an individual lens and personally designed boundaries; topics that we cover later in this book.

Key Points

- The organization of the book has three distinct focal points: knowledge (science), effect (well-being), and plan (mindfulness).
- In this book, giving is referred to as sharing one's money, time, possessions, or expertise.
- Empathy, the ability to put oneself in another's circumstance is an important ingredient to giving.
- Our privilege may interfere with our ability to see need.
- Our environments such as movies, music, and literature shape our understanding of giving.
- There are theories and research to help us to understand how giving gets "dialed up" versus "dialed down."

20 *Introduction and Giving Defined*

- There are many concepts involved in giving. Social science has studied these concepts enabling a multifaceted understanding.
- We all have our own views, desires, and motivations for giving; the key is to gain insight to them.

Action Steps

- Stay tuned for the following chapters to help you gain insight into your own giving along with identifying and evaluating needs, developing a plan for giving, teaching others about mindful giving, and creating a legacy.
- Reflect on your thoughts about giving. This will help with the start of developing your boundaries to giving and plan for giving explored in Chapters 7 and 8.

References

Aronson, E., Wilson, T.D., Sommers, S.R., Page-Gould, E., & Lewis, N. (2023). *Social Psychology*, 11th edition. New York: Pearson.

Batson, C.D. (1991). *The Altruism Question: Toward a Social-Psychological Answer*. Hillsdale, NJ: Erlbaim.

CNN. (2019). A college football fan's sign asking for beer money raised more than $1 million. He's giving it to charity. https://www.cnn.com/2019/09/22/us/carson-king-busch-beer-venmo-trnd/index.html

Cuddy-Casey, M. (Fall 2022). Why we chose to include PLT in our estate plans through the Legacy Circle. PLT Donor Spotlight. People's Light Newsletter. https://tracking.wordfly.com/view?sid=MjQzXzIwNzk1XzI5MDMzXzY4NzE&utm_source=wordfly&utm_medium=email&utm_campaign=DonorInsightsFall2022&utm_content=version_A&uid=1790443&promo=105702

Diprose, R. (2002). *Corporeal Generosity: On Giving with Nietzsche, Merleau-Ponty, and Levinas*. New York: SUNY Press.

Forster, M. (Director) (2022). *A Man Called Otto* (Film). Sony Pictures.

Giving USA. What is *Giving USA*? https://givingusa.org/

Goodier, S. (1999). *One Minute Can Change a Life: Sixty-Second Readings of Hope and Encourage*, 2nd edition. Highlands Ranch, CO: Life Support System Pub, Inc.

Lim, D., & DeSteno, D. (2016). Suffering and compassion: The links among adverse life experiences, empathy, compassion, and prosocial behavior. *Emotion*, 16(2), 175–182. https://doi.org/10.1037/emo0000144

Introduction and Giving Defined **21**

Lustig, J. (February 17, 2023). Best Movies About Philanthropy. https://jimmylustig.org/best-movies-about-philanthropy/

Rubin, B.J. (Director) (1991). *My Life* (Film). Columbia Pictures, Capella Films.

Schroff, L. & Tresniowski, A. (2012). *An invisible thread: The true story of an 11-year-old Panhandler, a busy sales executive, and an unlikely meeting with destiny.* New York: Howard Books.

Singer, P. (2009). *The life you can save.* https://www.thelifeyoucansave.org/mp3-book-downloads/

Spink, K. (2011). *Mother Teresa: An Authorized Biography.* New York: HarperOne.

2 Theories on Why We Give

Introduction

A plethora of social science and biological science exists that lends support to our understanding of our human tendency to give. After careful review of the existing literature, the below theories have been selected for their connection to the human tendency to give (or not to give). The intent in this selection was to offer a biological perspective, an individual's growth and wellness perspective, models on environmental influences, and theories on human tendencies. These areas are summarized in Table 2.1 with the theories to be covered in this chapter identified.

Biological Theory: Evolution Theory

Evolution theory focuses on human behavior due to our animalistic and biological influences.

Darwin's Survival of the Fittest

Many know the saying "survival of the fittest." This concept is part of Darwin's evolution theory, identified in 1859 (Darwin, 1982/1871). According to Darwin, a British naturalist, traits that aid a species' survival get passed onto future generations, whereas traits that do not enable survival fade. This process is known as *natural selection*. Strong, adaptive traits evolve to benefit environmental changes. Traits that aid adaptation survive. Those that have the adapted traits are better equipped to survive; thereby "survival of the fittest." Genes, the process by which traits are genetically passed down, evolve increasing offsprings' changes of survival.

DOI: 10.4324/9781003438359-2

Theories on Why We Give 23

Table 2.1 Theories Pertaining to Giving

Dimension	Theoretical model	Specific theory
Biological	Evolution	• Darwin's Survival of the Fittest
Individual growth and wellness	Humanistic theories	• Maslow's Hierarchy of Needs • Erick Erickson's Psychosocial Development • Positive Psychology • Health Psychology: Mindfulness Theory
Environment	Behavioral theories	• Skinner's Operant Conditioning • Pavlov's Classical Conditioning • Bandura's Social Learning Theory
Human tendencies	Social psychology theories	• Norm of Reciprocity • Social Exchange Theory

The more resources and the more equipped species are, the more likely they are to survive. Physical strength, intellectual endowment, etc. are all considered the fittest and most desirable traits. Fit genes enable one to physically overpower or outsmart another, increasing one's odds of gaining access to resources and safety, making their survival more likely. In the animal world, we see this as we observe the "runt of the liter" struggle for a position at the mother's nipples. Stronger and more physically fit liter mates have the advantage of speed, strength, and power to secure their position first in the feeding frenzy. The weakest run the risk of becoming weaker if they are not able to secure regular nutrients. Natural selection is based on competing for resources; survival depends on it.

The concept of giving directly conflicts with Darwin's theory. If the competition comes down to obtaining valuable resources, why would anyone share? How then does giving exist? According to the logic posed by Darwin, "giving" would be considered a weak trait as it often involves the giver sacrificing some resource. If only the strong survive, giving would hinder one's ability to survive. Darwin struggled too with this notion, pondering how giving or any "prosocial behavior" (behavior intended to help others) would last across generations. Fortunately, further research and development in evolution theory has offered several explanations such as "*Kin Selection*" (Hamilton, 1964, as cited in Britannica Encyclopedia, 2018), "reciprocal altruism" (Trivers, 1971), and "indirect

24 *Theories on Why We Give*

reciprocity" (Summers & Crespi, 2013). Kin Selection maintains that behaviors, such as altruism, that help promote the continuation of one's genetic material are favored in natural selection. Quite simply, helping family members helps us maintain our genetic legacy. An example of altruism toward family members is when one donates an organ to a family member. Their love for their family member is motivation; however, there is likely an added motivation for the donor to aid in the continuation of their genetic pool. Many surmise that giving occurs to aid the survival of one's group. This is evident in family members and our striving to maintain our genetic pool. However, giving can be reciprocal in an informal understanding that if I help you, you will help me (reciprocal altruism). But when it comes to helping strangers, the desire to maintain our species may be the motivation. Helping a stranger is supported in evolution theory as it helps ensure the strength of the human species. *Altruistic punishment* is a term used to describe those who give consequence to others that are not kind as it impacts the species. *Indirect reciprocity* shows that we are more likely to help others when we see them as helpful. We are, therefore, motivated to be viewed as cooperative and giving. The social norm to be kind is enforced for the betterment of all. We, therefore, engage in prosocial behaviors to avoid being punished as not helpful. Anonymous giving reinforces our sense of unity in our collective survival.

Research has offered interesting and compelling evidence for the positive physical effects of giving, making it seem as though nature is reinforcing behavior. These findings are reviewed in Chapter 5 on the benefits to giving. These benefits create incentive for giving and suggest that we are prewired to give.

Individual Growth and Wellness: Humanistic Theories

Humanistic theories focus on human behavior of empowerment and growth. These theories consider other aspects of human being beyond pathology. Humanistic theories are growth-focused and strength-based. Abraham Maslow (1943), a Humanist, has been accredited as the first to use the phrase positive psychology

Theories on Why We Give 25

in his theories. Since then, a vast array of research and theory have mushroomed to form a science devoted to strengths and well-being. This science is known as positive psychology.

Maslow's Hierarchy of Needs

Abraham Maslow's (1943) classic hierarchy of needs theory conceptualized human motivation in levels. These levels were later depicted by others in a pyramid with basic needs for survival, such as food and shelter, at the base. As the levels get higher, more complex needs occur, such as "acceptance." According to Maslow, humans cannot achieve higher levels of motivation, such as self-actualization, unless earlier levels have been secured. Even though one may have stability in their levels of need, regression to a lower level can occur throughout life due to loss, natural disaster, crisis, etc. Initial levels are foundational to the point that without fulfillment, they become an area of hyperfocus. So, if an individual is stuck in crisis mode, they are likely to be hyper-focused on survival needs, making prosocial actions toward others not an area foremost in their minds. I have summarized these levels in Table 2.2 in the order of most basic to highest. Also included in the summary is an application of each level to giving.

Table 2.2 Maslow's Hierarchy of Needs as It Applies to Giving

Need level from most basic to highest order	Description/ examples	Application to giving
Physiological needs	Food, water, shelter, clothing	At this basic level of need, an individual is struggling for resources making it difficult for one to share what limited resources they have. Many still do, as their situation makes them aware of others with a similar plight. Limited resources may also make people hold tightly to them out of fear and need.

(*Continued*)

26 Theories on Why We Give

Table 2.2 (Continued)

Need level from most basic to highest order	Description/examples	Application to giving
Safety needs	Personal security, employment, resources, health	Stability and safety allow us to think outside our immediate needs. Without such stability, "tunnel vision" (seeing only what is in front of you) can occur.
Love and belonging	Sense of connection with others, friends, family, intimacy	Giving to those we love can be symbolic representation of love. We may also give with the intent to be better liked/loved (see Chapter 7 on boundaries). We tend to be more comfortable giving to people and organizations in which we feel a social/personal connection. It is also why many start foundations or support causes focused on needs affecting their loved ones.
Esteem	Self-regard, respect, status, independence	Previous research and literature discussed giving with the intent of increasing one's status. This form of giving can still have a positive effect. Giving can be empowering for the giver as it enables one to have an influence on a situation. This is especially important for children, who often feel helpless.
Self-actualization	Drive to be the most one can be. To be concerned for others beyond the self. Leaving a legacy knowing your presence made a difference	Often people at this level of motivation know they have fulfilled a purpose. Giving is a large part of this fulfillment. They often know ripples to their giving have occurred – even if not seen directly. Some examples of giving for this level include caring for someone at the end of their life, leaving a legacy gift to an organization in one's will, raising a child not biologically yours.

Theories on Why We Give 27

When thinking about giving, we likely process through where we are on this hierarchy, navigating between others' needs and our own. Someone at the lowest level in this hierarchy, striving for basic physiological needs like food, has less resources to give. Their anxiety and concern for their ability to have enough for themselves creates a tension in their ability to give. Even still, we know that people who are in this position may also be givers. Their empathy moves them to share what they have. One who is stable at these levels likely finds it less of a sacrifice to give.

An example of Maslow's hierarchy of needs in education is the need for children to have a safe place to learn and to receive proper nutrition. A hungry or scared child is not able to focus on higher order needs, such as academics when they are preoccupied with more basic needs. To decrease child malnutrition and increase children's ability to focus on academics, then President Truman in 1946 enacted the National School Lunch Act (NSLA) in schools across the United States. Fueled by Carl Perkins', then a Kentucky Congressman, two-year pilot study and pressure from civil right groups and women's groups, President Lyndon Johnson signed in the School Breakfast Program (SBP) in 1966. An area of substantial need that continues to this day is meals for these students during breaks from school when they cannot rely on having them provided by the school.

Maslow's theory speaks to the importance of stability in needs before we can progress to higher order aspirations.

Erik Erickson's Psychosocial Development

Even Erik Erickson's (cited in Rathus, 2019) developmental theory on psychosocial development mentioned earlier has roots in Humanistic psychology. This theory is also considered the early foundation for positive psychology as Erickson did not agree with the thinking of the time, mainly Freud's view that personality was determined by the age of five years. Instead, Erickson claimed that people develop their personality across their lifespan by navigating a series of eight stages. These stages were deemed to be universal and sequential, meaning that all people globally experience them in the order noted. As mentioned previously, the seventh stage (generativity versus stagnation) is especially applicable to the concept of giving. However, I have defined and analyzed all eight stages in Table 2.3 to demonstrate how this theory and the virtues to be acquired apply to giving.

28 *Theories on Why We Give*

Table 2.3 Erik Erickson's Stage of Psychosocial Development as They Apply to Giving

Approximate age	Psychosocial stage	Virtue	Application to giving
Infant to 18 months	Trust vs Mistrust	Hope	Infants gain understanding of reciprocal interactions: give and take. When their needs are met consistently and they are given care, trust is developed. Creating a sense of hope fuels expectation for good things in the future.
18 months to 3 years	Autonomy vs Shame/ Doubt	Will	Children in this stage are experimenting with doing things themselves. Empower them to impact others in a positive manner. Restricted from acting in an area they see as a need would likely result in feelings of shame/ doubt. (See Chapter 9 on empowering children as givers.)
3–5 years	Initiative vs Guilt	Purpose	Acknowledge a child's concern when they see needs and encourage them to come up with ideas for giving. (See Chapter 9 on empowering children as givers.)
5–13 years	Industry vs Inferiority	Competency	New skills are being acquired, support them with strategies and techniques that are effective for giving, such as tracking successes. (See Chapter 9 on empowering children as givers.)
13–21 years	Identity vs Confusion	Fidelity	Encourage the identification of themselves as a giver. Work on one's plan for giving starting with awareness of needs and one's passions. (See Chapter 8 on developing a plan.)

(Continued)

Theories on Why We Give **29**

Table 2.3 (Continued)

Approximate age	Psychosocial stage	Virtue	Application to giving
21–39 years	Intimacy vs Isolation	Love	Giving is a very tangible way of expressing love which builds intimacy. Thinking of others and being aware of their needs reduces self-absorption.
40–65 years	Generativity vs Stagnation	Care	Giving is a direct form of generativity. When we have insight into our giving, we increase our sense of generativity. Reflect on the many ways in which you give. If you fall short of your desire for giving, create a plan. (See Chapter 8 on developing a plan.)
65 and older	Integrity vs Despair	Wisdom	Integrity comes when one believes they have lived a purposeful life. When conducting a review of one's life, be sure to reflect on giving and the many ripples that have occurred from acts of giving.

Positive Psychology

Positive psychology is a branch of psychology focused on a purposeful life. It has come to be known as the science behind happiness; rooted in empowerment and flourishment. Maslow and other Humanistic theories are believed to be the early roots of positive psychology. The founding father, Martin Seligman, noted that happiness is best achieved by nurturing one's strengths and developing meaning and purpose in life (Seligman & Csikszentmihalyi, 2000). To have truly *Authentic Happiness*, according to Seligman (2002), one needs a pleasant life, a good life, and a meaningful life. Peterson et al. (2005) stated that the happiest people are those that focus on all three elements. Positive psychology is known to center on the tenets that the more one feels a sense of meaning in life,

30 *Theories on Why We Give*

the higher the sense of happiness, self-esteem, and psychological well-being. I have reviewed these elements in Table 2.4 and added my thoughts on how each would apply to giving.

Seligman (2012) added to his theory the PERMAs levels: positive emotions, engagement, relationships, meaning, and accomplishment. Positive emotion includes more than happiness, but

Table 2.4 Seligman's Elements of Authentic Happiness as It Applies to Giving

Elements for authentic happiness	*Defined*	*Application to giving*
The pleasant life	Includes everyday pleasures, such as spending time doing a hobby, taking a walk, enjoying a cup of coffee. Seligman notes that these everyday pleasures are short lived.	Small acts of kindness, e.g., leaving a positive note, paying for a stranger's coffee, can help one live a pleasant life.
The good life	Occurs when one's strengths are utilized to the point of "flow." Flow, a concept developed by Csikszentmihalyi in the 1970s, involves a state of absorption in a task that matches our skills. The task is challenging enough to engage our efforts and offers us satisfaction for the work we put into it. When we complete tasks that engage us to this level, we gain confidence and enrichment. Flow enriches us by giving us a sense of reward and fulfillment beyond wealth or material items.	Initiating a program or event to help a cause gives us challenge and fulfillment. Taking a challenge and working to solve the concern creates enrichment. Developing a program which utilizes one's strengths but also solicits the strengths of others engages flow.
The meaningful life	According to Seligman, we experience a meaningful life when we utilize our strengths for others.	Some examples include: volunteering time to help others; working for a nonprofit; careers in teaching and other areas of influence; donating at a scale of systemic impact; starting a nonprofit or other sustainable program; carrying out a plan for giving and legacy giving.

Theories on Why We Give 31

also hope, joy, compassion, to name a few. These emotions are best savored with an emphasis on flourishing for full expression. Engagement involves being in the present moment and getting lost in the stimulus to the point of absorption – flow. Positive relationships involve feeling love and support from others. Meaning consists of having purpose in life and grounding one's actions in values. Accomplishment is a sense one gains from working toward a goal, with intrinsic goals (internal growth) being more potent than external goals (tangible rewards) in the formation of well-being. Others have added to these five factors to include optimism, physical health, rest, and proper nutrition as additional ingredients to well-being. Research implications supporting this theory are provided in Chapter 5 covering the benefits to giving.

These theories beckon us to reflect on our degree of happiness. Is one area not as strong as another? In general, how is society doing with happiness? Fortunately, data is available to provide an answer. The 2023 World Happiness Report (https://worldhappiness.report/) is published by the Sustainable Development Solutions Network. Information is based on data from the Gallup World Poll. Noted on their website are many additional contributors reflecting the magnitude of this undertaking:

> ...the preparation of the *World Happiness Report* is at the Center for Sustainable Development at Columbia University, with research support from the Centre for Economic Performance at the London School of Economics; the Vancouver School of Economics at the University of British Columbia; the Wellbeing Research Centre at the University of Oxford; and the Helping and Happiness Lab at Simon Fraser University.

It is emphasized in this report that happiness should be the main marker of society's success. The data from the Gallup survey between 2006 and 2017 had approximately 1.4 million respondents from 161 countries. Life satisfaction, along with daily affect were key variables measured. Also measured was participants' involvement over the last month in donating money, volunteering, or helping strangers. As expected, results showed that life satisfaction and positive daily affect were positively correlated with generous acts. This means that those that reported higher satisfaction in life and were typically happier most days tended to give more than those that reported lower satisfaction and negative moods.

32 *Theories on Why We Give*

Regarding the 2023 worldwide rating of the happiest countries (https://worldhappiness.report/), the top and bottom 15 countries are noted in Table 2.5.

Looking ahead to Chapter 3, we see that four of the above happiest countries are listed in the top ten given countries. Highlighted in the World Happiness Report was the burst in charity giving, volunteering, and help provided around the world during the first year of COVID-19. This was a relative increase from the previous years. Generous acts were noted to have increased in 2022 worldwide by 25% compared to prior to the COVID-19 pandemic.

Also included in the report was an analysis of global language pertaining to happiness found on the online social media platform, *Twitter* (currently named *X*). This creative method for determining a dimension of expressed happiness was grounded in Seligman's five building blocks of wellness PERMAs: positive emotions, engagement, relationships, meaning, and accomplishment. This methodology offers some promise in measuring such a multifaceted concept like happiness.

Although positive psychology is typically defined as the science of happiness, the field of study includes a lot more, such as altruism, empathy, hope, satisfaction, grit, and resiliency, to name a few

Table 2.5 World Happiness Ranking 2023

Top 15	Lowest 15
1 Finland	123 Jordan
2 Denmark	124 Ethiopia
3 Iceland	125 Liberia
4 Israel	126 India
5 Netherlands	127 Madagascar
6 Sweden	128 Zambia
7 Norway	129 Tanzania
8 Switzerland	130 Comoros
9 Luxembourg	131 Malawi
10 New Zealand	132 Botswana
11 Austria	133 Democratic Republic of Congo
12 Australia	134 Zimbabwe
13 Canada	135 Sierra Leone
14 Ireland	136 Lebanon
15 United States	137 Afghanistan

Theories on Why We Give 33

(Seligman & Csikszentmihalyi, 2000; Seligman et al., 2005). Positive psychology theory continues to be a welcomed perspective as it differs from psychology's historical singular focus on pathology. The field continues to grow and has a variety of offshoots with other areas of science and applications to many disciplines, such as neuroscience, education, and business, to name a few.

Health Psychology: Mindfulness Theory

Health psychology is the study of the mind-body connection. As such, theorist and researchers in this area are interested in how one's psychology and behavior impact one's physical health and vice versa. They are also interested in the impact of the environment on our health and care. An example of a factor of influence is stress. Stress impacts one's physical and psychological functioning. The American Psychological Association (https://www.apa.org/topics/stress/body) identified the effects of stress on all systems of the body including the musculoskeletal, respiratory, cardiovascular, endocrine, gastrointestinal, nervous, and reproductive systems. Stress is a part of everyday life and in some dosages can be a necessary motivator. However, frequent and intense stress can cause significant health consequences. Moreover, research has found that **how** we think about stress is what matters. For example, in a TED Talk by Kelly McGonigal (2013), a health psychologist entitled *How to Make Stress Your Friend* (https://www.ted.com), neurochemical bases are explored. She highlighted a study of 30,000 people in the United States conducted over eight years by Keller et al. (2012) at the University of Wisconsin School of Medicine and Public Health. Participants were asked how much stress they experienced in the past year and whether they viewed the stress as harmful. Researchers then viewed the death records to see who died. They found that those that reported to have high stress had a 43% chance of dying, but only if they viewed the stress as harmful. Those that reported high levels of stress but did not view stress as harmful had a low percentage of dying, even lower than those with moderate stress. When we are stressed, we release a hormone called cortisol which results in an increase in heart rate and breathing. However, the neurochemical, Oxytocin, that is released when we perform kind acts such as giving, protects our heart from the

34 *Theories on Why We Give*

release of cortisol. So, when we feel stress, we would biologically do well to engage in a prosocial act, such as giving. Even just thinking about giving has been found to result in the release of positive neurochemicals, especially through the mesolimbic system, an area involved in reward but also cognitive processes. Oxytocin is our natural antidote for managing stress and anxiety. The obvious application to giving is to focus on problem solving, empowering one to tackle demands, and to have a mindset of gratitude to thwart negative effects of stress. We are social beings and seek others for comfort. Giving through volunteerism and working on projects with others can help us experience the positive physical and psychological benefits of giving.

A concept in both positive and health psychology that is applicable to giving is that of mindfulness. Mindfulness is the awareness of one's internal states and their surroundings. It is rooted in Buddhist traditions. The current western region of the world has recognized the benefits of mindfulness through the work of Jon Kabat-Zin who in 1979 developed Mindfulness-Based Stress Reduction (MBSR) programs at the medical school at University of Massachusetts (as cited in Niazi & Niazi, 2011). Since this time, mindfulness strategies have been a cornerstone of psychological treatments. The main points of mindfulness are to stay in the present and to put things in their proper context. Mindfulness is about being aware of one's internal states simultaneously while being aware of one's surroundings. According to the American Psychological Association (2024; https://www.apa.org/topics/mindfulness), mindfulness helps reduce negative thinking and behaviors.

Many interventions suggested by psychologists are considered mindfulness techniques, such as physical exercise, yoga, meditation, relaxation training, walks in nature, deep breathing, and more. These techniques help people become aware of their internal states and environments without judgment. People are encouraged to look closely at their surroundings and to appreciate beauty all around them. They are also encouraged to rest their minds. This can be difficult to do as our minds are often cluttered with competing thoughts. These thoughts may be negative and thereby weigh heavily on our mood. To be mindful, one's mind is calm, grateful, and compassionate. When our mind is in a mindful state, our mood follows. To ensure a balance in mind and body,

Theories on Why We Give 35

mindfulness techniques focus on good and optimism. Practice mindfulness by grounding yourself in the "here and the now." Focus on your environment. Notice the beauty around you. Nature offers a plethora of examples such as the beauty of the colors in the leaves, the fragrance of a flower, the sound of the rain, etc. Mindfulness is directly connected to gratitude as is explored further in Chapter 6.

Although not yet found in the scientific literature, there is a robust model for corporate professionals developed by Sabina Vitacca from Australia called *Meditate Now 1:1 Corporate Mindfulness* (https://meditatenow.com.au/four-rs-program/). Her model centers on Four Rs of mindfulness mediation. The Four Rs are described in Table 2.6 along with my applications to giving.

Table 2.6 Four Rs of Mindfulness with Application to Giving

Four Rs of mindfulness	*Defined*	*Application to giving*
Reflect	Thinking through one's thoughts and beliefs.	A large part of giving pertains to awareness of need and one's desired degree of involvement in a cause. Reflecting on one's intentions and desired outcomes can be rather fruitful as it may uncover unrealistic expectations.
Reenergize	Involves conserving and refueling one's resources.	When we give, we want to be aware of our means and boundaries (see Chapter 7). We also want to give without depletion of our resources and energies.
Reconnect	Involves socialization and the benefits we receive from interacting with others.	Through giving, we are providing a tangible indicator of hope to another. We are helping them been seen and realized that they matter. As givers, we also feel the social benefit from doing collective good.
Refocus	Occurs when we engage in activities consistent with our life's goals.	Seeing the outcome of our giving, feeling good about our actions, and becoming keenly aware of others positively changes our focus and creates a sense of meaning.

36 *Theories on Why We Give*

Regarding reflection, many of my interviewees commented "I never thought about that" or "I have not thought about giving at this depth before." Reflection takes time and mental energy, but the payoff is high in that self-discovery is a guiding force to our motives in life. Without reflection, we run the risk of acting on our biases and raw impulse. We also run the risk of being at the mercy of others' intentions. Having a conscious view makes decision making easier and more consistent with our internal goals. In terms of reenergizing, we also want to be aware of the resources we have available to give and the extent available for giving. Preserving our resources for self and others is a factor in this calculation. Resources need to be replenished, this is especially seen in the need to refuel one's passion, often needing a rest period to refuel to keep our passions strong. Reconnecting from the social level allows us to feel humanity and a sense of unity. Most people are socially driven and desire the comforts that can be obtained from the support of others. Once we experience refocus, it is nearly impossible to give without being moved emotionally. To this point, I was amazed that most of my interviewees were moved to tears as they recalled their experiences with giving. Once we see a need, our priorities are often altered. It is forever more difficult to unsee or unknow that such a need exists.

Positive interpersonal interactions are known to increase one's sense of well-being. More specifically, positive prosocial actions, such as giving, have been associated with positive well-being. The concept of flow, mentioned above, describes the pleasurable state of being when immersed in an activity. These moments of flow are said to contribute to one's happiness in life. When we give, we have several opportunities for flow, starting with identifying the need, thinking about the right course of action, conducting the action, and seeing the outcome of the action. Each step offers the chance for positive feelings to emerge. One of my interviewees, Lois, described flow in the process of giving:

> There is a joy to my giving. I enjoy the process of giving from thinking about the person to the actual giving when I'm watching their surprise. It gives me an injection of joy. If someone says that they enjoyed it or made their day – I feel good.

Theories on Why We Give 37

Mindfulness is involved in the energy we put into the process of giving. It involves the awareness of a need, the intention of one's gift, and the identification of who and what to give too. What are your thoughts behind a gift? Do you anticipate or hope to elicit a specific response or emotion from the receiver? Giving in a mindful manner requires a giver to think beyond themselves, outside of their own frame of reference, and to think with empathy – through another's lens. Mental energy is certainly needed; this level of thinking is often avoided as it requires effort and deliberation. Social psychologist note that we are "cognitive misers," preferring to reserve our mental efforts. For this reason and many others, gift giving can be rather superficial and done out of obligation, missing the potential beauty in the exchange. When one devotes mental energy to think from the receiver's perspective, with empathy and emotion, giving is meaningful. The beauty is often in the process and the mental energy believed to have been spent. This is why symbolic gifts, unexpected gifts, and personalized gifts are so memorable. Consider a meaningful gift you received. This gift is likely meaningful because who gave it to you rather than the object itself.

In thinking about meaningful gifts, I think about an interviewee's story. Barbara Gallagher, a retired university professor, grandmother, mother, and wife shared a story about her and her husband, John. She recalls:

John and I were struggling, living on one salary when the kids were young. I had to go somewhere and was putting on the same dress – I only had one. It was Christmastime and we agreed not to get each other anything so we could give gifts to the children. But he handed me a present – it was a new dress!

She teared up as she continued, stating: "It is still in my closet with a tag on it saying, 'bury me in it.' This is my most loving giving story." Decades later, Barb is still moved by the generosity and sacrifice her husband made. Giving to others while stressed provides a visual and tangible reminder of the proportionality of our problems. It helps place our problems in context. It could also very well give us a feeling of potential positive return. Perhaps our

38   *Theories on Why We Give*

kind act would be reciprocated, but in the least, we know that our problems are not the end all.

A saying comes to mind that is credited to too many to cite and goes like this: *If we all threw our problems into a pile, seeing what others have going on, we would rush to take ours back.* While we can easily come up with examples that would make us dispute this notion, let us think of the underlying message. This message is a reminder that we never quite know what another is going through. Perhaps their behavior or attitude can be explained by their current situation that is often unknown to us at the time. For example, witnessing a parent yelling at their child in the grocery store is not a pleasant experience. We may judge and think negatively about their parenting skills. But had we known that the parent is experiencing financial hardship, working extensive hours, is running late, etc. we would not see that as an excuse for their behavior, but it would certainly put their actions in context. Knowing this, or giving each other the benefit of doubt, would likely move us to help instead of judge. Another facet to this saying is that we ourselves often have problems that we think are unmanageable, until we see that others have it worse. Considering the beauty in the here and now, let's go back to how a mindfulness moment may help our previously mentioned overwhelmed parent in the grocery store. What if that parent could focus on the "here and the now" of what in their life is going right for them? What if they could build on their strengths and resources, empowering themselves to be problem solvers? Imagine if they were able to see their problem in a larger context, that it would pass. Imagine if they moved pass themselves to aid another. Notice the feeling of empowerment and positive control one can now seize with the step of a giving mindset.

Mindfulness theory involves clarity in thought. **How** we think about things matters in how we feel. Mindfulness serves to empower people to explore options and resources. It is not enough to consider the number and extent of one's problems; resources must also be considered. It could be that someone with a relatively small problem struggles more than someone with a larger problem because of a difference in resources. Resources are things like time, money, and support. Wherewithal and grit are also powerful resources. We all have problems. We all have resources. We all need help from time to time, especially when the proportion of resources to problems is skewed. A crisis can be described as when one's resources are less than their stressors/problems. Even someone with extensive resources can be in crisis and in need of help at some time or another. We are all susceptible to being skewed on this scale from time to time. This would suggest that we all have the potential of reaching crisis level if we do not replenish our resources or if our stressors exceed our level of resources. Mindfulness is a good way to be present with one's resources. Thinking once again about the parent in the grocery store, their "scales were tipped," their resources of time and finances were depleted, they enter crisis zone, an overwhelming emotional state. A small gesture of "can I help you find something" or "do you need a shopping cart; I am happy to get one for you" could be the "feather" that tips the resource side of the scale to make the situation manageable for the parent. So, how does all this pertain to giving and mindfulness? Our interactions with others contribute (or take away) from their balance. Giving can be the life preserver one needs to obtain equilibrium so that they can manage and apply their coping; it offers strength and hope. Giving can be the "here and now" beauty for another; a reminder to them of the humanity that exists. It can be a very tangible indicator that they are seen by others and valued. Mindfulness giving enables one to feel a sense of empowerment. It helps the receiver feel hope and love. A mindfulness act of giving declutters the mind of negativity and self-absorption. The act of practicing mindfulness is a gift to the self and to others. It is a gift of grace.

Environment: Behavioral Theories

Behavioral theories focus on the role the environment plays in shaping our behavior.

Skinner's Operant Conditioning

B. F. Skinner (1953) is credited as the founding father of operant conditioning. This behaviorism theory maintains that behavior is influenced by consequence. An "operant," which is an organism like an animal or human, behaves, then experiences a consequence. If the consequence is something the organism likes, the behavior is

40   *Theories on Why We Give*

likely to occur again. If the consequence is something the organism does not like, then the behavior is less likely to be repeated. This seems simplistic, but there are many factors to consider as it is not a perfect equation. When it comes to giving, or any behavior for that matter, we have all experienced unfavorable consequences, yet many continue to give. It could very well be that we are indeed getting something positive out of the behavior that is "reinforcing" our actions. Reinforcement is when a behavior occurs, and the outcome is positive. So, when we give to a person in need, and they say "thank-you." Punishment occurs when we act and receive a negative consequence as an outcome. An example being that we give up our weekend to help our friend move and they criticize how we helped. This negative consequence would make it less likely for you to help that friend again in the future. Here is where the need for gratitude, discussed in Chapter 6, is especially important as it can shape others' behavior. The theory is more complex in that removing a negative aspect can increase a behavior. This is known as negative reinforcement. It sounds like a punishment, but it is not. An example of negative reinforcement for giving would be the bank removing a hold on our account (negative stimulus) enabling you to donate funds (increase a behavior). Any consequence that serves to increase a behavior is reinforcement, whether the stimulus is positive or negative. Any stimulus that serves to decrease behavior is referred to as punishment.

According to this theory, people can influence others to give by providing the right reinforcement. Fundraisers that offer an opportunity to win a prize, a small gift, or a tangible incentive may increase the behavior of giving (more to come on this topic in Chapter 10). Knowing what an individual finds reinforcing is key. Reinforcement is only as potent as the individual's preference for it. What may motivate one may not motivate another. I recently went to a designer purse bingo. These are very effective fundraisers, fun, and appealing to many. However, I do not even carry a purse, let alone one that cost more than a month's mortgage. For that reason, I purchased less bingo cards as I was not interested in winning (except for the green Kate Spade tote to give to my friend). Motivated to support the animal food bank as the cause, I instead put money into their raffle baskets. Behavioral theories enable us to understand how our giving behavior has been shaped. Think about

Theories on Why We Give 41

a time you received praise for giving. Did this increase your giving behavior? By utilizing this behavioral theory, we can shape others' giving behavior! More to come about this topic as we do not want to externally reinforce behavior that is already internally motivated. I told you it was going to get a bit more complicated!

Pavlov's Classical Conditioning

Classical conditioning was first introduced by Ivan Pavlov (as cited in Rathus, 2019), a Russian physiologist. Pavlov stumbled upon animal learning serendipitously when he was testing the volume of salivating in dogs. In this theory, behavior is learned through association. When a stimulus that does not initially lead to a behavior is paired with a stimulus that does lead to the behavior, conditioning (learning) has occurred. In Pavlov's case, he noticed that the dog he had contained in an experimental apparatus to collect its saliva started to salivate at the sight of him entering the room. Pavlov would bring the bowl of dog food over to the dog, so the dog began to associate the sight of Pavlov with food. Any pet owner knows this to be the reaction to the sound of an electric can opener and in runs the pet! To investigate further, Pavlov conducted a series of experiments with the dog. He started with what should be a "neutral stimulus," something that does not elicit the behavior (in this case salivating). He chose a bell as a neutral stimulus. To ensure that the dog did not salivate to the bell, he rang it a few times in front of the dog to check. The dog did not salivate. Now to begin the pairing. Pavlov took the neutral stimulus (bell) and paired it with the food. He presented them together several times. The association had been made. Once the food was no longer present and he only rung the bell, the dog still salivated. Pavlov conditioned the dog to salivate to the ringing of the bell.

We can easily see how negative experiences, such as fears, can be conditioned. A child, not feeling any threat when near a dog, may witness their parent jump and yank them away from the dog. The pairing of this abrupt movement with the presence of the dog is likely to now cause fear when a dog is nearby in the future. There are many things that could be classically conditioned during the giving process, such as sounds, locations, mood, smells, and people, to name a few. Fundraising events often maximize

42 *Theories on Why We Give*

on conditioned aspects by serving food, playing music, providing opportunities to socialize, etc. When donors are satiated, comfortable and happy, they are inclined to give. They associated good feelings with the event and thereby the fundraising cause.

So, the million-dollar question – How many pairings (trials) is needed for learning to occur? Well, that depends on the behavior being conditioned. How potent is the stimulus? "One-trial learning" is a concept used to explain how some situations are so powerful and memorable that one only needs to experience it once for the solidification of the pairing to occur, such as a response to trauma. Other "trails" may need a dozen or so pairings before the learning occurs. This theory gets complicated too. As with the other behavioral theories, the premise is that all behavior is learned and thereby can be unlearned. This is true with operant conditioning too and indeed something we strive for when targeting naughty behavior. But when the behavior is "good," we want to keep the learning strong. To continue the strength of the pairing, the unconditioned stimulus needs to be periodically presented with the learned stimulus.

Social Learning Theory

Another theory in psychology that offers insight into why we give is the social learning theory (SLT), first developed by Albert Bandura (1977), a Canadian American Psychologist. SLT explains how people learn a variety of actions, thoughts, and behaviors, through observing others. Others serve as a model of the action, but also for the outcome. When we see that a model's behavior results in a positive outcome, we learn what we need to do to get a similar outcome (or what not to do when we see negative outcomes). Think about the first time you drove a car. Chances are no one needed to tell you to start the ignition, this is something you have seen drivers do for years. Imagine how much longer it would have taken you to learn to drive if every detail and every step needed to be explicitly taught.

In his classic "bobo doll" study, Bandura showed a group of children a video of a woman serving as a model. She was playing with a bobo doll (an inflated doll about 3 feet in size). The model engaged in physical aggression toward the doll by punching it, straddling it, and saying aggressive statements like "sock'em."

Theories on Why We Give 43

Another group of children did not see the video of this model. Each child was observed and videotaped playing alone in the playroom. The number of aggressive acts they conducted was tallied. Not only did the children who witnessed the aggressive model mimic her behavior and engage in more aggressive actions than the children that did not view the model, but they also mimicked her verbalizations. An additional finding that was not expected was that the children that witnessed the aggressive model manifested novel forms of aggression, meaning that they created new aggressive behaviors. The actions of the model were copied, but it seemed to have also opened the floodgates to other aggressive behaviors. Bandura maintained that children learn through modeling, both good and not-so-good behaviors. He also noted that they learn through "vicarious reinforcement" in that they see consequences given to others. So, when it comes to giving behaviors, the same elements apply. Others in the environment serve as powerful models for giving behaviors. How to give can be observed through the actions of others. Conversely, people that are not generous may not have had these models or did not witness the positive outcomes generosity had for the models.

Watching others informs much of our understanding of societal and cultural norms. These norms include beliefs and traditions on giving and receiving. If a child is not reared in an environment where they see generosity, they would not have a model for such acts and they would not learn to give. More social influences are discussed in Chapter 9 on empowering children to give. In the meantime, think about your earliest recollection of an act of giving. How old were you? What was the situation? Did the giver receive acknowledgment for their gift demonstrating vicarious reinforcement? Did the giver explain their actions to you so to create a teachable moment? Were there emotions involved in this giving exchange? Are there emotions involved now as you recollect these experiences? Have these examples served as a guide for your giving? These are the types of questions I asked interviewees while I worked on this book. Many of my interviewees shared that they gave for the purpose of lifting someone up. They also reflected that they were taught to help others when they could. Some referred to the "giving glow" to explain the good feeling they get from giving (discussed further in Chapter 5). Empathy, another concept that appears to be learned, was also a factor in interviewees' early

44 *Theories on Why We Give*

giving experiences. They reported learning to see the need in others through observing actions of givers. Interviewees also noted the influence of religion and explicit teachings. Teachings are often direct through statements guiding our developing sense of morality, implied in parables, and observational as we see models of giving through our families, churches, and communities. Direct messaging from religious entities, such as Dorothy Day (1952), a Catholic writer and activist, asserted that Jesus is seen in the face of the poor. How we treat the poor and those in need reflects our regard for Jesus. Figure 2.1 is of a picture I took during a trip to Washington, DC, in August 2023. I took this picture of the "Homeless Jesus" bench statue by Timothy P. Schmalz located outside the Old Carroll Hall.

This statute, similar ones located in other US cities, such as Philadelphia, PA, beckons debate and awareness of how we treat people who are homeless. Advocates for this awareness campaign point to the need for visual representation and reminders, declaring that society has become blind to the needs of the homeless. Bandura referred to this numbing of awareness and thereby concern as "desensitization." If you doubt this occurrence, reflect on

Figure 2.1 Homeless Jesus Statue.

Theories on Why We Give 45

your recent intake of events in the news. Chances are, like many of us, you were relatively unfrazzled by the horrendous stories reported on any news channel on any given day. Often, we feel overwhelmed by such magnitude and daily occurrences, that we insulate ourselves through cognitive acts of denial. We get so saturated by negative news that it no longer shocks us. This is desensitization. Desensitization can prevent us from seeing need. Mindfulness strategies mentioned throughout this book provide an antidote to desensitization. For when we are aware and focused on the here and now, we are grounded and attuned. From a social learning perspective, how others manage awareness of need can certainly serve as an influence on us, e.g., others modeling avoidance. Just as maladaptive behavior is modeled, so too is generosity. Interviewees reported learning to give directly from family members. They noted consciously giving to follow the example set.

Human Tendencies: Social Psychology

Social psychology theory and research focuses on the impact others have on our thoughts and behavior. Social psychologists are interested in a variety of human tendencies and attempt to find the multifaceted variables that create and maintain behavior. Our behavior is viewed as a series of variables that can "dial up" or "dial down" an action. Many factors impact whether we act or not; this is what social psychologist are especially interested in studying. They are not only interested in human tendencies, but also the various points on the dial. The dial of "prosocial behavior" includes many points. Social psychologist research these points on the dial to offer scientific explanations for a behavior. Social psychologist also study human tendencies in thinking. In the case of homeless, many "make it right in their heads" but using faulty self-justification beliefs such as one being a better person than another or that one deserves their circumstances, mentioned above as the "just world effect." Social psychologist noted that we are faulty in our justifications when we attribute dispositional (personality) factors to others instead of situational factors. This is known as a fundamental attribution error. Another component to this tendency is for us to give ourselves the benefit of the doubt by attributing "situational factors" to our own unfavorable actions. Our psyche is protected by the assumption that people are homeless because of something

46 *Theories on Why We Give*

they did or did not do; within their own degree of control versus situational factors such as losing a job or having major medical expenses. For us to focus on situational factors for the homeless, we run the risk of being vulnerable, knowing that we too could experience circumstances that create financial devastation. So instead, we protect our psyches and attribute one's state of homelessness to their personality aspects, such as poor motivation.

Aronson et al. (2023) summarized research on the variables involved in prosocial behavior. Some individual factors include one's mood, the cost-reward ratio, level of empathy, gender, and confidence level of the helper. Other variables involve the influence of the presence of others, such as in the bystander effect, interpretation of need, diffusion of responsibility, and desensitization. The Urban Overload Hypothesis is a form of desensitization due to constant bombardment of poverty, crime, and aggression seen in inner-city regions. These factors serve to dial down giving and other prosocial behaviors. Social psychology research finds other variables can dial up prosocial behaviors, such as increasing awareness of human tendencies, telling bystanders exactly what is needed, assigning a role to others, determining one's role/responsibility ahead of time, not underestimating one's influence, and empowering self and others.

Specific social psychology research identifies two reasons for giving, egoistic and altruistic (as cited in Pietraszkiewicz et al., 2017). Egoistic giving serves to benefit the giver by increasing their sense of esteem or image. Altruistic giving is motivated by the desire to improve another's well-being. Both reasons can occur simultaneously. Pietraszkiewicz and colleagues summarized a series of studies that have found that people who spend money on others are happier than those who spend it on themselves. Benefits to the giver are likely not the reason most people give, but it is fine to obtain some benefit from giving. It would make the act more likely to occur again. Social psychologists also acknowledge the reinforcing effects of reciprocation in giving, such as in the norm of reciprocity theory.

Norm of Reciprocity

The norm of reciprocity theory (Aronson et al., 2023) offers some insight where evolution theory fell short, specifically as to why we give to strangers and why we give anonymously. The norm of

Theories on Why We Give 47

reciprocity accounts for giving to others as we tend to hold a belief that the giver will be helped in the future. Other concepts along these lines include "Karma." Many forms of Indian religion, e.g., Buddhism and Hinduism, believe that one's actions now and in previous states of existence will come back to impact the individual. Even if not versed in these religious underpinnings, many see actions to be "what goes around comes around." Like a boomerang, what is manifested and projected onto the universe gets returned to the individual. So, someone who gives and spreads positive energy is likely to have reciprocated positive energy back from their environment. Think about people you know, likely there is someone you know who seems to be in perpetual crisis with a series of misfortunes. Their energy and thoughts are consumed with their current crisis state. They cannot think ahead, let alone outside their own immediate needs. Their energy is consumed with managing the chaos of their current crisis. Their thoughts are panicked and inevitably lead to negativity. They are taking in the negative energies and focus of their environment, spiraling internally with their thoughts, then projecting negative energy through their actions and words. What they collect (from the environment) is what they produce (send out to the environment). They become too preoccupied with the negative that they are not able to see any positives. They become emotionally paralyzed. In this state, they cannot see beyond their immediate concerns. Noticing other's needs is not likely as they are in "fight, flight, or freeze" mode. Their thinking affects their actions creating a circular pattern of negative energies, inputs, and outcomes. Their tendency to be in perpetual crisis is the result of this patterned loop. Cognitive behavioral therapies target these beliefs and work to help people neutralize their thinking, making it more objective.

The norm of reciprocity is also used to explain how solicitations that provide a small token to the potential donor can spark the urge for the donor to reciprocate. Receiving a gift from an organization in need creates the idea that the receiver should be the giver. The social psychology concept, cognitive dissonance, fits here too as people feel a sense of discomfort when they hold two conflicting thoughts. So, in an example of a fundraising campaign that sends a small gift to potential donors, the donor has the thought "this organization needs my money" while also thinking "this organization spent money on this gift for me." To resolve cognitive

48 *Theories on Why We Give*

dissonance and enable the state of dissonance/discomfort to be resolved, the individual needs to minimize one thought over the other. They need to "get their head around" one of the ideas/thoughts, thereby solidifying the potency of the selected thought. In this case, the potential donor takes the gift, has thoughts of dissonance, then resolves it by deciding that the cause needs the donation more than they do, and they donate. Developmental psychologists Kristina Olson and Elizabeth Spelke (2008) studied children 3.5 years of age regarding the "norm of reciprocity." These researchers found that children evidenced understanding of fundamental laws of exchange and the expectation to return a favor.

Social Exchange Theory

Social exchange theory (Aronson et al., 2023) maintains that we are motivated to maximize our rewards and minimize our costs when we help others. When giving comes at a cost that is too high, many do not give. An example of this is when someone needs money well beyond your means and more than your giving boundary, you will (and should) refrain from giving. Many in this situation will offer other supports and ideas to help an individual in need, such as volunteering to help with fundraising events. On the other hand, when we do give, we often feel that we have gained more than we have given. This model specifically speaks to the balance in giving and receiving in interpersonal relationships. The more balanced interactions, the healthier the relationship. Imbalance is believed to lead to distress in both the giver and receiver. The giver may feel frustrated and angry when their efforts are not reciprocated. The receiver may feel guilty and ashamed when they receive more than they give. There are certainly some people who take more than they give and do not feel remorse. Some may even prey on the generosity of others. However, most people feel the urge to reciprocate. Creating boundaries around giving, a topic covered in Chapter 7, will lessen the likelihood of being exploited. On the other hand, there are people that give without the desire for reciprocity. These exchanges may seemingly be imbalanced; however, it is likely that the giver does indeed receive a benefit to their giving. The giver experiences good feelings and meaning from their action which helps keep the balance to the scales.

Theories on Why We Give 49

Think about an example in which you have given and received seemingly nothing in return. Perhaps it was an anonymous gift you left for a random recipient. You may not have been there to see the response from the receiver, however, you felt good about doing this kind act. Even thinking about it now likely makes you feel good. We will discuss in Chapter 5 the biological aspects, such as the brain functions, when giving. The physical feeling creates a gain for the giver. Recently, I saw a post on social media of a colleague whose daughter was turning 21. I have met this young lady before, but do not know her personally. Her mother and friends wanted to surprise her for her 21st birthday with a network of 21 books donated by random people. What an interesting and meaningful idea! I was especially compelled by the opportunity to give her a book as I thought it carried extra special meaning to have someone basically unknown to her send a birthday greeting. I signed right up to be involved and to receive my book title. The cost of the paperback book was minimal, but the return I felt from doing this was huge. It felt great to be able to send a tangible gift to a young person to let her know there are others that care for her outside her immediate awareness. I was delighted by the idea that she would be bombarded with a pile of books to celebrate her 21st birthday. To know I took a small part in that was exciting. Plus, it was a fun and creative way to celebrate! I clearly received much from the experience.

Social exchange theory has not only been used to gauge the balance in personal relationships, but also with relationships in the workplace. If employees feel imbalanced, that they are getting less than their efforts they are putting in, they are likely to feel unhappy; morale in the workplace suffers. Employees give their time, effort, and passion. What they receive is a paycheck, but ideally so much more. Keeping the scales balanced and a healthy dose of reciprocation would include more than a paycheck, things like praise and recognition can be powerful rewards. Cardiovascular health has been associated with the balance (or imbalance) in social exchange. Employees that have low rewards relative to their efforts have been found to have higher levels of heart issues, even death (Kivimäki et al., 2002; Kuper et al., 2002).

The understanding of exchange involved in giving, known as reciprocal giving, typically occurs by the age of two years (Olson & Spelke, 2008). Reciprocal interactions are evidenced much earlier

50 *Theories on Why We Give*

through games like "peak a boo" and "patty cake." These interactions require a "give and take" and volley to and from one individual to another. These reciprocal interactions are known to build human connection and attachment.

In 2014, Becker, Goodman, and Macdonald published an article regarding their thoughts on giving and whether it could theoretically ever be "aneconomic," meaning free of expectation. Givers and receivers tend to have transactional patterns that are usually reciprocated. Economist, anthropologist, and philosophers alike have contemplated cost analyses on human interactions and behaviors. A ledger exists in all our psyches on cost versus benefit ratios. We typically act when the benefits are higher than the costs. Becker et al. (2014) cite philosopher Gary Becker who quantifies marriage when the utility exceeds the demands and thereby the opposite occurs when one decides to divorce. Economic logic is often seen in giving. Upon receiving a gift, we may question the intent and likely activate a feeling of obligation to reciprocate. Struggling between these two concepts creates cognitive dissonance. The cognitive dissonance is rarely resolved by realizing that giving was a selfless act, typically we view it through an economic lens. We expect to reciprocate and have a hard time accepting a "no strings attached" gift.

In their rather philosophical article, Becker et al. (2014) noted that the giver is always a receiver first. I sat with this, rereading sections of their argument, and find that I agree with this statement. As noted, givers receive various benefits to giving, both internally and externally (discussed more in Chapter 5). This process starts prior to the act itself. As one thinks about making a gift, they likely release neurochemicals that make them feel good. They are likely to have positive thoughts regarding their decision to give. I know this to have happened firsthand on numerous occasions. One of my examples was when my daughter was having a fundraiser and was looking for donation items to raffle. I was in possession of a pair of concert tickets for a well-sought-out music performer. I almost did not order such tickets as I was experiencing an "existential crisis" with this musical artist and his seemingly increasing greed running contrary to his musical messaging. I questioned whether I wanted to even attend the concert and risk contradicting my own views, so I donated the tickets. As soon as I made the decision to do so,

Theories on Why We Give 51

I felt a tremendous wave of relief and boost of dopamine. I felt great! I felt good that my donation would help raise money, but also offer another – without the same existential conflict – to attend what promised to be an amazing show. As the neurochemicals released and my positive thinking transpired, I realized that I got more out of giving the gift than I would have going to the concert. Becker et al. (2014) argued that being a receiver first is even more abstract in that the gifts we possess have been bestowed to us through inheritance; that what we have to give is a commodity that has first been given to us. They also make the philosophical point that giving lies outside economic logic as it does not always have reciprocal intent. The authors cite examples such as giving through a Last Will and Testament where the beneficiary does not reciprocate to the giver. They add that gifts are not always quantifiable, e.g., love. Of further emphasis, they argue that authentic gifts are often overlooked, their true value missed, as humans tend to focus on economizing the gift – they miss the true value. To this last point, I think of the "*Gold Paper Box*" fable, about a poor little girl that gives her parent a shoebox wrapped in gold paper. Her parent, struggling financially and not pleased to see that the daughter used (in her eyes wasted) the wrapping paper, became enraged when the parent opens the box to see nothing inside. The parent yells are the little girl asking the girl why she wrapped nothing, wasting the paper. The little girl, through her sobbing tears, cries out that it is not nothing – she blew kisses into the box until it was filled. Her parent feels horrible having missed the symbolism and begs the daughter for her forgiveness.

Key Points

- A variety of theories contribute to our understanding of giving behavior.
- Chapter 2 focused on four dimensions to giving from the biological, individual growth and wellness, environment, and human tendencies perspectives.
- Biological theory indicates some incentive for us to give to others to sustain the species.
- Humanistic theories indicate that we are driven toward generativity and caring for more than just our own needs.

52   *Theories on Why We Give*

- Positive psychology theory offers research and theory on the positive benefits to giving, aiding in living a fulfilling and authentic life.
- World giving data has shown a decrease prior to the COVID-19 pandemic, but since has increased starting in 2022 worldwide by 25% compared to prior to the pandemic.
- Behavioral theory maintains that we learn to give (or not to give) based on the environment, what was modeled or what was reinforced or punished.
- Social psychology theories emphasize many variables that can dial up or down giving behavior.
- The human tendency to reciprocate is a common human tendency along with equity in exchange.

Action Steps

- Consider the reasons for your giving.
- Contemplate – What theory best explains your giving patterns?

References

APA. (retrieved January 14, 2024). *Mindfulness.* American Psychological Association. https://www.apa.org/topics/mindfulness

APA. (March 8, 2023). *Stress Effects on the Body: Stress Affects All Systems of the Body Including the Musculoskeletal, Respiratory, Cardiovascular Endocrine, Gastrointestinal, Nervous, and Reproductive Systems.* Washington, DC: American Psychological Association. https://www.apa.org/topics/stress/body

Aronson, E., Wilson, T.D., Sommers, S.R., Page-Gould, E., & Lewis, N. (2023). *Social Psychology*, 11th edition. New York: Pearson.

Bandura, A. (1977). *Social Learning Theory.* Englewood Cliffs, NJ: Prentice-Hall.

Becker, B.W., Goodman, D.M., & Macdonald, H. (2014). A thought on giving: Towards an aneconomic relational subjectivity. *Journal of Theoretical and Philosophical Psychology*, 34(4), 214–228. https://doi.org/10.1037/a0037759

Darwin, C. (1982). *The Descent of Man, and Selection in Relation to Sex.* Princeton University Press. (Original work published 1871)

Day, D. (1952). Poverty is the face of Christ. *The Catholic Worker*, 3(6). https://catholicworker.org/641-html/

Theories on Why We Give 53

Hamilton. (1964; as cited in Britannica, T. Editors of Encyclopedia; 2018, April 14). *Kin selection. Encyclopedia Britannica.* https://www.britannica.com/topic/kin-selection

Keller, A., Litzelman, K., Wisk, L.E., Maddox, T., Cheng, E.R., Creswell, P.D., & Witt, W.P. (2012). Does the perception that stress affects health matter? The association with health and mortality. *Health Psychology*, 31(5), 677–684. https://doi.org/10.1037/10026743

Kivimäki, M., Leino-Arjas, P., Luukkonen, R., Riihimäki, H., Vahtera, J., & Kirjonen, J. (2002). Work stress and risk of cardiovascular mortality: Prospective cohort study of industrial employees. *British Medical Journal*, 325, 857–860. https://doi.org/10.1136/bmj.325.7369.857

Kuper, H., Singh-Manoux, A., Siegrist, J., & Marmot, M. (2002). When reciprocity fails: Effort-reward imbalance in relation to coronary heart disease and health functioning within the Whitehall II study. *Occupational and Environmental Medicine*, 59, 777–784. https://doi.org/10.1136/oem.59.11.777

Maslow, A.H. (1943). A theory of human motivation. *Psychological Review*, 50(4), 370–396. https://doi.org/10.1037/h0054346

McGonigal, K. (June 2013). *How to make stress your friend.* https://www.ted.com/talks/kelly_mcgonigal_how_to_make_stress_your_friend?language=en

Niazi, A.K., & Niazi, S.K. (2011). Mindfulness-based stress reduction: A non-pharmacological approach for chronic illnesses. *North American Journal of Medical Sciences*, 3(1), 20–23. https://doi.org/10.4297/najms.2011.320

Olson, K.R., & Spelke, E.S. (2008). Foundations of cooperation in young children. *Cognition: Science Direct*, 108, 222–231. https://doi.org/10.1016/j.cognition.2007.12.003

Peterson, C., Park, N., & Seligman, M., (2005). Orientations to happiness and life satisfaction: The full life versus the empty life. *Journal of Happiness Studies*, 6(1). https://doi.org/10.1007/s10902-004-1278-z

Pietraszkiewicz, A., Soppe, B., & Formanowicz, M. (2017). Go pro bono: Prosocial language as a success factor in crowdfunding. *Social Psychology*, 48(5), 265–278. https://doi.org/10.1027/1864-9335/a000319

Rathus, S. (2019). *Psych: Introductory Psychology*, 6th edition. Kentucky: Cengage Learning.

Seligman, M.E.P., & Csikszentmihalyi, M. (2000). Positive psychology: An introduction. *American Psychologist*, 55(1), 5–14. https://doi.org/10.1037/0003-066X.55.1.5

Seligman, M.E.P. (2002). *Authentic Happiness: Using the New Positive Psychology to Realize Your Potential for Lasting Fulfillment.* New York: Free Press.

54 *Theories on Why We Give*

Seligman, M.E. (2012). *Flourish: A Visionary New Understanding of Happiness and Well-Being*. New York: Atria Paperback.

Skinner, B.F. (1953). *Science and Human Behavior*. New York: Macmillan.

Summers, K., & Crespi, B. (2013). *Human Social Evolution: The Foundational Works of Richard Alexander*. Oxford University Press. https://doi.org/10.1093/acprof:osobl/9780199791750.001.0001

Trivers, R.L. (1971). The evolution of Reciprocal Altruism. *The Quarterly Review of Biology*, 46(1), 35–57.

Vitacca, S. *Meditate Now 1:1 Corporate Mindfulness*. https://meditatenow.com.au/four-rs-program/

World Happiness Report. (2023). https://worldhappiness.report/

3 Who, What, Where, How, and Why to Giving

Introduction

Chapter 3 dives into the specifics on giving to help the reader identify the "who, what, where, how, and why" to giving. How much we give globally is reviewed along with the tremendous need for giving due to worldwide poverty. Motivation to give is discussed along with examples of organizations fulfilling various needs. Focusing on these specific aspects will aid the reader in identifying areas of need that may match their experiences and passion (who). Carefully determining "what" is needed, "where" to best donate time, goods, or money, and "how" to get these resources to those in need will be reviewed. It is expected that the reader may be surprised by some of the needs and ideas mentioned here and throughout the book. That is the goal. A further aspiration is for the reader to be enticed to research other need areas, expanding on their knowledge and awareness.

Once an area of need is identified, the reader will know further the "what" to giving. They will be encouraged to ask the potential recipient directly or research what the most pressing need may be for that entity. For example, very often needs vary in organizations such as seasonally for foodbanks. In the United States, foodbanks have especially higher needs in the summertime when schools are out of session and in-school free breakfast and lunch programs are not available for those in need. The "what" to giving is not always money. Gifts can also be "in-kind."

Throughout the chapter, interviewees share with the reader their experiences with giving. Some interviewees are organization founders themselves.

DOI: 10.4324/9781003438359-3

56 *Who, What, Where, How, and Why to Giving*

How Much We Give: Global Statistics

Guo et al. (2020) studied the impact religion has on the World Giving Index (WGI) in a sample of 96 countries/regions. Giving was analyzed across three categories: giving money, volunteering time, and helping a stranger. The researchers hypothesized that as the level of religiosity of the nation increased, so would the rate of national giving. The results showed that nations deemed highly religious, such as Italy, Iraq, Iran, Puerto Rico, and Tanzania, were more inclined to help a stranger than less religious nations. However, religiosity did not relate to their willingness to volunteer time. Even more interesting, higher religious nations showed the opposite effect than predicated, donating less money the more religious they were deemed. Digging a bit deeper, the researchers found that this negative trend was not true for poor nations. In poor nations, there was a positive trend in religion and giving. In affluent nations, other variables were believed to impact giving, to the point of taking a positive trend and making it negative. Perhaps one such variable is less direct experience with need, thereby less empathy. In researching this finding further, I found that in 2021, more affluent nations have bounced back with some of the nations in the top ten highest givers (World Giving Index 2022: A Global View of Giving Trends). As noted in the report, "The global increase is most marked amongst high-income countries, many of which first recorded a decline in 2018 that was sustained until 2021." As a matter of fact, this more recent report noted that Indonesia and Myanmar continued to have strong traditions of religious giving. The WGI found that the top ten countries for giving were all in Africia, South and Central America, and the United States. Indonesia was the most generous country in the world for the fifth year in a row. From a cultural standpoint, Indonesia is very collectivistic with philanthropy and helping others deeply rooted in the culture, known as "gotong royong." The year 2021 showed the highest participation in giving ever with one in three (35%) individuals around the world reporting giving to charity. Volunteering also increased to 23% of people around the world. The report noted that 80% of people in the United States reported helping a stranger, 61% donated money, and 37% reported donating time through volunteering. In looking at giving overtime, since 2009, similar trends were found each year across the three categories of

Who, What, Where, How, and Why to Giving 57

Table 3.1 2022 Global Giving Trends across Three Types of Giving

To 10 overall giving	Rank helping stranger	Rank donating money	Rank time volunteering
1 Indonesia	76	1	1
2 Kenya	7	20	2
3 United States	4	9	7
4 Australia	34	6	20
5 New Zealand	46	10	14
6 Myanmar	83	2	36
7 Sierra Leone	1	76	3
8 Canada	50	13	33
9 Zambia	18	53	4
10 Ukraine	13	29	54

giving: helping a stranger, donating money, and time volunteering. The overall trends show helping a stranger had the highest percentages across all years, then donating money; the lowest form of giving year after year is volunteering.

I have provided in Table 3.1 a summary of the data from the 2022 WGI report of the overall top ten giving nations, across the three areas of giving, as follows:

Wealthier countries are intuitively believed to be the highest in giving, but this is not what the WGI data shows. The COVID-19 pandemic also changed the topography of giving. Previously, in 2018, most of the top ten giving countries (seven) were rated by the United Nations as high-income countries. But during the height of the COVID-19 pandemic in 2020, seven of the ten highest givers were from countries with low and middle economies. As noted further in the WGI report, the trend continued as in 2021, only four of the top ten most generous countries were from high economies.

Remember in Chapter 2, the happiest and least happiest countries were listed? Notice that the United States, Australia, New Zealand, and Canada were all listed in the top ten giving countries were also listed in the top 15 happiest countries. Many factors impact happiness and correlation does not necessarily mean causation, but trends are interesting to explore. Likewise, it is worth exploring how some of these countries, known to be relatively underprivileged financially, rate so high in their giving. What does

58   *Who, What, Where, How, and Why to Giving*

psychology say about why those that have less give proportionately more? Researchers agree that a core tenet is compassion. Those that have fewer financial resources understand and see need far better than those that do not experience the same level of need. Their own need enables them to be attuned to the needs of others. Once aware, action is prompted. Piff et al. (2010) explored research studies that have shown consistently more prosocial acts, such as giving, in those of low socioeconomic status compared to those of higher socioeconomic status.

Motivation for Giving

The term *altruism* infers that there needs to be a sacrifice and a cost to giving. It can be argued that all giving comes at a sacrifice in time, money, or other resource. However, knowing that there are many benefits to giving (to be discussed in Chapter 5), the benefits seemingly outweigh the costs. The psychological and neurological benefits infer that humans are prewired to give. If giving were merely sacrificial, we would be depleted of resources and motivation to give. Giving would seem like a chore. As an interviewee, Lois stated days before Christmas: "I have friends that have said that they are so exhausted in thinking about giving. If it makes them feel this way, why would they want to do it?" Indeed, we can dread giving if our intentions are mixed with contaminants, such as expectations of reciprocation or an ulterior motive. Perhaps we give with the goal of being liked or to be recognized. Perhaps we give with the desire to fall in one's good favor in hopes of receiving some benefit. Notice that these motivations avert the joy one could receive without such expectations. To give for the sake of helping another, lifting them up, without expectation of benefit to self is one of the purest forms of giving. Exploring one's intent to giving is an important aspect in defining boundaries (see Chapter 7) and in creating a plan for giving (see Chapter 8). Intention involves a focus to reach an outcome for giving behavior. Consider your expected outcome prior to giving. Notice commonalities and themes in your intentions over the course of your giving. Are there patterns you can identify? Intent is the goal. We operate with goals all the time, although not always with full awareness. Without reflection of our true intent, we will miss a salient piece to understanding our cognitive and behavioral patterns. A goal to our

Who, What, Where, How, and Why to Giving 59

behavior that is often outside our immediate awareness is "secondary gain." Secondary gain has long been understood in psychology to pertain to the self-serving outcomes one gets as residual effects to their behavior. Since they get X from their behavior, behavior is continued. Understanding the X is key to understanding one's motivation as it relates to secondary gain. Applied to giving behavior, if one receives personal recognition for their act of giving, they may continue to give, not because they are trying to help a cause, but because they are getting secondary gain of being praised.

Motivation is the drive to a giving act. Passion is typically seen as the fuel. What fuels you to give? Fuel for giving behavior is typically seen as a passion. We are motivated by many diverse reasons, usually categorized as "internal" or "external" motivations. Internal motivation for giving is when one chooses to give because it is a cause that they deem important or necessary. Contributing to this cause is the reward in its own sake as opposed to any external accolades. External motivation for giving is for the benefit of praise or recognition from others. An example of external motivation is a fundraising event that awards prizes for the highest sales. We think giving is intrinsically motivating, but this is not always the case – nor does it need to be. Perhaps an extrinsic motivator serves as a gateway to internal motivation. An example of this is a runner that joins a fundraising marathon, not because they are familiar with the cause, but because they are looking to earn a medal. The motivation may stop there. The race ends and the runner is awarded their medal. The runner, having been exposed to others during the event, may have learned more about the need – sparking an intrinsic interest. Intrinsic motivation tends to be the strongest as this is the motivation that comes from our beliefs. Once we believe in something and "get our heads around it," we tend to be motivated to act consistently with our beliefs. To do otherwise would create cognitive dissonance (a social psychology concept discussed in Chapter 2). When attempting to enhance motivation, one must be careful not to create an *Over Justification Effect* (Aronson et al., 2023). This occurs when external rewards are given for something already internally motivating. This causes the internal motivation to weaken. School programs that have children fundraising focus a great deal on external motivation, assuming that internal motivation is not present, and perhaps even preventing it from developing. My suggestion for enhancing motivation is to communicate

60 Who, What, Where, How, and Why to Giving

information about the cause at a developmentally and emotionally appropriate level, encouraging perspective taking. Stories of those in need, personal accounts through videos, etc. offer sensory connections. Specific discussion on empowering children to give is covered in Chapter 9. In brief mention here, offer ideas for fostering cognitive and emotional processing without overwhelming or making a child feel guilty. The empowering aspect is offering children (and others) tangible steps to make a difference. Once intrinsic motivation is sparked, the drive for action likely follows. Verbal praise is also a way to increase internal motivation. Although praise comes from outside, it helps us develop a sense of direction shaping our internal dialogue and thereby motivation. We feel good about doing the right thing, which is verified by others, serving as a guide for us to repeat our actions. Perhaps external incentives can be given for internal steps like knowledge of the cause, advocating for the cause, and participation/effort.

Sometimes our giving is motivated by the social example set for us by another. Social psychology identifies a concept known as "pay it forward." Pay it forward harnesses the power of social influence whereby recipients of a kind act are encouraged to pass

Figure 3.1 Pay It Forward Coffee Shop Program. Image Courtesy of How You Brewin® Coffee Company.

Who, What, Where, How, and Why to Giving 61

the good deed onto others. A coffee shop in Long Beach Island, New Jersey, offers a "pay it forward" program where customers can donate money for another customer to use (see Figure 3.1). How much money and for what reason is determined by the customer/ donor who pays the cashier and writes on a cardboard cup holder the amount and reason. An example could be $5.00 donated to someone "who is having a bad day." Cupholders are posted on a bulletin board, near the cashier, for all to read and take to cash in with their order. See below a picture of this bulletin board and the variety of reasons for the gift:

Some restaurants, often pizzerias, around the country allow customers to pay for a meal for someone in need. The customer decides what they would like to purchase, such as a slice of pizza and a soda, and the receipt is posted on a bulletin board for someone in need to claim. Motivation for this type of giving is often to help others in need anonymously, but to also keep a collective experience going. It is a form of a positive contagion effect where behavior is repeated due to the model being provided.

One's intention has a lot to do with their motivation to give. Researching philosophies on the intentions when giving, I came across levels of charity identified by the 12th-century Jewish philosopher, Maimonides. Maimonides Ladder of Tzedakah (Hebrew word for charity) identifies eight levels of charity (translated by *Dr. Meir Tamari*). Juxtaposed in these levels is the balance of two factors, the desire to do good with various degrees of recognition with balancing the potential embarrassment to the recipient. The first level giving is deemed the highest, most munificent, where the eighth is the least. On the first level, giving occurs to enable the recipient to be self-sufficient. Examples of this level of giving include giving one's time to mentor a student or providing an interest-free loan to help someone start a business. An example of level one giving comes from one of my interviewees, Georgette, who was a teacher. This example fits well here as do many examples from the world of teaching. Georgette recalled a student who was engaging in challenging behaviors at school. One such behavioral incident occurred around him not having money in his cafeteria account. Georgette recalled:

I anonymously put money into a student's lunch account. My understanding is that this student was never placed in school

62 *Who, What, Where, How, and Why to Giving*

until he was in the 5th grade when his parents were arrested. He did not know of the expectations. He was placed in a behavioral support classroom and lacked hierarchical and social/emotional skills. I would observe his interactions (with staff was tough) and the whole situation was unfamiliar to him.

I was assigned to work with him 1:1 with math one day. He cursed at me. He swiped items off the desk and took a swing at me. Realizing his anger was not at me, but at the situation, I set clear boundaries that his behavior was not okay.

There was talk about him being sent to another school for students with intense behavioral concerns. One day he had a fit when he was declined a snack because he did not have money in his lunch account. I asked the cafeteria worker if anyone ever explained to him that he needs money in the account for snacks as the free lunch plan he was on only included the meal. My co-worker said that she had no idea if anyone ever explained anything to him. All she knew was that he yelled and cursed at her and was sent to the principal. So, I put money in his account. He lost his parents and everything that was familiar...he needed an ally. I sent him an anonymous note explaining that he has money for snacks in his lunch account and if he uses it responsibly, it will be renewed in the New Year. His behavior shifted.

I thought about him and how he must have felt when others pulled out their snack later in the day and he did not have one. He must have felt different. Another situation with this boy occurred when he needed help and another one-to-one staff tried to help, but he cursed at her. When I went over to assess the problem, I noticed that he threw all of his work on the floor. I offered to show him how I would complete the task, step by step, which he accepted. He did it! After accepting my help, I told him that I am proud of his perseverance.

He never did get placed in the other school.

In level two, neither the donor nor the recipient knows each other. This is often referred to as "double blind" donation, such as when one leaves hats and scarfs in the park for the homeless. Many of my interviewees gave examples of level two giving, such as putting donations of food and clothing in a collection box. However, in level three, the donor knows the recipient, but the recipient does not know the donor. An example of level three giving is when

Who, What, Where, How, and Why to Giving **63**

one leaves cash or a gift card in the mailbox of a neighbor who is struggling. An example from one of my interviewees, Gary Downing, comes to my mind. Mr. Downing, an African American single father of two, is a behavioral specialist for troubled youth. When asked about giving anonymously, he said:

> I put things in their mailbox to help out: clothing, food, gift cards, etc. When I was a schoolteacher, I had an imaginary uncle. He was extremely wealthy and would "send" in gifts for the kids. This allowed me to maintain a boundary while also being a giver. It also allowed the students to be empowered as I would tell them that I was telling my uncle how good the students were doing. It really meant the world to these students. "Mr. Butterbee" was his name.

The opposite is the case in level four giving in that the recipient knows the donor, but the donor does not know the recipient. An example of this is the Gates Foundation sponsors an educational program, the students likely know who is funding the program but the Gates themselves do not know the recipients. The fifth level is when the donor gives without being asked. This is seen when a donor researches an organization's mission and supports the cause such as the case with MacKenzie Scott Bezos' team. Unbeknownst to the recipient, her team researches an agency and their needs. If deemed suited for the goals Ms. Scott has identified, the organization is awarded funds without them even soliciting her. A *New York Times* June 15, 2021 article by Nicholas Kulish and David Gelles explained:

> Little is known about how Ms. Scott selects her grantees, and there is no formal method for groups to apply for funds. Instead, most grant recipients first learn of their potential windfall when they are approached by representatives of Ms. Scott, often from the nonprofit consulting firm the Bridgespan Group, and told that they are under consideration for a substantial sum from an anonymous giver. They are sworn to secrecy at first but are allowed to talk about the money once Ms. Scott's latest letter is posted.

Another example of level five is when one sees a customer in the grocery line that does not have enough to pay for their bill and the

64 *Who, What, Where, How, and Why to Giving*

giver covers the amount. This happened numerous times to Mike Ciunci, one of the leading real-estate agents in Pennsylvania. While Mike offered numerous examples of his giving philosophy, noting "I am just scratching the surface (to my giving)," the below fits well as an example to level five giving:

> I was in an ice cream shop that was cash only. This guy ordered like 10 things and went to pay but did not know they were cash only. I discreetly covered him. It was a bit awkward, I did not want to embarrass him, so I was subtle. A month ago, I was there again, and the same thing happened, but I was not close by and could not be subtle, so I did not intervene.

The key to this level of giving is to maintain an individual's dignity. Mike did this so well by being discreet.

The sixth level is when the donor gives after being asked. An example of level six would be when one is asked by a cashier if they would like to "round up" their purchase giving the change to a predetermined charity. Level seven is when the donor gives less than they can but does so happily. An example being a change drive at a local retail store. When making a purchase, the cashier asks if the customer would like to round up (the change goes to a particular charity). Most people opting to give could likely give more than just the change; this is a minimal sacrifice to them. Level eight, the least robust form of giving, is when the donor gives reluctantly. An example of this is when one feels social pressure in a group where others are giving, such as a fundraising auction. In this setting, identities are also known. The extent of one's involvement or lack of involvement is visible. There is a degree of social pressure or perceived pressure in that one may assume expectations from others. Even if one does not subscribe to the Jewish faith, these levels can be adopted and explored. As Maimonides would implore, we can all strive to give as close to level one as possible.

Social admiration and recognition received as a giver can be very motivating. It may indeed be a powerful motivator. But what are the downsides to being identified as a giver? De Freitas et al. (2019) conducted a series of experiments to measure how others perceive donors who give anonymously versus when identities are known. The researchers referenced Maimonides Ladder, noting that traditionally, anonymous giving is held at the highest esteem.

Who, What, Where, How, and Why to Giving 65

In a series of six experiments, the researchers found that even with increments of increasing donation sizes, donors who revealed their identity were perceived by others less favorably than anonymous donors. Participants also believed that anonymous donors were more likely to donate again compared to other donors. The explanation for these findings is that when a donor makes their identity known, the intent of the gift is perceived to be shared with the desire to do good and the desire to be praised. The anonymity of the donor does not refute the benefit to the recipient. Additionally, an anonymous donation is not always completely anonymous as often someone, say in a development office, knows of the donation coming in and from whom. Anonymous donations are often perceived by others as righteous in that nothing is expected in return. There remain many schools of thought on this complex concept of anonymous giving.

Adding further complexity to our motivation to give are our beliefs. Our beliefs about why we give and who deserves such giving are subject to errors and biases. Recall the social psychology concept *Fundamental Attribution Error* mentioned in Chapter 2. This error highlights the tendency to think about other's intent differently than we think about our own. Often, we tend to give ourselves the benefit of doubt and put ourselves in the "best possible light" having the purest of intentions. This bias also results in us making personality attributes for other's circumstances. If we think a homeless person is lazy, then our motivation to help is diminished, versus seeing the people as a victim of environmental circumstances. Our belief also impacts our perception of the outcome. Research has shown that people tend to value giving actions over the actual outcome (Yudkin et al., 2019). This finding is consistent with the literature that states that givers enjoy the act of giving regardless of the outcome from the giving. These points indicate that giving, as an act, is a powerful action. The outcome does not necessarily need to be grand.

Social exchange theory (covered in Chapter 2) maintains that people in general tend to strike a balance between giving and receiving. This theory also accounts for the ledger we all keep in our minds as to what is owed to whom. Some people are more explicit with this accounting and write it down, others keep it in their minds. At any given time, we tend to have a general sense of who owes what to us. Researchers (e.g. Ouyang et al., 2018) have

66 *Who, What, Where, How, and Why to Giving*

dug further into this theory by identifying three types of favor giving: generous, stingy, and matched. When people give more favors than they receive, it is referred to as "generous favor giving," whereas receiving more favors than one is giving is referred to as "stingy favor giving." Ouyang and colleagues added the third type, "matched," to describe those that give favors to a similar degree that they receive. Social exchange theory would maintain that people strive to restore balance when they receive more than they give. This is motivated by our human tendency to reciprocate. Matched giving is believed to be more common than the other two types. Taken a step further, generous givers are given higher status than stingy givers. This is often seen in the workplace. The rationale is that people feel gratitude for the favors given, earning the giver credit in the pay it forward figurative ledger. This credit is stored as the receiver has not returned the favor. When matched favors occur, the credit of social status is no longer "credited" as the favor is matched (returned). This thinking suggests that we elevate people to a higher social status of being kind and competent when they give without receiving. A higher social status provides us with respect and influence; things that are very valuable in the workplace. Ouyang et al. (2018) maintained that one can elevate their status by giving, especially favors.

Sometimes our intention is not fulfilled. This is a question I asked in my interview: "Was there a time you gave and regretted it?" Returning to the powerful words spoken by Georgette, she replied:

> Yes. But giving can be risky when you expect a particular outcome. My regret is not in the gift, but with the ideas I had about the possible outcome taking a turn in another direction. I don't settle into regret. I either set new boundaries or accept the outcome for what it is once it was out of my hands.

She offered more insight while discussing her boundaries to giving, noting:

> I believe we need to be willing to give freely without expectations, otherwise you are just adding stress to the receiver. No sick person or poor person has ever done better due to added stress. Society often donates with "terms and conditions" put on others.

Who, What, Where, How, and Why to Giving 67

This last statement was a theme throughout my interviews. Many interviewees shared having more regret not giving than when they did give.

Regardless of the reason, level, and intention, all giving can reap positive outcomes for the receiver. Benefits also occur for the giver as will be discussed in the next chapter. To this point, giving is good at all levels. Even when giving is motivated by an outcome, such as the giver receiving credit for giving, it can serve to reinforce and thereby increase one's inclination to give in the future. It feels good to receive praise. Also, giving the findings in social psychology on the power of modeling, when we share our generous actions with others, it can serve as a powerful influence on others' behavior. There certainly is a need for balance, perhaps the answer is for one to establish a giving portfolio with a variety of levels. See Chapter 8 for more discussion on creating a giving plan.

Who to Give To?

There is a tremendous amount of need all the time and in all environments. Needs are in our local communities, national regions, and across the globe. Some people have identified a preference for where their giving is allocated, others have not. Some refuse to give globally, preferring to see immediate outcomes by giving to those they know. Others give through large global organizations for a variety of reasons, perhaps one of the most pressing being that financial giving stretches furthest is more impoverished areas. Still others give to both local endeavors and worldwide entities. The choice is personal and linked to an individual's interests and goals to prioritize one need over the other. The choice is even more difficult when we think of our limited resources and try to allocate them efficiently. This is more the reason for an explicit reflection on one's goals and desires.

To explore the various areas of giving, Post and Neimark (2007) developed a Love and Longevity Scale and sampled 339 Floridan undergraduate students from diverse cultures. The scale spans four domains of giving, to: family, friends, community, and humanity at large. While family and friends describe one's inner circle, community includes one's neighbors and humanity, including strangers and those in a larger circle, such as global. This scale can be used to reflect on one's giving practices and help determine who they are most comfortable giving to.

68 *Who, What, Where, How, and Why to Giving*

The "who" varies. Deciding on the "who" is an individual choice. One of my interviewees, Ms. Majorie Dawkins, assistant enrollment director for a precollege program at Carnegie Mellon University, poignantly noted that it is "very tricky not to judge what others prioritize – we all have our own passions and can cover more bases that way." When we think about who to give to, we often think of those unable to help themselves. However, anyone can be a noble target for giving. Even someone of more than adequate means can be lifted by the act of giving. If the priority is to help those most in need, individuals living in poverty, homelessness, food insecurity, abused and neglected, are a few areas to start. The Department of Health and Human Services Office of Assistant Secretary for Planning and Evaluation (2023; https://aspe.hhs.gov) has identified the 2023 poverty levels in the United States as provided in Table 3.2.

People who fall below these levels are living in poverty. The *National Poverty in America Awareness Month: January* 2024 report showed that in the United States in 2022, the poverty rate was 11.5% with 37.9 people living below the above guidelines (https://www.census.gov/). Globally, *World Vision* noted in their *Global poverty: Facts, FAQs, and how to help* article that 1.2 billion people worldwide live in poverty (https://www.worldvision.org/). This accounts for 19% of the world's population. Given the magnitude of this problem, giving to those in poverty is an important place to start to make a powerful difference.

Table 3.2 US 2023 Poverty Levels

Number of people in family/household	Poverty guideline if less than:
1	$14,580
2	$19,720
3	$24,860
4	$30,000
5	$35,140
6	$40,280
7	$45,420
8	$50,560
More than 8	add $5,140 for each additional person.

Who, What, Where, How, and Why to Giving 69

Exploring who to give to takes awareness. Once you become aware of a need, it is now difficult to not know. Most people are moved to action once a need is known and they have the power/resources to help. Communities devastated by natural disasters rebuild together, enhancing their sense of community. Hardships shared can lead to emotional bonds with others. However, if the stress and devastation is long-term, communities can crumble and lead to despair. This occurs in impoverished cities and towns. In addition to lack of resources to purchase adequate amounts of food, many of these communities are in a "food desert." Food desserts describe areas with limited access to affordable and nutritious foods. Remember Maslow's hierarchy of needs. It is difficult to focus on anything other than basic needs when they are not being met. In impoverished areas, the focus is on securing food and safety/shelter for themselves and their loved ones. Giving to causes that serve to fulfill basic needs are often at the forefront of many peoples' mind when thinking about "who" to give to. It pains us empaths to image someone going without food and shelter. Making matters worse, envisioning a child hungry is too much to fathom.

The cost of poverty is much more than hunger. Poverty effects physical and mental health; recently, data from over 32,000 Canadian households were analyzed for the effects of childhood poverty (Anderson et al., 2023). The results found that children and adolescents in food-insecure households had 55% more medical visits for mental health concerns and substance use disorders than children and adolescents living in food-secure homes. They were also found to have 74% acute care visits.

Organizations, like *Save the Children* (https://www.savethe-children.org/), exist to end childhood hunger globally. They recently helped pass the Global Food Security Act allowing for $5 million to go toward emergency food shortage relief. This organization also provides clean water and medicine to those in need. They prominently display their financials on their website for ease of location and transparency. In 2022, most of their leadership staff earned yearly salaries in the 200,000 range with the CEO and Chief Human Resource Officer earning just over 500,000. These salaries seem within proportion to the industry and size of the organization in that their revenue was reported to be 1,051,387,892.

70 *Who, What, Where, How, and Why to Giving*

However, the "other compensation" column of the IRS 990 form (a resource available to evaluate nonprofit organizations to be discussed in the next chapter) seemed a bit exorbitant with additional amounts between $44,000 and 107,000.

Another entity trying to tackle food insecurity is that founded by rock star, Jon Bon Jovi. He and his wife run three restaurants with the theme "pay what you can" as part of his JBJ Soul Foundation (https://jbjsf.org/). Their mission statement is displayed on their website as follows: "Since 2006, the Jon Bon Jovi Soul Foundation has worked to break the cycle of hunger, poverty and homelessness through developing partnerships, creating programs and providing grant funding to support innovative community benefit organizations." Their three restaurants are in New Jersey, open to in-need and paying patrons. Paying patrons are encouraged to "pay it forward" to cover the cost of in-need customers. All customers are treated with dignity and respect. In addition to these restaurants, JBJ Soul Foundation works in partnership with New Jersey Anti-Hunger Coalition (NJAHC) to educate the public and policy makers on the food needs in New Jersey. In addition to providing food pantries, they instituted a project in which they gave cameras to participants for them to document what hunger meant for them. JBJ Soul Foundation is even tackling food insecurity issues on a college campus. As noted on their website, a startling one in three college students have food insecurity concerns. JBJ Soul Foundation provided a "pop-up" restaurant on campus to provide meals for the spring semester at New Jersey University. But wait, there is more! JBJ Soul Foundation also partnered with other entities such as the New England Patriots Foundation (football team) to offer a housing program in Massachusetts. Other housing programs have been initiated in 12 states providing close to 1,000 affordable housing units.

I crossed my fingers as I opened their easily accessible IRS 990 forms located on their website. Their 2022 revenue was reported to be $1.6 million. No leadership staff or board member earned a salary except for one executive director in charge of treasury and their salary was under 100,000. Approximately, 660,000 was paid in salaries to non-executive positions, which is a strong indication that funds are going to the frontline workers and the people in need. So, how does Charity Navigator (an online tool to be discussed in the next chapter) rate JBJ Soul Foundation? They give it a four-star, 100% compliance rating.

Who, What, Where, How, and Why to Giving 71

Help No Kid Go Hungry (Helpnokidgohungry.org), also known as Save the Children Federation, is another nonprofit organization tackling food insecurity. The statistics listed on their website note that in the United States, one in five children live with hunger, totaling over 13 million affected children. With the rising costs in food and the increasing wage gap in the United States, many are finding it difficult to secure basic needs. Of the households with children under the age of six years, 16.7% faced hunger on a regular basis. *Help No Kid Go Hungry* organization provides free meals, summer food programs, and feeding kids in school and at home programs across the United States. They also work to educate and change public policy to eliminate hunger. Their financials were clearly depicted, showing their 2021 IRS 990 form a revenue of $84.6 million. Their top 22 salaries ranged from 163,000 to 477,000 with other compensation for them ranging from $8,000 to 45,000. Charity Watch gives them an A rating, noting that 84% of their revenue goes to programming and that it costs them $16.00 to raise $100.00.

Exploring local causes, I came across 41 Days (https://41days. org/About-us/), an organization located in Chester County, Pennsylvania, that helps people that have "fallen in the cracks" and do not qualify for other supports. An excerpt from their story shared on their website is as follows:

It takes just 41 Days to change a life. My family knows that reality firsthand. On Feb. 13, 2021, my husband David walked down the steps of our home and asked me to take him to the ER "because something felt very, very wrong." 41 days later he was dead.

It took just 41 days for my life to be shattered. With Dave's death, every aspect of my life, and the lives of our children, were changed forever. That left me with a question, "how could so much change so quickly?" After all, it was just 41 days.

Now, think of this: if a life can be shattered in 41 days, it can also be restored. And with that simple thought, the ministry of 41 Days was born!

In addition to providing monetary support to community members in need, they also conduct workshops and classes on landscaping to teach job skills. In 2023, they provided help to 19 families

72 *Who, What, Where, How, and Why to Giving*

in need, totaling $16,329.00. Funds were provided for a variety of needs such as hearing aids, a week at a hotel for a family in transition, rent and utilities, the construction of a walk-in shower, a new mattress for a nine-year-old, Christmas gifts for children of a cancer patient, and family counseling to name a few. Unfortunately, there were other needs that could not be fulfilled as the funds ran out.

Other ways to fulfill basic needs and help those that have low financial resources is through community and church clothing drives. Donating clothing to these drives enables those in need to obtain clothing for free, making it one less expense for them and their families to worry about. If you cannot locate a place collecting clothing for free distribution, start your own in conjunction with your religious community or community center. Another way to give is to contact your local school and ask to speak with their case worker or residency coordinator. These professionals work with students and families in need, some of whom are homeless. They will have a list of unique needs that you and your network can support. Perhaps you are interested in donating directly to an individual, but abroad. Kiva loans, mentioned later in this chapter, allows donors to be lenders of loans to underdeveloped regions. Potential lenders can peruse proposals to select what may be of interest to them.

What to Give?

Truly, anything can be given and valued by a recipient. Gifts of time, money, and attention carry powerful symbolism to the recipient, sending messages of love and care. Most giving through this book focused on monetary giving. Some attention has been paid to volunteering time and expertise too. The reader is reminded that giving items "in-kind" is also an amazing way to give; in-kind donations are items like clothing. These items fill a need, help to purge the unnecessary accumulation of belongings, and keep landfills from being filled. This section covers examples of a variety of items to give. Several of these items are identified as a reminder of the value in things and the powerful message that can be sent when we share our resources with others.

It is surreal to realize just how fortunate we are to have resources and experiences. We often forget this until we hear of needs in others. Without insight into our privilege, it is likely that

Who, What, Where, How, and Why to Giving 73

we do not know what it is like to be without a basic need. There-fore, we will miss opportunities to give. We may be surprised by another's experience (or lack of experience). This rings true in a story told to me by one of my interviewees. She recalled volunteer-ing years ago in an inner-city program that brought children "out to the country" for a few weeks. The interviewee said: "It was an eye-opening experience; one girl was afraid of butterflies as she never saw one!" This same interviewee noted another example of an especially meaningful gift she observed was years ago when she was in New Orleans. She recalled:

> It must have been meaningful because I remember it, it left an impression on me. I saw a homeless man with a sign. A woman ahead of me gave him a sandwich. He opened it with glee and said, "a ham and cheese sandwich!" I thought, "Why did I not think about that?" I feel better giving something other than money. It never occurred to me to give like that.

Another interviewee, Kristine, stated:

> When I was volunteering at the Food Pantry, I remember the day that I learned that each family was receiving just two rolls of toilet paper for the month. This was shocking to me because I knew how much toilet paper my family used, and I knew that these families couldn't use food stamps to buy toilet paper or sanitary products. Plus, learning this triggered memories of my foster sister who refused to buy paper products, like tissues, nap-kins, or paper towels as they only get thrown away. Some things in life appall you to the point of action, and this did that for me.

Kristine noted that her mother and a woman she called Mrs. W. were her most influential role models for giving. When Kristine's husband fell off a roof when he was in his twenties, Kristine was told that he may not survive and if he did, that he would never work again. Kris-tine needed to rely on others for various things, one of which was finances. All they had to live on was her paycheck until her husband started receiving social security disability. She shared that:

> Mrs. W., a family friend who used to work for my father-in-law would check on us through my father-in-law. Mrs. W. was

74 *Who, What, Where, How, and Why to Giving*

very wealthy and wanted to know if we needed help. Once a month I would let her know how much I was short on bills and Mrs. W. would send her a check. Mrs. W. did this for a year. She gave me a check for whatever amount that was needed; sometimes it was for hundreds, sometime a thousand. I came to find out that Mrs. W. had a habit of doing this for people. She set a boundary as the months went on and said that she has other people to help.

About ten years later, Kristine and her husband received a settlement for the injury, and they tried to repay Mrs. W., but she refused to take the money.

Another interviewee, Tom, reflected on an early recollection of a gift he received and shared the following:

When I was little, like 4 years old, my aunt visited me when I was in the hospital with pneumonia. She brought me *Colorforms* to play with. We couldn't afford to have things like that, so it meant a lot to me that she thought to do that.

When asked further about early experiences with giving and the types of things he saw given, he stated:

In my neighborhood, people were always giving to each other. We were on welfare, our neighbors were on welfare, even still giving was standard. Clothing, food, help, fixing things. Time, effort, and money were the things we gave. Clothing was a huge thing; it was something people passed around a lot.

Tom also pointed out:

There is always something out there that someone needs. The act of recognizing the need can be random. Like when I put things on *Facebook Marketplace* for free: rocks from the property popping up creating a hazard to the horses and the blades on the lawn mower, we get dozens of people who want them. I have listed for free and given away mature evergreen trees from the property for someone in need of a Christmas tree, wood from fallen trees, bricks from an old patio, old fence posts and rails to name a few things. Other ideas are items people can use

Who, What, Where, How, and Why to Giving 75

for crafts like empty toilet paper rolls or for fundraisers like the *Box Tops for Education*.

The Box Tops for Education (https://www.boxtops4education.com/s/) is a program that gives money to schools for each box top collected from participating grocery store products. A similar program used to be in effect from *Campbells* soup company called *Labels for Education*. This program was started in 1973 and continued for 43 years until it was closed in 2016 due to reported decline in participation. They boast that $110 million in supplies was awarded over this time to tens of thousands of schools in the United States. Labels for Education program in Canada followed suit and closed in 2018 with the company once again citing the reason being due to decline in participation. Clearly there is a substantial need for more funding for schools and Campbell's acknowledgment of fulfilling some of this need with its $110 million contributions would be considered successful. So why does their reasoning seem like an excuse? Why does it seem like the customer is being blamed. Why did the company not stay up with the technology and offer an app for uploading. The company offered no explanation, as far as I could find, of the cost involved in keeping the program running. I could not help but think, what else might be the motivation? So, I researched further into what changed in 2015/2016; a press release posted on their website in 2015 noted:

> President and Chief Executive Officer Denise Morrison, will meet with investors today to outline steps the company is taking to alter its growth trajectory and its plans to drive growth in fiscal 2015, which include the launch of more than 200 new products.

Was the new focus on prosperity part of the reason for ending this giving program? Shortly after this prosperity plan was announced, Campbells also changed their signature recipe on a few classic soups and did a bit of executive reorganization. Campbells continues to be involved in corporate giving through awarding grants to nonprofit organizations that match their mission of food accessibility and healthy eating, employee matching gifts, and partnerships with nonprofit organizations to build healthy communities. The beauty of this program and others like it is that they are relatively free to

76 *Who, What, Where, How, and Why to Giving*

consumer. They purchase the item and send in the labels. Low cost giving makes it easier for people to participate. A free resource we all have is the powerful use of our words. On April 18, 2023, the ABC News reporter Todd Haas (https://6abc.com/philadelphia-pa-compliment-squad-celine-mcgee-rittenhouse-square/13150008/) reported a story on the *Compliment Squad* located in Philadelphia started by Celine McGee after her father died. McGee walks around town giving compliments to strangers. She then hands them a card encouraging them to spread kindness to others.

Other programs tackle matters that money cannot resolve, such as grief. Several programs offer support for grieving families that have lost a baby. Each program is unique in their offerings and worth exploring to determine the best fit for utilization and/or donation. Three such programs are reviewed below. All three programs accept donated wedding gowns that are repurposed by the organization to make infant burial gowns. Two founders/presidents responded to the request to be interviewed. Excerpts from these interviews are also provided. The programs include (1) The NICU Helping Hands Angel Gown®Program, (2) Emma and Evan Foundation, and (3) Sweet Grace Ministries.

1. *The NICU Helping Hands Angel Gown®Program: https://nicuhelpinghands.org/programs/angel-gown-program/*

Based in Fort Worth, Texas, this program was founded by Lisa Grubbs in 2010. The program offers education and support to families in neonatal intensive care units (NICUs). The support includes helping families bring the baby home and to support families that have lost the baby. According to their website, NICU Helping Hands has also provided over 15,000 bedside visits, conducted over 600 parent support groups, and has also provided education and support to siblings.

More recently, NICU Helping Hands added the Angel Gown®Program. In the event of infant death, custom-made burial gowns are available, made from donated wedding gowns. Gowns are donated globally. NICU Helping Hands has over 180 volunteer seamstresses. Their website notes three team members. The Board of Directors are listed on the IRS 990 form. No compensation is listed for any of these roles.

Who, What, Where, How, and Why to Giving 77

2.   *Emma and Evan Foundation: https://www. evefoundation.org/angel-gowns*

The founder and president is Sherri Howe. The organization is based in Montana but helps families throughout the United States and beyond. In 2023, they sent 456 angel gowns and 157 NICU Graduation sets to hospitals throughout the United States. Services are provided free of charge. Sherri noted during the interview, "we sent a shipment to South Africa three years ago of about 200 gowns different sizes and genders. Customs was expensive costing $85 plus shipping on top of it." Their website notes that 90% of their funding comes from their "Keepsake" orders where people can select a keepsake to be made from their gown as a memento. Options include ornament balls, framed lace patterns, pillows, christening outfits, to name a few. When asked about the start of this organization, Sherri noted:

Eight years ago, I was led down the path when I was an admin assistant at Verizon, had a good paying job, but was downsized and lost my job. I was depressed for three months, felt lost and did not know what to do with myself. I was cleaning out my garage and was moving my wedding gown again wondering what to do with it. I was scrolling through Facebook when I found a girl in Washington that was making these gowns and I thought that is what I will do and prepared it in a box, but I could not send it. I wondered if anyone did this in my local community. I could not find anyone doing it and thought it would be a good way to honor my mom and the community. I put a teaser on Facebook of me taking a pair of scissors to my wedding dress. Then I cut it up and made my first angel gown. Shortly after, I delivered 6 gowns to Community (the local hospital), around June. In September at a church fair, someone had a table with their ministries, so I presented my ministry and overnight I had ten people wanting to help. Put it out on Facebook and started getting requests. Now it is a 501c3 and it is my fulltime job.

She stated that memory boxes are sent out that include "a gown, journal, grief processing book, a blanket, ornament, and picture frame and a mother's bracelet with birthstone of the child, all free of charge, even the shipping." Sherri noted the need for more

78   *Who, What, Where, How, and Why to Giving*

seamstresses to keep up with the demands and the keepsake orders. She provides a private Facebook site for volunteers to process and manage their feelings as they provide this much-needed service. She explained that volunteers feel a strong sense of purpose in the work. Sadly, she noted:

> I have found that some seamstresses sign up then look at the little gown pattern, the smallest pattern is for an infant less than a pound about 8″ tall and realize that they cannot do it. I try to help them look at it from a different perspective – that is it is a gift to the family. 90% of my team are Christian and believe that the child was born into heaven.

3.   *Sweet Grace Ministries: https://sweetgraceministries.com/*

The founder and president, Katy Dortenzo. Located in Pennsylvania. Sweet Grace Ministries offers services to families experiencing loss. As noted on their website, Sweet Grace Ministries' mission statement is "We offer resources to families enduring ectopic pregnancy, miscarriage, stillbirth, life limiting diagnosis, and infant death. We offer help and support in the form of baskets, comfort bags, photography, support groups, remembrance events, mentor couples, and more." They too accept donations of wedding gowns and have volunteer seamstresses that turn these wedding gowns into infant burial gowns. In 2023, they provided 824 early loss bags to families and 480 infant loss baskets to families. There were 118 photography calls dispatched and over 100 families attended support groups in four in-person locations and one online location.

In January 2024, I had the pleasure of a phone interview with Mrs. Katy Dortenzo. When asked to describe the work, she does at Sweet Grace Ministries, Mrs. Dortenzo stated:

> Sweet Grace is different. When it was established in 2010 and got 501c3 status in 2011, I knew I wanted to do something different. I wanted hospitals to have a concise package. I wanted Sweet Grace to fill all the gaps. It is a partnership with the hospitals. My main goal is to partner with hospitals. We ship multiple times per week. Services are free and are available to individuals too through our online form for services.

Who, What, Where, How, and Why to Giving 79

When asked what was the organization's current most pressing need? Mrs. Dortenzo stated:

> Recently, we have received ten out of state requests for hospital partnership. I am working with my team to figure out how we can extend to other states and be able to be present to support the needs in person. We currently have 22 partner hospitals in PA, Montana, and Maryland. We are looking at what the out of state model looks likes. We need to explore how to get the local support.
>
> The organization has grown immensely in the past 10 years – mostly because families are able to find our information easily, they get our support, and then come back to give the cause support. We just added a 4th employee. Currently, there are two full-time and two varying hours part-time employees. We have 170 volunteers, 29 photographers, 10–12 seamstresses, and a Board of Directors, some who have financial and business backgrounds.

Sweet Grace Ministries partners with hospitals and supplies them with baskets and comfort bags, photography, gowns, and referrals. They also provide training for hospitals staff to help them work with families who experience loss.

Regarding seamstresses, she noted that they have a team of 10–12 regulars who are mostly retired women. She added that they love it, and it keeps them busy, that they feel a sense of purpose. Mrs. Dortenzo notes that they currently have enough wedding gowns but can accept more. They are selective to ensure that the condition is good. Unfortunately, some gowns that have been donated were too damaged to use. They seem to be in good balance with having enough seamstresses for the wedding gowns donated. I then asked: "Are there requests that you cannot fill?" To that, she replied: "No, we never had to turn anyone down in the 13 years I have been doing this, for any of the resources. We never had to say no."

I was curious about the work of the photographers, appreciating the emotionally challenging job that would be to photograph a deceased infant. Mrs. Dortenzo noted that there is an application progress for the photographers and that they "are very picky about

80 *Who, What, Where, How, and Why to Giving*

the quality. We want the photographer to tell a story. This is the only opportunity the family will get to create a remembrance of their child."

I also asked: "Does Sweet Grace Ministries receive external funding?" She replied:

> No governmental funding. All donations come from families. We have a huge annual walk in Chambersburg, Pa. About 1,000 people are in attendance. Local businesses sponsor items for bags. People want to see that businesses care about the community. Since COVID, we now have a virtual option with families watching from all over the world like Africa, England, and Ireland. The virtual walk allowed them to be part of the event. It is heart breaking but beautiful.

She also noted that families send monetary donations that sponsor baskets and bags that are sent to the hospitals. The child's name is attached on these baskets and bags to leave a legacy.

Regarding the name of the organization, Mrs. Dortenzo graciously shared that while pregnant with her daughter in 2003 she and her husband picked her name, Cicely Grace. Sadly, Cicely Grace was stillborn. The Dortenzos have had three other children since, one boy and two girls. Both girls have the middle name "Grace." I shared with Katy that my daughter's middle name is also "Grace," selected after a discussion with a nun who said the name meant "undeserving," meaning that grace is something given to us without having to be earned. The philosopher Aristotle defined grace as helpfulness for the purpose of another without any other return. Therefore, grace is giving not because someone is good or because they earned it. Grace speaks to the purpose of the giver wanting to give as opposed to the receiver earning it. Grace is not concerned with whether an individual "deserves" the gift or not.

All three of the above programs fill an important need. They are a testament to the power of giving in the process of healing. Much giving comes from loss as those experiencing hardship are keenly aware of the need in others. These programs, and others like it, show the involvement of the community and businesses. The creation of a good network is essential for shouldering the enormity of needs. People want to see companies support causes such as these.

Who, What, Where, How, and Why to Giving 81

The compounding effects of these types of programs are insurmountable. The sense of purpose and fulfillment the donors of their wedding gowns must feel knowing that their special possession will be transformed to give comfort and compassion to a previous infant and their family. The fulfillment the founders, volunteer, board members, hospital staff, funeral directors, local businesses providing support, etc. must feel knowing they are part of something that matters. If one was in the position to donate funds or a wedding gown to any one of these sources, the challenge would be to determine which one. This is a personal decision that can be guided by some of the elements already discussed. Once again, I recommend reaching out to organizations by phone, email, online question forum, or visit if possible. This will give you a sense of what they do and the way they do it. You can see or hear firsthand more than what is on a website. Organizations that are not transparent may not want their processes to be known or open to scrutiny. Allow for grace when reaching out to nonprofit organizations as they may be taxed with high demands and limited resources, impeding their ability to return calls and messages in a timely manner. Careful not to assume that an organization is not doing great work just because they cannot get back to you. Use other valid methods to research the organization.

Other ways to give small for big results is to give anonymously through random acts of kindness. For example, leaving *Post-it* notes on the kitchen cabinets in the lunchroom at work with positive words of encouragement such as "you matter," "you are beautiful," "you are enough," and "thank yourself today" with the tag line "pass it on." Image if you were to leave ten notes in one day. Chances are all ten recipients (and more if the note is read but left on the cabinets for others to read) felt a touch of positivity when they read it. Now, estimate that two to three out of ten pass it along, perhaps leaving for another group of people to view and so on. Such as small act can mushroom into larger effects (an example of a ripple effect).

Another way to make a big splash is to use your influence in a group to inform and educate. Ensure that you are not in a role that would prohibit you from doing so. Spreading the word about programs and needs you have researched is a great way to compound the support. These days there is a role for just this task, known as an *Influencer*. An *Influencer* has over a million followers

82 *Who, What, Where, How, and Why to Giving*

on social media and utilizes their popularity to persuade and "influence" people on product selection, fashion, fanfare, and more. Why not use your influence for good and market for organizations and needs. One such Influencer, MrBeast, discussed previously, has quite the sway on his followers.

You do not need to have millions of followers to make a difference. Tapping into one's network can encourage others to get involved. Returning to one of my interviewees, Georgette, she started a shoe collection in her classroom for *Soles4Souls* (https://soles4souls.org/give-shoes/). Georgette recalled:

> When I worked at the YMCA, I read a story to the children about an African boy who became lost while looking for "the best thing." When the boy's family found him, he realized that family was the best possible gift. One of the boys listening to the story asked why the boy did not have shoes. I offered him an explanation about how some people cannot afford the same things we can. He continued to ask, "why not?" I shared that some people may just need a little help sometimes. I asked the class if they think that we can help people who need shoes? They said, "yes!" So, I researched this further and found *Soles-4Souls*. We started a collection of shoes to be donated. We collected about 100 pairs of shoes. We connected it to MLK day of service. The parents loved the whole idea. A reporter came into the classroom and took a picture. I was so proud of the kids for taking such an interest.

Soles4Souls collects shoes and clothing for distribution to those in need worldwide. They have seven global facilities. They also work with other entities in a global program called *4Opportunity* which assists local entrepreneurs in selling donated items in their small businesses enabling stability in income. In researching this organization, I found them to be transparent with their website posting the organization's financials including their IRS tax form 990 and their annual plan across many years. According to their 2022 IRS 990 tax form, the senior administration made a modest, yet robust, salary in mid-350,000. They report over $92 million in gross receipts with approximately 5.7 million paid in salaries for a percentage of 6% of income going toward salaries. Charity Navigator gives

Who, What, Where, How, and Why to Giving 83

them a 99% rating. Charitywatch.org did not have them rated. The BBB's evaluation indicates that all 20 metrics are met.

Another type of donation is that of blood and organs. Curious as to what motivates people to donate organs sparked the interest of researchers Ruggieri et al. (2023). Considering that the number of people in need of donated organs exceeds donors, a method for capitalizing on motivation may help solicit more donations and thereby close the gap. They studied thousands of Italian participants, south of Italy, between the ages of 14–89 to create a scale to determine the variables involved in one's consideration to donating an organ. The researchers cited previous research findings that the social norms of one's family are quite influential in the decision to donate an organ and to know the wishes of family members in this regard. This gift of life is also viewed as a method to extend one's own life by giving life to another. They also noted that previous literature identified factors of religion, knowledge, and general attitude as pertinent to the decision. Through statistical validation and reliability analyses, the researchers found 21 items on seven factors that impact the decision. The seven factors include bodily integrity, fear of death, familial beliefs, altruism, medical mistrust, trust in the health institution, and emotional support. Each factor had three items measuring it. The researchers included the entire scale in their article. Readers are encouraged to view this scale for specific item content. The scale is nice and concise, but also offers a few questions that are scenario-based. The factor "bodily integrity" measured concern over being buried not whole. "Fear of death" measured the degree of difficulty one has in thinking about their own death or that of their loved ones. "Familial beliefs" gauged the social norm of one's family pertaining to organ donation. "Altruism" factor was to measure a respondent's inclination to help others and feeling good for doing so. The factor of "medical mistrust" measured the extent they viewed the doctors benefiting from the process, resulting in a dehumanization process. "Trust in the health institution" measured confidence in the experience and judgment of the healthcare system. "Emotional support" gauged the value of the support one would need to decide from the medical staff. Interestingly, this current study did not find the factors of religion, knowledge, and general attitude to be salient in deciding to donate an organ. This is contrary to previous

84   *Who, What, Where, How, and Why to Giving*

research. The researchers noted that the concept of religion is complex in that life is highly regarded, however, many religions do not view it to be an individual's decision to make regarding the extent of medical intervention to save a life. The National Kidney Foundation states that most religions do have specific permits for donating organs. Research in this area highlights many interesting aspects involved in the consideration of organ donation. However, these results need to be viewed with caution as self-report is subject to social desirability in that participants are inclined to answer as they deem socially appropriate. An important piece to this type of research would be to follow up with participants and see how many became a designated organ donor on their driver's license or report authorizing an organ donation for their loved one.

Individuals interested in designating themselves as an organ donor in the United States are encouraged to go to the federal government website: https://www.organdonor.gov/sign-up. Often, this option is listed when one gets or renews their driver's license. According to the University of Penn's Penn Medicine blog from March 21, 2023, *6 Quick Facts About Organ Donation* (https://www.pennmedicine.org), there are 170 million organ donors registered, however, approximately three out of 1,000 die in a manner that would allow for the donation to occur. There are currently over 100,000 people waiting for a transplant. Given my inclination for numbers, especially when faced with overwhelming topics, I did the calculations: 17 million donors assuming donate at the same time and what is donated matches the recipients' need and type (which is a big "if" as blood type and other factors apply), the percentage of donations is 3% yielding a total of 510,000 possible donations. This would be half the need, but remember, that this calculation is based on the highest outcome if the organ available for donation is what the recipient needs and is a match for them. This site also reviewed how one organ donor can save up to eight lives!

Speaking of saving lives, donating blood and platelets is another way to give. America's Blood Centers (https://americasblood.org/) is a national association of independent blood centers. Currently, there are 53 community blood centers and 90 hospital-based blood centers in the United States that collect approximately 60% of the nation's blood supply and the American Red Cross collects approximately 40% (2022 Americas Blood

Who, What, Where, How, and Why to Giving 85

Centers). It is also noted on this website that only about 3% of the eligible population donates blood each year. Some people hesitate to donate the much-needed blood because it is sold by these collection sites to hospitals. The hospitals then charge the recipients for the blood transfusion. While this venture may seem profitable, consider the overhead cost to the organization. To contemplate further, even if this noble act of giving created a profit for an organization, the payoff to saving a life is priceless. The donor themselves receive a sense of goodwill and at times a T-shirt or small gift card as additional incentives. A donor card lists the number of lifetime pints of blood donated and a running tab of the lives saved. The US Department of Health and Human Services (Levine, 2023) noted that for every pint donated, three lives can be saved!

In addition to blood donations, the American Red Cross and other collection facilities collect donated platelets. Platelets create an additional urgency as donations must be used within five days. Platelets are small cells in the blood that stop bleeding. They are needed to fight cancer and other diseases along with traumatic injuries. The procedure for donating platelets is a bit more involved and takes approximately three hours. It involves drawing blood from one arm, extracting the platelets, then returning the remainder of the blood to the other arm. A small needle is used to aid comfort. Most people sit back and relax, watching a movie to ease the time. One platelet donation helps two to three patients according to the Red Cross webpage.

Giving time is another valuable way to give. It is deemed to be a form of giving that not only increases happiness and well-being in the giver but also enriches social connection. Some have indicated that giving time is the deepest way to self-actualize (Reed et al., 2016). Time seems to be a more valuable resource than money to many. One can always theoretically increase their money; however, time is nonrenewable. There are psychological costs involved with forfeiting one's time, likely higher than any other resource. We want to know one is worthy of our sacrifice. As noted above, there are potential benefits to giving of time that could be enriching, such as the satisfaction one gets from watching their mentee develop. Understanding "time aversion," the hesitancy to give time to a social cause, needs further exploration. Reed et al. (2016) studied this very topic in a series of four studies

86 Who, What, Where, How, and Why to Giving

with college undergraduate students. They hypothesized that people who are more aware of their moral identity would have less time aversion. As people know who they are and what they stand for, they are more likely to allot time consistent with their beliefs. The authors explained further that high psychological cost causes one to act consistent with their moral identity. In other words, when faced with two options of giving time or money, people will ask themselves which option provides the best reflection of their identity. For causes that align with one's moral identity, the more potent resource would be allotted as a form of self-expression. Additionally, time being such a precious commodity makes us more inclined to spend time on people we know as opposed to strangers. As we get older, preserving our time becomes even more salient. To test their hypothesis on the impact of moral identity in giving time, four studies were conducted. The first study found that participants, who had their moral identity activated by a writing task, had less time aversion than those that were in the non-activated moral identity group. This effect was also seen for giving time to strangers or distant others. This finding held up even when the task was deemed unpleasant as measured in the second part of the study. In the third part of the study, the researchers tested time aversion when time was scarce, and money was abundant. People in the moral identity active group showed lower aversion to giving time rather than money when compared to people in the group that did not have moral identity activated. In the fourth part of this study, participants had the choice to donate real money ($5.00) or the equivalent in time performing a charitable act. The results showed that those in the moral identity activated group did not differ in their method of giving whereas those in the moral identity not activated group were more likely to donate money than time. The researchers concluded that time and money are not psychologically equal.

Many of the studies on giving are based on self-report of what people believe they would do or are measured through a computer-simulated giving game. Social psychology is interested in determining further as to what it is that people do in the real-world setting. Fortunately, the study noted above by Reed and colleagues added an experimental component to their research enabling them to measure actual giving.

Where to Give?

As will be reviewed in Chapter 4, there are several resources available for determining the most suitable organization to give to. Not all organizations will be nonprofit, nor do they need to be. A benefit to giving to a nonprofit is that they are expected to have financial transparency through the IRS tax form 990 (to be explored further in the next chapter). Plus, donations made to a 501(c)(3) can be claimed on a donor's individual tax form. Organizations that are for-profit or not established as a formal organization can also be a good place to give if they are doing the work you deem to be of value. Examples of these types of giving opportunities are collections in the workplace for a sick employee, a neighborhood fundraiser for a family that lost their home due to fire, a beef and beer event to raise money for a travel aboard service-learning experience, etc. These causes are usually for one isolated need that is time-sensitive, creating an official organization and filing for 501(c)(3) status would be time-prohibitive. Giving, though, makes sense as you know where the money or time is going, and the outcome is clear. Many people like this form of giving as it is less removed from the individual in need, and they can see where their resources are going. A further advantage is that typically close to 100% of donations go directly to the cause as opposed to salaries and overhead.

When asked what organizations she felt needed more support, one of my interviewees noted:

> A big one I give too, that needs more support is UMCOR (United Methodist Committee on Relief) global ministries responds quickly to global needs where disasters and wars have done so much damage that communities cannot recover on their own. They are sometimes on the ground before American Red Cross. Once a year the methodist churches earmark the offering to help cover the administrative costs for UMCOR. Then 100% of all funds received the rest of the year go for response and rescue efforts.

I was curious about UMCOR and did a quick search for their IRS 990 form. I found one from 2020 although it noted that they were

88 *Who, What, Where, How, and Why to Giving*

not required to file the 990, as they are church-affiliated, unless these were reporting unrelated business income. Their total yearly revenue was over 44 million, down by 13 million from the year prior. Out of their 17 listed trustees, only the last two received a salary, that being under $150,000. Many of the trustees consisted of reverends and bishops, so I suspect that funds were made to the church at large. Charity Navigator (an online tool to be reviewed in the next chapter) did not have a rating for this organization.

How to Give

The how to give can be viewed from the perspective of giving on-line, in person, anonymously, to name a few. Additionally, various categories on how we give were identified by Post and Neimark (2007). Their scale categorized ten ways to give as celebration, generativity, forgiveness, courage, humor, respect, compassion, loyalty, listening, and creativity. Celebration are occasions in which most people think of when they think about giving. These are birthdays, holidays, etc. that often spur people to gift to another. Generativity, as mentioned earlier in Erickson's theory, is also a cornerstone of positive psychology in that when we empower and nurture others, it enhances our well-being. Forgiveness also corresponds with well-being in that when we forgive others or ourselves, we become more at peace. There are ways in which we may give forgiveness directly to an individual or postmortem, such as writing a letter of forgiveness to someone deceased or even reading it to them at their gravesite. Courage is a gift of advocacy as it often involves saying and doing things for the betterment of others, but often hard. Courage is also seen in one's advocacy and speaking out. It is involved in giving feedback to others to aid in their personal growth. I think about the wise statement made by Randy Pausch (2008) in his book *The Last Lecture*. He noted that when people stop giving you feedback, it is a bad place to be, as that means they have given up on you. Giving humor is a wonderful gift to yourself and others. Humor can lift another's mood and distract from unpleasant ruminations. It brings us all a bit "out of our heads" and back to the "here and now," a very important place for our wellness. Giving respect to others shows that they are valued and that they matter. Respecting another allows them to be "seen."

Who, What, Where, How, and Why to Giving 89

It can be easily given through words of appreciation or recognition. This form of giving is free; a bottomless resource we all have at our disposal. Compassion is being calm and present when things are hard. Experiencing empathy and sharing one's understanding to help mitigate another's struggle is expressing compassion. A core to mindfulness theory is the need for one to give compassion to themselves. I encourage individuals I treat in psychotherapy to be kind to themselves and to treat themselves as they would treat their friend. Loyalty involves giving faithfully across time. Think of those in your life who have been loyal to you. They may not be those you are in daily contact with but are certainly the ones that stand out as being consistent and reliable in their regard for you. We give loyalty to others when we are there for them, in some manner or another, in times of need. Perhaps one of the most powerful gifts one could give another is to listen. With all the competing distractions these days, it is easy for one to feel low in priority. Actively listening is how we truly understand others. It is the core of all forms of psychotherapy. This is what a psychotherapist spends most of the time doing, listening to the individual. Most of the time, individuals know that they want or need to do about a problem, listening gives them a sounding board and validation. Listening is not only necessary in psychotherapy but in all our relationships – co-workers, friends, children, significant others. It is the vehicle for developing depth to relationships. I interpret creativity as a form of giving to be centered in mindfulness too in that we are noticing the gifts all around us. We can gift creativity to others in a formal craft, such as a sculpture, baked good, or through creative problem solving, to name a few.

There are so many ways to give, in person, virtually and beyond. A new idea I discovered is "micro-lending" in which you can lend money, usually to an individual in a Third World country. You can select who you lend the money too. Kiva (https://www. kiva.org/) is one organization that coordinates such loans. Kiva's website boasts that they have a 96% repayment rate. Lenders are encouraged to repeat their lending with other opportunities once they are repaid. This allows for the same initial loan to benefit many. I researched their IRS form 990 and found one from 2020. I found their top annual salaries (highest being almost 450,000) being typical for similar size organization, I was surprised with the

90 *Who, What, Where, How, and Why to Giving*

added bonuses, some got a whopping additional 350,000 in bonuses. I had envisioned using Kiva as a model to carry through with my own donation and share the steps along the way with you, the reader, but at this time, my research has given me pause as I am not comfortable with knowing where some of my money is going. I am a bit torn as I really like the idea of providing micro loans that could repeatedly serve others. I am also very curious about the process, and I would enjoy following what I envision a running tab of those benefited. I also found a bit of controversy in researching in that there were claims that not all loans got to the individuals. These concerns warrant further consideration and research.

This form of giving is relatively new, but there are other organizations filling this need. To this point, many have challenged the way giving has traditionally occurred. Starting with the intent, Joy Son (2014) has challenged others to think differently about donating. In her TEDtalk, *Should you donate differently?* (https://www.ted.com/), Son refers to what economist call "unconditional cash transfer," having no expectation on the outcome of an exchange. When we have an intention in mind with giving, a motivation for a specific outcome, we become attached to that outcome. Our sense of good, in this case, would be determined by the outcome as opposed to the act of giving itself. She adds that government aid operates in a manner that assumes recipients cannot do for themselves. She challenged her previous belief, also held by many, that poor people could not do for themselves, that they needed her and others to do for them. She added that she realized she had two assumptions:

> One, that poor people are poor in part because they're uneducated and don't make good choices; two is that we then need people like me to figure out what they need and get it to them. It turns out, the evidence says otherwise. In recent years, researchers have been studying what happens when we give poor people cash. Dozens of studies show across the board that people use cash transfers to improve their own lives.

Son added that none of the studies showed that people spent the funds on alcohol or that they worked less, findings showed that they worked more. A further valid point made by Son was how do we know the right resource to give and for that reason channeling

Who, What, Where, How, and Why to Giving 91

funds directly to the person for them to decide is best. She offered the example of elderly in Vietnam using their cash transfers for coffins. Admittedly, something she noted not realizing would have been a priority for them. This model is what GiveDirectly (https://www.givedirectly.org/) was founded on in 2009. It started as a private giving circle, then became public in 2011. Michael Faye and Paul Niehaus are the co-founders of GiveDirectly, the first unconditional cash transfer to the poor global program. GiveDirectly's financials were easily found on their website with highest salaries in 2022 less than $500,000 and additional compensation column between $3,000 and $15,000.

Prior to GiveDirectly, the Grameen Bank https://grameen-bank.org.bd/ program was launched in by Muhammad Yunus as a giving program for small loans to the poor, known as "micro-credit." His lending started in Bangladesh during the 1974 famine. Later, Grameen Bank was established in 1983. In 2006, he was awarded the Noble Peace Prize for his humanitarian work (https://www.nobelprize.org/). As of this writing, the Grameen Foundation continues to provide micro-credit around the world. Most recipient are women using funds for business ventures, such as basket and clothing making. Their website notes a stable repayment rate of 98%. They have emphasized their purpose more as a foundation over the years than a bank, now identified as the Grameen Foundation. This program has also inspired similar programs around the world.

Online giving has a plethora of forums such as https://www.gofundme.com/ and https://fundrazr.com/, where donors choose from a variety of profiles requesting support for people with medical expenses, housing and food insecurities, burial expenses, and team uniforms. Existing online businesses, such as eBay, enable sellers to designate a percentage of their profit to a selected charity. On that note, some charities utilize the online forum to sell items donated "in kind" with the mention that the sale goes to charity. Facebook users can elect to post a link to their social network to raise money for charities; a popular post for those celebrating a birthday, encouraging others to donate to their selected cause in lieu of sending a birthday gift. The Internet also provides games or activities for people to engage in at no cost to them, but their involvement leads to donations, such as http://freerice.com/. On this site, multiple choice vocabulary questions allow the player to

92   *Who, What, Where, How, and Why to Giving*

earn a piece of rice for each correct answer. The rice is donated around the world, based on the "greatest need" at the time. The program is funded by private sponsors who pay the World Food Programme (WFP) for the number of rice grains each player earns. Freerice declares that 100% of all funds go directly to WFP. This is a great way to engage children in the act of giving along with helping them learn! (More to come in Chapter 9).

As will be reviewed in Chapter 8, giving can be in remembrance of another. It can be through the start of a foundation or through collection drives to support a cause. It can be through a prepared Will or legacy plan. When thinking about how to give in remembrance of a deceased, think about what they were passionate about. What causes mattered to them? Perhaps the individual enjoyed walking in the community park. The donation of a park bench with a plaque noting the name of the deceased is a nice way to leave a person's legacy. How you choose to give to honor a deceased could allow for opportunities for healing. This is especially true when done collectively, leading to social support from family and friends, even strangers.

Another "how" to giving is to incorporate the family into the giving plan. This will be discussed more in Chapters 8 and 9. Working collaboratively with one another, the family can brainstorm ideas and set goals. Working together serves to model giving behavior and reinforces members in this prosocial behavior. Social learning theory mentioned in Chapter 2 applies here as prosocial behavior is learned through observation. Children are especially influenced by positive role models, but so are adults. Children's passion and optimism is contagious. When we work together as a family unit on how to give, we establish tangible indicators of our family values.

Another way to give is through matching gifts. Some employers offer to match an employee's monetary gift up to a predetermined amount or percentage. Life insurance policies naming a person or organization as the beneficiary are a low-cost way to make a big impact. We will return to some of these ideas in Chapters 8 and 9.

When considering the "how," be sure to make it fun! Make it joyful, not a chore. Challenges or competitions, such as bowl-a-thons, walk-a-thons, provide a social and motivational incentive for givers. "Coin wars" are coin collections. There are many variations such as whoever has the greatest number of coins

Who, What, Where, How, and Why to Giving 93

wins, or the highest value wins, or points are assigned to colors or sizes of coins yielding a total point count. I have also seen a competition where the winner is the team that has the **least** number of coins. This encourages the teams to fill up their competitor's jar as much as possible.

Another fun fundraising challenge is to offer donors the opportunity to challenge other donors to donate. An example of this is Marywood University's Giving Day Challenge 2023 (https://www.marywood.edu/support/events/giving-day/). As noted on their website, donors are encouraged to challenge others to donate by posting a commitment as a challenge goal, class goal, or social media challenge goal. The website offers these three examples:

Setting a challenge goal: "If we reach 50 donors, I will donate $5,000."
Making a class challenge: "If 25 alumni from the class of 1970 donate, I will donate an additional $1,000."
Making a social challenge: "I will make a gift of $1,000 to the fund choice of the Giving Day Volunteer with the most Facebook shares."

The campaign also solicits others to be "giving day volunteers" and offers a "giving day tool kit" to download which consists of ways to reach out to others and maximize social media presence. These creative "how" to give enables a variety of opportunities for giving. The challenge method is a smart way to enable smaller donors to make a larger impact by getting others involved. Typically, these types of challenges were reserved for large donors that could afford to offer a match incentive.

Another how of giving is through corporate "co-ops" philanthropy workplace programs. These are workplace sponsored collections and volunteering. The "co-ops" stands for "cooperatives" meaning a group of people working together toward a shared interest. This may be raising money or volunteering their time. Many businesses are realizing their social responsibility to give back and are supporting employees to do so. Some companies offer time off to volunteer. One such company is Johnson and Johnson (J&J), the world's largest healthcare products company. They started the *Talent for Good* (https://www.jnj.com/) program in 2017 which encourages employees to volunteer time in service to

94 *Who, What, Where, How, and Why to Giving*

the community. One avenue for volunteering is to help a community organization have a better online presence. Another program provided support to frontline healthcare workers, and another helped women and girls get involved in STEM (science, technology, engineering, and math) fields. J&J declares on their website that since 2020, approximately 4,890 employees have volunteered 55,000 hours.

Some billionaires are actively exploring their "who, what, where, and how" of giving as they have made a substantial commitment to giving. Many people are aware of *The Giving Pledge* (https://givingpledge.org/), started in 2010 by billionaires Warren Buffet, Melinda French Gates, and Bill Gates. The concept is for billionaires to committee to giving away most of their money in their lifetime or upon death in their Wills to causes to make the world a better place. As of the writing of this book, 240 people have signed this pledge from 29 countries. Those that make the pledge are encouraged to write a letter to share their decision to commit and to identify the causes that most move them. I was intrigued by the people on this list and the eclecticism of their letters, each hovered on the theme of the collective and the joy experienced with giving. MacKenzie Scott (formally married to Jeff Bezos) signed on May 25, 2019. She writes in her letter:

> I have no doubt that tremendous value comes when people act quickly on the impulse to give. No drive has more positive ripple effects than the desire to be of service. There are lots of resources each of us can pull from our safes to share with others – time, attention, knowledge, patience, creativity, talent, effort, humor, compassion.

She continues with "These immediate results are only the beginning. Their value keeps multiplying and spreading in ways we may never know" (https://givingpledge.org/pledgers). Mala Gaonkar, an Indian American businesswoman who started *SurgoCap*, the largest hedge fund run by a woman, signed the Giving Pledge in 2022. She writes in her letter:

> Giving money away is often termed generous. But if being generous means sacrificing a great deal, then I do not qualify. If anything, doing this has richly rewarded me, not just with

Who, What, Where, How, and Why to Giving 95

ideas and insights, but also with bonds to some of the most important people in my life. People who work quietly, often at great risk, often at great cost to them and those they love, people who resist the misplaced value society places on fame and wealth as markers of talent or even virtue. Such people are some of the most fulfilled people I know.

(https://givingpledge.org/pledgers)

Exploring this list, there currently does not seem to be any representatives from the entertainment industry. Many signatories are extremely successful business entrepreneurs, technology developers, or finance giants.

Social media can be used for good when it comes to "how" to give. It is a relatively free resource with limitless reach. Kindness can be spread with little effort but results in a big impact. *Social Media Kindness Day* occurred on November 9, 2023. The site encouraged people to pledge that they would post a message encouraging others to be kind on social media and to invite three other friends to post the same message. The website notes that there were 1,126 people who signed the pledge. Kindness Pandemic (https://www.thekindnesspandemic.org/) was started in March 2020 by Dr. Catherine Barrett who thought it especially important for people to find support online due to struggles with the COVID-19 pandemic. A survey of members was conducted and found that 86% reported improved mental well-being being part of the group. The scientific validity of this study is not known as there is limited information about it posted on their website. The website also boasts that they were awarded the 2021 "Most Uplifting Group in the World" by whom it does not say. It is more than possible that surrounding oneself with positive images and messaging makes them feel good. Engaging in positive actions such as giving can also be a great boost to one's mood as mentioned in Chapter 5. It is also possible to use giving to make negative feelings dissipate as the focus becomes less on the individual's concern and more toward others. Giving to others puts our own needs into perspective.

Another online source, Donors Choose (https://www.donorschoose.org/) is specifically for teachers. It was founded by a previous schoolteacher, Charles Best, with the goal of "connecting the public with public schools." The need being filled are funds for

96 *Who, What, Where, How, and Why to Giving*

school supplies and resources. Best notes that teachers spend an exorbitant amount of their own money on supplies and products for their students. Donors Choose allows teachers to post their proposals for classroom and school projects for potential donors to browse. The search function allows donors to search by amount, proposals from low-income schools, projects with no donations, proposals from never-before-funded teachers, etc.

How to give involves being aware of needs. One of the first things I did when my family and I relocated to a horse farm in Chester County, PA, was to research the area, specifically for needs within my community. I came across "Al's Warming Center" in the town of Pottstown. A few years ago, the center was renamed Pottstown Beacon of Hope Warming Center. This center provided a few dozen homeless men overnight lodging and meals during the winter months. Although this center has been approved for a permanent shelter, they have faced numerous zoning struggles leading to last minute openings and closing along with relocations. For the 2023–2024 winter season, they creatively arranged to rotate the center across four churches. The political struggle continues as some residents and business owners shun having the homeless gather in their vicinity. Financial struggles are a constant worry for many 501(c)(3) organizations; this one is no exception.

Other opportunities may seem small and everyday occurrences but can have compounding giving effects. One summer day, my husband and I were out for a ride venting our frustrations. We could not resist stopping upon seeing a yard sale sign. A preteen Indian girl was manning her stand displaying her handcrafted bracelets. She pridefully explained that she made them all. She was selling individual bracelets and sets to share with a friend. Eager to support her entrepreneurship, I purchased a set of blue and black bracelets. Interestingly, one was smaller than the other, enabling the fit for me and my husband (getting the larger one) to be perfect. I came back to the car and gave my husband his bracelet which I identified as our "Karma bracelets." The joy I felt supporting this young lady's business lifted my irritable mood to the point that I could not even remember what I was frustrated about. I told my husband that we will wear these all day and be sure to feel the good Karma. My husband, being a good sport, agreed and for the rest of the day, our moods having been changed, the Karma bracelets did their job.

Figure 3.2 Karma Bracelet.

Every time something good happened that day; I reminded him that it was the Karma bracelets! This is an example of what I call "compound giving." Compound giving benefits more than one person or entity. I gave by supporting this young lady, then shared with my husband, and felt a lot of good Karma in return. See Figure 3.2 for a photo of the two beautiful Karma bracelets.

Never underestimate the impact of giving or limit the opportunities for giving. I came across a post on Facebook by @jaysondbradley that stated:

> I hate that when the discussion turns to helping people there's always someone who takes the most ungenerous, contemptible stand towards others. If by helping legitimately needy people, I accidentally help some lazy people, so what? How is that worse than helping no one?

Motivational speaker, Steve Maraboli notes: "A kind gesture can reach a wound that only compassion can heal."

98 *Who, What, Where, How, and Why to Giving*

Key Points

- The World Giving Index found that the top ten countries for giving were all in Africia, South and Central America, and the United States.
- Indonesia was the most generous country in the world for the fifth year in a row.
- In 2021, only four of the top ten most generous countries were from high economies.
- Maimonides' Ladder is used to conceptualize the various forms of giving with the best form being that which makes the recipient self-sufficient.
- Poverty is a global issue.
- Included in this chapter offered several stories and ideas for giving including donating wedding gowns to be turned into infant burial gowns, using your influence on social media to support causes, donating blood and platelets, and so much more.
- We all have something to give!

Action Steps

- Consider the who, what, where, and how of your giving.
- What resources do you have in excess that can be given to another in need?
- Think creatively and consider what you have to give.
- Research areas of need that may be of interest to you.

References

Americas Blood Centers. (2022). *U.S. Blood Donation Statistics and Public Messaging Guide.* https://americasblood.org/wp-content/uploads/2022/05/Whitepaper-National-Stats_5.22.pdf

Anderson, K.K., Clemens, B.L., Zhang, L., Comeau, J., Tarasuk, V., & Shariff, S.Z. (July, 2023). Household food insecurity and health service use for mental and substance use disorders among children and adolescent in Ontario, Canada. *Canadian Medical Association Journal*, 195(28), E955–E955. https://doi.org/10.1503/cmaj.230332

Aronson, E., Wilson, T.D., Sommers, S.R., Page-Gould, E., & Lewis, N. (2023). *Social Psychology*, 11th edition. New York: Pearson.

Box Tops for Education. https://www.boxtops4education.com/s/

Who, What, Where, How, and Why to Giving 99

De Freitas, J., DeScioli, P., Thomas, K., & Pinker, S. (2019). Maimonides' ladder: States of mutual knowledge and the perception of charitability. *Journal of Experimental Psychology: General*, 148(1), 158–173. https://doi.org/10.1037/xge0000507

Department of Health and Human Services Office of Assistant Secretary for Planning and Evaluation. (2023). *2023 poverty guidelines computations.* https://aspe.hhs.gov

Donors Choose. https://www.donorschoose.org/

Emma and Evan Foundation. https://www.evefoundation.org/angel-gowns

41 Days. https://41days.org/About-us/

GiveDireclty. https://www.givedirectly.org/

Grameen Bank. https://grameenbank.org.bd/

Guo, Q., Liu, Z., & Tian, Q. (2020). Religiosity and prosocial behavior at national level. *Psychology of Religion and Spirituality*, 12(1), 55–65. https://doi.org/10.1037/rel0000171

Help No Kid Go Hungry. https://Helpnokidgohungry.org

JBJ Soul Foundation. https://jbjsf.org/

Johnson and Johnson. *Talent for Good.* https://www.jnj.com/

Kindness Pandemic. https://www.thekindnesspandemic.org/

Kiva. https://www.kiva.org/

Kulish, N., & Gelles, D. (June 15, 2021). MacKenzie Scott gives away another \$2.74 billion even as her wealth grows. *New York Times.* https://www.nytimes.com/2021/06/15/business/mackenzie-scott-philanthropy.html

Levine, R. (2023). Giving blood saves lives. *US Department of Health and Human Services.* https://www.hhs.gov/

Noble Peace Prize. https://www.nobelprize.org/

Ouyang, K., Xu, E., Xu, H., Liu, W., & Tang, Y. (2018). Reaching the limits of reciprocity in favor exchange: The effects of generous, stingy, and matched favor giving on social status. *Journal of Applied Psychology*, 103(6), 614–630. https://doi.org/10.1037/apl0000288

Pausch, R. (2008). *The Last Lecture.* New York: Hyperion Books.

Penn Medicine. (March 21, 2023). *6 quick facts about organ donation.* https://www.pennmedicine.org

Piff, P.K., Kraus, M.K., Cote, S. Cheng, B.H., & Keltner, D. (2010). Having less, giving more: The influence of social class on prosocial behavior. *Journal of Personality and Social Psychology*, 99(5), 771–784. https://doi.org/10.1037/a0020092

Post, S., & Neimark, J. (2007). *Why Good Things Happen to Good People: How to Live a Longer, Healthier, Happier Life by the Simple Act of Giving.* New York: Broadway Books.

Reed, A., Kay, A., Finnel, S., & Aquino, K. (2016). I don't want the money, I just want your time: How moral identity overcomes the aversion to

100 *Who, What, Where, How, and Why to Giving*

giving tie to prosocial causes. *Journal of Personality and Social Psychology*, 110(3), 435–457. https://doi.org/10.1037/pspp0000058

Ruggieri, S., Boca, S., & Ingoglia, S. (2023). Willingness to donate organs after death: Development and validation of a multidimensional scale on organ donation. *European Journal of Health Psychology*, 30(2), 51–64. https://doi.org/10.1027/2512-8442/a000118

Save the Children. https://www.savethechildren.org/

Soles4Souls. https://soles4souls.org/give-shoes/

Son, J. (2014). *Should you donate differently?* https://www.ted.com/

Sweet Grace Ministries. https://sweetgraceministries.com/

Tamari, M. (Retrieved November 2023). Maimonides' ladder of Tzedakah: The best form of charity make the recipient self-sufficient. *My Jewish Learning Newsletter*. https://www.myjewishlearning.com/article/maimonides-ladder-of-tzedakah/

The Giving Pledge. https://givingpledge.org/

The NICU Helping Hands Angel Gown®Program. https://nicuhelping-hands.org/programs/angel-gown-program/

US Census Bureau. (2024). *National Poverty in America Awareness Month: January 2024*. From the U.S. Census Bureau, Current Population Survey (CPS), Annual Social and Economic Supplement (ASEC). https://www.census.gov/

World Giving Index. (2022). *A global view of giving trends*. https://www.cafonline.org/docs/default-source/about-us-research/caf_world_giving_index_2022_210922-final.pdf

World Vision. (Retrieved March 1, 2024). *Global poverty: Facts, FAQs, and how to help*. https://www.worldvision.org/sponsorship-news-stories/global-poverty-facts

Yudkin, D.A., Prosser, A.M.B., & Crockett, M.J. (2019). Actions speak louder than outcomes in judgement of prosocial behavior. *American Psychological Association*, 19(7), 1138–1147. https://doi.org/10.1037/emo0000514

4 Evaluating Where We Give

Nonprofit Organizations

Introduction

Now that several points about giving have been reviewed, let's consider how we regard certain methods of giving. I encourage the reader to reflect on their initial thoughts as they often illuminate potential biases and assumptions. Do you view one method of giving better than another? Do you prefer to give in person instead of online? Is one method more legitimate than another? Are the viral clips posted in social media rehearsed and, therefore, not true acts of giving? Do online platforms such as *GoFundMe* detract from the cause? What about giving to entities that are registered as nonprofit, those that are not, and giving to organized religions – is one entity better than another? All forms of giving should follow similar levels of scrutiny and research. In this section, we will explore a few of these methods to gauge their potential influence and capacity for helping. The methods for evaluating organizations are based on the resources available as of the time of writing and largely for organizations in the United States. However, strategies can be generalized and serve as a prompt for researching in one's geographical setting. Likewise, the analysis provided for church giving can serve as a template for evaluating other religious entities.

Rehearsed or Fake Viral Clips

Many of us see short videos in our social media feed of people recording themselves giving to strangers. The lack of anonymity makes one suspicious of their motives. It also makes one suspicious of the genuineness of the scene. Is that young man pulling up in a fancy sports car, being recorded handing food to a homeless man

DOI: 10.4324/9781003438359-4

102 *Evaluating Where We Give: Nonprofit Organizations*

for real? Or is this scene rehearsed for the sole purpose of gaining "likes?" Even if the scene was "real," publicizing of the act makes us view the action less favorably. Even still, let us consider the possible good that could come from this video. First, if the scenario was real, a homeless person was fed. This enabled the person to be fulfilled at Maslow's most basic level of need; at least for the time being. But what other good may have come from this example? How does the giver feel having gifted food to someone in need? (See Chapter 5 for more on the positive effects of giving.) It is very likely that the giver had a burst of good physiological arousal, in addition to positive thoughts. The giver likely felt less helpless over the enormity of need-taking action to make a difference. The potential good does not stop there. Now, consider the viewer of this video. Even with a healthy dose of skepticism, how do you suppose the viewer feels after watching the video? As you view such acts, do you feel contentment, hope for humanity, even a sense of peace? For various physiological, cognitive, and emotional reasons, the viewer feels good after viewing the scene. The viewer is also reminded or made aware of a specific need. Awareness of a need creates a powerful ripple. As one of my interviewees stated, "awareness creates intention." Social psychologist would suggest that these videos create a stage for modeling that leads to replication. Good feelings are a good thing! Perhaps viewing an act of generosity has lifted your mood, inspired you to do for others. The online world is full of causes that have sparked exponential amounts of people to get involved. Of all the material on social media to view, these acts, albeit it real or not, have potential to create good. I know I would rather see rehearsed or staged social media clips of kindness than violence and negativity.

There is certainly something to be said about the viral effect of social media. This is evidenced in Jimmy Donaldson's "MrBeast" YouTube channel. With over 152 million subscribers, Jimmy is considered an *Influencer* and YouTube's "biggest philanthropist." His philanthropic channel displays videos of him giving away large sums of money, paying for eye surgeries, paying for hearing aids, etc. If his other videos are anything like the "I rescued 100 abandoned dogs" that I viewed, I can see (through my tear-filled eyes) why he has such a following. He has a charismatic and creative way of channeling himself and his viewers to make a collective difference. And yes, all 100 dogs were successfully adopted! His success

Evaluating Where We Give: Nonprofit Organizations **103**

is not short of controversy with critics accusing him of "inspiration porn." Inspiration porn is defined as objectifying a disability or need for the benefit of another. Such as posting a picture of someone with a prosthetic leg running a marathon with the caption "What is your excuse?" This type of ad is deemed to reduce the disabled person to an object of inspiration (Prange-Morgan, June 28, 2022). A less controversial social media presence is a TikToker, @traashboyyy. This young man posts brief videos of him picking up trash. He encourages his 101.3K followers to do the same. @traashboyyy posts videos of his viewers picking up trash all over the world in support of National Geographic's Sling Shot challenge by picking up 500,000 pieces of trash. Even with such an innocent action, criticism ensues as to whether these online celebrities are doing what they do just to get ratings, likes, or to maintain their status. I cannot help but think that there is worse messaging out there!

Crowdfunding: Giving through Online Platforms

"Crowdfunding" is a term used for fundraising through the internet, often utilizing social media. The idea is that small amounts from a large scale of people add up quickly. Some popular crowdfunding sites include *GoFundMe*, *Kickstarter*, and *Indiegogo*. Some sites have an "all or none rule" meaning that if funding does not reach the recipient's goal, no funds are distributed, and the money is not deducted from the donor's account. *Kiva* has an interesting model in which a donor can select from a variety of proposals. Donations are given in the form of a loan. Recipients repay the loan allowing the original donator to fund more proposals.

To evaluate these methods objectively, advantages and disadvantages are considered based on information from interviewees, research on these companies, and my own assumptions. Three main disadvantages I surmised are the cost involved in using these platforms, the social tendencies we experience when we see a fund making too little or too much, and the fear of providing financial information online. To the first point, *GofundMe*, like many other platforms, is a for-profit company. They charge 2.9% payment processing fee plus $0.30; another site says 8% for every donation (check these numbers). So, for a fund totaling $1,000.00 raised

104　*Evaluating Where We Give: Nonprofit Organizations*

across ten donors, the fee would be approximately $32 (recalculate with different numbers like $10,000 and after fees are checked). People rightfully do not like to pay fees. We do not like to pay for something when we do not see it as a tangible product. Plus, "fees" seem arbitrary and thereby not trusted. There is some social psychology to our thinking, especially in the concept of "lose aversion" in that we are more averse to the thought of losing money than to not gaining it. Several of my interviewees stated that they will not give through these methods due to the fees. Fees are important to consider. One needs to determine for themself their comfort level with such fees. To offer another perspective, as I mentioned earlier about replacing the noun/pronoun, I like to think about situations from multiple angles. Do we consider the postage on a stamp and the cost of a written check when we mail a donation? Do we consider the time, wear on our cars, and gas when we drive to volunteer our time? We absolutely should consider these things. We should consider the cost to our giving across all methods and weigh our options accordingly. The fees incurred from donating online pay for the overhead cost of the technology infrastructure and employees to create and maintain the platform. Sure, there is a profit to be made for the company, but how does that compare proportionally to the salaries of nonprofits. The internet is full of valuable information, be sure to use valid sources in your research process. As of this writing, the annual salary of the CEO at *GoFundMe* was reported as $264,300 (https://www.glassdoor.com). This is markedly lower than the salaries of many nonprofit CEOs mentioned later in this chapter. If we are okay with one, we should be okay with the other. Online platforms are especially good for reaching a broad array of people. Strangers can be made aware of a need and donate to it. This potentially increases the number of donations and thereby the amount raised. Why pay the fee if you do not need to?

There may be times when you become aware of an online fundraiser but know that you will see the person directly. It may be best to give to the person directly as they will get 100% of the gift. This needs to be weighed by the giver's intent and consideration of the receiver. The receiver may be more comfortable having the funds collected virtually in a discrete manner as opposed to seeing donors face to face. I recently had the opportunity to hand deliver a check to the grandmother of a nine-year-old girl undergoing brain

Evaluating Where We Give: Nonprofit Organizations 105

cancer treatment. I weighed the above considerations and determined that it was best for them to have as much of the donation as possible by hand delivering it. The decision to not send the money through the *GoFundMe* account was made easier by the fact that I knew I would be seeing her and that I wanted to gift it directly to the grandmother who has served such an active role in this little girl's life. This grandmother needed her spirits lifted and to be reminded that there are people cheering for her granddaughter, but also for the entire family. Even though it was the first time meeting her in person, the gratitude on this grandmother's tear-filled eyes and extra-long hug, were proof enough that she understood the purpose of bypassing the virtual fund.

Another disadvantage of virtual platforms for fundraising can be explained by social learning theory in terms of modeling. If a fund has too little support, the model for giving is not there. The model of social influence created in low supported funds activates the belief that others know someone we do not about the cause, resulting in low support. Whereas too much support may activate a belief that the need is not dire. Social psychologist would explain the effect of hesitancy to support a cause already well supported as due to the assumption that the need has already been met. Both beliefs are often fallacies and difficult to challenge if one is not attuned to their thinking. I encourage readers to reflect on their immediate thoughts when they see a need or solicitation. As stated throughout, this reflection will likely bring forth assumptions. It is now up to you to determine if the assumptions are correct or not. Think about the social learning theory on modeling and observational learning noted in Chapter 2. We can be the models of giving to funds that have no or few donations. When I see coin collections in the community such as the Muscular Dystrophy "boot drive" or the Salvation Army "red kettle" drive, I do what I can to contribute and watch afterward to see if others have followed my lead. Would donors have donated anyway even if I did not model it, I will never know. However, the probability of a ripple effect could be realized by seeing if others gave after your donation. When the donations are high and well supported, the psychological tendency is for people to think that their donation is not needed. This may or may not be the case (see MacAskill's notion of diminishing return later in this chapter). Further consideration is necessary by asking the following: What is the goal

106 *Evaluating Where We Give: Nonprofit Organizations*

of the fundraiser? Have they reached their goal? Will they need more? Ponder the example of a fundraiser for a medical need such as surgery. The cause may have already received $50,000 but the surgery costs exceed $100,000. In this case, the amount collected so far seems large, but it is not enough, any further donation counts. Medical fundraisers are further complicated in my experience as there are costs that are known, such as co-pays and surgeries, but then there are also unknown and unexpected cost such as loss of employment, lost pay for the person recovering but also for the caregiver missing work, gasoline, tolls, and parking fees (many hospitals now validate parking) for the commute to and from medical appointments, the expense of eating meals out while commuting or for caregiver in the waiting room post operation, the list goes on. Often additional funds, beyond the established goal, are needed and much appreciated. Sadly, if the goal is not met, even if it appears to be close, surgery may not be obtained. This is commonly true with pets in need of expensive surgeries. Fortunately, there are credit lines for such expenses, but not all people are eligible. Other fundraisers with dire "all or none" implications are funds for rent, food, automobile repair, fuel for home heat in the winter, etc.

The last consideration for online donation is the fear of giving financial information to the platform. As with anything, the legitimacy of such a site must be researched and securitized. Not only is the site an entity one may be concerned with misusing financial information, but the fear of hackers infiltrating the site is something to consider. While I am far from an expert on cybercrime, I can say that reputable sites provide robust security of personal information. That is part of the overhead cost paid with fees. However, anything is possible and there are sites that get hacked, have security breaches, and are even held hostage (known as ransomware)! But this is true anywhere. I am not suggesting throwing caution to the wind, only to consider "what is okay for one is okay for the other." Let's explore further from other angles. Do you shop online? Do you do banking and pay bills online? How about purchasing concert or sporting tickets online? The same level of risk applies. Some advantages to donating through online platforms is that the donation can register instantly. Online donations "strike while the iron it hot" meaning that it capitalizes on a person's initial passion to be involved. "Out of sight out of mind" is a common human

Evaluating Where We Give: Nonprofit Organizations 107

phenomenon. If we wait and put things off, they are less likely to occur (see Chapter 5 on gratitude). Another benefit to contributing online is ease of tracking for your banking and total giving. It is a nice way to organize and collapse gifts for year-end totals for accounting purposes, but to also assess progress toward your giving goals (see Chapter 8 on creating a giving plan). Online fundraisers allow us to watch the progress of the fundraiser, seeing donations add up, and even receive special messages posted from donors as well as the receiver.

A "feel good" example of the power of online funding platforms is that of a barber who cuts hair, free of charge, for the homeless. *Empowering Cuts* (https://empoweringcuts.org/) was started by Joshua Santiago from Philadelphia, PA. In 2017, he started asking people in a very impoverished area of the city, Kensington, if they would like a free haircut. He cut their hair right there on the side of the road with his clippers plugged into an extension cord connected to his car. He estimates that over the past six years, he has given over 8,000 haircuts to people in need. He now has a nonprofit organization called Empowering Cuts and has received $70,000 in donations through *GoFundMe* which has enabled him to purchase a recreational vehicle (RV) and all the tools needed to continue his charitable work. Santago's passion is fueled by the mission to lift others up. This is especially relevant to him as he grew up in a home where both his parents struggled with drug addiction. Santago had some run-ins with the police and was incarcerated on drug-related charges. He now devotes himself to empowering others and helping them get a second chance. Dignity is a power element, something he provides for those in need by helping them feel better about their presentation.

What Are Nonprofit Organizations?

Many, if not all, the causes listed through online platforms are not established nonprofit organizations. They are individuals or groups that have an immediate need for which they are soliciting funds. They are not organizations or other entities registered with the government nor are they eligible for tax benefits to the recipient or the giver. This section reviews information on what it means to be a nonprofit organization and how to evaluate nonprofit organizations.

108 *Evaluating Where We Give: Nonprofit Organizations*

In the United States, official nonprofit entities are identified as 501(c). The Internal Revenue Service (IRS) recognizes 28 types of 501(c)s organizations (2024 Publication 557 https://www.irs.gov). These types are listed in Table 4.1.

If an organization meets requirements for a 501(c)(3), they are exempt from paying federal taxes. The IRS lists organizations (https://www.irs.gov) exempt from paying federal taxes as follows:

1 Charitable organizations
2 Churches and religious organizations
3 Private foundations as qualified by a 501(c)(3)
4 Policial organization for accepting and expending donated funds
5 Other nonprofits, such as social welfare, and social clubs.

The donor too receives a tax benefit and that is the ability to write off on their federal income taxes a percentage of their monetary and/or "in kind" donations made to a 501(c)(3) nonprofit organization. A specific aspect of the tax law requires the donor to subtract any benefit they receive from the donation, such as a dinner or free tickets, from the allowable tax deduction. Some 501(c) nonprofits are also exempt from taxes, but their donors cannot claim a benefit on their taxes, such as donations made to political campaigns. Note that depending on the type of 501(c), donor contributions may be made public. The campaign may be free of paying taxes on that donation, but the giver cannot write the donation off on their personal income taxes unless the donation was made to a 501(c)(3).

Organizations, such as PANO (Pennsylvania Association of Nonprofit Organizations https://pano.org/), provide a comprehensive list of nonprofit organizations in the state. This information is utilized for grant writing and solicitation. The National Council of Nonprofits (https://www.councilofnonprofits.org/) is a network of nonprofit organizations in North America.

How to Evaluate Nonprofit Organizations

Large organizations tend to have large expenditures. It behooves one to research an organization prior to donating time or money. This section will cover strategies for researching nonprofit organizations of any size. But first, a note about small nonprofits.

Evaluating Where We Give: Nonprofit Organizations 109

Table 4.1 List of the US IRS Publication 557 Organization Reference Chart of Nonprofit Organizations

Section of 1986 code	Description of organization
501(c)(1)	Organized by act of congress, e.g., credit unions
501(c)(2)	Holds a title of property for exempt organizations
501(c)(3)	Entities that operate for Religious, Educational, Charitable, Scientific, Literary, Testing for Public Safety, to Foster National or international Amateur Sports Competition, or Prevention of Cruelty to Children or Animals Organizations
501(c)(4)	Civic Leagues, promote Social Welfare, and Local Associations of Employees: often used in politics
501(c)(5)	Labor, Agriculture, or Horticulture Associations
501(c)(6)	Associations organized for business such as Chambers of Commerce
501(c)(7)	Social and Recreational Clubs such as the YMCA
501(c)(8)	Fraternal Beneficiary Societies that operate under the lodge system
501(c)(9)	Voluntary Employees Beneficiary Associations
501(c)(10)	Domestic Fraternal Societies
501(c)(11)	Teachers' Retirement Fund
501(c)(12)	Benevolent Life Insurance Associations, Mutual Ditch or Irrigation Companies, Mutual or Cooperative Telephone Companies, etc.
501(c)(13)	Cemetery Companies
501(c)(14)	State-Charted Credit Unions
501(c)(15)	Mutual Insurance Companies or Associations
501(c)(16)	Cooperative Organizations to Finance Crop Operations
501(c)(17)	Supplemental Unemployment Benefit Trusts
501(c)(18)	Employee Funded Pension Trust
501(c)(19)	Member Organization for previous or present members of Armed Forces
501(c)(21)	Black Lung Benefit Trusts (coal mine)
501(c)(22)	Withdrawal Liability Payment Fund
501(c)(23)	Veterans Organizations (created prior to 1880)
501(c)(25)	Title holding corporations or trusts with multiple parents
501(c)(26)	State-Sponsored Organization Providing Health Coverage for High-Risk Individuals
501(c)(27)	State-sponsored Workers' Compensation Reinsurance Organization
501(c)(28)	National Railroad Retirement Investment Trust
501(c)(29)	CO-OP health insurance issuers

* Other organizations are listed such as 501(d)–(q), 521(a). and 527.
** 501(c)(20) and 501(c)(24) are no longer listed in the IRS chart.

110   *Evaluating Where We Give: Nonprofit Organizations*

Small nonprofits run the risk of folding (closing). This is a concern I have witnessed repeatedly in the field of social service. Wonderful, creative, and innovative services may not last – not because they are not effective, but because they lack the financial means to continue. Many nonprofit entities are dependent on volunteers and donated funds, especially those smaller in size. Large, and even some resourceful small nonprofits, apply for and may receive grants from their local municipalities, state, or federal government. There is a database at the library and other resources (discussed in Chapter 8). However, there is a never-ending chase for these funds as they are usually only awarded for a few years at a time. Some of these grants are renewable, others are not, making their reliance unpredictable for long-term budgetary considerations. It is no wonder small- and medium-sized nonprofits struggle to exist long enough to complete their mission. An online article from Bloomerang "Common reasons why new nonprofits fail and how to avoid it" (https://bloomerang.co/blog/common-reasons-why-new-nonprofits-fail-and-how-to-avoid-it-part-one/) noted various sources indicating that 30–50% of nonprofits fail. Highlighted in the article were five key reasons: (1) failure to keep up with technology, (2) failure to invest in infrastructure, (3) "nonprofit founders syndrome" in which the founder is not open to new ideas creating stagnation, (4) hallowing of the core if ethical guidelines are not established from the beginning, and (5) small details not attended too such as logos, updated website, environment – as all details create impressions that can impact a donor's willingness to give. As an example, Boles' (2009) book *The Everyday Philanthropist* offers wonderful ideas and is well worth the read. However, many of the specific organizations mentioned in the book have closed their doors since the date of publication.

So, what are the strategies for evaluating and researching a nonprofit prior to donating time, money, or property? I recommend starting with the organization's tax records (if in the United States), reliable online resources explored here, an organization's website, and their annual report. The US IRS tax form 990 is required to be submitted annually by all 501(c)s with revenue over $50,000, except for the 501(c)(1) and 501(c)(28). Form 990 is a valuable and accessible tool for the public to review. It is highly recommended that you review online a nonprofit's 990 form prior to donating. This form can be easily found through an online search

Evaluating Where We Give: Nonprofit Organizations 111

"IRS 990" and the name of the organization. You can also research nonprofits directly through the IRS at https://apps.irs.gov/app/eos/. Some organizations post their 990 directly to their webpage – now that is transparency! Typically, the form posted is two-three years delayed but can still prove informative in aiding your decision to support or not.

Now that you have access to the 990, what do you look for? It can be a lot like opening the hood of your car when it fails to start. Looking under the hood can be intimidating if you are not sure what to look for. (I would suggest starting with the battery. Hopefully, it is not the alternator!) When reviewing form 990, I tend to scroll straight to the end where it requires the organization to list the top earners' salaries and bonuses. The US IRS does not regulate the percentage of a nonprofit's income it can spend on salaries. However, it does consider their fiduciary patterns when deciding if an organization can keep its tax-exempt status. I factor in the size and responsibility of the organization, while considering proportionality of salaries for those on the "front lines." I want to see that most of the revenue goes toward the cause. I personally do not support nonprofits with excessively high salaries. This is something each person must decide for themselves (see Chapter 7 on creating boundaries around giving). There are many other factors to consider in one's research. Fortunately, there are tools to aid in the inquiry.

While looking at the 990, remember that not all expenditures and salaries are exploitative. It costs money to run an organization and to hire and maintain talent. It would be wonderful if these organizations could be fueled by love and volunteerism only, but that is not always practical. Additionally, employees should not feel shame for earning a reasonable salary while serving a cause they are passionate about…. read that again…. "earn a **reasonable** salary while serving a cause they are passionate about." In Chapter 7, we will explore one's personal boundaries with giving. This is where we all have potentially individualized perspectives. My gauge is for a substantial percentage of the donations go to the cause. I expect there to be "overhead" expenses such as building and operations along with salaries; however, I am disenfranchised with exorbitant salaries and fringe benefits.

The *Better Business Bureau* (https://www.bbb.org/all/charities-donors) evaluates charities/nonprofit entities across 20 standards

112   *Evaluating Where We Give: Nonprofit Organizations*

(BBB Standards for Charity Accountability) across four categories: governance, results reporting, finances, and truthful and transparent communications. Regarding the percentage of a nonprofit's spending on programming, they recommend at least 65%. Program expenses also include salaries. No more than 35% should be spent on fundraising. Another source, Charity Navigator, maintains that less than 10% of revenue should be spent on fundraising where less than 35% spent on programming would be considered deficient. *Charity Watch* considers at least 75% of the revenue spent on programming as ideal. (Note on Charity Watch: The site requires the creation of a log in and repeatedly directs viewer to donation site. Even with a log in created, I was not able to find any further information of value to my research, other than the metric listed above). These sources are consistent in their percentages providing a gauge for our own evaluation. However, programming is a wide category that includes salaries, which can be steep at times. Both Charity Navigator and Charity Watch rank organizations based on their proportion of spending on their mission's work versus administration. Charity Watch claims that organizations spending less than a third of their income on their mission are ineffective.

The BBB offers a plethora of information on charitable giving, including reports to aid the donor in making wise choices. Their website offers tips for donors (https://www.bbb.org/article/news-releases/24788-basic-giving-tips). These include:

1   "Confirm the charity's exact name": this is important to do as many charities share similar name and causes but are not the same nor are they necessarily connected with one another.
2   "Resist pressure": giving on the spot does not allow the donor to think through their decision nor have time to research the cause.
3   "Be wary of heart-wrenching appeals": sad stories trigger empathy and the impulse to help, without the cognitive component of considering one's giving plan and researching the legitimacy of the need.
4   "Press for specifics": the BBB recommends that a donor ask questions about the charity and quite specifically where the money is going and what types of programming is occurring.
5   "Check websites for basics": review the charity's mission statement, programming, and financial reports. The BBB notes that

Evaluating Where We Give: Nonprofit Organizations 113

all this information should be on an organization's webpage for transparency. If not, a potential donor should use their Give.org website for information.

6 "Check the charity's registration": each state in the United States tracks nonprofits. A potential donor can check to ensure that the organization is in good standing or if there are any restrictions placed on the organization. In Canada, nonprofit entities are tracked by the Canada Revenue Agency. Organizations or fundraising groups must also be registered with the Gaming Commission if they are holding event that involve games of chance with money such as Bingo, casino, raffles, poker games. An organization would need to apply for a license or permit prior to holding such an event. Organizations that do not comply with this state-by-state process are subject to steep financial penalties. For example, in the state of New Jersey, a first-time offense can be upwards of $750,000!

7 "Don't assume that every soliciting organization is tax exempt as a charity": a charity in the United States needs to be a 501(c)(3) for donations to be tax deductible. A volunteer may even be able to claim mileage on their taxes for commute to and from volunteer work at a nonprofit. Donations to organizations that are not a 501(c)(3) cannot be claimed on one's personal income tax. An example is a fundraiser for a neighbor to raise fund for their medical expenses. Although a needed cause, it would not be tax deductible on a donor's taxes as the fund is not a registered nonprofit (501(c)(3). Even still, the cause is noble and likely one you will choose to support, especially if you know the individual and are confident in how your money will be utilized.

8 "Research the charity with BBB": the BBB offers evaluations of approximately 11,000 national and local charities. The BBB website also has a tab for filing a complaint. Among its many resources, it provides lists of scams.

I was curious about the rating system utilized by BBB and researched a variety of nonprofits I have worked for, some I have donated too, and a few I recognized. I encourage you to do the same to see the variety of feedback and information provided. In looking at the Red Cross (https://give.org/), I found the following information with the first screen showing the 20 metrics depicted in Figure 4.1.

114 *Evaluating Where We Give: Nonprofit Organizations*

Figure 4.1 Screen Shot American Red Cross BBB Rating.

Selecting the "financial" tab, a breakdown of income to expenditures is provided as noted in Figure 4.2.

Although the BBB gives the Red Cross favorable rating on all 20 metrics, I see that the CEO earned $640,484 in 2020, which is rather high for my comfort, but perhaps not for others. Many make the case that salaries need to be high to attract the best of talent. But from my three decades in the nonprofit healthcare field, I can attest to the point that the positions most in need of the best talent are the direct providers. They are the ones that deliver the services and the ones who fulfill the organization's mission every day. Unfortunately, these are the positions that are often paid the least. As a result, turnover is incredibly high, leading to more demands on the workforce that remains. The additional work placed on the remaining employees further hinders morale and increases burnout, further impacting employee turnover (see Chapter 7 for more information on burnout). Perhaps what I experienced is only

Evaluating Where We Give: Nonprofit Organizations 115

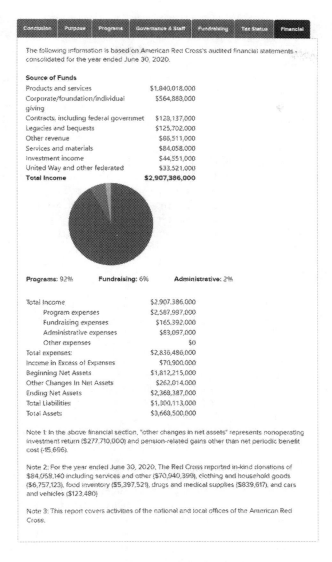

| Conclusion | Purpose | Programs | Governance & Staff | Fundraising | Tax Status | **Financial** |

The following information is based on American Red Cross's audited financial statements - consolidated for the year ended June 30, 2020.

Source of Funds

Products and services	$1,840,018,000
Corporate/foundation/individual giving	$564,888,000
Contracts, including federal government	$128,137,000
Legacies and bequests	$125,702,000
Other revenue	$86,511,000
Services and materials	$84,058,000
Investment income	$44,551,000
United Way and other federated	$33,521,000
Total Income	**$2,907,386,000**

Programs: 92%   **Fundraising: 6%**   **Administrative: 2%**

Total Income	$2,907,386,000
Program expenses	$2,587,997,000
Fundraising expenses	$165,392,000
Administrative expenses	$83,097,000
Other expenses	$0
Total expenses:	$2,836,486,000
Income in Excess of Expenses	$70,900,000
Beginning Net Assets	$1,812,215,000
Other Changes in Net Assets	$262,014,000
Ending Net Assets	$2,368,387,000
Total Liabilities	$1,300,113,000
Total Assets	$3,668,500,000

Note 1: In the above financial section, "other changes in net assets" represents nonoperating investment return ($277,710,000) and pension-related gains other than net periodic benefit cost (-15,696).

Note 2: For the year ended June 30, 2020, The Red Cross reported in-kind donations of $84,058,140 including services and other ($70,940,399), clothing and household goods ($6,757,123), food inventory ($5,397,521), drugs and medical supplies ($839,617), and cars and vehicles ($123,480)

Note 3: This report covers activities of the national and local offices of the American Red Cross.

Figure 4.2 Screen Shot American Red Cross Financial.

116 *Evaluating Where We Give: Nonprofit Organizations*

anecdotal, but I believe it is not. I challenge anyone in the nonprofit industry to reflect on their employee retention rate and dissect it. Compare the front-end staff with that of administration. Are the retention rates different? Are the salaries disproportionate?

I have seen many organizations struggle with high turnover, low pay for those on the front line, and disproportionately high salaries for those in leadership positions. One specific direct care staff comes to my mind. He worked with behaviorally inclined individuals with intellectual disabilities. His "clients" were so aggressive that they could not be safely maintained without direct supervision and coaching by staff. As a direct care staff, this individual would pick up a client from their new part time job and take them to the bank to deposit their paycheck. The staff confided in me that he was shocked to see that his client was making more money per hour than he was after having more years of experience and working in a high-risk position. So, when I look at a salary as high as 640,000, I cannot help but divide that by 50,000, 75,000, even 100,000 to see how many more average salaried frontline workers could be added to an organization if such high salaries were not paid out to senior administration.

Exploring the Red Cross further, I found their IRS 990 form from 2020 showing that they estimate having 300,000 volunteers and over $3 billion in total revenue. The five highest salary earners each made over half a million dollars a year. Fundraising events totaled over $8 million. Total program expenses were approximately 2.5 billion. Charity Navigator (I find to be the most helpful online source) maintains that at least 35% of revenue should go toward programming, whereas Charity Watch claims 75% should. Note that BBB report placed the program percentage at 92% and the program revenue at 2.9 billion. Having access to the full 990, I used the total revenue reported for the year which included contributions and grants, program revenue, investment income, and other revenue, totaling $3 billion. Using the separate line item for salaries and benefits, I see that they totaled over 1.3 billion. Dividing that into the total revenue of 3 billion shows that 43.33% of the revenue goes to employee salaries and benefits. Salaries and benefits are factored in as program expenses, so ratings can lead one to believe that more funds are going to recipients than they really are. Therefore, I like utilizing the IRS 990 information to dig a little deeper and factor out salaries to see what is left.

Evaluating Where We Give: Nonprofit Organizations 117

Another large nonprofit in the United States and Canada is Goodwill Industries; known by most as Goodwill. Goodwill's website notes that they have a presence in 12 countries, partnering with organizations around the world to implement their retail model and training focus. Goodwill accepts donations "in kind" of gently used clothing and household items. Funds raised from selling donated items in their retail stores go to training and rehabilitation programs for individuals that have limited employability. Their 2022 annual report (https://www.goodwill.org/annual-report/) noted that there are 155 Goodwill organizations with 3,300 stores across the United States and Canada. They boast that over 2 million individuals have received services and training to overcome barriers. In addition to helping to fund valuable programs, making a purchase at Goodwill helps keep materials out of the landfills. The 2022 annual report notes that more than £4 billion of goods were rehomed through the Goodwill retail stores. Of course, another advantage to thrift store shopping is the opportunity to find a hidden treasure and a good deal!

In researching Goodwill online through the strategies recommended, several separate entities are listed with different CEOs and senior administration. Although the Goodwill model is consistent across thousands of stores, their financials can look quite different.

Researching the Goodwill Fort Worth, Texas organization (https://give.org/) shows that all 20 standards rated by the BBB are met. These ratings are shown in Figure 4.3.

Exploring deeper with the 990 from 2020, the total revenue was reported at 3.6 million. Salaries and benefits were noted at 2.2 million. While BBB reports the CEO making 385,000, the 990 notes 325,000 (likely the difference being the year of reporting).

Another Goodwill 2021 IRS 990 from Maryland shows the CEO made $605,362 which included a $38,760 bonus. A 2022 IRS 990 for the Goodwill in Los Angeles shows the top earner made $749,593 which included a $178,125 bonus. Perhaps focusing on salaries is being too hyper focused as there are plenty of other metrics to consider. However, a human inclination when being asked for money is to consider **who** is asking and what are their means. To what degree are they able to fund the need themselves? When organizations ask us for support when they themselves are of more than sufficient means, we may feel a sense of exploitation. These salaries are likely higher than most readers. Certainly, many

118 *Evaluating Where We Give: Nonprofit Organizations*

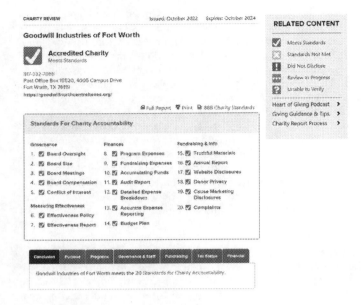

Figure 4.3 Screen Shot Goodwill Fort Worth, Texas BBB Rating.

US families are living off the amount of these CEOs bonuses alone. Just to put it in further proportion, according to the US Consensus (Shrider et al., 2021) in 2020, the median household income was $67,521.00. This means that 50% of the entire US households fell below this number and 50% were above.

The Salvation Army, started in 1865, provides support in 133 countries. Their mission statement from their website (https://www.salvationarmyusa.org) is as follows:

> The Salvation Army, an international movement, is an evangelical part of the universal Christian Church. Its message is based in the Bible. Its ministry is motivated by the love of God. Its mission is to preach the gospel of Jesus Christ and to meet humans needs in His name without discrimination.

Some of their programming consists of serving meals, providing financial assistance, life skills education, afterschool program, and

Evaluating Where We Give: Nonprofit Organizations 119

giving shelter to those in need. Like Goodwill, they have retail thrift stores that help raise funds to support programming. Researching the Salvation Army, as with the Goodwill, there are many entities listed. The Charity Navigator gives the Salvation Army a score of 100 but does not have specific data available as with other organizations. The Salvation Army is a nonprofit 501(c)(3) but is considered a religious organization. Therefore, they are not required to file an annual 990 (see the next section on church giving). Very little information is available online regarding the financials for the Salvation Army. Their website posts multiple years of annual reports. A company's own website can be biased, or at least puts them in the best possible light. It is also good to search for additional information through valid sources. Once source for salaries that is commonly used is Glassdoor.com. A search on December 31, 2023, on the Glassdoor finds the salary of the CEO (the Salvation Army calls this position the General) to range from $99,000 to $185,000 with the median (midpoint range) being $132,292. The reason for the low reported salary for the General seems to be that salary is paid in living expenses, such as housing, which is also tax exempt.

The ASPCA, the American Society for the Prevention of Cruelty to Animals, is a long-standing nonprofit, incorporated in 1866, even before animal protection laws were passed. The Animal Welfare Act (AWA) was passed in 1966. Although this is a relatively recent law, it still predates the Child Abuse Prevention and Treatment Act (CAPTA) of 1974. The ASPCA is a well-known nonprofit entity in the United States. They are known for not only prevention and rescue, but also for lobbying for laws for the humane treatment of animals. They air television commercials that are extra-long in duration and show sad depictions of abused animals, making the viewer feel like they just want to look away, then guilty for feeling that way. What makes the commercials even more compelling are the celebrity endorsements, like the iconic singer, Sarah McLachlan. Is the appeal too much? Does it fall within the bounds of inspirational porn? Just how far does an advertisement need to go to get noticed? This can be debated from the moral and ethical stance, but there is no denying that the appeal has been effective for the ASPCA fundraising efforts.

Their 2021 tax form (990) notes that the ASPCA has given away over $190 million to thousands of animal rescues and shelters. The president/CEO made a combined total of $990,525

120 *Evaluating Where We Give: Nonprofit Organizations*

in 2021. Included in that amount was $108,750 in bonuses. As anticipated, other senior leadership was awarded bonuses ranging from $20,000 to $76,000, where a few VPs received $0–$8,9000. I am curious what bonus structure is in place here. In the for-profit sector, bonuses are linked with percentage sales. What might the incentive base be here? It gets better for those at the top as in 2022, the president/CEO made a total of $1,117,171 which included a bonus of $154,440. Additional income is also earned from the ASPCA's subsidiaries. It must have been deemed a "good year" as all other senior staff listed received a bonus ranging from $7,500 to $57,217. Interestingly, comparing the reported revenue from 2021 to 2022, we see that there was a decrease in revenue in 2022 as the 2021 amount was noted as $389,934,885 compared to 2022 of $376,416,316. That is a difference of $13,518,569! What must have been cut or reduced in funding to support these increased salaries and bonuses for those at the top? There is a saying: "If you're not mad, you are not paying attention."

What do the other sources say? The BBB rated them as adhering to all 20 standards. In the "Program" section it lists their 2021 program expenses, consisting of shelter and veterinary services; public education and communications; and policy, response, and engagement at $228,580,572. Interestingly, the BBB site did not list the percentage amount going to programming. No fear, this is easily calculated by dividing program expenses into the revenue for 2021 then multiplying by 100 to get a percentage ($228,580,572/$389,934,885 = $\times$ 100). We see that 58.62% of the funds went toward programming. This is considered satisfactory according to both the Charity Navigator and Charity Watch. The BBB report did note the percentage of funds going to fundraising as 17%. Charity Navigator rated the ASPCA for the 2021 fiscal year as four stars with a score of 99%. Their rating was slightly shy of a perfect score of 100% as they received only partial credit for not having donor privacy statement listed on their webpage. Charity Navigator calculates program expense ratio differently than I did above. First, they use the average over three years and even more importantly, they divide program expenses into total expenses. This tells us how big programming was in comparison to their other expenses, not (as I calculated) how much of the money they receive goes to programming. Certainly, both figures are important to consider, but not to confuse

Evaluating Where We Give: Nonprofit Organizations 121

one's definition with another. It behooves us to know how metrics are defined to understand how to best use them and determine whether they are reliable/valid. So, the Charity Navigator reports ASPCA's percentage of expenses going to programming in 2021 as 75.3% ($227,836,676.00). You may be wondering what the other "expenses" were, as was I. The other expenses were reported as fundraising at 19.8% ($59,992,191.00) and administrative at 4.8% ($14,616,729.00). So, what exactly does the administrative cost include? Although it does not define, it can be assumed that a large chunk would be salaries and benefits. Given that I like to work with numbers and to consider an analysis from all sides (as I tell my statistics students, explore data from multiple angles like you would a beautiful gem), I took the salary of one employee, the president/CEO and divided it into the total administrative costs to see the amount taken out. Sticking with the 2021 reporting total salary (even though we know 2022 was more) and comparing it with the 2021 administrative costs, we see the percentage is ($990,525/$14,616,729.00 = $\times$ 100) 6.78%. This means that one person is earning 6.78% of all the money allocated for salaries. Of course, there are many ways to look at data; it is valuable to run your own calculations based on the information provided as not all metrics you may be interested in will be provided by these tools. Other questions I typically ask, and research are: How much have the CEOs donated to their own cause? How much have they donated to other causes? For ASPCA, I was not able to find any information. My searches kept going back to prompts to donate to ASPCA.

Salaries and expenditures are not the only indicator of whether one should or should not support a particular organization or cause. In addition to the financials, one should review the mission statement, programming provided, and the organization's goals as evidenced in their strategic plan. Information should be easily accessible online. For full transparency, these elements are a minimum. If you are so inclined, dig a bit deeper. Review the background of the founders and leaders. Do they come from a business background or personal experience with the cause? Either way, knowing the senior leadership's background will give you an idea of their mindset. Do they have personal stories associated with the cause? A personal reason for being involved? Look for rates of retention for employees/volunteers, this can offer very telling

122 *Evaluating Where We Give: Nonprofit Organizations*

information about the "culture" of the organization. Other ways in which the organization spends funds can be enlightening, just like that of for-profit organizations. The causes they sponsor are directly connected to your time and money. Some organizations sponsor programs that you may find conflicts with your personal beliefs. To this point, it is important to research the organization itself, starting with the organization's annual report. IRS records will also show some indication of grants the organization has provided to other entities. Looking outside an organization is important too for a balanced perspective; however, one must use valid sources. The internet can be a rampant barrage of biased and ill-informed information, be sure to use credible sources. Additionally, organizations evolve (as least the viable ones do) and learn from their mistakes. Organizations that once were exclusionary may now be more inclusive; ones that historically only filled senior positions with individuals of the same demographic may now be more diverse, and organizations that previously mismanaged funds may now be more fiscally responsible. Organizations are only as good as the people in it. Drastic shifts in employees/volunteers can significantly affect the organizational culture, not only from bad to good but from good to bad. So, the same warning should be heeded for organizations you have "always supported." When was the last time you looked critically at what they are doing (and not doing)? It is important that one does not only attend to the history and possible scandals, but to the current focus and potential good. Likewise, organizations in which one has always given needs to be reviewed periodically to ensure that they are being efficient with your money and their mission matches with your passion. Individuals change and organizations change. It could very well be that it is time to place your resources elsewhere to be more consistent with your giving plan (see Chapter 7 on boundaries and Chapter 8 on developing a giving plan). Entities like Charity Navigator (most accessible), Charity Watch (requires account to be created) and GuideStar (will also require an account to be created) can assist with this, but they are only as good as the metrics being used – you may have other metrics in mind necessitating that you do a bit of digging.

Now a counter-argument regarding high salaries is worth considering. First is the point that the IRS requires nonprofit organizations to justify high salaries and to establish that they are in line with the industry standards. A second point is that leaders of

Evaluating Where We Give: Nonprofit Organizations 123

large nonprofit organizations have a tremendous responsibility and oversee many workers and volunteers, facilities, and operations, that they should be compensated for this level of responsibility. They juggle complex budgets and regulatory requirements along with setting future goals for the organization to ensure its sustainability. Another argument made is that high salaries attract high talent. Some have even suggested that the higher the leadership compensation, the higher the revenue. This seems like a correlation which, if true, could be interpreted in another way and that is as the revenue of an organization increases, so does the leadership pay. If either statement is true, it still does not mean "causation" in that one variable (higher pay) is causing the other (more revenue). As I mentioned earlier in this chapter, the best of talent is needed on the front lines of an organization.

Other ways to evaluate charities are to look at their financials online, annual reports, tax records. Do quick calculation of percent revenue versus salaries and other expenditures. Charity Navigator evaluates US charities reporting that most causes spend 75% or more on programming and 25% or less on operational/administrative costs. Consider how much the top earner(s) makes in salary and other compensation (numerator) and divide it into the total expenditure (dominator) to get a sense of the percentage taken by the one or few compared to all other expenses. Do a similar calculation for the CEO plus several of the highest salaried and compensated employees (numerator) and the total amount revenue (dominator). This will show the proportion of the donations that are going directly to the top. MacAskill (2016) and others would argue that these calculations are not enough to determine whether a cause should be supported or not. The example of purchasing the newest iPhone is given as case in point that we as consumers do not care how wealthy the CEO is when we evaluate products which we purchase for ourselves, so why should we care what higher ups at a nonprofit make? MacAskill's comparison does create some need for consideration and reflection. However, the modern consumer is mindful of the tremendous salary gaps and is likely to consider company salaries, ethics, community giving, and social consciousness in their consideration of purchasing a product. Capitalizing on this are campaigns to "buy local" and "support small businesses." In the United States, the Saturday after Thanksgiving has become known as "shop small" in support of small local businesses.

124 *Evaluating Where We Give: Nonprofit Organizations*

Mindful consumers care about where their money is going and do not like to support businesses that support political and social views that conflict with their own. We live in a boycott and cancel culture where information about an organization that is not flattering could make consumers recoil their support. Consumer reaction can shift organizational climate, such as the case with Walmart, a large retail store operating in 19 countries, and customer outrage over low salaries. Although not a charity organization, employees started a food pantry for one another which was reportedly shut down by management to avoid the shame associated with the fact that such a resource was needed. Now, salaries appear to have improved. Salary deficiencies resulting in the "working poor" does demand evaluation of pay structures throughout organizations be it for-profit or nonprofit.

Attracting and maintaining high talent is important, but how can a nonprofit justify exorbitant salaries and perks? The whole concept of "nonprofit" is that the organization is not about making a profit but in putting everything back into the organization and its mission. I think most people are taken aback at the exorbitant salaries thinking that "if their salaries were not so high, the organization would not need to solicit from me, someone of much lesser means." We see our donations going toward excess as opposed to the cause itself. Our suspicion and skepticism are especially triggered as we are being asked to pay without exchange of a product. When making a purchase through a for-profit company, we tend to care less about the salaries within a company because we are getting a product in return. That tangible aspect enables us to better manage the discrepancy between purchase amount and CEO salary. Of course, there are times, as noted above, that we opt to not purchase a product because of what we know about a company. Other times, we are likely to reflect on the "drop in the bucket" we create for large for-profit companies like Amazon. Now image if Jeff Bezos, founder of Amazon, reached out to us asking for donations to a charity he is spearheading. Might we think, "you fund it!" Note that Amazon used to have an *Amazon Smiles* program that allowed customers to identify nonprofit organizations to support their purchases. If customers logged into *Amazon Smiles* instead of the Amazon site, and made a purchase, Amazon would donate 0.5% of the purchase to a nonprofit of your choice. Amazon ended this program on February 20, 2023,

Evaluating Where We Give: Nonprofit Organizations 125

claiming that despite half a billion dollars in global donations made during the ten-year program, "our ability to have an impact was often spread too thin." This is different from asking for donations, from "everyday people" to support a cause that Bezos himself is fully equipped to fund.

Other ways to evaluate a nonprofit and for those organizations in other countries that have different tax requirements, the organization's annual reports are a good place to start. A suave consumer could search for other trusted sources, often available on the internet. Another way to investigate a nonprofit organization is to go to the organization and see their operation. Ask for a tour or attend one of their events. When in doubt, give elsewhere. Unfortunately, there is plenty of need. When I asked interviewees, "What percent of donations should an organization use to run the organization?" I received a variety of responses. Many stated "none." Interestingly, interviewees did not have the same restriction when asked about using donations to run the church.

Charity Navigator assesses organizations across four metrics: Impact and Results, Accountability and Finance, Leadership and Adaptability, and Culture and Community. Similarly, William MacAskill, author of *Doing Good Better: How Effective Altruism Can Help You Help Others, Do Work That Matters, and Make Smarter Choices about Giving Back* (2016), identified five questions donors should ask before donating. Each of these questions is a separate chapter in his book. MacAskill's questions include: (1) What does this charity do? (2) How cost-effective is each program area? (3) How robust is the evidence behind each program? (4) How well is each program implemented? and (5) Does the charity need additional funds? These two sources provide good questions for evaluating the efficacy of an organization and its cause. In Chapters 7 and 8, I provide further points to consider as it pertains to developing boundaries around giving along with creating a plan for giving. For now, I would add that when looking at the merits of an organization or a cause, I suggest considering how much attention and publicity the cause receives. Causes with a small reach likely need your support more. MacAskill commented on this as being in direct relation to "the law of diminishing returns." This economic term describes the tendency for a benefit to be smaller the more investment it receives. Theoretically, causes with less awareness and spotlight are often the ones where the most difference can be made.

126 Evaluating Where We Give: Nonprofit Organizations

Looking deep into what an organization stands for is recommended and something we all should try to be attuned to. Once we learn about an organization's misdoings or support of controversial issues, we tend to withhold our support. This is true of for-profits as well as nonprofits. MacAskill debates the efficacy of "ethical consumerism" and has a whole chapter in his book devoted to it. Ethical consumerism involves choosing what to purchase based on where and how the items are made, how it is distributed, and the equity of trade involved in producing the product. While MacAskill acknowledges the need for human rights and improvement in working conditions and wages, he questioned whether boycotting products was the best way to do good. He, as many others have, made the point that eliminating sweatshops (work environments around the world with low wages and often unhealthy work conditions) and the like undermines this class of workers as it leaves them even more destitute with less options. Many consumers look for the "Fairtrade" endorsement on products such as coffee and other consumable goods. MacAskill's questions the actual impact Fairtrade has on the manual laborer, noting that owners are often the beneficiaries. He mentions further that Fairtrade certification is expensive to obtain, preventing some of the poorest countries from securing.

Many organizations do not provide the level of detail one would need to really ascertain their effectiveness in programming and financial responsibility. The mindful donor will likely need to do some digging. Transparency is important, without it, I would be suspicious as to how your money is being used. Reach out to the organization, ask questions, and take a tour of the facility. Are they open to your questions and requests for more information? If not, that answers your questions. To these points, I offer Table 4.2 additional metrics to consider while researching a nonprofit organization.

Table 4.3 provides a summary of several online entities available for evaluating nonprofit organizations.

Giving to the Church

Churches are not required to file tax returns but are encouraged to write annual reports covering finances across the entire institution. In researching church annual reports for this book, I started locally, mainly with the churches I knew and were at one time affiliated.

Evaluating Where We Give: Nonprofit Organizations **127**

Table 4.2 Additional Metrics to Consider When Evaluating Nonprofit Organizations

Finances	• What proportion of funds go to individuals served after taking out for salaries? • Are financials accessible to the public? • Environment: Are properties/rents excessive? • Is it clear what portion of each dollar goes to the cause? • Will your donation of time or money make a difference?
Programming	• How urgent is the need? • Is the need not covered by others or other entities? • Is programming accessible to those in need?
Culture	• Is there a lot of turnover in employees and volunteers? • Are they open to donor inquiry? • Do they provide transparency to donors? • Do they have events for donors outside fundraising?
Add your priorities and parameters (explored further in Chapter 7)	

Table 4.3 Online Tools for Researching Nonprofit Organizations

Sources for evaluating charities	*Website*
Better Business Bureau	https://give.org/
Charity Navigator	https://www.charitynavigator.org/
Charity Watch	https://www.charitywatch.org/
GuideStar	https://www.guidestar.org/
Consumer Reports	https://www.consumerreports.org/money/charities/best-charities-for-your-donations-a4066579102/
IRS 990	https://www.irs.gov/charities-non-profits/tax-exempt-organization-search
IRS nonprofit table	https://www.irs.gov/statistics/soi-tax-stats-charities-and-other-tax-exempt-organizations-statistics
Organizations website and annual reports	Various websites specific to the organization to review their mission statement, programming, and goals. Review background of leaders and rates of retention for employees/volunteers

128 *Evaluating Where We Give: Nonprofit Organizations*

It struck me as odd that most of these churches did not have their annual reports posted on their websites. Some did and made them easy to find and across multiple years. One church (and I am sure many others that I did not go on to research) had their annual reports easily accessible online, but when I reviewed the report, all areas were covered in detail, except for the finances. Instead, in the finance section, it listed the names of five financial reports with the note: "available to members upon request." How many members would take the extra step to ask for these reports? Why not include it in the report? Churches that do not post their reports or limit them to "members only" may argue that this is an internal document that perhaps only members should have. I counter by saying that the donation button was active, easily accessible, and at the forefront for non-members – why not information on how that money is being used? Plus, churches receive a tax benefit of being deemed exempt from taxation. They are not required to post financials; however, doing so would seem prudent and go a long way toward earning trust. Knowing where one's money is going and the percentage that gets put toward the cause are my first two considerations. In my mind, churches are not excluded from these criteria. Annual reports can be incredibly helpful to a potential donor who is not a member as they would not necessarily know what the church does by way of programming, etc. We all know that some places of worship do more than others for the community, this would be reflected in the annual report. Since annual reports are important to review for all organizations, religious or secular, it warrants mentioning that annual reports are written in the best possible light. It is a bit self-serving that these reports are written by members of the organization themselves, just like shareholder reports, with the view of the stakeholder in mind. This is not to discount the report, just to put it in a perspective worth knowing.

In asking about how financials are reported and how churches spend donations, many interviewees reported not thinking about it previously. One interviewee stated: "Putting money into a collection, I am not always sure where it is going." Other interviewees commented on the programming they see occurring through the churches as a direct indicator of where the donations went. Others did not see this type of evidence.

Church fraud is a real issue with devastating consequences. It tears apart congregations and leaves members with deep feelings

Evaluating Where We Give: Nonprofit Organizations **129**

of betrayal. Existentially, members experiencing fraud within the church question, "if a person or entity of God cannot be trusted, then who can?" Some defend the poor behavior and refuse to believe the charges levied against the church or leadership. Psychologist call this "denial." Certainly, misuse of funds can and has occurred in any organization. The undertone to the need for research and creating boundaries to giving is due to the need to protect oneself from being exploited and to ensure, as best as possible, that resources are going where one believes them to be. However, if one does not know where their resources are going or blindly believes in what could just be a good sales pitch or idea, they run the risk of being exploited. What is further devastating to contemplate is that fraud could occur through the guise of a valid cause, e.g., an individual raising money for the March of Dimes, Special Olympics, etc. How does one know that the money they give is going directly to the organization? One solution is to write a good old fashion check with the organization's name on it, not the name of the person collecting the donation.

Ministry Watch (https://ministrywatch.com/) is one organization that provides ratings of churches based on review of their 990 forms (if filed), an audited financial statement, and membership in the Evangelical Council for Financial Accountability (ECFA) for churches over $1 million in revenue. Table 4.4 offers some tools for researching churches.

Table 4.4 Tools for Researching Churches

What to do/where to go	How to access and what to look for
Ministry Watch	Website: https://ministrywatch.com/
Read annual reports	Typically published on church's website
Attend budget and planning meetings	Dates, times, and location should be listed in newsletters and the church's website
Serve on administrative teams to be involved directly in decisions for spending	Volunteer or apply for task forces, boards, and governance bodies at the church
Ask leaders at the church for information on programs/ project spending	Go to the leaders of the church and ask for specific information, such as a financial report. Follow up in writing, such as in an email too

130 *Evaluating Where We Give: Nonprofit Organizations*

Difficulties option information with any of these sources or others is telling about the level of transparency. Lack of openness to responding to questions is telling and not a good indicator.

Key Points

- Caution and research are needed before giving resources to an individual or organization.
- Online tools, such as Charity Navigator, Charity Watch, reviewing US IRS form 990, *Better Business Bureau*, and organizations annual reports are a few ways to research an organization.
- Expenses paid to salaries and perks should be considered when investing resources in a nonprofit, or any entity for that matter.
- Another factor to consider is how much money is the organization putting into programming, minus salaries?

Action Steps

- Select an organization or two that you currently give to or have considered giving too. Now using one of the tools mentioned in this chapter, explore their financials and programming.
- Identify your own parameters around what you find acceptable regarding percentage of resources going to salaries versus programming.

References

Better Business Bureau. *Charity & donor resources.* https://www.bbb.org/all/charities-donors

Better Business Bureau. (2021). *BBB tip: Advice for giving to charity.* https://www.bbb.org/article/news-releases/24788-basic-giving-tips

Bloomerang. *Common reasons why new nonprofits fail and how to avoid it.* https://bloomerang.co/blog/common-reasons-why-new-nonprofits-fail-and-how-to-avoid-it-part-one/

Boles, N.B. (2009). *How to Be an Everyday Philanthropist: 330 Ways to Make a Difference in Your Home, Community, and World-at No Cost.* New York: Workman Publishing Company.

Empowering Cuts. https://empoweringcuts.org/

Glassdoor. https://www.glassdoor.com

Evaluating Where We Give: Nonprofit Organizations 131

Goodwill. (2021). *2022 annual report*. https://www.goodwill.org/annual-report/

IRS. https://www.irs.gov

IRS Publication 557. (2024). 2024 Publication 557 Tax-Exempt Status for Your Organization https://www.irs.gov

IRS Tax Exempt Organization Search. https://apps.irs.gov/app/eos/

MacAskill, W. (2016). *Doing Good Better: How Effective Altruism Can Help You Help Others Better*. New York: Penguin Random House.

Ministry Watch. https://ministrywatch.com/

National Council of Nonprofits. https://www.councilofnonprofits.org/

Pennsylvania Association of Nonprofit Organizations. https://pano.org/

Prange-Morgan, C. (June 28, 2022). What is "Inspiration Porn" and why does it matter? *Psychology Today*. https://www.psychologytoday.com/us

Salvation Army. https://www.salvationarmyusa.org

Shrider, E.A., Kollar, M., Chen, F., & Semega, J. (September 2021). *Income and poverty in the United States: 2020*. Report Number P60–273. https://www.census.gov/library/publications/2021/demo/p60-273.html

5 Benefits to Giving

Introduction

Included in this chapter are the benefits to giving for the giver and the receiver. The effects of giving on the giver are reviewed through the lens of positive psychology and physiological processes. Biological functions create feelings of joy and emotional wellness when we give. Psychological effects from giving show increased mood. Along with the positive burst of pleasurable emotional states, giving creates a positive shift in a giver's mindset to that of solution-focused instead of problem-focused. Through giving, we become active agents of change. In modeling this action, we communicate positive messaging that creates awareness in others, leading to a ripple effect.

Benefits to the Receiver

Surprisingly, little research is available on the effects of being a receiver. It may seem obvious. To most people, receiving a gift is a positive thing. It could even be life changing. However, to some, receiving a gift can be awkward and trigger embarrassment, even shame. The next chapter covers material on being a recipient and the importance of gratitude. Gratitude is a central aspect to wellness and a core of positive psychology theory. For now, it is important to mention that the response to giving can vary among receivers. When asked about benefits to receiving, my interviewees reported feeling seen, validated, and hopeful. The receiver may be processing opposing feelings regarding a gift, such as gratitude and pride. However, most people report experiencing a tangible benefit to being a recipient as it fulfills a need such as food, money,

DOI: 10.4324/9781003438359-5

Benefits to Giving 133

or shelter. Usually, a gift provides an opportunity for the receiver to advance beyond their current circumstance. To the receiver, the gift reminds them that there is compassion in the world and offers them hope. As noted in the World Happiness Report (2023) cited earlier, recipients of help reported improved trust, empathy, and view of human nature. Noted in the same report was that recipients' well-being was highest when they perceived the giver to be intrinsically motivated to give.

Exploring the benefits of receiving, Chancellor et al. (2017) conducted a study in a Spanish corporation. Employees were assigned to one of three groups: givers, receivers, or control group. The control group served as a comparison group that did not undergo the same experimental procedures as the other two groups. The "givers" were instructed to do five acts of kindness a day for the "receivers." Ideas were provided and included sending a thank-you email, bringing receivers a drink, cheering them up, etc. The results showed that both the givers and receivers had improvements in their emotional well-being. Additionally, receivers engaged in three times more prosocial acts than those in the control group. Wow, talk about the power of being a recipient! This study supports the contagion effect giving has on the recipient.

But is it better to be the recipient or the giver? Liang et al. (2001) conducted research to find out. Their sample consisted of over 1,000 individuals aged 65 years and older. Although both giving and receiving were found to be advantageous, the researchers showed that being in a reciprocal relationship that is relatively equal in "give and take" leads to contentment. These researchers found that receiving support may increase distress and have a negative impact on wellness when the support is excessive and when the receiver is not able to reciprocate. The social exchange is important to consider when determining benefit on recipients. Based on their findings, the researchers recommended that older adults place themselves in helping roles to offset potential distress of being a recipient. Monin et al. (2019) also studied caregiving and the effects of giving and receiving support to a spouse with health concerns. This study found that husbands benefited most from the spousal support in that their blood pressure and reported distress decreased. The wives too showed a reduction in their blood pressure and distress when they provided support to their husbands. Interestingly, the same benefit was not found for wives in recovery

134 *Benefits to Giving*

receiving support from their husbands. In fact, husbands and wives in this study showed elevated heart rates when the wives received support from the husbands. Wives in this situation also reported more distress. However, both husbands and wives reported feeling closer to each other while giving support. These findings are likely the result of a gender role expectation that females are presumed to be the caregiver. As females continue to be placed in the role of caregiver, it may very well be difficult for her to accept being the recipient of care.

Exploring the research on benefits to being a recipient, a common factor of concern is the human tendency for givers to underestimate the effect of their giving. In a recent study, Kumar and Epley (2023) had research participants give away small gifts by way of random acts of kindness. They were then asked to rate how the receiver felt about the gift. The receiver was also asked to rate how they felt about the gift. The findings showed that receivers rated the impact statistically higher than what the givers thought. The givers underestimated the impact of the gifts. The researchers concluded that this was because the giver is focused on the **value** of the gift whereas the receiver looks at the value of the gift but is focused on the **intention** of the gift. The givers then reported on their frequency of random acts of kindness, reporting that they performed them less often than they would like. Given that they also underestimated the positive impact of such acts, it is likely that their erroneous belief impeded their motivation to conduct more kind acts. This research is salient in aiding our understanding of a potential barrier to giving; thinking that the recipient would not value it. Another study by the same authors found that participants underestimated how positive the recipient of a gratitude letter would feel when compared to how the recipient felt (Kumar & Epley, 2018). The participants even overestimated how awkward the recipient would feel. I know this to be the case in my own perceptions of the receiver. To ensure an accurate assessment of whether they benefited or not, I make a conscious effort to look and listen for their reaction. Think about your most recent act of giving and the recipient's response. Did you see the recipient receive the gift? If so, did you stay in the interaction long enough to determine if they benefited from the gift? Did you exit the interaction quickly to avoid anxiety or embarrassment? Recently, I found myself feeling empathic while interacting with a salesclerk. I shared with her

Benefits to Giving 135

that I was on my way to see a movie. She shared that she had not seen a movie since "pre-Covid" which would have been about three years. She added that she and her mother were struggling financially. There was no intention in her sharing, no expectation of support. My empathy soared as I envisioned her and her mother living paycheck by paycheck. I was not moved to action until I got into the car and realized I could do something to create a bit of joy in her life and to reinforce her working through her struggles. I decided to purchase a gift card while at the theater for her and her mother to attend a movie with a bit left over for a snack. After the movie, I rushed back to the store hoping to catch her still at work. She remembered me and resumed our discussion, noting that she was working late as she got on the wrong bus this morning and got to work late. To make it up to her boss, she agreed to stay later at work. I reached into my wallet and pulled out the gift card. I slide it toward her and stated: "Take your mom to the movies." I intentionally stopped myself from running out the door, feeling a bit flustered with my adrenaline soaring. I wanted to see her reaction so I could remember it. Her face was full of surprise. She immediately filled up with tears, stumbling for words. "Thank-you" was heard between sobs. She said, "You don't know how much this means." I started to worry about embarrassing her at work and drawing attention to her. Then I thought, perhaps this would make for a good model for others to witness. I asked her to come around the counter so not to be in the spotlight, and I offered her a hug. She hugged me, a stranger, so tightly. I walked away without turning back. I do not know what others might have thought, nor their reactions. I do not know how my dear receiver reacted after that, but what I can be assured of is that she and others will remember that moment. I am confident that when she thinks about this interaction, she feels seen and valued. I think of the unexpecting mother who will now be enjoying a movie with her daughter. I think of how this mother likely sacrifices daily for her family; even when the financial pressure eases up, I imagine she is the last to treat herself. Thinking about it now, a mother-daughter gift benefits two for the price of one! Compound giving strikes again. I envision the mother excited to spend a few carefree hours in the theater with her daughter. Yes, I could be wrong about this daughter and mother; after all, I do not know them. But chances are, they will be slightly better off with this gift than

136 *Benefits to Giving*

without it. There is something powerful about giving to a stranger. When we receive something from someone that has no obligation to give, it tends to have added potency.

Returning to the study by Kumar and Epley (2023) mentioned earlier, several experimental variations occurred involving a giver and receiver. The giver consistently underestimated the positive effects on the receiver. In one of the variations, participants were paired and seated separately from their partner. They were shown five small gifts such as a chocolate bar and lip balm. They were told that the items came from the "Lab store" and that there was enough for each pair to have one item. The participant could keep the item for themselves or select an item for the experimenter to give to the participant's partner in the next room. Of the 51 pairs, only two chose to keep the item for themselves. Forty-nine participants opted to give the item to their partner, however, when asked to rate the receiver's mood after receiving the gift, givers once again underestimated the positive benefit. The receivers themselves rated their mood statistically higher than the givers thought. The researchers concluded, across the experimental variations, that givers undervalued their kindness.

To test more explicitly whether the giver's underestimate of the receivers' benefit served as a barrier to giving, the researchers (Kumar & Epley, 2023) ran a correlation to see if expectations on the impact related to performance of a random act of kindness. Participants were asked to think of five people they could perform a random act of kindness. They then rated how each would feel about the gift, then they were asked to score each person on how likely they would be to perform an act of kindness. One hundred and one college students participated in this study. A statistically significant positive correlation was found in that the higher the expectation of positive impact on the recipient, the more likely the participant would perform a kind act. While this result does not come as a surprise, remember all the studies finding that the giver underestimated the impact on the recipient. This being the case, givers may give less often as they believe that their gift is not as valued as much as it is to the recipient. These findings should caution the reader to not reserve giving to only grand acts that they think their recipient would value. But instead, give without concern for the size of the gesture. An interviewee, Kristine, spoke words of

Benefits to Giving 137

gratitude being a recipient of the support of her mother-in-law by stating, "I feel blessed every time my mother-in-law rings my doorbell. She has been a gift beyond measure in my life."

Not all research finds positive effects on receiving. One study (Koo et al., 2022) narrowed the effect down to **when** the giving occurred, in the beginning or end of a situation. In a series of nine studies, Koo et al. found that when giving occurred at the beginning of a situation, the receiver felt more positive. However, as time passed and giving occurred later in a situation, the receiver felt more negative effects as a potential shift in responsibility occurred. This shift to negative effects is not believed to occur when the giving is "autonomy-oriented," such as offering resources and ideas as opposed to doing completely for another. It seems that timing is a critical aspect to how the receiver will feel. The thought behind giving may create a positive or negative effect on the recipient. Returning to powerful words from my interviewee Lois who stated:

> Whether the gift of time, money, or energy – the gift is the thought that you personally put into the whole process. It doesn't matter what it is – but the process you put into it. In receiving, I don't get that same feeling. If people ask me for a list – it takes away from that process. If the thought is not there. It goes back to spending time and understanding someone and paying attention. It is not very personal when they do not put in the time and thought. I have friends that have said that they are so exhausted in thinking about giving. If it makes them feel this way, why would they want to of it?

Benefits to the Giver

While there are certainly costs to giving (explored further in Chapter 7), however, the benefits are numerous. Research has shown that we experience physical changes in our bodies, such as chemical releases in the brain when we engage in giving behaviors. Chemicals released give us a boast in mood. This section will start with a review of the psychological benefits, including increased well-being, mood, and self-image. The last part of this chapter covers the physiological benefits to the giver. Given that our minds and body interact, these benefits are not deemed to occur in isolation.

138 *Benefits to Giving*

Psychological Benefits to the Giver

Referring to the World Happiness Report (2023), positive effects of giving occur for the giver, but also for those who witnesses giving. Observing altruistic behaviors has been found to result in "moral elevation," the boast in mood that comes with the desire to be a better person. Simply hearing about (or reading) altruistic actions can influence others to be more altruistic in the future. This is quite a powerful influence that is consistent with psychological theories of social influence and social learning. Further noted in the report was the finding that the more altruistic acts observed, the more positive the witness felt about humanity. Even just recalling previous experiences with giving or thoughts of future acts can prompt emotional responses and motivation to help others (Gaesser & Fowler, 2020). When we think about our good fortune or think about our future in favorable ways, we are more likely to help others. These vivid memories trigger positive emotions compelling us to action.

Positive psychology focuses on emotional and physical well-being. Giving has been found to be related to many aspects of well-being. Amy Novotney (2022) provided a summary of the research on the benefits of giving on happiness and noted that many studies have been found to demonstrate that spending money on others increases happiness. She added that the positive feelings experienced when giving to others and feeling intrinsic reinforcement is known as "warm glow." Recall the Chancellor et al. (2017) study mentioned above in the benefits to the receiver section, well the benefits continue. Givers were found to have an increase in autonomy and competence. Two-month follow-up with the giver group found that they had higher rates of life satisfaction, fewer depressive symptoms, and higher job satisfaction than the control group. The researchers further noted that the givers had more and longer lasting positive effects than the receivers or the controls. Novotney (2022) highlighted one study from Switzerland that gave college students 100 dollars. One group was told to spend the money on themselves. The other group was told to spend the money on someone other than themselves. Participants in the "spend the money on others" group showed more brain activity in areas associated with pleasure than the group told to spend on themselves. The "spend on others" group also reported higher levels of

Benefits to Giving **139**

happiness compared to the "spend on self" group. Research and strategies on spending money to enhance well-being are included in the book *Happy Money: The Science of Happier Spending* (Dunn & Norton, 2014). Dunn and Norton place mindfulness spending at the forefront with more joyful giving experiences being linked with spending on experiences and others.

Research has shown a plethora of benefits to giving. Jenny Santi (2015), in her book *The Giving Way to Happiness: Stories and Science Behind the Life-Changing Power of Giving*, writes about interviews she conducted with extremely wealthy and generous donors. When asked about benefit to giving, a theme across interviewees was that of fulfillment. Fulfillment was described as a level higher than what one could obtain through material possessions. Benefits from material items were often described as fleeting, especially when luxuries were easily acquired. Post and Neimark (2007) in their book *Why Good Things Happen to Good People: How to Live a Longer, Healthier, Happier Life by the Simple Act of Giving* summarized findings from their research institution, Institute for Research on Unlimited Love (IRUL) funded. These findings of the benefits of giving are summarized in Table 5.1.

Table 5.1 Summary Findings on Benefits to Giving by Post and Neimark (2007)

Post and Neimark's research findings	Researchers noted by Post and Neimark
A 50-year study found that those that are givers in high school have good physical and mental health throughout adulthood.	Paul Wink
Mortality rates were found to be lower for adults studied in a five-year period for those that volunteered.	Doug Oman
Adolescents who give were found to be happier and more involved than less giving peers.	Peter Benson
Offering help to others reduces one's financial stress.	Neal Krause
Self-forgiveness is improved when we help others, increasing personal well-being.	Neal Krause
Giving support, including emotional support, increases mortality; however, receiving the same support does not.	Stephanie Brown
Adults over 65 years old who volunteered had reduced symptoms of depression.	Marc Musick and colleagues

140   *Benefits to Giving*

Interviewees shared their comments on why they give, highlighting the impact on their wellness. Some replies include:

- "One hundred percent, I get more than I give. Periods of my life in which I haven't volunteered, and I feel discontent."
- "I have so much more than so many people do – I am blessed. It feels good (to give), gives me pleasure and satisfaction. Makes me feel good that I can help someone in that way. When it comes to giving tips, I tell myself: "I will do as long as I can"."
- "Joy. I get a lot out of it."
- "Can come back via karma if I need anything. It feels good to be helpful."
- "My giving is directly related to my mental health and how I feel about myself."

Consider why you give. Does giving impact your well-being? Research has consistently found that caregivers report a higher sense of well-being. This is especially true for givers of emotional support. The findings do not hold for givers of "instrumental support." Instrumental support involves tangible levels of support such as helping with hygiene and preparing meals. These findings have been seen in "individualistic" cultures such as the United States. Tsai and Kimel (2021) were interested in exploring whether similar findings would occur in a "collectivistic" society. They studied 178 Chinese exchange students and found the same pattern in that givers of emotional support had higher well-being but not for givers of instrumental support.

One of the first cross-cultural studies on the effects of giving for the giver (Aknin et al., 2013) found positive effects on the giver in 120 out of the 136 countries studied. The authors reasoned that their small sample for the 16 countries that did not demonstrate a positive correlation may be why their results did not follow suit with the majority. Giving of financial resources, regardless of income level, was found to increase ratings of happiness. In a series of studies, these authors also showed that having participants recall a time in which they gave was enough to induce happiness ratings.

Wellness also involves mood, a variable studied for effects of giving on the giver. Although not the initial focus of Kumar and Eply's (2023) study mentioned above, they found that participants reported a higher mood than usual after completing a random act

Benefits to Giving 141

of kindness. Lanser and Eisenbergrer (2022) studied the positive benefits of giving to both the giver and the receiver. They noted previous research findings of improved mood for the giver and the receiver. However, they wondered if giving would improve feelings of loneliness. The researchers conducted two studies, one involved being assigned to a group to either give a gift card, keep a gift card, or control condition in which no gift was involved; the second study involved participants being in either writing a letter of gratitude, reflection-only group, or control group. Three-hundred participants in each study responded to survey items regarding their mood and loneliness before and then again after experimental activities. The findings from the first study showed that the giving group had statistically less loneliness scores after the giving task than the keep and control groups. The giving group also reported higher scores on happiness items than the keep or control groups. For the second study, the results showed that loneliness scores were significantly lower in the letter of gratitude group compared to the reflection-only and control groups. Likewise, the gratitude group scored higher mood scores than the other two groups. The results of this two-part study highlighted the potency of giving behavior. Studying depressive symptoms in adolescents, researchers (Schacter & Margolin, 2019) found that on days adolescents rated themselves more prosocial, they also rated their moods as more positive. Aknin et al. (2015) studied adults on their happiness when giving. The adults were found to be more gratified when they purchased items for others versus when they bought items for themselves.

Giving can also have positive effects on how givers are viewed by others. Small acts of kindness have been shown to improve one's reputation (Milinski et al., 2002) and raise one's social status in a group (Flynn et al., 2006). Willer (2009) explained these tendencies occur because generous people are more valued in a group. Generous people are also noted to elicit respect (Williams & Bartlett, 2015). Economists agree with social science in that giving produces benefits to the giver. "Utility" is a term used by economist to describe the degree to which one gets something in return from giving. The benefit to this return is based on how good the giver feels about giving. Michael Norton's 2011 TED talk (https://www.ted.com/talks) on *How to Buy Happiness* is from the business perspective. He recommends spending more money on other people. He stated that money makes us selfish and antisocial.

142 *Benefits to Giving*

He conducted a study on the Vancouver college campus where they measured how happy the participant reported being, then handed them an envelope with cash in it and one of two instructions. One group received the instruction to spend the money on themselves by 5 pm that day. The second group was instructed to spend the money on somebody else by 5 pm that day. The amount of money differed across both groups being either $5 or $20. The results showed that those who were instructed to spend money on others reported being happier when their before and after self-reported happiness ratings were assessed. Those that were instructed to spend the money on themselves showed no difference in their self-reported happiness. Additionally, it did not matter how much money they were given. What did matter was that they spent it on someone else. He and his research team replicated these findings in Uganda, then later in a workplace setting with sales groups. Giving to others was found to increase their sales. Prosocial giving was also found to have positive effects on sport teams as it increased performance. Norton noted that it is not what you spend on other people, but the fact that you do that leads to the increase in happiness.

Negative Psychological Effects to Giving

Scott Rick (as cited in Novotney, 2022) noted that gift giving also has the potential for stress and anxiety, especially around the concept of paying for the gifts. This construct he coined "the pain of paying." Stress, he noted, can also occur when one receives a gift they did not expect and does not have one to reciprocate. Stress will negate the positive potential experience of giving. Stressful giving is likely outside one's boundaries or may very well be due to poor boundaries or having no boundaries set. A topic we will return to in Chapter 7.

Smith and Davidson (2014) noted that ungenerous people tend to be unhappy. But what comes first? Is it that they are not happy to begin with and, therefore, do not give or is it that they are not engaging in generous actions toward others and miss out on the wellness benefits of socialization and mood elevations? Smith and Davidson rationalize that many ungenerous people feel overwhelmed and regardless of actual income level, feel an overarching need to hold onto their resources. Resources, such as money, likely provide them with a sense of security.

Benefits to Giving 143

Smith and Davidson (2014) stated in their book *The Paradox of Generosity*:

> Generosity does not usually work in simple, zero-sum, win-lose ways. The results of generosity are often instead unexpected, counterintuitive, win-win. Rather than generosity producing net losses, in general the more generously people give of themselves, the more of many goods they receive in turn. Sometimes they receive more of the same kind of thing that they gave – money, time, attention, and so forth. But, more often and importantly, generous people tend to receive back goods that are even more valuable than those they gave: happiness, health, a sense of purpose in life, and personal growth.
>
> (page 11)

These authors note that a second paradox exists regarding giving. Not only do givers tend to receive, but many Americans do not engage in the kind of giving that enhances wellness. They explain that the American culture, being rather "individualistic," sends contradictory messages about giving. Messaging has tones of materialism and fending for oneself. Other societies are "collectivistic" in that the focus is on the unit working together for the success of all. This individualistic versus collectivist culture is seen in companies. Organizations tend to have a "zero-sum" belief that to be successful, competitors need to fail. This line of thinking is consistent with an individualistic mindset. Researchers Chernyak-Hai and Davidai (2022) studied this belief in 102 Israeli employees and found that participants were likely to give help that was deemed "dependent," but not so for "autonomy"-building assistance. This seemed to serve the benefit in the workplace of securing one's position of being in the know.

So, with all the benefits to giving yet the need to reserve resources, how can we "have our cake and eat it too." This is the topic of research by Kardas et al. (2018). These researchers suggest that we can receive the benefits of being generous while also preserving some of our resources by merely offering another the choice. This is known as "abdicating." For example, if there is one piece of chocolate cake remaining, you know, the kind with moose frosting dripping in the middle between layers and spread generously on the top, and you and your spouse are foraging for dessert.

144 *Benefits to Giving*

If you offer your spouse the last piece, you are seen as generous. If they conduct the selfless act of offering it to you, you now have acquired a resource and not experienced a "loss." You would still be deemed generous and now have your cake. Of course, sharing the slice of cake is also an option. This too will enable you to be perceived as generous and allow for the obtainment of a resource (delicious cake), albeit a moderate portion. These researchers also found that abdicating was seen as generous and increased the tendency for participants to reciprocate. These researchers also reviewed previous research on generousness versus selfishness which consistently notes that people form positive evaluations of people who are generous and negative evaluations of people that are selfish. As a result, people tend to reward those they deem generous and punish those that are not. For this to be the case, actions would need to be known to be credited and perceived as genuine. If an ulterior motive is perceived, the giver is considered less genuine, and a negative evaluation may occur.

Giving behaviors have been shown to impact emotional well-being. It can lead to a sense of empowerment, allowing us to seize a bit of control in seemingly otherwise overwhelming situations. The tendency for people overwhelmed by need exceeding resources can create a feeling of "learned helplessness" (discussed further in Chapter 7). A helpless mindset affects motivation and thereby results in inaction. Giving enables us to ward off learned helplessness. A positive focus is created by shifting our mindset from focus on a problem to focus on the solution. We become active agents of change. Plus, we are likely to communicate our actions, creating awareness in others, leading to a positive ripple effect from giving. The positive effects of giving are not only in those self-reported but are evident in biological responses.

Neurobiological Benefits to the Giver

A bit of neuroanatomy background is important to lay a foundation to the biological benefits to giving. Our brains send and receive messages throughout our bodies using a neurochemical process. The basic unit of this communication signal is a neuron. We have billions of neurons, but none to spare! The neuron consists of the cell body (soma) where the nucleus is housed, axon, and dendrites (Kolb et al., 2019). The nucleus holds the messaging material. The axon carries messages to other neurons where the dendrites receive those messages. Neural messaging involves both an electrical signal and a chemical signal. Once a neuron is activated, an electrical signal (the message) travels down the axon like a car speeding down the highway in an "all or nothing" manner. The message reaches the terminal end of the axon, and causes release of chemicals, to carry the signal on to the dendrites of a receiving cell. The chemicals released spill out into the synaptic cleft, a gap between the sending neuron and neighboring receiving neuron, to bind with corresponding receptors on the adjacent neuron. These chemicals are called neurotransmitters (Kolb et al., 2019). There are a variety of neurotransmitters, leading to different biological responses. A few neurotransmitters have been linked to the process of giving, namely, dopamine, serotonin, and oxytocin. Figure 5.1 depicts the parts of the neuron and the synaptic transmission where the neurochemicals are being relayed to the neighboring neuron.

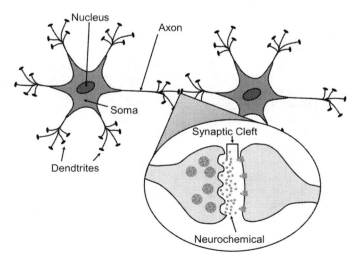

Figure 5.1 Parts of the Neuron: Synaptic Transmission.

146 *Benefits to Giving*

Research has shown that neurotransmitters, such as dopamine, are released during the process of giving. Dopamine is produced by cell bodies in two midbrain areas, the ventral tegmental area (VTA) and the substantia nigra. Dopamine produced by midbrain VTA cells is part of our natural reward system. Santi (2015) noted that peoples' reward (dopamine) pathway was activated during the process of giving. A second area that Santi (2016) said was activated was the subgenual area in the frontal lobe. This area is involved in emotional attachment and autonomic responses to social material (Lockwood et al., 2016). Together, these two systems reward us with "feel-good" neurochemicals when we engage in giving behavior. Dopamine release is associated with positive feelings and creates a pleasurable "rush." This feeling is highly rewarding, creating motivation to repeat behaviors. It is not surprising to find that dopamine is also involved in addictive behaviors, as these activate the reward system more strongly than natural rewards.

This rewarding experience from giving has been termed "warm glow" (Moll et al., 2006). An online article by Jo Cutler (2018), at the time, a doctoral student in the Social Decision Lab at the University of Sussex, discussed brain imaging findings as they are related to giving. The striatum, located in the forebrain, was noted to be involved in experiencing reward. It has been found to be active when we receive, but also when we give, creating the feeling of "warm glow." The positive neurobiological effects of giving have been shown to occur with just thinking about giving! This region was shown to be active for both altruistic and strategic (when giving is motivated by an outcome) giving (Lockwood & Cutler, 2022). However, more neural activity was noted for when giving was altruistic, compared to strategic. Since this region is involved with both giving and receiving, it is believed that rewarding giving behavior may stimulate the "warm glow" reward naturally felt. As noted previously in Chapter 3, this is suspected in behavioral theory, with the caution against rewarding intrinsically reinforcing behavior (Over-Justification Effect) as it makes the act contingent on external reward (Aronson et al., 2023). Additionally, the positive effects of giving can be offset or even eliminated if stress accompanies giving. Therefore, giving should be within one's means and of free will. It should not be done to relieve guilt or a sense of obligation. Science now knows these physical feelings to be associated with neurochemical secretions and cardiovascular elevations.

Benefits to Giving 147

I know these physiological effects firsthand while giving, experiencing the increase in energy and physiological reactions, such as elevated breathing. While collecting items for someone in need, I typically experience a flood of good feelings. The energy level makes me feel as though I cannot get the items to the individual fast enough.

Another neurotransmitter found to be involved in giving is serotonin. Serotonin impacts mood and leads to what has been termed the "helper's high." Allan Luk (1988) coined the term "helper's high" to describe the lifted mood and warmth that comes over the giver when they give. Kindness has been shown to increase serotonin release, improving mood. Low levels of serotonin are involved in some forms of depression. As a matter of fact, medications such as selective serotonin reuptake inhibitors (SSRIs) which serve to block the reabsorption (reuptake) of serotonin, allowing for more natural serotonin to remain available, are often prescribed for individuals with depression. Activities known to naturally increase serotonin include exercise, socialization, light, healthy nutrition, and even giving.

A third neurochemical involved in the giving process is oxytocin, considered the "love hormone." Oxytocin is a hormone produced in the hypothalamus. The pituitary gland releases oxytocin into the bloodstream during childbirth, breastfeeding, sexual activity, even hugs. Due to the feel-good effect, oxytocin is known to enhance bonds with others. It is involved in the attachment process. Zak et al. (2007) found that when participants were infused with oxytocin were 80% more generous than those not receiving the injection. More recently, Zak et al. (2022) noted that oxytocin is associated with trust, altruism, charity, and generosity and that it increases with age. Ritvo (2014) concluded that the combination of these three neurochemicals: dopamine, serotonin, and oxytocin create the "*Happiness Trifecta*." As such, nature has found a way to physically reward good deeds with the release of pleasurable chemicals. It is no wonder some have referred to this reward cycle as the "miracle drug," "natural detox," and our "pre-wiring to give" system. Ritvo further noted that these neurochemical benefits are experienced in both the giver and the receiver. Regarding giving versus receiving, Novotney (2022) summarized that the research indicates that similar brain patterns result. Receivers have been found to have increased oxytocin release when their

148 *Benefits to Giving*

partners allocated money to them during an economic game (Zak et al., 2005). Additionally, the release of oxytocin increased as the amount of money allocated to them increased.

Ritvo (2014) also reported on a very special type of neuron, mirror neurons, and their involvement in giving. Mirror neurons are activated when we witness others engaging in an activity. Our neurons fire just as if we were engaged in the activity ourselves. Mirror neurons enable us to use nonverbal cues to recognize the feelings of others; they help us feel empathy. As a matter of fact, mirror neurons have been found to be plentiful in empaths; people who are incredibly sensitive to the feelings and emotional states of others (Orloff, 2022). Given this neurobiological structure, it seems reasonable to assume that witnessing giving activates our mirror neurons, producing feel-good neurochemical release. We feel good and are motivated to repeat this feeling through action of our own. Here, we not only learn by example, but are neurobiologically reinforced for such learning, adding further motivation to give. Research has shown that giving, even when "mandated," evidenced some neurobiological benefit as seen in participants' functional magnetic resonance imaging (fMRI) results (Harbaugh et al., 2007).

Psychological feelings of wellness are frequently reported by those that give. Additionally, neurobiological indicators have been found to reinforce giving behavior. This mind-body connection shows how our mood is enhanced while giving.

Key Points

- The experience of being a receiver can vary.
- Positive effects of receiving are like those of giving.
- Research shows that givers underestimate receiver benefits from their giving.
- Givers and receivers show increases in emotional well-being when they give/receive.
- Positive effects of giving are felt by those that witness giving behaviors.
- Research shows givers to have high rates of life satisfaction, happinesses, and positive mood.

Benefits to Giving 149

- Givers have been found to have increased mortality and a high sense of well-being while having fewer financial concerns and less mental health concerns than those that give less.
- Research shows evidence of giving behaviors reducing negative mood states, such as loneliness and depressive symptoms.
- Being generous has been associated with a positive reputation.
- There is believed to be a paradox to giving in that the giver tends to get from giving.
- Neurochemicals dopamine, serotonin, and oxytocin have been shown to be activated in the giving process, creating powerful chemical releases producing positive feelings.
- Since giving is emotionally and biologically rewarding, caution is warned in externally rewarding giving.
- Stress, such as giving beyond one's means, will offset the positive effects of giving.
- Thanks to mirror neurons, simply witnessing giving behavior can activate positive neurochemical release.

Action Steps

- Think about your own benefits to giving.
- Observe your emotional and physical state when giving, when thinking about giving, recalling giving experiences, or watching giving behavior.
- Experiment with increasing mood by conducting a generous act when feeling low in mood. Note the results. Was your mood elevated?

References

Aknin, L.B., Broesch, T., Hamlin, K.J., & Van de Vondervoort, J.W. (2015). Prosocial behavior leads to happiness in a small-scale rural society. *Journal of Experimental Psychology: General*, 144(4), 788–795. https://doi.org/10.1037/xge0000082

Aknin, L.B., Dunn, E.W., Helliwell, J.F., Biswas-Diener, R., Nyende, P., Barrington-Leigh, C.P., Burns, J., Kemeza, I., & Ashton-James, C.E. (2013). Prosocial spending and well-being: cross-culture evidence for a psychological universal. *Journal of Personality and Social Psychology*, 104(4), 635–652. https://doi.org/10.1037/a0031578

150 *Benefits to Giving*

Aronson, E., Wilson, T.D., Sommers, S.R., Page-Gould, E., & Lewis, N. (2023). *Social Psychology*, 11th edition. New York: Pearson.

Chancellor, J., Margolis, S., Jacobs, K., & Lyubomirsky, S. (2017). Everyday prosociality in the workplace: The reinforcing benefits of giving, getting, and glimpsing. *Emotion*, 18(4), 507–517. https://doi.org/10.1037/emo0000321

Chernyak-Hai, L., & Davidai, S. (2022). "Do not teach them to fish": The effect of zero-sum beliefs on help giving. *Journal of Experimental Psychology: General*, 151(10), 2466–2480. https://doi.org/10.1037/xge0001196

Cutler, J. (October 19, 2018). The neuroscience of philanthropy. *Impakter*. https://impakter.com/the-neuroscience-of-philanthropy/

Dunn, E., & Norton, M. (2014). *Happy Money: The Science of Happier Spending*. New York: Simon and Schuster Paperbacks.

Flynn, F.J., Reagans, R.E., Amanatullah, E.T., & Ames, D.R. (2006). Helping one's way to the top: Self-monitors achieve status by helping others and knowing who helps whom. *Journal of Personality and Social Psychology*, 91, 1123–1137. https://doi.org/10.1037/0022-3514.91.6.1123

Gaesser, B., & Fowler, Z. (2020). Episodic simulation of prosocial interaction: Investigating the roles of memory and imagination in facilitating a willingness to help others. *Psychology of the Consciousness: Theory, Research, and Practice*, 7(4), 376–387. https://doi.org/10.1037/cns0000232

Harbaugh, W.T., Mayr, U., & Burghart, D.R. (2007). Neural responses to taxation and voluntary giving reveal motivate for charitable donations, *Science*, 316(5831), 1622–1625. https://doi.org/10.1126/science.1140738

Kardas, M., Shaw, A., & Caruso, E.M. (2018). How to give away your cake and eat it too: Relinquishing control prompts reciprocal generosity. *Journal of Personality and Social Psychology: Interpersonal Relations and Group Processes*, 115(6), 1054–1074. https://doi.org/10.1037/pspi0000144

Kolb, B., Whishaw, I.Q., & Teskey, G.C. (2019). *An Introduction to Brain and Behavior*, 6th edition. Worth Publishers.

Koo, M., Jung, S., Palmeira, M., & Kim, K. (2022). The timing of help: Receiving help toward the end (vs. beginning) undermines psychological ownership and subjective well-being. *Journal of Personality and Social Psychology: Interpersonal Relations and Group Processes*, 124(4), 772–795. https://doi.org/10.1037/pspi0000403

Kumar, A., & Epley, N. (2018). Undervaluing gratitude: Expressers misunderstand the consequences of showing appreciation. *Psychological Science*, 29(2), 1423–1435. https://doi.org/10.1177/0956797618772506

Benefits to Giving 151

Kumar, A., & Epley, N. (2023). A little goes a long way: Underestimating the positive impact of kindness on recipients. *Journal of Experimental Psychology: General*, 152(1), 236–252. https://doi.org/10.1037/xge0001271

Lanser, I., & Eisenbergrer, N. (November 10, 2022). Prosocial behavior reliably reduces loneliness: An investigation across two studies. *Emotion*, 23(6), 1781–1790. https://doi.org/10.1037/emo0001179

Liang, J., Krause, N.M., & Bennett, J.M. (2001). Special exchange and well-being: Is giving better than receiving? *Psychology and Aging*, 16(30), 511–523. https://doi.org//0882–7974.16.3.511

Lockwood, P.L., Apps, M.A.J., Valton, V., Viding, E., & Roiser, J.P. (2016). Neurocomputational mechanisms of prosocial learning and links to empathy. *Proceedings of the National Academy of Science*, 113(35), 9763–9768. http://www.pnas.org/cgi/doi/10.1073/pnas.1603198113

Lockwood, P.L., & Cutler, J. (2022). Four reasons we give to charity: Giving can be motivated by empathy, the positive impact, and protecting others. *Psychology Today*, May 10, 2022. https://www.psychologytoday.com/us/blog/the-helpful-brain/202205/4-reasons-we-give-charity

Luks, A. (1988). Doing good: Helper's high. *Psychology Today*, 22(10), 34–42.

Milinski, M., Semmann, D., & Krambeck, H. (2002). Donors to charity gain in both indirect reciprocity and political reputation. *Proceedings Biological Sciences*, 269, 881–883. https://doi.org/10.1098/rspb.2002

Moll, J., Krueger, F., Zahn, R., Pardini, M., deOliveira-Souza, R., & Grafman, J. (October 17, 2006). Human fronto-mesolimbic networks guide decisions about charitable donation. *Proceedings of the National Academy of Science*, 103(42), 15623–15628. www.pnas.orgcgidoi10.1073pnas.0604475103

Monin, J.K., Manigault, A., Levy, B.R., Schulz, R., Duker, A., Clark, M.S., & Ness, P.H. (2019). Gender differences in short-term cardiovascular effects of giving and receiving support for health concerns in marriage. *Health Psychology*, 38(10), 936–947. https://doi.org/10.1037/hea0000777

Norton, M. (2011). *How to buy happiness.* https://www.ted.com/talks/michael_norton_how_to_buy_happiness?language=en

Novotney, A. (December 9, 2022). What happens in your brain when you give a gift? Gift-giving activates regions of the brain associated with pleasure, social connection, and trust, creating a "warm glow" effect. https://www.apa.org/topics/mental-health/brain-gift-giving

Orloff, J. (June 28, 2022). How the Brain's mirror neurons affect empathy: The relationship between empaths, compassion, and mirror neurons. *Psychology Today*. https://www.psychologytoday.com

152 Benefits to Giving

Post, S., & Neimark, J. (2007). *Why Good Things Happen to Good People: How to Live a Longer, Healthier, Happier Life by the Simple Act of Giving.* New York: Broadway Books.

Ritvo, E. (April 24, 2014). The neuroscience of giving: Proof that helping others helps you. *Psychology Today.* https://www.psychologytoday.com

Santi, J. (2015). *The Giving Way to Happiness: Stories and Science Behind the Life-Changing Power of Giving.* New York: Penguin Random.

Schacter, H., & Margolin, G. (2019). When it feels good to give: Depressive symptoms, daily prosocial behavior, and adolescent mood. *Emotion,* 19(5), 923–927. https://doi.org/10.1037/emo0000494

Smith, C., & Davidson, H. (2014). *The Paradox of Generosity: Giving We Receive, Grasping We Lose.* New York: Oxford University Press.

Tsai, W., & Kimel, S. (2021). When and how supporting others can improve life satisfaction: A longitudinal study examining collective values. *Cultural Diversity and Ethnic Minority Psychology,* 27(3), 505–510. https://doi.org/10.1037/cdp0000433

Willer, R. (2009). Groups reward individual sacrifice: The status solution to the collective action problem. *American Sociological Review,* 74, 23–43. https://doi.org/10.1177/0003112240907400102

Williams, L.A., & Bartlett, M.Y. (2015). Warm thanks: Gratitude expression facilitates social affiliation in new relationships via perceived warmth. *Emotions,* 15, 105. https://doi.org/10.1037/emo0000017

World Happiness Report. (2023). https://worldhappiness.report/

Zak, P.J., Curry, B., Owen, T., & Barraza, J.A. (April 21, 2022). Oxytocin release increases with age and is associated with life satisfaction and prosocial behaviors. *Frontiers in Behavioral Neuroscience Behavioral Endocrinology,* 16, 846234. https://doi.org/10.3389/fnbeh.2022.846234

Zak, P.J., Kurzban, R., & Matzner, W.T. (2005). Oxytocin is associated with human trustworthiness. *Hormone and Behavior,* 48, 522–527. https://doi.org/10.1016/j.yhbeh.2005.07.009

Zak, P.J., Stanton, A.A., & Ahmadi, S. (2007). Oxytocin increases generosity in humans. *PLoS One,* 2(11): e1128. https://doi.org/10.1371/journal.pone.0001128

6 Gratitude and Being a Recipient

Introduction

For most people, it is hard to be a recipient of giving. It can be embarrassing, ridden with guilt and shame. Often the receiver is processing opposing feelings regarding a gift. This chapter explores social science research on being a recipient with a focus specifically on gratitude. To start, social psychology research has shown that we like people better when they allow us to do a favor for them (Aronson et al., 2023). Read that again! People like us better when they do us a favor. This is in part due to a concept called "cognitive dissonance." Cognitive dissonance is when we hold two conflicting thoughts. It creates an uncomfortable emotional state until resolved. We resolve this tension by placing more validity on one of the beliefs over the other. In other words, we make one thought more right in our heads. When we do a favor for someone, we need to justify it in our minds. We need to convince ourselves that this person was worthy of our effort or resource. For us to spend our time and/or money doing another a favor (or giving a gift), we would not want to believe it was a waste of resources. As a result, conflictual thoughts (cognitive dissonance) are diffused with the thought that the recipient was worthy of the favor/gift. The giver now views the recipient even more favorably, justifying their decision to invest resources.

Accepting a gift graciously adds to the positive feelings experienced by the giver. Showing gratitude will likely reinforce a giver's future acts of giving. Gratitude is fundamental to one's emotional well-being and, therefore, is important for the recipient to embrace.

DOI: 10.4324/9781003438359-6

154   *Gratitude and Being a Recipient*

What Is Gratitude?

Gratitude is one of those terms that we all seem to know but may define differently. A common element to gratitude is being thankful for one's good fortune. Positive psychology literature is grounded in this concept. At its core, gratitude is a way of being. It is mindfulness at its very best. Mindfulness is the practice of attending to the here and now, to the environment and to one's current thoughts and feelings. Gratitude is a state of being, in the here and now, that requires awareness and reflection. It is a positive way of viewing the world and is indeed a conscious effort. It is therefore a choice. It involves recognizing the good in the moment. It is an art, a practice, and something we can all hone. The benefits of living a life of gratitude are numerous. It not only helps us feel good in the moment, but it also helps us live longer and healthier lives (Ross, 2023). Once again, the power of **what** we think matters. Simply adjusting our thinking with a mindset of gratitude releases oxytocin, improving our mood and feelings of being loved. The experience of gratitude has been found to be associated with increased activity in the medial prefrontal cortex and the anterior cingulate cortex regions of the brain associated with moral judgment and social cognition (Sawyer et al., 2022). Gratitude makes us think of others and is involved in drawing us near to one another to be socially affiliated. Healthy thinking creates healthy states socially, emotionally, and physically. We would all do well to be grateful for what we have, as opposed to what we do not. Think about what is working over what is not working. Challenge yourself further by thinking of an obstacle as a puzzle to be solved as opposed to a stressor. A positive psychological mindset opens our mind to problem solving, helping us derive healthy solutions. Gratitude is known to be one of the strongest traits associated with good mental and physical health. Through mindfulness exercises, such as appreciation of nature, physical exercise, or daily writing in a gratitude journal, research has shown improvement in mood, blood pressure, physical health, coping with stress, willingness to help others, ability to process trauma, and higher resiliency, to name just a few of the benefits.

A disposition of gratitude is seen in individuals that find beauty in their everyday lives. Even hardship can lead to "collateral beauty." Some have referred to collateral beauty as a form of a silver lining,

Gratitude and Being a Recipient 155

a good that comes with the bad. Mr. Rogers, an iconic American children's television show host from 1968 to 2001, is famous for his gentle manner and humanity. As a child, his mother would tell him to "look for the helpers" when difficult times occurred. This is a powerful example of the collateral beauty around us even during devastation. Rescuers rushing toward the Twin Towers in New York City during the US 9/11 terrorist attack is evidence of the beauty of helpers. Those with a disposition of gratitude tend to think "every day is a gift" and "I have more blessings than worries." Ask yourself, "Do I focus more on what is working or more on what is not working in my life?" "Do I see others as having more than I do?" "Do I feel like I have been cheated or slighted more than most?" These are all signs of an "upward comparison." According to social psychologist, upward comparisons occur when we compare ourselves to people we deem to be better whereas "downward comparison" occur when we compare ourselves to others that are deemed less better off (Midgley et al., 2020). People who regularly make upward comparisons tend to have a negative view of self, lowering their feelings of wellness. This way of thinking creates a tendency to be less grateful for what one has while focusing on what they do not have. Failing to recognize the good around them, they are less happy than those that focus on the positives. Many know this as "the glass is half empty versus half full" distinction. While this speaks specifically to optimism, gratitude shares a similar mindset. Gratitude requires insight and appreciation. Even just an acknowledgment to the self, such as in our thinking, can create a sense of well-being and gratitude. Ideally, we share these insights with others, show our appreciation, and spread the joy that comes from the beauty all around us. Showing appreciation is an outcome of gratitude. It makes us feel good to appreciate others and it certainly makes others feel good to be appreciated.

To further put this concept into perspective, consider the 2016 movie *Collateral Beauty*, starring Will Smith. The plot centers on the notion that kindness can be seen in the face of tragedy. The movie depicts grief through powerful symbolism and personification, beckoning the viewer to key their eyes open for similar messages of beauty in their own lives. There are healing qualities in collateral beauty as evidenced in communities that come together for vigils, parents who start scholarships in moratorium for

156 *Gratitude and Being a Recipient*

their deceased child, neighbors rebuilding homes that have been devastated by natural disasters, the list goes on. Perhaps the most compelling example of gratitude over hardship is that of Victor Frankl's 1946 book *Man's Search for Meaning*. Frankl was a prisoner in the Nazi concentration camp. He credits his survival to his ability to find purpose and meaning in his circumstance. He maintained that one always has the freedom to choose their meaning and to see value in every experience. The focus on choice in and of itself is empowering. No matter what was being taken from him, restricted, and destroyed, he had control over his mind and will. He envisioned how his life would be and exerted choice over how he led his life. The key to positive living is to find meaning to one's life. We all have a purpose. Giving is a tangible way to express one's purpose and to effect positive benefits on self and others. However, is it better to give or to receive?

Is It Better to Give or Receive?

Determining what is better, to give or receive, is a topic of research interest. Väänänen et al. (2005) studied this question between men and women. Women were found to be healthier when they gave support in their intimate relationships, even without reciprocation. The authors speculated that this was due to the value women place on social relationships. Interestingly, men who reported being "over-benefited" (receiving more support than they gave) were found to be healthier than men whose support was like what they gave. These findings, going back almost two decades, highlight the power and influence of social role expectations.

More recently, a study was conducted to measure the perception of whether it was better to give than to receive (Flynn & Yu, 2021). In a series of seven studies, researchers found that more favorable status was placed on individuals that initiated a generous act over individuals that reciprocated one. This was explained in that observers saw the reciprocated act as an obligation. Participants who did not reciprocate in a simulation were given lower status than individuals who did not initiate an act of giving. These results showed that participants who did not give to begin with were perceived more favorable, albeit still low, than individuals who were the recipient of an act but did not reciprocate. More status was granted to participants that reciprocated anonymously.

Gratitude and Being a Recipient 157

The authors concluded that we judge the actions of others using a series of factors, including any history known about the exchange, such as whether the act was initiated and whether the act was reciprocated. There seems to be a hierarchy in how we view a kind act with anonymous acts and initiated acts having the highest value, whereas reciprocated giving is expected and viewed unfavorably if it does not occur. These findings are in line with the levels of Maimonides Ladder noted earlier. Positive physical and emotional effects noted in Chapter 5 occur for both the giver and the receiver. Noted here are the social expectations for reciprocation and gratitude.

Benefits to Gratitude

In a wonderful TED Talk (https://www.ted.com/talks) by Kelly McGonigal (2013), mentioned in Chapter 2, called *How to Make Stress Your Friend*, compelling research findings were reviewed on the benefits of positive thinking at the cellular level. McGonigal noted that changing the way we think about stress, to that of gratitude and positivity, has significant benefits to our health. When we think positively about our bodies preparing us to respond to a stressor, the negative physical effects of stress are diminished. Negative mindsets and beliefs were shown to have detrimental impact on one's health, such as damage to the heart resulting in higher rates of death than those that did not view stress as harmful. Whereas, research participants who had a lot of stress, but did not review it as harmful, had the least number of negative effects on their body – even less than people who had little stress! These findings show the power of positive thinking. Stress and giving behavior are related in their shared neuropathways and neurochemical release. Giving can be the antidote to stress! McGonigal further noted the concept that stress makes us social. Our neurochemistry is set up to secret oxytocin, which makes us crave social contact and is released when we hug. It is a stress hormone, released to motivate us to seek support when we are stressed. It protects our body in that our heart has receptors for this hormone which helps us heal when under stress. It is released when we reach out to others when stressed **and** when we help others under stress. Both giving and receiving provide healthy natural chemical states protecting our bodies and emotional states. Included in the research

158 *Gratitude and Being a Recipient*

she reviewed is the finding that people who engage in "caring creative resilience" (caring for others) showed significantly diminished negative effects of stress. Once again, the power of our minds and what we think is compelling. A mindset of gratitude and caring can literally add time to our life.

Chowdhury (2023) summarized the neurological and other benefits of gratitude. The benefits were organized in three categories: psychological benefits, social benefits, and physical benefits and are summarized in Table 6.1 along with my thoughts on the applications to giving.

When we express and receive gratitude, neurochemicals (dopamine and serotonin) are released. This, in turn, leads to a positive mood. Being grateful has been repeatedly shown to change the neural structure of our brains in positive and healthy ways. These neurological findings fit well with elements of gratitude noted in the field of positive psychology. Positive psychology maintains that

Table 6.1 Chowdhury's (2023) Summary of Benefits of Gratitude

Benefit category	Examples of benefits summarized by Chowdhury	Applications to giving
Psychological	Better mood, positive thoughts, reduced anxiety, mindful awareness, improved satisfaction, gives a sense of hope especially during grief. Regulates stress hormone reducing negative feelings of fear and stress. Evoking positive thinking helps with shifting one's mindset.	Reflect on your circumstances and find aspects to be grateful.
Social	Increased empathy, sense of belonging and teamwork, enhanced communication. Better workplace environment, employees more inclined to be involved and volunteer for projects.	Join groups and fundraising activities: volunteer with others.
Physical	Reduction of pain, better immune system and cardiac functioning, enhanced sleep quality-wakefulness. Increases release of neurotransmitters related to feeling good. Gray matter in the right inferior temporal gyrus increases. Also results in new neural connections to pleasure centers of the brain.	Be present in the here and now, calming oneself with deep breathing.

Gratitude and Being a Recipient 159

for happiness to occur, one needs fulfillment in elements of optimism, selflessness, spirituality, empathy, and self-esteem. Gratitude is the starting block to these elements, especially optimism. Gratitude comes from receiving but also from the awareness and recognition of what one already has. Post and Neimark (2007) noted research on participants who kept daily journals of gratitude were found to be happier, more optimistic, and more connected to others and had less difficulties with sleep.

Showing Gratitude

Returning to Maslow's hierarchy of needs covered in Chapter 2, it seems logical to predict that people would be more inclined to give and think outside their immediate needs once their own basic needs are met. If we are struggling to meet a need and someone offers us assistance, we are likely to feel a sense of gratitude and relief. Having received a gift can lead to the recipient gaining stability, enabling them to be able to give to others. Showing one's gratitude can close the gap in a giver's tendency to underestimate the impact of a gift (Kumar & Epley, 2023). Showing gratitude is good for the recipient and for the giver.

Robert Emmons (2013), author of *Gratitude Works! A 21-Day Program for Creating Emotional Prosperity*, offered strategies for enhancing the practice of gratitude. He views the concept as a journey in "growing gratitude." The reader is encouraged to develop a disposition, a way of thinking, which cultivates a life of gratitude. The steps to the program first involve assessing one's current level of gratitude. A brief ten item scale is provided for readers to rate themselves from strongly disagree to strongly agree. A sample statements is "I have so much in life to be thankful for." There are plenty of surveys available, many free online, to provide a baseline and even a comparison with others on just how grateful one may be. A six-item questionnaire was published in 2002 by McCullough, Emmons, and Tsang and is available online (https://ggsc.berkeley.edu/). The next step identified by Emmons was to start a gratitude journal. He leads the reader with seven prompts, one for each day of the week. The advice is for the reader to complete this exercise over three weeks, hence 21 days. On the first day, the reader writes three blessings. The second day the focus is on identifying "to whom for what." The third day of the week

160   *Gratitude and Being a Recipient*

prompts the reader to identify gifts they have received throughout their life. Day four journals something positive in one's life that is ending soon. This step is likely to encourage one to embrace the time remaining. The prompt on day five is to think about a positive experience and reflect on how it may not have occurred. This step helps reduce the tendency to take things for granted. Day six prompts the reader to write a letter to someone in their life. The final day encourages the reader to "remember the bad." This is done so that the reader can focus on the fact that they survived an experience and may have even received a positive outcome from the experience. Once the full seven days are completed, the reader will repeat the steps for two more weeks.

Barriers to Gratitude

Kumar and Epley's (2023) study previously mentioned had another layer to it. To test the potential barrier to giving being underestimating the impact of givers due to focus on the value of the gift, the researchers conducted yet another variation of their experiment. This time, they had the participants in either a "competence-focused" (the value of the gift) group where the instructions emphasized choosing "just the right gift" or the "warmth-focused" (meaning of the gift) group where the emphasis was on the kindness behind an act. Participants were offered the option of keeping a $5.00 coffee shop gift card or to give it to someone in their life. Participants in the warmth focus group were more interested in giving their gift card away than those in the competence focus group. These results supported the hypothesis that participants were less likely to give when they were focused on the value of the gift instead of the meaning.

Along with strategies for improving gratitude, Emmons (2013) noted that one must recognize their barriers to gratitude. A barrier may be that we forgot to express our gratitude or perhaps we did not think of an act or gift as "praiseworthy." Another barrier is that we may assume one already knows we are grateful. As a psychologist, I know that humans may experience guilt and shame, even embarrassment, as a recipient. These factors could serve as barriers to gratitude. I can certainly relate to this as a few years ago, while dining out for a late meal, my husband and I went to pay the bill. Our waiter informed us that another patron had already taken care

Gratitude and Being a Recipient 161

of the bill. We quickly looked around the restaurant to try to figure out "who," but as it was minutes from closing time, the restaurant was emptied. My initial response was surprise. I said to the waiter: "This is something we do! I am not used to being the recipient." My husband wondered: "Why us?" "Did we appear to be in need?" He began to feel a bit guilty that this generous gift could have been given to someone more in need. I shared my interpretation with him that someone conducted a random act of generosity to spread kindness. They gave, without expectation of reciprocation, a gift that we were not required to deserve or earn. It was not an issue of whether we needed the gift or not; whether we deserved it or not, it was "unconditional." Inferred in this random act is the hope that we would "pay it forward" by doing a kind act for someone else. Imagine if all kind acts were compounded! How different might our world look?

Embarrassment can serve as a barrier to our graciousness and impact our comfort in expressing words of gratitude. Giving compliments is hard for this reason, many feel awkward in initiating words of kindness. We may worry that saying a compliment to another person may be misinterpreted as flirting. Another barrier could be the confidence needed to speak up and out to initiate such an act. Even to people we know, we sometimes hesitate to mention the good. At some level, we may worry that mentioning the good may make one realize they are "too good for me." Ironically, without mentioning the good in others, relationships fail. Research on couples, such as Gottman (2006), shows that couples that stay together have a 5 to 1 ratio of positive to negative feedback. This means that for every one negative comment, such as "you're late for dinner," there needs to be at least five positive comments to offset the effect. Similar findings exist for parent-child interactions. The job of a parent is to give feedback. Most parents find themselves particularly focused on pointing out the areas in need of improvement. However, are the negatives balanced with words of gratitude? Have they invested enough in the interaction to be effective in that plenty of positive feedback has been given to balance the construction feedback? Notice that this research is only referring to constructive feedback. It does not claim to balance or erase the effects of degrading or mean comments. Without a healthy dose of positives, relationships erode. One is left feeling unappreciated, invisible. Therefore, my challenge to you is to consider

162 *Gratitude and Being a Recipient*

the implications of **not** acting generously and **not** showing one's gratitude. Ask, "Is my current feeling of embarrassment more important than taking a chance to make someone feel appreciated?"

Emmons (2013) noted in his book a significant barrier to gratitude is a sense of entitlement. This is often a concern parents experience with their children. Chapter 9 covers empowering children to give, one way to ward off potential entitlement. When children are taught to see others and their needs, it puts their own situation into perspective. Young children think egocentrically in that they see others through their own lens and experience. If you ask a four-year-old what to get their mother for Mother's Day, they will confidently state the newest and greatest toy. It is not until they develop neurologically that their cognitive development enables them to take another's perspective. Theory of Mind is a concept used to describe one's ability to understand their thoughts and feelings as separate and possibly different from others. This is an important area of development for empathy. Without understanding others' perspective, egocentrism occurs. Egocentrism is a developmental limitation in young children where they have not yet developed the cognitive ability to take another perspective or to see the world through another's frame of reference. Therefore, children need to be explicitly taught.

Another barrier to expressing gratitude is that it can be hard. Recipients may struggle with feelings of guilt, shame, and inferiority when they receive without giving (Remember the Social Exchange Theory mentioned in Chapter 2). The desire to reciprocate is a typical human tendency. This could lead to or exacerbate feelings of low self-esteem and a sense of indebtedness in a relationship. These feelings can be resolved by balancing the scales when possible. Paying back the giver in an even exchange or by other means such as a thank-you letter, an act of kindness, or exchange of work, can rebalance the scales. If the giver is not known or accessible, the receiver can "pay it forward" to a stranger.

Those that receive more than they give may experience a sense of guilt (Liang et al., 2001). According to the equity theory on relationships, it is best that we allow for some reciprocation. As the receiver, think of how you can reciprocate a gift. This is in no way to indicate an equal exchange, instead the focus should be on the acknowledgment of the kind gesture. A thank-you note or

Gratitude and Being a Recipient 163

follow-up to the giver on the progress made since the gift is a nice way to reinforce the act and create a balance in the relationship. Simply repaying the favor or a gift is not the answer as it may be detrimental to do so in relationships such as friend and family. In less close relationships, the exchange theory calls for more balance. Family and friends are considered communal relationships and often operate under the rule of doing what is needed when needed as opposed to balance of equity. It is important though in all relationships to be aware of the need and appropriateness of reciprocating. It is unnecessary and even harmful to return the favor with a gift equally expensive, thereby diminishing the intent of the initial gift.

Here are some strategies I recommend for managing barriers to gratitude:

1 Know your barriers: ask yourself what is stopping me from expressing gratitude? What am I worried about?
2 Think of the bigger picture. Like an investment, what is the potential gain from your initial cost? Yes, expressing gratitude may be hard, but the payoff is good.
3 Consider what would happen in the situation, relationship, etc., if you do not express gratitude.
4 Reverse the situation and ask yourself how you would want someone to acknowledge a kind act you did.
5 Ensure that you are alert to the kind act. Look for opportunities to "catch" someone doing good.
6 Recognize negative tendencies such as envy. Practice "thought stopping" when you catch yourself thinking negatively.
7 Reword negative statements to make statements that are more neutral or even positive. For example, instead of thinking: "I am not able to make it on my own without help." Reword to: "I am fortunate to have people in my life that are willing to help me."
8 When anxiety or shyness are a barrier, start small. Encourage yourself to take small steps, start with an expression of gratitude that is not face-to-face, such as a note.
9 Practice once a day expressing gratitude in some fashion. This will aid your fluency and comfort.
10 Observe someone's reaction to your expression of gratitude, this will likely reinforce your efforts.

164 *Gratitude and Being a Recipient*

Relationships are a series of exchanges. Most people want these exchanges to meet their needs of the three As: attention, appreciation, and affection. We all vary in the degree of need for these areas. As a partner or a friend, ask yourself: "How much attention, appreciation and affection am I providing?" "Is this amount what the other needs?" Better yet, ask the person directly for feedback as to whether the amount is congruent with their needs. This may be hard to do and rather vulnerable for you both, but the payoff will be worthwhile.

Ways to Cultivate Gratitude

Gratitude can be elicited. Research has shown that small reminders of humanity are enough to activate feelings of gratitude. Rubin (2011) conducted a study with 122 undergraduate students. It was found that students who were cued with a picture of two people holding hands (a reminder of human connection) were found to be more likely to ask for help on an assignment than students shown a picture not of hand holding. The timing of the gift is also a factor when considering gratitude. Further review of Koo et al.'s 2022 study, mentioned in Chapter 2, is relevant here. The type of giving and the timing of the gift are important regarding the impact it has on the receiver. As already mentioned, giving earlier is better for the recipient than later. Additionally, when the gift enables the receiver to remain autonomous, the receiver feels more gratitude as they are empowered. Combining these two points, when help is received toward the end of the situation, the dependence on the giver is more predominate, resulting in the receiver feeling less independent. Receiving help can undermine one's independence and create feelings of inadequacy and dependency. The receiver may feel overwhelmed by the desire to reciprocate the gift or to return the favor such as in the reciprocity norm mentioned earlier. Ideally, the recipient will know and agree to the terms of the gift. Is the giver giving a loan? Is the expectation for the receiver to return or exchange the gift for service? Is there an expectation that the gift will be returned only if the individual is in the position to do so? These questions are important for the exchange and can have a tremendous impact on gratitude. Chapter 7 will cover strategies for maintaining boundaries as a giver, but the receiver too must be comfortable with the circumstances of the exchange. The receiver

Gratitude and Being a Recipient 165

can add in their own caveat, especially when it helps them preserve their autonomy. It is, therefore, incredibly important for the receiver to be able to return the favor/gift if they can. Sometimes, a "pay it forward" expectation is stated. Knowing what we have so far covered of the science and human tendencies, I suggest that paying it forward would be through any method available to the recipient. "Pay it forward" does not, and should not, mean to repeat the act of giving in the same manner to another. It should not be a "pay-it-back" mindset. Instead, it should be, give to another when you can in a manner they may need.

In a series of six studies, researchers Walker et al. (2016) found that gratitude is more likely experienced when people reflect on a purchase made for experiential items like tickets to an event over material items like jewelry. The reason for this is believed to be threefold, experiential purchases typically provide social connection, contribute to an individual identity, and are less likely to create a negative social comparison than a material purchase. Additionally, they found that people were more altruistic when thinking about experiential purchases over material purchases. There were a variety of interesting methods used in this series of six studies. First, the researchers surveyed the 95 US participants on their purchasing and gratitude, then they looked at online reviews for comparison of words of gratitude mentioned in either type of purchase, then 48 college students were tested using the electronic Dictator Game to assess whether they gave more in the game when they were instructed to think about an experiential purchase versus a material purchase. These researchers also summarized the literature demonstrating the benefits of gratitude on increasing well-being, life satisfaction, socialization, and sleep while decreasing feelings of envy and visits to the doctor (as cited in Walker et al., 2016). It is further noted that gratitude can encourage generosity and paying it forward to others. In discussing their findings, the researchers mentioned previous research on "targeted" versus "untargeted" gratitude. Targeted gratitude is what we feel when we are given a specific gift from another. We are inclined to want to return the favor to that person (norm of reciprocity). Whereas untargeted gratitude occurs when there is not a specific person to express one's gratitude toward, such as when we feel a general sense of gratitude for our way of life. Untargeted gratification is more broadly felt and as such is likely to result in the desire to not only reciprocate

166   *Gratitude and Being a Recipient*

but to pay it forward. Untargeted gratitude can spark the urge to want to give to others, even anonymously. Of further interest summarized by Walker and colleagues, is the previous finding that people tend to feel closer to those that have given them experiential gifts versus material gifts. This is a very interesting "point on the dial" to consider when selecting "just the right gift" for others.

Returning to our tendency to make social comparisons, it is important to note that how we think about our giving has a tremendous impact on our feelings but also on the type of giving we do. Montal-Rosenberg and Moran (2022) studied the extent to which envy impacted one's willingness to give help and the type of help given as fostering dependency or autonomous. They explored two methods for giving help: dependent and autonomous. Dependent giving aids with a current need and tends to keep the recipient reliant on the giver whereas autonomous help entails providing support to the recipient so that they can provide for themselves in the future. The researchers hypothesized that people who engage in upward social comparison (comparing themselves to others they deem to be better) and result in feelings of envy will engage in more giving that is dependent. The thought is that the giver would still benefit from the appearance of generosity, while subtly maintaining a receiver's dependency. The researchers viewed this as "malicious motivation" and cited the word "schadenfreude" to describe one taking pleasure in an envied person's suffering. Giving in this manner is thought to be a way for the person with low self-esteem to give themselves a boost. Since this type of giving perpetuates dependency and is motivated by less-than-ideal motives, it is not held in high regard. However, giving to those better off than us can be a true act of grace when the intent and type of giving serves to aid autonomy. Motivation would play a large role in determining qualifying the goodness in such an act. The researchers did find that participants (134 US residents) were less likely to give autonomous help to envied peers than non-envied peers.

Culture seems to have some impact on people's comfort in accepting gifts. When the gift is small and from an acquaintance, Asians may refuse the gift due to the expectation of reciprocation (Shen et al., 2011). This finding does not hold true for accepting gifts from close friends. The rationale for the rejection of the gift is that Asian culture is collectivistic, making them more

Gratitude and Being a Recipient 167

sensitive to the need to reciprocate. Northern Americans, being an individualistic society, are noted to accept gifts based on the attractiveness of the gift over the need to reciprocate. These potential cultural differences may also have an impact on gift giving. People from collectivist societies may be more inclined to expect reciprocation when a gift is given versus individualistic cultures like the US and Canada.

When it comes to the idea of "it is the thought that counts," researchers have demonstrated that a receiver is not automatically inclined to think about the motivation of the giver unless cued by the social environment, such as when a parent says: "Isn't that thoughtful that your sister took the time to make that for you?" This is because the receiver evaluates the gift concretely based on the nature of the gift as opposed to the more abstract unseen measure of the giver's intent. Zhang et al. (2012) noted that the giver is more likely to overrepresent the receiver's focus on the thoughtfulness of the gift. They recommend that the giver should

> focus on getting a good gift and ignore whether it is a thoughtful gift or not. But if you want to feel closer to the person you are giving a gift to, then put as much thought into your gift as you possibly can and do not be offended when your thoughtfulness is overlooked.
>
> (page 679)

What do you think? We all can think of gifts we have received that have little to no monetary value but were incredibly meaningful. Think of Otto's quarter mention in Chapter 1. Perhaps this is a different process as the receiver themselves associated the symbolism rather than the giver. It is not to say that givers cannot "nail it" when finding the perfect sentimental gift, many often do. But the challenge is real in that the giver's idea of thoughtfulness and symbolism may not be the same as the receiver's. The receiver, on the other hand, can associate their own symbolism of a gift. Think of the little mementos we have collected over the years that remind us of others. A few years back, there was an *Extra* gum commercial (https://www.youtube.com/watch?v=NemtQx0m0Ss) showing a young woman giving her boyfriend a stick of gum when they first meet, then on a date, and various times throughout their relationship. The man doodled the moment on the wrapper and

168 *Gratitude and Being a Recipient*

displayed the sequence of doodles during a marriage proposal. The commercial ends with the statement: "Give *Extra*, get extra." Clearly, the symbolism is not lost on either the giver or the receiver, nor the audience! It is not the value of the gum wrapper, but the thoughtfulness in the man capturing and saving precious moments with his love.

Gratitude can also be cultivated in the workplace. Research has shown that there are many benefits to gratitude in the workplace. It behooves us to first know the barriers. A recent study (Sawyer et al., 2022) pointed out many dynamics in the workplace that interfere with the expression and experiencing of gratitude in the workplace. A few examples include the need for hyperfocus and attention in most workplaces to manage the sleuth of inputs and demands that become ever increasing. This fast-paced environment constricts our focus, often to the neglect of the world around us. Our focus becomes narrow, making us lose awareness of the grace surrounding us. Mindfulness strategies provide a shift away from the self. These researchers utilized mindfulness strategies to help employees experience gratitude. They found that when employees journaled for ten days, received cues to focus on positive occurrences and taking the perspective of others, their rates of helping increased.

The positive effects of gratitude have also been shown in college students. In 2017, researchers (Wong et al., 2017) studied the effects of a *Gratitude Group Program* on 20 college students. Students participated in five group sessions to aid in the expression of gratitude. Through the tenets of positive psychology and mindfulness theories, these researchers designed the *Gratitude Group Program* based on existing literature that demonstrated that gratitude is more powerful when practiced with others. A meta-analysis, a summary of existing literature, by Davis et al. (2016) noted only slight increases in gratitude when exercises were conducted alone. Wong et al. (2017) continued this endorsement of the benefits of group practice and noted that individual exercises can go only so far. These researchers further noted that activities, such as writing letters of gratitude, often provide minimal instruction and are not typically overseen by others that can offer guidance. People who struggle with socialization will tend to struggle with the completion of such a task. In person, group activities provide face-to-face encouragement and examples most people need to get started on such tasks, along with seeing them through to completion. The

Gratitude and Being a Recipient **169**

Gratitude Group Program boasts a vibrant curriculum where feedback and suggestions are provided along with a variety of exercises for expressing gratitude that are shared in a group environment.

The Gratitude Group Program consists of five sessions as follows.

Session One

Micro gratitude: After introductions, the benefits of gratitude are reviewed, mindsets and barriers to gratitude are discussed along with practicing gratitude for the little things. Group members are then encouraged to express gratitude to one another. Daily journaling is encouraged with the prompt of listing three things they are grateful for each day.

Session Two

Gratitude savoring: Focuses on paying attention to the benefits of gratitude and the pleasure one receives. Activities include volunteers sharing one thing from their gratitude journal as other members respond to the information shared. The "savoring" activity involves the use of food or beverages to practice awareness of one's senses connecting to enjoyment and gratitude. Attempts to prolong the good feelings are practiced by creating an awareness and expression of these feelings. Using further mindfulness techniques, the group then goes outside to practice savoring techniques through expressions of gratitude for nature. Members are encouraged to identify two savoring activities to practice between the sessions.

Session Three

Interpersonal gratitude: The importance of interpersonal gratitude is discussed. The activity starts with a "positive mental subtraction" exercise where participants image a positive influence in their lives and what their life would be like without that individual. The group receives instructions, ideas, and coaching on writing a gratitude letter. They are encouraged to take note of how they feel while writing the letter. They are encouraged to plan out how and when the letter is to be sent to the recipient.

170 *Gratitude and Being a Recipient*

Session Four

Redemptive gratitude: The focus of this session is on participants reflecting on a stressful experience that they felt gratitude, known as redemptive gratitude. I liken this to the "collateral beauty" concept. Experiences are shared and participants journal their experiences with redemptive gratitude.

Session Five

Marco gratitude: The focus of this session is on gratitude for the big things in life such as loved ones, life, and shelter. Reflecting on and expressing gratitude for these people, places, and things occurs through group discussion and the making of a "gratitude habit for life." The group ends with saying good-bye to members, sharing reflections and gratitude to one another.

This program was shown to be effective for these 20 students as they had a significant decrease in psychological distress along with an increase in gratitude, life satisfaction, and meaning of life. Although the size of this study was small, the findings and program proposed are encouraging. The researchers recommended that future users of this program add a sixth session to focus on further opportunities to build gratitude. The applicability of a program of this nature is evident with any group such as schools and the workplace. It is an ideal model to modify for group work with children too, a topic we will return to in Chapter 9.

Whether in a group or individual, one may be interested in further ways to cultivate gratitude. Here are a few strategies of my own for cultivating gratitude:

1 Gratitude journal. Write on paper or electronic notes on your cellphone a list of things you are grateful for. Keep this list going, adding to it often. There are a variety of techniques one can use to add to the challenge of growing this list. For example, I have clients write a list of things they are thankful for, experience joy from, or see beauty for every letter of the alphabet or for each letter of their name.

2 Review your list regularly, especially when feeling down.

3 Make a list of everyday heroes. This is a class exercise I give to my undergraduate students. I have them make a list of ten everyday heroes; someone that they look up to or noticed has

Gratitude and Being a Recipient 171

made a difference in the world – no matter what size. I then have them select one person from the list to send a message to. I ask them to reflect on how they feel while making this list, how they feel in writing a note of thanks, and what the response was from the recipient.

4 Celebrate successes and steps along the way. Do not wait until a project is completed or a destination is reached before rejoicing – celebrate the progress.

5 Identify the joys around you. Take a moment to marvel in the wonder of nature and the smallest of beauties. This mindfulness task not only enhances gratitude but enables one to focus on the here and the now. This focus is a counter-pose to anxiety and negative thinking.

6 Compliment others and congratulate them on their successes. When we build up others, we too are strengthened.

7 Count among your blessings feedback from others for they are the ones that care about our success. They are often the ones that tell us what we need to hear, even when we are not necessarily ready to hear it. As Randy Pausch, an American educator and professor, said, it is a bad place to be when people stop telling us we are messing up because that means they have given up on us.

8 View failure as an opportunity to learn. Be glad for the opportunity to try and to be lucky enough to try again.

9 Eliminate judgments and negative assertions of others. We never know what another is experiencing; what weight they may be carrying. Negativity brings us down. Like a magnet, these thoughts collect and create negativity in our thinking. Instead, be the one that offers kind words of encouragement or compliments to build another up.

10 Look for the collateral beauty in things. Was there a time in your life that was particularly difficult? At the time, its purpose may have been unknown. As you look back on this experience, can you detect where you have developed? It is not to say that you are glad the event occurred, just that you have grown from it. What are the life lessons that can be extracted? How has the experience made you stronger?

11 Keep your eyes wide open and your ears perked to the world around you and where opportunities exist to be gracious.

12 Appreciate yourself with extra doses of self-care and positive affirmations.

172 *Gratitude and Being a Recipient*

Gratitude helps us build resiliency for life's hardships. It allows us to think about the positives and place things in their proper context. The more we practice gratitude now, the better equipped we are to withstand adversities. As with any practice, the more we train and condition, the more automatic the response becomes. There are so many ideas for expressing gratitude. Ask others to share their ideas and experiences; try them on for size. I was fortunate to interview Andie Summers, the host of the *Andie Summers Show* on the country radio station 92.5 XTU. Her show is very popular with a faithful fan base. Many of her fans attend fundraisers broadcasted on her show. Thinking about her fans, she noted: "It's a country station; the listeners have big hearts." Regarding how giving impacts her show, she stated: "On the radio, I work to make listeners aware. I get the message out and work with organizations that are like minded." On a personal note, Mrs. Summers shared with me an experience she had. Her friend invited her and several other friends to a dinner party before Thanksgiving to express how much they meant to her. The friend went around the table and said words of gratitude to each person. She then had each guest write ten cards to a stranger to express gratitude with the challenge of giving each card out before Thanksgiving. These ideas for expressing gratitude are so powerful.

Many of the research findings summarized were echoed in my interviews. A theme that merged was a need for appreciation. Interviewees overwhelmingly noted that they give without expecting anything in return, however, gratitude was what they craved. A few of my interviewees recalled feeling overlooked when not given credit for their generosity. Initially, this made them feel bad and question their giving. Interestingly, none of the interviewees reported that it was enough to make them stop future giving behaviors. This was true even for those who thought it would change their behavior. It seems that if a giver feels unappreciated in the moment, that may not be enough to stop their giving heart. It tended to make them readjust their boundaries around giving. When asked about their experiences being a recipient, interviewees reported feeling "seen." They felt noticed by others and restored their views on humanity. Interviewees reported feelings of gratitude that have lasted years after the kind act. Many interviewees cried tears of gratitude while recalling their experiences as a recipient.

Gratitude and Being a Recipient 173

Gratitude is a mindset. It is a way of thinking that is shaped throughout our development. Often, we mimic what we see as we tend to learn by example. Our thinking impacts our behavior. With reflection and work, one can alter patterns of thinking. The first step is to reflect; something we do not do enough, causing us to repeat patterns we have learned without properly exploring them. To have a sense of congruence, our thoughts need to be consistent with our actions, and require reflection.

Influencing Gratitude in Children

Parents and the family unit are children's first social network. It is here that children learn patterns of relating to others. As mentioned earlier, according to the social learning theory, the environment teaches children through modeling. Children learn generosity through observation of those around them. Children are especially influenced by models of generosity. Many of us can remember early experiences of witnessing generosity. One of the questions I asked interviewees was to recall their earliest recollection of giving. Returning to my interview with Mrs. Summers, she recalls her father donating blood frequently. She remembers him coming home with a cotton ball on his arm. He would say: "I'll make new blood." Mrs. Summers fondly reflected on the role models she had in her life. She was proud to know that she had modeled giving for her children. Giving is an important part of her life and the life of her family. When asked about her thoughts on giving, she noted:

> When I think of giving, I think of the *Disney* movie *Princess and the Frog*, the scene where they share gumbo on the stoop with the community. It is my favorite movie. I said to husband 'that is the life I want for people, to share the only pot of soup with one another'.

Another example comes from my 83-year-old mother, Dorothy Cuddy. When I asked her to recall an early experience of witnessing giving, she told the following story:

> When I was about 12 or 13 years old, my youngest brother was born. I noticed that he had blonde hair...then I realized that

174 *Gratitude and Being a Recipient*

all my siblings had blonde hair as babies, I became so upset because I thought I was adopted. I could not be calmed. My parents could not find my birth certificate to prove I was not adopted, so I went on being upset. My dad took me out to the store and said I could buy whatever I wanted. I selected a white fur hat with a rose on it. That was his way of making me feel better, to give me something.

In further reflection of her early role model for giving, my mother shared:

When I was a child between 8–11 years old, I used to go into the neighborhood on trash day and pick broken toys out of the trash. I would bring them home for my mom to clean and put on dresses for the dolls and brush their hair. My dad would fix what was broken. Come Christmas time, we would go the orphanage or give to neighbors who did not have much.

A specific note of interest is that several of my interviewees mentioned stories that were told to them, ones that they themselves did not witness. These stories were passed down to them yet were still potent as it meant so much to the family member sharing the story. It is amazing how even talking about kind acts can make us feel good and can serve as valuable lessons. One of my interviewees shared a story that her father-in-law shared with her. When he was young and his family was just starting out, he struggled financially. He told his friend that he did not know how he would make it to the end of the week. The friend gave him his paycheck. After all these years, the father-in-law felt grateful for this kind act. The interviewee had tears in her eyes as she shared this story. A similar "by proxy" experience of gratitude was expressed by Mike Ciunci, one of the leading real-estate agents in Pennsylvania. He noted being very influenced by Tony Robbins, a famous life and business strategist. Mike noted that Tony serves meals to 5 million people a year. Mike stated:

I remember him talking about how he grew with his giving, that affected me positively. Tony tells a story of how he was poor as a child. He started to give a few meals at a time and just started adding to where he is now serving millions.

Gratitude and Being a Recipient 175

Mike remains inspired by this story of another's giving. Our models are powerful teachers. Mike, himself, is an inspiring model for giving. However, he only claims: "I am just scratching the surface (of my giving)."

Another component to this social learning is how parents shape children's behavior through their responses. Parents' response to children not being grateful was shown to have a significant effect on children's gratitude and internal symptoms three years later (Hussong et al., 2021). One hundred and one parent-child pairs were part of a study on *Raising Grateful Children*. Ingratitude was described by parents in a focus group to occur when the child does not say "thank you," when child assume others will act on their behalf, when they want something immediately or not what was offered, and when they complain about something not being enough. Data was collected in a series of assessments, observations, and interviews. Six parental responses to their child's ingratitude were measured: self-blame, let-it-be, distress, punish, give-in, and instruct. Parents that scored high on "self-blame" responded high on questions wondering if they did something wrong in their child rearing. They felt as though the child's behavior was their fault. The "let-it-go" subscale measured a parent's tendency to not pay attention to the behavior as the parent would attribute the ingratitude to the child's developmental level. The "distress" subscale indicated parents that would get frustrated, upset, or annoyed by the child's ingratitude. Parents that scored high on the "punish" subscale were inclined to give a consequence for the ingratitude. "Give-in" subscale measured parents' response of letting the child lead the outcome. These parents reported that they would make a substitute meal if that was what the child wanted or give in to purchase something they originally said "no" to. Parents that scored high on the subscale of "instruct" would remind their child of the things they already have, encourage them to realize how lucky they already are, they explained that we all need help at some time, and to think about the things they like instead of what they do not. Statistics were used to collapse these six categories into four (combining let-it-go with give-in and combining self-blame with distress). This scale is now deemed a reliable and valid measure for gauging parents' response to ingratitude.

The results showed that parents responded differently depending on the child's age. Parents of younger children responded with

176 *Gratitude and Being a Recipient*

more "let-it-go" responses than parents of older children who responded to ingratitude with more "self-blame." To test which responses led to more gratitude three years later, the researchers had parents track gratitude. Children of parents who initially responded with distress over ingratitude had more gratitude three years later. Children of those that punished less and gave-in less also had higher gratitude at follow-up. Parents high on punishing responses had children with higher internalizing symptoms such as feelings of sadness, hopelessness, and worry three years later. The clear takeaway points are that children learn how to be grateful from the responses they receive from their environment. Additionally, when these responses are not emotionally healthy, children are likely to internalize them with negative feelings. There is a right way to teach gratitude and a wrong way. The right way is through concern, consistency, and nonpunitive methods. Think of the opportunity as a teachable moment where the adult can shape and model the response for the child. Just as gratitude is learned, so is generosity.

Key Points

- Social psychology has shown that people like us better when they do us a favor.
- Gratitude enables us to live happier, healthier, and longer lives.
- Giving can be the antidote to stress! Per research findings.
- Gratitude needs to be expressed at a 5 to 1 ratio of positive to negative feedback for relationships to be robust.
- Small reminders of humanity are enough to activate feelings gratitude.
- Paying it forward shows gratitude and means giving to another in a manner they may need to carry on the positive benefits of receiving.
- Research support has been found for the tendency for people to feel closer to those that have given them experiential gifts versus material gifts.
- Comparing ourselves to others deemed better hinders sense of well-being.
- Giving is a tangible way to express one's purpose and to effect positive benefits on self and others.
- Women were found to be healthier when they gave support in their intimate relationships, even without reciprocation.

Gratitude and Being a Recipient 177

- Research has shown that more status was granted to givers that reciprocated anonymously.
- Changing our mindset about stress to that of gratitude has been shown to have positive benefits on health and well-being.
- Gratitude has been shown to have positive effects on mood, reduced anxiety, increased socialization, enhanced sleep, reduced physical pain, to name a few.
- Barriers to gratitude include not thinking a gift is praiseworthy. Other variables include embarrassment, feelings of guilt, shame, inferiority, to name a few.
- Gratitude can be activated by thinking about an experience.
- Interviewees overwhelmingly noted that they give without expecting anything in return, however, gratitude was what they craved.

Action Steps

- Ask yourself, "Do I focus more on what is working or more on what is not working in my life?"
- Challenge any negative thoughts you may experience by countering with statements of gratitude.
- Engage in gratitude strategies covered in Chapter 6; find several that work best for you.
- Reflect on your barriers to expressing gratitude.
- Think about your early model of giving behavior. What did you learn?

References

Aronson, E., Wilson, T.D., Sommers, S.R., Page-Gould, E., & Lewis, N. (2023). *Social Psychology*, 11th edition. New York: Pearson.

Chowdhury, M.R. (October 3, 2023). The neuroscience of gratitude and effects on the brain. *Gratitude*. https://positivepsychology.com/neuroscience-of-gratitude/

Davis, D.E., Choe, E., Meyers, J., Wade, N., Varjas, K., Gifford, A., Quinn, A., Hook, J. N., Van Tongeren, D.R., Griffin, B.J., & Worthington, E.L., Jr. (2016). Thankful for the little things: A meta-analysis of gratitude interventions. *Journal of Counseling Psychology*, 63(1), 20–31. https://doi.org/10.1037/cou0000107

Emmons, R.A. (2013). *Gratitude Works! A 21-Day Program for Creating Emotional Prosperity*. California: Jossey-Bass.

178 *Gratitude and Being a Recipient*

Flynn, F., & Yu, A. (2021). Better to give than reciprocate: Status and reciprocity in prosocial exchange. *Journal of Personality and Social Psychology: Interpersonal Relations and Group Process*, 121(1), 115–136. https://doi.org/10.1037/pspi0000349

Frankl, V. (1946). *Man's Search for Meaning*. Boston: Beacon Press.

Gottman, J., Schwartz Gottman, J., & DeClaire, J. (2006). *10 Lessons to Transform Your Marriage*. New York: Crown Publishers.

Hussong, A.M., Halberstadt, A., Langley, H.A., Thomas, T.E., & Coffman, J.L. (2021). Parents' responses to children's ingratitude are associated with children's gratitude and internalizing 3 years later. *Journal of Family Psychology*, 36(1), 80–91. http://doi.org/10.1037fam0000855

Koo, M., Jung, S., Palmeira, M., & Kim, K. (2022). The timing of help: Receiving help toward the end (vs. beginning) undermines psychological ownership and subjective well-being. *Journal of Personality and Social Psychology: Interpersonal Relations and Group Processes*, 124(4), 772–795. https://doi.org/10.1037/pspi0000403

Kumar, A., & Epley, N. (2023). A little goes a long way: Underestimating the positive impact of kindness on recipients. *Journal of Experimental Psychology: General*, 152(1), 236–252. https://doi.org/10.1037/xge0001271

Liang, J., Krause, N.M., & Bennett, J.M. (2001). Special exchange and well-being: Is giving better than receiving? *Psychology and Aging*, 16(30), 511–523. https://doi.org/10.1037//0882-7974.16.3.511

McCullough, M., Emmons, R., & Tsang, J.A. (2002). *The gratitude questionnaire – Six item form (GQ-6)*. https://ggsc.berkeley.edu/

McGonigal, K. (June 2013). *How to make stress your friend*. https://www.ted.com

Midgley, C., Thai, S., Lockwood, P., Kovacheff, C., & Page-Gould, E. (August 13, 2020). When every day is a high school reunion: Social media comparisons and self-esteem. *Journal of Personality and Social Psychology*, 121(2), 285–307. https://doi.org/10.1037/pspi0000336

Montal-Rosenberg, R., & Moran, S. (2022). Envy and help giving. *Journal of Personality and Social Psychology*, 122(2), 222–243. https://doi.org/10.1037/pspi0000340

Post, S., & Neimark, J. (2007). *Why Good Things Happen to Good People: How to Live a Longer, Healthier, Happier Life by the Simple Act of Giving*. New York: Broadway Books.

Ross, M. (April 26, 2023). *Expressing gratitude has been scientifically proven to help you live longer, says a world leader in longevity research*. https://www.wellandgood.com/benefits-of-gratitude/

Rubin, M. (2011). Social affiliation cues prime help-seeking intentions. *Canadian Journal of Behavioral Sciences*, 43(2), 138–141. https://doi.org/10.1037/a0022246

Gratitude and Being a Recipient 179

Sawyer, K.B., Thoroughgood, C.N., Stillwell, E.E., Duffy, M.K., Scott, K.L., & Adair, E.A. (2022). Being present and thankful: A multi-study investigation of mindfulness, gratitude, and employee helping behavior. *Journal of Applied Psychology*, 107(2), 240–262. https://doi.org/10.1037/apl0000903

Shen, H., Wan, F., & Wyer, R.S. (2011). Cross-cultural differences in the refusal to accept a small gift: The differential influence of reciprocity norms on Asians and North Americans. *Journal of Personality and Social Psychology*, 100(2), 271–281. https://doi.org/10.1037/a0021201

Väänänen, A., Kivimäki, M., Buunk, B.P., Pentti, J., & Vahtera, J. (2005). When it is better to give than to receive: Long-term health effects of perceived reciprocity in support exchange. *Journal of Personality and Social Psychology*, 89(2), 176–193. https://doi.org/10.1037/0022-3514.89.2.176

Walker, J., Kumar, A., & Gilovich, T. (2016). Cultivating gratitude and giving through experiential consumption. *Emotion*, 16(8), 1126–1136. https://doi.org/10.1037/em0000242

Wong, Y.J., Blackwell, N.M., Mitts, N.G., Gabana, N., & Li, Y. (2017). Giving thanks together: A preliminary evaluation of the Gratitude Group Program. *Practice Innovations*, 2(4), 243–257. https://doi.org/10.1037/pri0000058

Zhang, Y., & Epley, N. (2012). Exaggerated, mispredicted, and misplaced: When "It's the thought that counts" in gift exchange. *Journal of Experimental Psychology: General*, 141(4), 667–681. https://doi.org/10.1037/a0029223

7 Ill Effects of Giving and the Need for Creating Boundaries

Introduction

This chapter will provide several examples of the negative effects from giving. Interviewees share experiences of when their giving was not appreciated, exploited, or when given a gift in mean spirit. Additionally, other negative experiences from giving such as burnout, secondary trauma, compassion fatigue, and giving fatigue are addressed. These concepts are defined, and mindfulness strategies are offered to prevent their occurrence. The second part of this chapter covers the need to create and maintain personal boundaries to giving. Elements of positive psychology and mindfulness theories are integrated leading to the development of boundaries through worksheet applications.

Theory and research are covered to assist the reader in identifying their own giving patterns and experiences. These insights are used to help with the construction of personal giving boundaries, enabling the reader to make choices aligned with their priorities and to ward off ill effects from giving too much or to the wrong entity. Decisions made through the lens of established boundaries make saying "yes" or "no" easier. The reader is prompted to reflect on the many ways in which they already give and to give themselves credit for these acts. They are reminded to replenish themselves as a giving resource by providing self-care and maintaining their boundaries to giving. To this end, this chapter has two distinction sections, the ill effects of giving and strategies for preventing and developing personal boundaries to giving.

DOI: 10.4324/9781003438359-7

Ill Effects of Giving

Negative Experiences with Giving

While working on this book, thinking more than usual about giving and the many facets involved, I had a dream. In this dream, I was bringing bags of clothing and household items to a woman in transitional housing. She complimented my wedding ring, saying how beautiful it was. My empathy soared as I believed this woman was not currently in the position to own such a valuable item, so I offered it to her! I took the ring off and heard it drop into the bag of items I was giving her. At the sound of the ring falling into the bag, I immediately felt regret. I asked for the ring back as I recognized that I overextended my boundary. I was giving away something that I wanted; something very valuable to me emotionally and monetarily. The dream ended there. Did I get the ring back in my dream? The end of the dream may seem abrupt, but not necessarily as the issue was resolved – I had made my realization of violating my own boundary. The giving away of the ring was the "manifest" content; the content that was on the surface, what seemingly the dream was about. The "latent" content, psychoanalytic theorists like Freud would say, is the real meaning behind the dream. It is what lies below the surface, often lying deep in our unconscious, outside our immediate awareness. The latent content, seems to me, is the strong desire to help. This desire can result in a detriment to myself if I do not adhere to my personal boundaries. Perhaps you have been in a similar situation where you did not feel right before, during, or after giving. Exploring the elements involved in this situation will help you understand more about your patterns and motivations. Consider your reasons for giving and the amount of your gift. Was the gift proportionate to the need and your available resources? Notice that in my dream, the giving of the ring came at an enormous sacrifice. Also, the aspect of me giving such a personally valuable possession without being asked gives suspicion to my motivation to give, at times too much (more latent content). How would I have felt if I did not ask for the ring back? This type of giving would no doubt leave me feeling regretful and exploited. How may I have viewed the receiver if she

182 *Ill Effects of Giving and the Need for Creating Boundaries*

kept it? Unfavorably for sure, thinking she should have declined it. Negative outcomes to giving can occur due to regret, shame in receiving, and a slew of other dynamics. Exploring further, consider your beliefs regarding the outcome to a gift. Does it always need to be positive? Does a negative outcome deflect from a kind gesture? Negative outcomes often speak more about the recipient's place in their life than the giver's intent. Perhaps we should ask: "Is the recipient able and ready to see the kindness underlying the kind act?" If not now, then maybe later. The stark reality is that there are people that will exploit and take without having a legitimate need. There are still others that may even exploit the need they have to play on others' sympathies. Sadly, there are some occasions in which your gift of time, effort, or money does not appear to be appreciated. Strategies for avoiding negative outcomes and their ill effects are included later in this section.

There are costs to giving that go beyond the expense of the time or money offered. Giving can lead to feelings of frustration and regret, especially if there are expectations associated with the gift. Monitoring one's expectation about giving is important. It is not realistic or fair to expect giving to be without expectations. The key is to be aware of one's expectations prior to giving so not to be disappointed. This insight can be used to communicate expectations ahead of time to the recipient to prevent miscommunication as expectations are rather individualized.

To empathize how individualized our expectations and personal comfort levels are, I think of a time I gave a van full of clothing, household items, and furniture to a transitional home for women and children. This facility housed a dozen or so families at any given time. The facility's goal was to support them and provide services to help transition them to their own homes or apartments within a few months. The facility, therefore, always had an influx of families coming in and families leaving; there was always a need for items in kind. When I pulled up to the back door located in a narrow alley, some of the women and children came out to help me and the staff unload the van. The items were brought to a common area where the women (and children) started to divide up the items. They were ecstatic; there was something for everyone! The staff member pulled out a long sweater and asked if she could have it. I said, "yes." Some may say that I should have said, "no." Some organizations have rules around this too. Although I brought the items for the residents of

Ill Effects of Giving and the Need for Creating Boundaries **183**

this program, my expectation was that those in need would benefit. My thinking was that I know what direct care staff earn in nonprofit organizations; it is not much. Perhaps this staff too needed support. Perhaps she would benefit from the item and the kind gesture. Additionally, I noticed that she encouraged all the residents to go through the items and take what they needed as opposed to her going though it first. In private, she could have taken anything she wanted. The fact that she asked, instead of taking or assuming, I saw as humility of someone in need. Giving can benefit more than the initial intended recipient. It was a small ask that hopefully gave her some joy; I am certain it did lend some warmth as the building was rather cold!

Regret was a topic of interest during my interviews. I wanted to get a candid view of peoples' experiences as givers, so naturally some of the not-so-favorable feelings emerged. For the most part, interviewees were not deterred from giving, even when the outcomes were not what they thought. Negative experiences seemed to make them more mindful in future giving. Interviewee, Sheree, said while discussing any regrets:

> Even times I felt it was not appreciated, I did not regret doing it, but noted that I would not do it again. Like an organization that is happy to receive the money but is not interested in my involvement or perspective.

When she was asked if there are any reasons why she would not give, Sheree said: "Sometimes I feel like I am being directed by God towards or away from giving."

Sometimes giving feels wrong or forced. This can occur with obligatory gift giving during the holidays, birthdays, weddings, baby showers, the list is endless further adding to dread some feel with giving. Forced giving can be of your time and expertise. My husband, Tom, can attest to that as I frequently volunteer him to help with projects that need fixing. He acquiesces as a favor to me, and typically feels good about helping when the job is completed. Other times, he feels regret over doing so. To this point, Tom noted a negative experience with giving being:

> Forced giving by my wife. I am forced to do it when I do not want to do it, then I feel bad about it because I did not want to do it. There was recently a woman who lost everything in a

184 *Ill Effects of Giving and the Need for Creating Boundaries*

house fire and was living at a hotel. We gave her clothes, shoes, and household items. I felt annoyed because she was not respectful of my time, arriving late, and making us wait. I feel taken advantage of when not appreciated or when I know the giving benefits the wrong person.

When I asked Tom more specifically if there was ever a time he gave and regretted it? he said:

Yes. The accumulation of negative responses and lack of respect and appreciation from the past has made me slow down and focus more just within family. Lack of respect for what I have done – not reciprocating. Respect has been little to none.

He mentioned a mutual friend and noted: "I gave her my time, expertise, listening ear, and she gets upset and angry at me for not taking her side in a dispute she was having with someone." When it came to his expectations around the outcome of his giving, he noted: "The closer I am to the person or the organization, the more I expect to have some respect and acknowledgment for what I have done. Could be a simple thank you, good job."

Negative experiences can occur when giving to an individual, but also when giving to an organization. There is a lot of suspicion regarding how donations are utilized. It is wise to research causes and individual circumstances as mentioned in Chapter 4 to ensure, as best as possible, the legitimacy of the organization and the need. Returning to my interview with Mr. Downing, like so many of my interviewees, he noted trust being a factor he needs to support a cause. He questioned the concept of church tithing, stating:

Tithing…we got it all twisted, it should be clothes and food for the needy. I do not see a whole lot of that at the church, but this is how it should be. I see more of it being about the church's needs. Today we see on social media mega churches and homeless on the same block.

In discussing his use of boundaries in giving, he noted:

…this whole giving thing is good, but sometimes people take advantage of it. They try to guilt you into giving more, like

Ill Effects of Giving and the Need for Creating Boundaries **185**

your last leg – when they know it is your last leg and they still want it! I now walk away. Sometimes say flat out: "no." I have learned that silence can speak louder than all the words in the dictionary. So, saying nothing you have said everything.

When asked specifically about views on giving to the church, one interviewee stated:

> I haven't been to church in a long time. When I was a member, I thought my two obligations were time and money. I would give my time to children's programs. The monetary is a personal conflict to me – I don't have issue giving my money but there is a huge disconnect that I am a giver of the church because they tell me too. But my money is excluding others in need. What the church says is good welfare. There is a bubble about what service means. Why is it worthy because it is attached to a church – you should "walk the walk" outside the church too. It kind of pigeonholes who deserves and who does not deserve help.

Several interviewees felt strong connections with their church and the service that came from their religious community. A few noted being aware of the financial operations of their church, whereas others acknowledged not knowing where their offerings went. A couple of interviewees noted that their churches had a tremendous local community outreach. Others emphasized the international service and support their church community provided. One interviewee noted that her church supported both local and international projects. One interviewee did not see evidence of service and support outside the church and noted that the emphasis was internal on building the church. From these varied responses and experiences, it seems logical to conclude that church, like nonprofit organizations, should be subject to the same transparency and critique. Some experiences giving to the church were deemed positive, whereas others were deemed negative – to the point of members leaving the church over the experience(s). The extent of the support you offer to your church, or any entity, should be in proportion to the match of shared values and focus. If accountably is not there, it is nearly impossible to know the true outcome to one's giving efforts.

186   *Ill Effects of Giving and the Need for Creating Boundaries*

One interviewee spoke about her time volunteering. When asked if there was ever a time she gave and regretted it, she stated:

"If I kind of regretted it, I think I have learned something from it." She thought further and noted: "I was on a Board of a nonprofit for years. They had a new member come in that I had frequent disagreements with, and I started to feel like I was a naysayer. I voluntarily stepped off the board. I regretted it, that I made my decision because of my negativity. My initial instincts were correct, I should have stuck it out. I wondered if it was worth it when I would come out of the meetings feeling so negative. I used to always feel good about being there but did not anymore. I was conflicted."

Another interviewee said that they were taken aback after they made a large donation to a colleague's fundraiser, but the colleague did not later call on them for business, utilizing someone else. The interviewee noted thinking about the experience and realizing: "… that I would have still donated because it fits my parameters. It's the right thing to do." One of my interviewees spoke about her husband John. She recalled a "time I was mad at him, we were short on cash – at my cousin's bar mitzvah, we came out and a woman was saying she did not have money for diapers – he gave her his last $15. John said: "How do we know, but we both feel better."" John's words express a poignant way to think about giving outcomes; we may not know of the good our giving is doing, so why not trust that it is doing good and enjoy the feeling it gives.

Sometimes giving is to an individual that has a previously established pattern with you, other times it is an isolated situation that arises. We have varying ideas on the extent that we should give to others. It helps you to have an idea of your own view so when the need presents itself, you will know how to respond. Even when you know whether you will give or not, the question of what you expect in return should also be explored. Here too, we all have varying answers depending on who we are giving to, what we are giving, how much, our expectations for what they do with the resources we give, etc. Start by asking yourself why you give. Ask what you hope to get out of giving. These questions can help you gain insight into your motivations and expectations. Patterns

Ill Effects of Giving and the Need for Creating Boundaries 187

of giving that result in negative experiences can occur with those closest to us. I asked another interviewee if they ever regretted giving, she stated:

> Yes, my daughter struggled with addiction. She spent her rent money on her addiction. I had to pay her rent 2–3 times as there were children involved. After that, I had to cut it off. To this day we do not give her money. She calls me a "poo-poo mom."

Statements like this spark guilt and are often said to make someone feel bad until they give. Use the feeling of guilt as a radar for whether you should give or not. If you are giving just to avoid feeling guilty, you should not do it. Also, notice how you feel after you give. If you feel lousy, that is likely an indication that you know you were taken advantage of. These exchanges can become patterns, especially when it involves family or friends. Parenting is especially hard to navigate once children become adults. It is hard to know when to stop giving or when to stop some forms of giving, or if to give at all. Allow your feelings before, during, and after to be an indicator of whether you should give or give again. When you notice discomfort with giving or a pattern forming that you do not want to continue, alter your behavior. See the below strategies for ideas on preventing negative dynamics. When it comes to parent-child giving, additional strategies include having the child raise half the money needed or to work off the amount doing chores. These ideas are applicable to adult children too! Have them work to raise the money first before the money is given. This not only allows them to be empowered and preserve their dignity, but also cuts back on possible resentment and feeling taken advantage of as a giver.

Expectations identified before giving occurs can help ward off a negative experience. Here too, we all have varying views on what we expect in return (if anything) when giving. Kristine, an interviewee previously mentioned, poignantly stated:

> Thing about a gift – once it is given, it is not mine anymore. I have no power or control over it anymore or where it goes too. It is the gesture that is the gift. You cannot have any expectations about it.

188 Ill Effects of Giving and the Need for Creating Boundaries

She added that she did not realize this when she was younger and gave money to someone that was "in a dire situation." She found out years later that that person's sibling stole the money. To that, Kristine stated:

> Anyone in desperate need will go to any extent to get what they need. Giving must be free, you cannot control it. Was I sorry I gave the money, no – it was the gesture that matters... When you give money, you need to always think of it as a gift.

This last sentence is one that I have heard from many others. It is a mindset some people choose to adopt, not necessarily to be ultra generous but to protect themselves from negative feelings that may arise after giving a gift. Having this mindset, they are less burdened by the expectation of repayment and strains on the relationship if debt is not resolved. However, some may not be able to afford to make a loan a gift. Knowing this is a good start to candid reflection on giving. Can one afford to give a loan in the first place needs to be honestly considered for they run the risk of it not being repaid. Others may be fully able to make a loan a gift but choose not to as a method for preserving dignity to the receiver. Or perhaps they keep it as a loan to empower and motivate the recipient. Some are in the position to not need repayment but accept it so that they can use it to help the next person. If you deem a loan to be the best outcome, create a document and plan for repayments. Both you and the recipient should review and sign the plan, ideally in front of a notary. I will review more specific strategies later in the chapter and the next chapter.

When thinking about negative experiences with giving, we may think about scams and devious malice intent of others who take from us. While this can certainly occur, other scenarios can be negative even though the intentions of the recipient did not start out as such. Take, for example, the lending of money to a friend between jobs. Suppose they are behind on their mortgage and car payments. They owe money to their utilities and are about to lose their electric and phone services. They come to you for monetary support for their immediate needs of food and gasoline for their car. You generously loan them $500 to get a supply of groceries and to fill their gas tank a few times as they travel to job interviews. What are your expectations about being repaid? How

Ill Effects of Giving and the Need for Creating Boundaries 189

much and when? Assuming they land their next job at the end of the week, they will likely need to work a week or two before their paychecks start coming in. That adds another week or two to their debt as they are still behind on their bills. As they start to catch up on their expenses, where should their priority be? Certainly, the mortgage to prevent foreclosure and utilities are important (remember Maslow's hierarchy of needs identifying shelter at the most basic level). Also, the basic need for food is obvious, making grocery shopping of high importance. Getting caught up on the most pressing priorities could take months! It should not surprise you that your friend does not immediately start to repay you. Perhaps this was factored in with the repayment plan (see below). Perhaps you also accounted for their other debt and priorities and made the repayments start small and later. Often lenders get frustrated that they are not paid back as quickly as they believe they should be. It behooves a lender to establish their expectations on repayment in the beginning and make it part of the plan. Givers, having the desire to help foremost in their mind, likely do not factor in the above logistics when lending money. Lenders may not factor in the embarrassment one feels when they need help. This embarrassment may lead the receiver to avoid conversations about repayment. They may avoid contact with the lender attempting to stall until they can get caught up in paying their main priorities first. In this case, avoidance is more about the recipient's shame than it is about them trying to deceive the lender. As time goes on, this dynamic gets more and more solidified, making it even harder for the recipient to face the lender. The relationship is likely to suffer and may even be severed.

Here are five options for preventing a negative dynamic when giving/lending money:

1 Decide not to give: Dave Ramsey, Suzi Orman, and many other financial gurus would advise against loaning money to family and friends. Dave goes as far as to say that the chance of being repaid is low when it is someone you know. However, both advocates being generous. Suzi's tag line from her previous television show was "People first, then money, then things." However, generosity should not cause risk to the giver. Since relationships are at stake and emotions are involved, the dynamics are high stakes when lending money. It may be that the best

190   *Ill Effects of Giving and the Need for Creating Boundaries*

option is to say "no" and empower the individual to get support in another manner. Perhaps brainstorm with them about other options.

2   Give as a gift not a loan: If the need and parameters fit your plan, are in line with your boundaries and **if** you can afford to do so – consider giving as a gift. This takes the pressure off the recipient and ideally allows them better chances of getting caught up, and it also takes the pressure off the relationship. On the other hand, a gift could make the recipient feel beholden to the giver or could affect their sense of independence. Consider the individual and the relationship to determine if this is the right option. Perhaps dialogue with the individual will help inform the decision.

3   Give with a plan to work off the amount owed: Why not have the best of both worlds – helping someone financially and protecting, as best as possible, their dignity. When the recipient can work for the money, it enables them to preserve their pride. If the need fits your plan, is in line with your boundaries, and **if** you can afford to do so – consider a trade of money for work. Perhaps the recipient has a skill or asset that you can barter. You may want to devise the exchange in a written agreement, signed by both parties. Notarizing documents is always a smart move.

4   Give with a plan for repayment that is manageable: As the individual begins to pay back other debt, if possible, make the payments small initially, with a later start date, and/or over a longer period. Schedule payments at regular intervals, such as monthly. Ideally, have the individual set up their bank account to automatically withdraw per the schedule you both agree to. Most banks have in their online banking an option to set up automatic payments and the bank will mail a check to the recipient per the schedule you create. This is all at no cost, not even for shipping! It is also possible to set up bank-to-bank automatic payment where the payments would be sent electronically; however, I suggest against this option as your bank account number would need to be shared with the recipient.

5   Give with a combined plan: Take from the above strategies to tailor a plan that fits the needs of both the recipient and the giver. The plan may be that the recipient works off half the money needed and takes a loan with the giver for the remainder. Or half is considered a gift and half is worked off or repaid.

Ill Effects of Giving and the Need for Creating Boundaries **191**

Considering the psychology of the recipient is important in understanding why negative experiences may occur. Two psychological concepts involved in being a recipient are **shame** and **pride**. Shame is associated with a negative self-evaluation and can have cultural implications. Cultural expectations could be a good thing in that a bit of shame tends to motivate people to adhere to their cultural expectations on giving. For example, giving to charity is expected in the Islamic culture. It is one of the Five Pillars of Islam known as Zakat (Davis et al., 2023). In African cultures, there is the spirit of Ubuntu which involves giving as an important part of collectivism and well-being (Sobell, 2015).

However, cultural expectations may create high levels of shame. It behooves us givers to be aware of a recipient's comfort with being a recipient and be as gracious as possible. If a recipient is not responding to a gift as expected, it does not necessarily mean that they are not grateful. It could very well be that they are feeling embarrassed about needing help. An example comes to my mind of a very cold Christmas Eve. My husband and I were driving home from my best friend's (Michele) annual gift exchange party when we stopped to fill our tire with air. Next to us was an Indian family of four. The two girls went inside the store, watching their parents try to figure out what to do about their flat tire. I jumped out of the car and asked if we could help. I learned that they were told that the tow truck would not get there for another two hours and that they had a flight to get to. I "voluntold" (mandatory volunteering) my husband to help change the tire. This was not an easy task as our fingers were numb from the cold. Attempting to work smarter, not hard, I suggested to my husband a strategy that would help spin the lug nuts quicker – to which he gratefully adopted. We took turns taking off, then putting back on, the lug nuts. We were quite the team! We have worked on many projects together and under his tutelage, they have all been successful. I did not think to incorporate the husband and wife who owned the vehicle as we felt confident in the job at hand. I noticed that the husband was looking uncomfortable, pacing behind me. He offered to help. I said that it was not a problem, "I got it." He asked again, and that was when I realized I may have been offending him.

Initially, I did not take into consideration his cultural and his possible gender views. As an Indian man, it is likely that he held strong collectivistic views. As such, he likely believed that it took

192 *Ill Effects of Giving and the Need for Creating Boundaries*

many hands to get a job done. However, there is also a strong Indian cultural expectation on self-sufficiency. Additionally, there exists a social hierarchy that may have made him hesitant in accepting assistance for a manual labor task from a woman. This view clashes quite a bit with my own. It still does, even as I write this, I cannot help but think, "Why should I alter my view and back off from helping because I am a woman?" This clash is easily resolved as I weigh in with the intent of my assistance. My goal was to enable this family to get safely to where they were going. This task can be accomplished in many ways. Manually changing the tire was not my only option for helping. The tire was getting changed by my husband with or without my assistance. The most important step in the giving of our time and expertise was to get the process started. It truly did not matter who changed the tire – me or my husband or both, the important part was that it got done. I stepped aside for the man to finish. Hopefully, I caught on quick enough to enable the man to feel less awkward about the situation. Perhaps it led to him thinking more about why he may have felt uncomfortable. Hopefully, he was able to resist feeling shame for needing help. I believe the story ends well as his wife kindly texted me when they got safely to the airport and were able to board the plane in time to see their family for the holidays.

Pride is also at the core of an individual's experience in needing help. Most people consider themselves self-sufficient and want to be seen that way. When we struggle, but overcome these struggles, we feel a sense of accomplishment. We feel strength and empowerment. Together this equates to pride. Pride is a sense of satisfaction with what we have achieved and earned. It is a belief that we are doing well. It creates expectations of the self, having to alter from these expectations can be a real shot to one's ego. When someone's pride is hurt, they feel vulnerable and insecure. Self-doubt may take over and affect one's thinking. It is important to give in a way that protects the recipient's dignity. This is done through putting yourself in another's frame of reference when giving. Ask yourself, would you like to receive a gift in this manner? Preserving dignity is why many organizations ask for new items in their collections. It is also why food pantries are mindful of the experience of their customers and provide small amenities, such as shopping carts, to make their experience feel like a trip to the grocery store. To this

Ill Effects of Giving and the Need for Creating Boundaries **193**

point, below are a few strategies for enhancing dignity when giving. See if you can add anything to this list.

Strategies for enhancing dignity while giving:

1 Keep their identity private! Their need is not your story to tell.
2 See them as equals and treat them with humanity.
3 Put yourself in their frame of reference, how would you like to receive?
4 Work with the individual in creating a plan/solution/repayment plan.
5 Be aware of their individual personality and cultural views for receiving. Check for comfort.
6 When possible, provide guidance on how to get their need met on their own before offering to give.
7 Ask if you can teach them how to prevent or solve the problem in the future.
8 Show care and empathy, not pity.
9 Treat them with respect empowering them to make choices themselves.
10 Create an open and accepting environment that imparts no judgment.
11 Enter you own here, continue the list.

Knowing these factors and exploring precautions will help reduce the likelihood of negative effect to self and others when giving. Interestingly, having negative experiences in giving does not seem to stop givers from giving. Instead, negative experiences serve to help givers define their boundaries. There will always be reasons for not giving. Critics to giving will rationalize that people are takers. These critics tend to not give, preferring to criticize those trying to make a difference. I rather "mistakenly" help someone who is not in need, than run the risk of not helping someone who is. Some believe that *Karma* will balance it out. Most people regret the times they did not give over the times they did.

One final example of a negative effect of giving is the person that gives with the intent to harm. A few of my interviewees noted such occurrences. Interestingly, the experience did not seem to hurt them as the giver may have intended, but only served to make the receiver more empathic. I know this

194 *Ill Effects of Giving and the Need for Creating Boundaries*

to be the case as in my teenage years, I was dating a boy whose stepmother was rather mean toward him. By association, she did not like me. As a teenager, I was not allowed to get my ears pierced, so she teased and mocked me for not having pierced ears. Come Christmas time, she handed me a gift – as you may have predicted, a set of pierced earrings. Being young and naive at the time, I did not make the connection that she was being cruel. I commented on how beautiful they were, thanked her, and told her I would save them until I eventually got my ears pierced. It was not until years later that I realized her mean-spirited gesture and glad that my naivety enabled me to be gracious in my response. Another example was provided by my interviewee, Georgette. She recalled:

> When I was 5 years old, my stepdad's father bought me a baby doll that you could feed. It was black. I thought it was the most beautiful baby. I learned later that he was taking a jab at my mother as she was "one of those kind" (referring to my mother being accepting of others). The joke was on him that his intention fell short.

Why would someone do such a thing? Why would they spend money and time just to take a jab at another? Passive-aggressiveness comes to mind. Passive-aggressiveness describes personality traits and behaviors of a person who struggles to express their feelings, especially negative ones, directly and thereby does so in a more covert fashion. Typically, this style of communicating is repetitive and occurs in a pattern throughout the individual's relationships. Passive-aggressive behaviors are noted to be difficult to detect at times but can have detrimental effects on relationships. Another reason for such negative intentions in giving is how bullying is conceptualized. People dealing with internal pain and doubts may target others as a way of releasing some of the pain. They try to make themselves feel better by bringing others down. This is not a healthy thing to do for the individual or those with whom they are interacting. Mean-spirited people have difficulties appropriately expressing their emotions. They may struggle to be assertive or may have a fragile view of themselves, protecting their fragility with a hard shell.

Ill Effects of Giving and the Need for Creating Boundaries **195**

How to manage mean-spirited giving?

1 Do not let it change who you are. It is not a reflection on you as it is more a reflection on them as the mean-spirited giver.
2 Use your skills with empathy to try and understand their ill-intended gift.
3 Do something positive with the gift such as giving it to someone that would appreciate it.
4 You could also consider reaching out to the person to try and build a better rapport.
5 You could ask for clarification on how they feel about you or if there is a conflict of which you are not aware. It could be that this person is carrying beliefs about you that are misinformed.
6 Do not feed the fire and end up validating their negative beliefs.
7 When all else fails, sometimes the healthiest thing to do is to let it go.

Reflecting on your experiences with giving, answer the following questions:

1 Do you feel your giving has made a difference? _____

_____

2 Do you feel appreciated for your giving? _____

_____

3 Were any of your giving experiences negative? _____

_____

4 Do you notice any commonalities, any themes, with these experiences? _____

Burnout, Secondary Trauma, Compassion Fatigue, and Giving Fatigue

Other ill effects from giving have been identified in scientific literature. These experiences typically occur with continual giving of time, money, and other resources. They may also occur in extreme settings causing emotional reaction from the giver.

196　*Ill Effects of Giving and the Need for Creating Boundaries*

Four such phenomena, burnout, secondary trauma, compassion fatigue, and giving fatigue, are described below followed by strategies for management and prevention of these ill effects.

Burnout

Psychologist Herbert Freudenberger is credited with first identifying the term "burnout" in 1974. It consists of three components: loss of empathy, decreased sense of accomplishment, and feeling emotionally exhausted. Burnout is a state of physical and mental exhaustion. It is seen in the workplace, volunteering, and caring for loved ones. It can be brought on by working consecutive days without sufficient breaks, being understaffed, under-supported, working long hours, etc. The nonprofit field is especially susceptible to burnout as employees and volunteers often have too much work and not enough resources. Think about the medical field during the COVID-19 pandemic. Professionals, paraprofessionals, and nonprofessional staff worked around the clock. Some even slept at the hospital. Even when breaks were provided, people felt compelled to continue to work as the needs were so high. Many people I spoke to in the nonprofit fields struggle with taking breaks. They see the needs are never-ending and the limited staff already available, that they forgo vacations, breaks, and take on extra hours to try and fill the gap. For years working in the nonprofit sector, I was "on-call" every day, even during vacations. I was even on call in the delivery room having my first child! This was a quick recipe for burnout!

Burnout is a significant concern in the workplace. It has even led to a new phenomenon known as "quiet quitting." Quiet quitting is when an employee or volunteer continues to work but puts in minimal effort. The employee is not satisfied with the setting and becomes disengaged from it and its mission as noted in Cal Newport's (December 29, 2022) article, "The Year in Quiet Quitting: A New Generation Discovers That It's Hard to Balance Work with a Well-lived Life," in the *New Yorker*.

The US 2022 Bureau of Labor Statistics (https://www.bls.gov/) provides some indication of the impact of burnout in nonprofit sectors. First of note was the finding that nonprofit organization workers held the highest level of education compared

Ill Effects of Giving and the Need for Creating Boundaries 197

to for-profit industry and government agencies. Most (2/3) of these nonprofit workers worked in education or healthcare settings. Across all three groups (for-profit, nonprofit, and government agencies), women earned less than men. Interestingly, men were noted to be paid highest when in the nonprofit sector as opposed to the for-profit or government sectors. This could very well be due to their level of education being higher as educators and healthcare professions are often in nonprofit sectors. However, this finding was not true for women. Of the three sectors, women were paid similarly in nonprofit sectors as they were in government agencies. Women were paid least in the for-profit sector; again, this finding does not account for positions held and types of fields. When it comes to ethnicity, "Asians" were paid the highest across all three sectors, with "Whites" second highest. "Blacks" earned the least in nonprofit and government sectors and only slightly more than the lowest paid group, "Hispanics" in for-profit fields. This information provides important insights regarding the demographic differences in workplaces. These differences are related to the settings and how equitable employees are and are not treated. The fairness with which one deems their work to be regarded adds to their satisfaction, but can also subtract from it, leading to feelings of burnout.

Signs of burnout may be physical, emotional, or both. Physical symptoms include fatigue, low energy, and changes in sleeping or eating patterns. Exhaustion can also be experienced psychologically with symptoms of depression and anxiety. Specific symptoms may include negative thinking, hopelessness, helplessness, irritability, and feeling overwhelmed. The individual experiencing burnout may be more argumentative than usual. They may feel that their value and purpose are limited in their current workplace setting. They may feel that they do not enjoy the work like they used to and may even dread going to work. Their irritability may increase as the workday approaches. Many have identified experiencing "Sunday night blues" when the weekend is coming to an end, and they are scheduled to return to work on Monday morning. Feeling relieved when appointments are canceled or an individual they are helping does not show up or cancels is another indicator of burnout. Behavioral indicators may include calling out of work, not showing for scheduled shifts, or showing up late.

198 *Ill Effects of Giving and the Need for Creating Boundaries*

Secondary Traumatization

Secondary, also known as *vicarious*, traumatization is a form of indirect trauma. It is brought on by being exposed to another's trauma. It is especially concerning when the witnessing of other's trauma is frequent. The psychological effects experienced by the volunteers, workers, or caregivers are like those experienced with burnout in that anxiety and depression are often at the core. Witnessing trauma can lead to feelings of learned helplessness, as mentioned in Chapter 5. Fear of the trauma could lead to anticipatory anxiety and hypervigilance. Anticipatory anxiety is an uncomfortable psychological and physiological response experienced by worrying about the future. Hypervigilance is a heightened physiological state in which an individual feels on constant guard. An "on-edge" response, such as a startled response, in which a person seems "jumpy" may be observed. These symptoms are caused by activation in the brain. Midbrain structures, such as the amygdala, have been shown to cause an exaggerated response in individuals who have experienced trauma. Witnessing trauma can be as potent as experiencing it firsthand. The brain is responding to our experiences and thoughts, creating a physical impact. Remember the phenomena created by mirror neurons mentioned in Chapter 5? As we witness someone engaged in positive experiences our brains activate mirror neurons that produce pleasurable neurochemical sensations as if we were the ones completing the action. The same effect can occur when we witness negative events. Our mirror neurons create physiological arousal and fear responses. Witnessing or being exposed to another's trauma is difficult to manage. For once we know, we cannot undo and unknow that such trauma exists. Often, nonprofit workers and volunteers are in the position that they know explicit details and information about others' traumas, making the experience more and more vivid for them. Over time, these experiences can impact the worker's view of the world. Volunteers at crime victim centers hear constant stories of trauma. Likewise, police, fire rescue, EMTs, emergency room staff, etc. see what seems a never-ending flow of people who have been traumatized. These workers run the risk of developing a skewed perception of the world and the prevalence of crime and emergencies. The tendency to over-estimate the frequency of an occurrence because it is perceived through one's experience is a known as the

Ill Effects of Giving and the Need for Creating Boundaries 199

"availability heuristic" in the field of social psychology (Aronson et al., 2023). It is a shortcut our brain takes to derive at a conclusion; however, it is biased by one's experiences. As a result, the perception of crime/emergencies/trauma are likely to be overestimated in individuals working in these settings.

Signs of secondary trauma include physical and emotional symptoms, like those that have experienced the trauma directly, can occur in those exposed to the trauma. These symptoms include hypervigilance, anxiety, depression, fear, and flashbacks. Hypervigilance was described above and applicable here. Flashbacks are the sensory re-experiencing of the event, such as seeing, hearing, smelling, and feeling sensations they felt when exposed to the trauma. These experiences occur when the trauma is no longer occurring, thereby revisiting the event through images, sounds, and physical sensations when not in the situation. Changes to sleep and eating patterns may also be evident. One may experience guilt, such as "survivor's guilt", in that they were spared the trauma directly. Secondary trauma is also triggering to witnesses that have experienced their own trauma. The witnessing of another's trauma or hearing the individual who experienced the trauma recall the events may remind the observer of a time when they felt scared and vulnerable. As these underlying feelings are the common denominator, the traumas do not need to be the same for the response to be triggered. For these reasons and more, an organization should be very careful when considering who is hired and assigned to what type of work. Trauma informed care for the individuals served, but also for the employees and volunteers, is essential. Training and a supportive environment are necessary for all involved. Having a sense of an employee's or volunteer's coping mechanisms and aptitude for the work is important to obtain. As a professor, I have worked with hundreds of students over the years. I have directed their research interests and have had some students work directly with me on my research. Advising dissertation students always involved a discussion about their readiness to be "married" to the topic for a few years. Was this a topic they would want to work on and think about most days for the years it would take to complete? Likewise, is the topic something they can emotionally manage and if so, what are their self-care strategies to ensure management? When considering the fit for student workers in my research, a similar conversation ensued. Since some of the topics I explored were sensitive with a

200 *Ill Effects of Giving and the Need for Creating Boundaries*

risk of secondary trauma, I was always mindful to get a sense of a student's readiness for the material. This can start with a question regarding their interest in the topic. If the student expressed previous experiences that seem to have a potential to be traumatizing or retraumatizing, it warranted a direct question to them about how they planned to manage the material they may be exposed to during the research process. As a psychologist and college professor, I must ensure that I do not create a dual role nor create a situation in which they are disclosing personal information. The balance of privacy and information is essential. Along with this is the need to balance assumptions, so not to assume that someone with prior experience with a trauma is not able to handle material that is traumatic. This balance is needed not only in research but as a volunteer or employee in a setting that has exposure to trauma.

Compassion Fatigue

Compassion fatigue is sometimes used interchangeably with secondary trauma. However, this concept is a bit more distinct in that it involves a form of desensitization often developed by a gradual loss of compassion over time. It occurs when one experiences both burnout and secondary traumatization (Lee et al., 2021). Desensitization refers to the emotional reduction to repeated exposure. Helplessness and desensitization occur over time and create a state of numbness affecting motivation.

Compassion fatigue has been well researched and found especially in caregivers who give not only physical support but emotional support as well. Strazdins and Broom (2007) considered the giving of social support as a form of emotional labor. Social support, defined by these authors, as companionship or helping. They conducted a study surveying 398 Australian participants on their frequency in giving support to family or friends, companionship (showing affection and appreciation), helping (involving direct problem solving and emotional expression), and their responses on a depression scale. The findings showed that the giver reported fewer depressive symptoms when they spent time aiding another in building positive emotions and inclusion (companionship), whereas those who engaged in listening to others' problems (helping) emoting worries, sadness, and anger were found to have more

Ill Effects of Giving and the Need for Creating Boundaries 201

depressive symptoms. The emotional toll giving can take on the giver runs the risk of developing compassion fatigue. Compassion fatigue is the result of giving too much to the point of wanting to give up. Instead of giving up, perhaps healthy intervals of break would be just the rejuvenation needed. Developing a boundary to good self-care and detection of exploitation or one's own tendency to overdo it may be the best way to ward off compassion fatigue. Just like the instructions given by a flight attendant on a plane, if the plane loses pressure and oxygen masks deploy, put on yours first before securing others. Similarly, a caregiver must engage in regular self-care to preserve their ability to care for others.

Signs of compassion fatigue are a combination of burnout and secondary trauma, symptoms of both can occur. It is often heavily weighted with hypervigilance, anxiety, sleep disturbances, and flashbacks. Burnout symptoms of agitation, anger, feelings of helplessness, feelings of hopelessness, fatigue, feeling overwhelmed, feeling resentment, feeling numb, disconnected/withdrawn socially, and loss of interest in previously enjoyed activities may be experienced. People often feel like they have nothing left to give, that they are "empty."

Organizational structure and dynamics often add to compassion fatigue. Employees and volunteers working in nonprofits may feel that the needs are not being met or that the mission of the organization is not adequately being served. Additionally, they may see larger systems like the government and society have negative views on the individuals served such as the homeless, criminals, and the poor. These overarching views create cognitive dissonance (as described in Chapter 2 and throughout) and dissatisfaction. The magnitude of need can also be crushing to one's spirit. These existential realizations can leave one feeling discouraged, wondering what is the use?

Giving Fatigue

Giving fatigue is also known as donor fatigue as identified in philanthropic work by the Indiana University's Lily family School of Philanthropy and on the NonProfitPRO website (https://www.nonprofitpro.com). In their article (Elsey, October 2, 2023) "The Reality of Donor Fatigue and Strategies to Overcome It,"

202   *Ill Effects of Giving and the Need for Creating Boundaries*

it is noted that "donors get tired and pull back on their giving."
It is the result of:

1 Bombardment of requests
2 When the same donors are asked repeatedly
3 Burnout due to constant emotional appeals
4 The donor does not clearly see the outcome of their efforts

Donors are noted to stop giving to nonprofits due to donor fatigue. The fatigue is described as the result of becoming desensitized to all the needs and appeals for help. Donors become overwhelmed with the enormity of requests. This experience is especially crippling if one does not see the benefits to their efforts. It makes them believe that the problems cannot be solved. Without feedback demonstrating outcomes, the donor is left to their own assumptions and suspicions.

As mentioned in Chapter 1, the children's story *The Giving Tree* (Silverstein, 1997) further illuminates the depletion a giver can experience. There are many interpretations of this story and its meaning behind the selfless giving the tree provides to a boy who goes repeatedly back to the tree throughout his life, into manhood, taking from the tree. The tree always seemed to have what the boy/man needed, from its apples to sell, branches to build a house, the trunk to build a boat, to the stump which provided the now old man a place to rest. All along the tree proclaimed that it was happy to provide. There are different views on "Did the tree give too much?" "Did the boy/man ever learn to be self-sufficient?" "Did the tree experience giving fatigue?" At minimum, we can all agree that the tree was depleted, and a better balance could have been made.

Signs of giving/donor fatigue include:

- Feeling empty
- Resources depleted
- You do not feel appreciated
- Feeling taken advantage of
- You are not able to or no longer able to see benefits from your contribution
- Bombardment of requests and solicitations

Ill Effects of Giving and the Need for Creating Boundaries 203

- Feeling indifferent toward your previous passion (desensitization and/or helplessness)
- Feelings of guilt and excessive responsibility

Giving fatigue can accompany any of the other ill effects of giving and since it is linked with the depletion of resources, I conceptualize it to be at the root of burnout, secondary trauma, and compassion fatigue. See Figure 7.1. for a concept map on the ill effects of giving.

Mindfulness Strategies to prevent ill effects of giving:

- Create and maintain personal boundaries.
- Daily self-care using mindfulness strategies such as focusing on nature, deep breathing, and taking in sensory experiences.
- Monitor thoughts: avoid extremes and expectations that are unreasonable. The US culture tends to value those that "work hard" to the sacrifice of a personal life and other self-care tasks. Messaging is constantly sent in the workplace and beyond. Push back! Ask yourself if you are being fair to yourself? Would you believe this to be true (that they need to constantly work) for a friend?

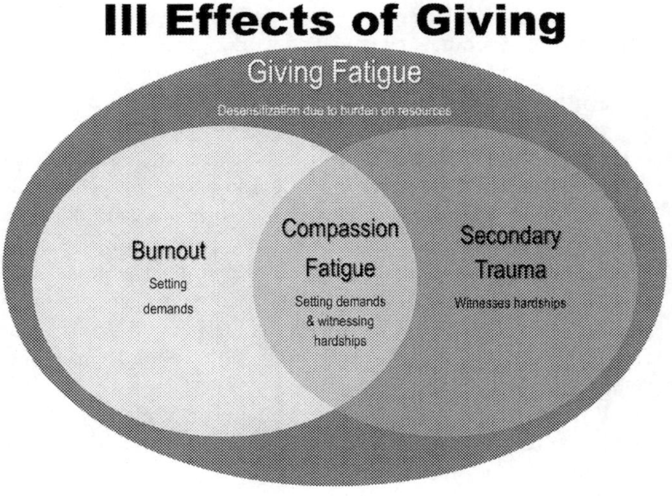

Figure 7.1 Concept Map of the Ill Effects of Giving.

204 *Ill Effects of Giving and the Need for Creating Boundaries*

- Ensure you have a hobby or two and carve out time for it on a regular basis. Schedule it in your calendar so that nothing interferes with it.
- Exercise, go for a walk, participate in yoga, etc.
- Take time to focus on something or someone different. Tell yourself that it is time to do XYZ, a mundane task for positive distraction.
- Give or offer a kind act: notice the immediate neurological chemical release.
- Be assertive of your time: say "no." Be sure to concurrently tell yourself "I do a lot," "I do enough," and "I am enough."
- Delegate even small tasks to competent others. Remember the research from Chapter 6 that noted that people like people more when they help them – let someone help you. Even small tasks can help shed some time and frustration.
- Positive affirmations: say kind words to yourself. Praise yourself for the difference you are making.
- Laugh, dance, sing: physically engage in joy.
- Allow yourself to make mistakes and to be human. Remind yourself that it is ok.
- Celebrate small successes.
- Adjust your schedule – change days working, reduce hours, etc. Assess the climate in the setting, do you prefer some tasks more than others? Working with some people more than others? If so, adjust as you are able too.
- One may want to dive deeper into the cause, such as advocacy or working directly with an individual in need. If you are feeling frustrated with your administrative role in a cause and are not seeing where the emotional payoff is, try getting more at ground level. I have seen administrative support workers start celebration programs, such as holiday parties, to get an opportunity to be in contact with the individuals being served at an organization. This is a nice way to remind oneself what (and who) they are working for.
- Find support groups for caregivers: many are available online.
- Utilize apps such as *Calm*, *Aloe Bud*, and *Lumosity*, for reminders and ideas for practicing self-care.
- Find joy in everyday experiences.
- Connect with someone socially: talk or go out.
- Adopt the motto: "quality over quantity."

Ill Effects of Giving and the Need for Creating Boundaries **205**

- Process stressors about the experience with a supervisor, trusted co-worker, therapist, etc.
- Talk with family or friends about what you are going through. Let them know when a day or week is harder than usual. Ask for help, if they do not offer, in lightening your load in other areas, e.g., chores.
- Collect thank-you notes or create a document of compliments received. Review them periodically to remind yourself of the difference you are making.
- Protect your time. Keep separation between time working and personal time. Just because the online and cellphone capacities have made it easy to be accessible 24/7 does not mean we should be. Tell employers, co-workers, clients – whoever needs to know – that you are not available outside work hours. Do not check emails, voice messages, etc. during your time off.
- Find other sources of income if your passion is not paying the bills. Financial stressors can drastically increase one's sense of burnout. Since salaries are typically low in the helping industries, other sources of income can be helpful to supplement your income. Perhaps you could work a few hours at a for-profit job or one that offers tips. You may decide to switch nonprofit pay for for-profit salary and "earn to give" instead. Each person needs to decide what is best for them based on their own personal situation. This deliberation should be after ample time is spent reflecting as opposed to reacting to a practically stressful or a particularly joyful day.
- Reflect on your role; see where your role and tasks fit in the larger scheme of things. This puts your involvement in context. You are not expected to do it all, nor should you.
- Take a break for a few minutes throughout the day, a couple of times a day. Plan and schedule a vacation. Take off for a "mental health day."

Ill Effects Experienced as an Employee or Volunteer in a Nonprofit Organization

Although some information specific to volunteers and employees was included above, this section serves to emphasize additional factors within nonprofit organizations. Reflections here come from my decades of nonprofit employment and several years serving in

206 *Ill Effects of Giving and the Need for Creating Boundaries*

senior management roles, along with a review of the research available, and my course material on organizational development.

People working in nonprofit fields can experience any of the aforementioned ill effects. In addition to the constant flow of need, nonprofit organizations tend to work in areas that have few tangible indicators of success. Consider the for-profit technology sector as an example. Success (even failure) is tangible when the newest device is released as measured in profit (or loss). Whereas in the nonprofit sectors, the outcomes are less measurable. Sure, tracking how many people were provided aid can be measured, but what about the other factors less tangible such as hope and emotional wellness? Measuring outcomes is also a struggle as the "what would have happened otherwise" is difficult to predict. How can one know for sure how many lives were saved from freezing due to shelters or how many people did not die from starvation due to meal programs provided by churches, community centers, and shelters. Likewise for the many ancillary services nonprofit programs provide such as social work, medical triage, supportive counseling. Not having a full account of the positive outcomes to one's efforts can be deflating and add to ill effects.

Maintaining a career in the nonprofit sector is a challenge for many reasons, perhaps the most obvious is the relatively low pay (except for those in senior administration positions) with disproportionately high demands. The demands can literally mean life or death. An example that comes to my mind was when I was a full-time psychologist in a nonprofit organization while expecting my second child. I worked up to the very last day of the pregnancy. My last day being a long one as I worked with a youth who expressed suicidal intent. I needed to secure an inpatient hospitalization setting for him to make sure he was safe. Knowing I will likely not see this young man until returning from leave, I reassured him that he would be my first stop when I came back. For the rest of the time, I worked with him, he referred often to me being there for him and making sure he was safe. He felt seen. This is why we do what we do in helping fields. These nontangible moments of infusing hope in another cannot be gauged with a ruler. These moments fuel the nonprofit worker, who feels the success of their efforts. Many are motivated by this type of work. The satisfaction of a successful outcome by working through challenges gives an employee satisfaction, often despite the pay and other workplace demands.

Ill Effects of Giving and the Need for Creating Boundaries **207**

Struggles in nonprofit workplaces include not only the witnessing of the enormity of need, but also for the need for the worker to pivot in their role and take on tasks that stretch beyond their comfort zone. I found it to be empowering to be challenged with the need to think creatively and hone my problem-solving skills. Across my experience in nonprofit roles, I have dabbled in graphic arts, fundraising, marketing, accounting, recruitment, event coordinating, etc. These skillsets have helped me across my professional and personal life.

The above concerns are not limited to those working in nonprofit organizations. Likewise, nonprofits are not the only entities fulfilling community needs. Individuals and for-profit organizations also engage in charitable works. The entity alone does not determine the impact of ill effects on the giver. All forms of giving run the risk for detrimental effects if not detected and resolved.

It can be especially difficult to manage burnout and compassion fatigue in the nonprofit sector as there is a never-ending flood of people that need assistance. Competing for this assistance becomes the reality as resources are low. This creates disequilibrium when demands are higher than the resources, an equation for crisis! Having spent my entire clinical career in the nonprofit sector, I have had much exposure to this phenomenon with co-workers, but also my own personal struggles. I need to emphasize that even on the most challenging of days, I would always leave work knowing I made a difference. Perhaps this was even more obvious on the toughest of days. I certainly "earned my keep" (earned my day's pay). Given that resources in nonprofit organizations were often low, I had to be creative. As a psychologist my giving was in my service. Giving to specific individuals would violate professional boundaries. It was (and still is) hard to see basic needs not being met due to poverty or worse yet, neglect. As a psychologist, I could not hand my client money to buy the clothing so desperately needed. That was not my role, and a dual relationship would be created, ultimately harmful to the individual. My role in this situation was to help her find and use her voice of advocacy. This is an empowering method of giving; albeit one that typically takes time and perseverance. Considering Maimonides Ladder (mentioned in Chapter 4) with levels of giving, it would be easier to fix the need by making the purchase directly, but as noted, that would have

208   *Ill Effects of Giving and the Need for Creating Boundaries*

conflicted with my role and professional boundaries and would not have enabled her to be empowered.

I have brainstormed the following tips for aiding retention for employees in general, but especially those in the nonprofit fields:

1 Give them a role. When one has specific tasks to accomplish to fulfill a mission, they have purpose.
2 Pair a new volunteer or employee with an existing employee to help them acclimate and form a social connection. Have newer workers meet with existing employees to hear their account of why they do the work. This also reaffirms the existing employee's sense of purpose.
3 Offer flexibility to help balance work-life responsibilities. Flexibility allows the work to be sustainable. It is a perk that can be more valuable than additional pay.
4 Be transparent and open in communication. Let workers at all levels know how the organization is doing toward their goals. Ensure that communications are available to all and not just those that are full-time or have the organization's email or intranet. Some organizations utilize private social media sites for volunteers to get updates and to have a sense of community.
5 Provide training for the specific role and cross-training as appropriate, but also for how to manage the material they witness. Existing employees need these refreshers too.
6 Managers need to be trained in how to be leaders and how to support volunteers and employees, especially in the nonprofit sectors. Not all good employees make for good managers. This is a common mistake made in organizations, to promote a good employee to a management role without training and support.
7 Solicit feedback from workers. Workers are on the front-lines. They are the ones implementing the mission. It is very likely that they have a keen sense of what is working and what is not. Certainly, they have ideas on streamlining processes and aid in smoother operations. Plus, if it makes their job easier, then that is a bonus.
8 Empower employees by ensuring their influence in decisions and operations. Review issues with them, when possible, prior to making decisions. At times, the decision may be put to a vote.

Ill Effects of Giving and the Need for Creating Boundaries **209**

9 Invest in their development which may include outside training and have a monetary cost associated with it, however, there are plenty of free resources available online and in the community. Sharing these resources shows an interest and concern for a worker's growth.
10 Look for opportunities to build a social community such as team celebrations. These celebrations should not require more of their time away from their family and other demands. Organizations would be wise to integrate events to include the family of workers.
11 Show gratitude for service and recognition of achievements. Be specific to the individual and their contributions.

Chapter 10 provides tips for organizations to prevent giving/donor fatigue. Here, the focus is on preventing ill effects from giving on the worker or volunteer. A caregiver shoulders a tremendous array of responsibilities and constant demands. Some caregivers even provide care around the clock. Basic self-care needs of the caregiver may get neglected or lost while caring for another. Over time, depletion and drain are likely to occur. The caregiver may experience physical and emotional distress, as stated earlier. To prevent these ill effects and to ward off when symptoms are detected, the caregiver should practice regular self-care. Included below are some specific mindfulness strategies for the volunteer/worker themselves to prevent ill effects from giving of their time and care.

1 Ideally, practice self-care daily with an hour or so put aside for you as the caregiver. Identify this time and protect it. Block it out on your calendar and do not let anything be scheduled in its place. Use this time to get out into nature; a very mindful activity, where you can breathe in fresh air and observe beauty all around you.
2 Exercise, even brief stretching with cleansing breaths can be refreshing. When possible, incorporate the person you are providing care for so that they too can benefit and to also ensure that your time is carved out to complete it.
3 Schedule vacations and days off in advance. For what nonprofits lack in salary, they make up for in generous time off benefits,

210 *Ill Effects of Giving and the Need for Creating Boundaries*

presumably to help prevent burnout in employees. Employees tend to feel bad about taking time off and away from the need. They feel bad for their co-workers, already taxed, that would need to pick up responsibilities when another employee is out. We feel guilty, so we do not take the days we earn and desperately need.

4 Resist vacation "buy backs" which is when a company will pay the employee their hourly rate for each vacation day they do not use. This type of incentive is further enticed as it is often offered right before major holidays capitalize on employees needing extra funds.

5 Resist signing up for constant over-time or picking up double shifts. Due to relatively low pay, nonprofit employees are often tempted to supplement their income. However, care should be given to not create a habit or pattern that neglects your need for replenishment. Remember that the goal is to ensure patterns are healthy and sustainable. Balance is essential to prevent the ill effects but also feelings of regret and resentment.

Before volunteering or working for a nonprofit organization, interview others in the role. Ask them what their main struggles are in doing the work. This will likely give you an indication of whether it is right for you. If not, there may be other ways to help without direct contact. For example, I can barely manage to see (and hear) commercials soliciting funds to prevent animal cruelty. I know that I could not manage witnessing these acts as a rescuer. I, therefore, would not be good at volunteering for this role. Even with training and support, I cannot image being able to manage it. Therefore, my involvement should be reflective of my comfort level. Perhaps my level of involvement would be best suited in networking and aiding efforts to increase public awareness or fundraising for the organization. Perhaps it is supporting the organization through a monetary donation or a donation of resources, such as supplies. Giving needs to fit within our comfort zone and boundaries to prevent ill effects. As such, creating healthy boundaries is the focus of the remainder of this chapter.

Ill Effects of Giving and the Need for Creating Boundaries   211

Creating Boundaries

How Have You Already Given?

Before considering boundaries, it is important to explore how it is that you already give. Three specific reasons for this exploration are as follows:

1 Your Interest: Exploring how you already give is likely to indicate areas of interest you may not realize. What type of causes do you gravitate toward? Creating this inventory will also enable you to reflect on whether your giving is consistent with the causes you believe to be priority or because an appeal was made?
2 Replenish: Once you know a bit more about what you have given previously, you can assess your inventory and see what needs replenishing. What resources might you have in abundance? As those with business mindset would say: What are your "inputs and outputs?" meaning resources that you have and are regularly replenished, such as money from a weekly paycheck. Replenishment also refers to the giver's mindset and emotions. Consider the emotional costs to your giving along with the other more tangible resources like time and money. This will further help with your creation of your plan for giving in the next chapter. Consider this analysis a "baseline," a starting point, to what you may give.
3 Give yourself credit: Filling up on good, through the tenets of positive psychology, observe the here and now, creating balance and well-being. It would be difficult to maintain balance if not aware of one's scale. The scale here refers to boundaries as the fulcrum with a need at one end and resources at the other. We are congruent and balanced when the need is leveled with the resource we have available to give. Acknowledging steps already taken toward mindfulness giving is important for moving forward.

Now that you know why exploring your previous giving is important, let's begin with developing boundaries to giving. From this point forward, I recommend you keep a list, in a notebook, file, or electronic folder of your giving. Table 7.1 offers a template for

212 *Ill Effects of Giving and the Need for Creating Boundaries*

Table 7.1 Worksheet: Giving Ledger

A time I gave of my time, money, resources	Rank priority level (1 being highest)	Money amount	Time amount	In-kind amount
Example: local food pantry	1			Two grocery bags of food
Example: school fundraiser for library	2	$200		
Example: park clean up	3		two hours	

tracking your giving. Plugging in your experience to sections of a worksheet will help you "dig deeper" to begin to devise a personal code of giving. Start by identifying the many ways in which you gave in the past year. Explore over the past 12 months all the money you donated, time you spent volunteering, and trips made to donate goods in kind. This can be quite a long list once you get thinking about it. Do not worry about every detail, just start with the pieces of data that are readily available to you. Spend a few minutes looking over your banking ledger, reviewing your activities in your calendar, and using your sheer memory. Identify where your resources were given and what the resource was, again, every detail is not needed to get a sense of themes for the who, general frequencies of giving, and estimated totals. You may even benefit from asking a significant other, close friend, or family member to help you recall. I recommend you spend no more than 45 minutes on this task. Sure, you can truly spend substantially more time on this task, but that would be a deterrent for most, preventing you from getting to the next valuable steps. This initial step is to get an estimate of your "baseline" or current level of giving to determine trends and interest (or disinterest). Notice below a sample ledger that can be used for concise accounting of various gifts. Summarize your findings on the following ledger, adding more lines as needed:

Ill Effects of Giving and the Need for Creating Boundaries **213**

Review Your Entries Above and Answer the Following Questions to Extract Possible Themes:

1 What causes/people did you most contribute to? _____

_____

2 What causes are your highest priority (even if not noted on the worksheet)? _____

3 Were there causes/people you would not give to again or do not consider a high priority? _____

_____

4 What resource did you give more frequently/most in quantity? _____

5 Did you overextend with any of these resources, giving more than you had or should have given? _____

_____

Keep this worksheet handy as a template for tracking future giving. Again, it can be used to track some forms of giving or an exact accounting of all giving. It is up to you to decide based on your needs and goals. I recommend that the method you use is manageable so that it is sustainable. A system for tracking, such as this, that is concise and done right away/each time giving occurs, is a method that is likely to be most manageable. Perhaps this ledger can be paired with when you are paying your bills, biweekly or monthly. If the system of tracking is too detailed or time-consuming, it will likely not be maintained. Keep in a location that is readily accessible such as on one's desk, car, banking file. An additional benefit to this type of tracking is for financial accounting when reviewing one's budget but also for income tax purposes. We will return to this list at the end of this chapter as we continue to build boundaries. As noted above, ill effects to giving can occur, especially if boundaries are not created and maintained. Previous experiences can be important indicators for developing personal boundaries.

214 *Ill Effects of Giving and the Need for Creating Boundaries*

Lessons Learned

As reviewed above, there are certainly risks to giving and to giving too much or to the wrong entity. There may even be negative experiences associated with giving. However, there is much fulfillment to be had. When interviewees were asked specifically about these experiences, many commented that the benefits outweighed any detriment. Likewise, negative experiences did not seem to stop those interviewed from giving to others in the future but did serve as a reason for them to create boundaries to their future giving. These givers tended to consider negative experiences as "lessons learned." Considering lessons learned from not-so-favorable experiences is a good way to prevent similar experiences from happening again. There is no guarantee, but it is always best to be prepared than not. To that end, utilize the following worksheets to create your boundaries around giving. The below worksheet serves to help you identify times when you gave, organizations in which you volunteered, and people whom you may have given to that could have led to experiencing burnout, compassion fatigue, secondary trauma, and/or giving fatigue. Take a few minutes (limit to 45 at the most) and fill in as many examples as possible. Refer to your responses to Worksheet 7.1 to help you recall your giving. Table 7.2 provides a worksheet for lessons learned. Included in Table 7.2 only giving that created a sense of one or more of the four negative experiences.

Worksheet 7.2 provides a snapshot to assist you in detecting patterns, themes, and lessons learned to help build your boundaries moving forward. Without boundaries, we can lose focus on our priorities. If we do not know our priorities and boundaries, we run the risk of our time and resources being consumed by others' priorities. Our financial resources can be drained or spent out of portion with our budget. Having set boundaries makes decisions easier. Think of boundaries as an internal compass, helping you navigate toward your goal.

What Are Boundaries?

Boundaries are a set of expectations we have in our relationships. They describe behaviors that are acceptable and those that are not. These boundaries create metaphorical lines between what we

Table 7.2 Worksheet: Lessons Learned

A time I gave of my time, money, resources	Negative experience giving	Burnout (limited resources and high demands)	Secondary trauma (feelings & symptoms of trauma due to witnessing)	Compassion fatigue (desensitization due to constant exposure & limits in setting)	Giving fatigue (bombardment of requests)	Lessons learned
Volunteered for nonprofit with children		X	X			I needed to take more breaks for self-care. Remind myself that I am doing what I can as I see the never-ending needs. Focus on one to two examples of a positive outcome.
Donated to a cause not sure if it was legit/ if the person collecting sent it to the cause					X	Next time, research first before giving. Ask for literature or information on the organization. Ask for outcome from donation: where money went, etc. Make donation directly to the organization.

(*Continued*)

Table 7.2 (Continued)

A time I gave of my time, money, resources	Negative experience giving	Burnout (limited resources and high demands)	Secondary trauma (feelings & symptoms of trauma due to witnessing)	Compassion fatigue (desensitization due to constant exposure & limits in setting)	Giving fatigue (bombardment of requests)	Lessons learned
Donations to local food pantry			X			Hard for me to see the need, especially witnessing the long lines of people waiting for food.
Let money to family member	X					Make expectations for repayment clear from the beginning. Work out a contract.

Ill Effects of Giving and the Need for Creating Boundaries **217**

will tolerate and what we will not. Boundaries establish what one is willing and not willing to do. These lines change depending on the person and the relationship. The lines change in personal versus professional interactions. They vary across individuals and are influenced by life experiences and culture. Positive psychology encourages us to reflect on our boundaries to improve self-care. Healthy boundaries respect one's time and resources. Boundaries regarding giving are essential as our time, resources, and heart go into it. Having developed boundaries help maintain one's sense of self-worth and helps make decisions consistent with one's goals. Once set, follow through is essential, even when it is emotionally hard. Some people struggle to set boundaries and even if they do, they struggle to keep them. Struggles could be rooted in one's belief in their value. This is especially true when people fill their time with giving and volunteering as they feel that other's needs are more pressing than their own. To this point, I believe if one's experience is more negative than positive, it is time to stop giving in the same manner. Giving should not come as a sacrifice for your peace of mind or integrity. While considering boundaries, one needs to ensure that the balance is well distributed with a sense of well-being as opposed to detriment. Explore for a moment your ability to set and maintain boundaries. Table 7.3 provides examples of healthy and unhealthy boundaries pertaining to giving.

As you may have expected, I asked interviewees their thoughts on boundaries. Returning to Mike, he noted: "I do not think I have a hard time saying "no," but I don't want to let people down. I am working on how to say "no."" When Tom was asked if he has boundaries for giving, he stated:

> Yes, it has to be something I agree with. I don't give to things I do not feel right about, like money to politicians or blindly giving money to charities I know nothing about. Something where the need is important to life itself. I wouldn't be willing to give to an organization so a kid can play sports over giving to the homeless.

Reflecting on words shared by another interviewee, I think back to Kristine who was mentioned earlier. When she was asked about her boundaries in giving, she noted:

218 *Ill Effects of Giving and the Need for Creating Boundaries*

Table 7.3 Examples of Healthy and Unhealthy Boundaries

Examples of healthy boundaries around giving	Examples of unhealthy boundaries around giving
Saying "no" to giving when request does not fit your giving model/plan.	Giving even though you are not comfortable with the cause/organization.
Giving within your predetermined budget.	Exceeding your budget because you feel empathy, guilt, or pressured to give.
Not giving to people or organizations that have violated your trust.	Continuing to give even though you are feeling taken advantage of or used.
Protecting your time by saying "no" to a request for volunteering or adjusting the extent of time you offer.	Giving your time when you are overextended not leaving adequate time for your own needs.
Taking care of yourself first.	Taking care of everyone else first; rarely getting around to your own needs.
Not feeling guilty about enforcing your boundaries.	Changing your boundaries or giving in to others.
Knowing you have limits to how much you can help another versus how much they can help themselves.	Helping too much to the point of creating dependency and enabling instead of empowering and enhancing self-sufficiency.
Knowing that your giving efforts matter.	Feeling burned out or compassion fatigued.

One little word "no" I learned early on. I first decide if it is something I want to give too. It is a gift to myself to be able to say "no" because I am not giving all of myself all the time, so I have for when I want to give when it is most needed. I say: "I'll have to think about it" and take about a day to decide if it is something I really want to do. This affords me the opportunity to process if it is something I want to do. Especially as a woman I had to learn that people expect woman to say "yes" all the time. I have to say over and over again to create a boundary and to maintain it.

Why Are Boundaries Important to Set and Maintain?

There are many reasons for maintaining one's boundaries such as avoiding the depletion of resources and preventing ill effects

Ill Effects of Giving and the Need for Creating Boundaries 219

from giving. This depletion can be a slow subtle drain or a quick diminution. Depletion can have a physical and emotional toll. Keep in mind Maslow's hierarchy of needs as a reminder that you too need resources. Depletion can leave you feeling anxious, overwhelmed, and perhaps now in the same situation as the person you set out to help. Regret may ensue. Guilt may also occur as one realizes that they may have given impulsively and that the resources were needed elsewhere. Without boundaries to adhere to in giving, one runs the risk of being exploited. Negative patterns could be formed as repeated behaviors occur leading to problems like burnout, secondary traumatization, compassion fatigue, and giving fatigue. Givers, with their big hearts and high empathy, are especially vulnerable to these consequences. Those working in caregiving fields have additional boundaries they must adhere to referred to as professional boundaries.

Professional Boundaries

Many professions mandate professional boundaries in their code of ethics, and for good reason. Professions such as teachers, social workers, psychologists, medical doctors to name a few, meet people in need all the time. Boundaries are not to say that we, as professionals, ignore the need. Instead, we work to help the individual fulfill their needs as best as possible. We also advocate for systems change within an organization, community, policies, etc. to help the greater good. We also facilitate securing services of support, such as a caseworker/social worker whose role is to help an individual find resources. At times, a professional may find a very discrete and anonymous way to give to someone in need. Prior to engaging in such action, the professional should contemplate the intention behind their desire to give. Ideally, this process should include consultation with a colleague and/or supervisor. In the field of psychology, we undergo a process called "supervision" in which these urges to help are processed and explored.

Psychologist and counselors are licensed professions that follow ethics of their field, such as the American Psychological Association (APA) or the American Counseling Association (ACA). The 2016 Ethical Principles of Psychologist and Code of Conduct (https://www.apa.org/) Preamble Principal A: Beneficence and

220 *Ill Effects of Giving and the Need for Creating Boundaries*

Nonmaleficence is to do no harm. Psychologist must weigh their intent along with possible implications of their actions; all with the goal of not causing harm to the individual or the treatment process. The 2014 ACA Code of Ethics (https://www.counseling.org/) Preamble also notes safeguarding the integrity of the counselor–client relationship. Both ethic codes include sections on avoiding multiple roles with individuals served. An example of a multiple role that pertains to giving is if a counselor gives a client money for food. The counselor's role is to provide therapy, not to be the client's friend. As difficult as this is to refrain from providing this level of help, a counselor must resist doing so. Instead, the counselor should provide support to enable the client to fulfill their needs through other services. A counselor could facilitate starting an anonymous food cupboard at the location for all clients to benefit. That way, dual roles are prevented. Returning to "Uncle Butterbee," the pseudonym my interviewee, Gary, gave his students. Mr. Butterbee was a third party that enabled anonymous giving. Likewise, my other interviewee, Georgette, knew she could not give outright to her student in need of money for his lunch account, so she did so anonymously. Whether the boundaries are created via a professional association or on your own, the key is to have them established.

Setting Boundaries

This section of the chapter will aid the reader in developing boundaries around giving. Rebecca Clay (2022) from the American Psychological Association wrote about the work psychologist Heidi Allespach does in training medical students whom she recommends have a "semi-permeable membrane" around their hearts. As Allespach noted, too fluid of a boundary allows everything to come in creating a feeling of being overwhelmed. Certainly, too rigid of a boundary is not the answer as that does not allow for any human compassion to be experienced. Therefore, a semi-permeable boundary is deemed to be a good and healthy balance.

Boundaries around giving are essential. Let's face it, most of us do not have unlimited resources. Caring as we are, we probably find ourselves in the position of wanting to do more than we can. Creating a boundary will ensure that we do not go over our limit when giving. Also, we want a boundary to protect us from being exploited or regretful. Creating and sticking to one's boundaries will

Ill Effects of Giving and the Need for Creating Boundaries **221**

prevent stress and conflict. Time and resources will be balanced and preserved. Clear and consistent boundaries result in positive feelings about actions taken, with less experiences of regret. Boundaries create mindfulness giving enabling one to act in accordance with their comfort level. It allows for the positive benefits of giving to be experienced as opposed to focusing on negative aspects. This positive, mindful approach requires prioritizing yourself as a critical step. Boundaries help protect one's resources, preventing ill effects. Boundaries will assist you in asserting yourself and empowering yourself to say "no" when needed. Boundaries start with creating an awareness around the issues you find most pressing and where you see yourself within the solution. At times, the tendency is to take on other's problems which drains us and does not help the person learn to take care of their own needs. Giving can run the risk of enabling and lowing drive in the recipient, especially when it is continuous.

Positive psychology and mindfulness approaches focus on resiliency and optimism. If we give with this focus in mind, it is likely that we will experience more positive outcomes from giving than negative. Healthy boundaries pertain to not only actions but our mindset too. Objective and realistic thinking is important to joyful giving. Some cognitive statements I employ that keep me a cheerful giver are as follows:

- The act of giving itself is powerful, regardless of how the gift is received.
- I do not need to know the outcome of my giving as I can trust that it was good.
- If we all do a little, a lot happens.
- I do not need to fill the entire need; I just need to create a start.

Previous researchers and theory offer important considerations while contemplating one's boundaries. These concepts include being selective, effective, and mindful of resources. Each is reviewed in the below sections.

Be Selective

As Worksheets 7.1 and 7.2 strive to do, it is important to discover a few giving priorities as it is not likely that we can give to all needs. Considering priorities should include the wide range of resources

222 *Ill Effects of Giving and the Need for Creating Boundaries*

needed. It helps to think about the variety of resources you have as opposed to thinking that the only way to give is monetarily. It is okay to be selective about **who** you feel comfortable giving to and **what** resource you feel comfortable giving. Giving is a prosocial behavior, but that does not mean that we must always engage in this behavior.

Selective Prosociality (Stellar et al., 2014) is a concept used to describe the tendency to be prosocial in only some situations and to only some individuals that are likely to reciprocate or at least not exploit the generosity of others. Individuals in need deemed to be egoist (someone selfish and preoccupied with their own interests) are found to be less likely to receive compassion from potential givers. We give as a collective, to lift others up, but to also keep our communities viable. We must allocate our resources to guard against exploitation. In other words, it is okay to be selective; it is important to be so to protect your boundaries and to give in the most efficient manner.

Be Effective

A fascinating book by William MacAskill (2016), *Doing Good Better: How Effective Altruism Can Help You Help Others Better*, offers valuable and quantifiable insights into the impact of giving. MacAskill urges readers to reflect on their giving to ensure that it is the most effective use of their resources. He continued by noting that many fail to analyze their effectiveness in giving, thinking that it deflects from the virtue of the act. MacAskill encourages readers to do the "most good" with the resources they have by taking a scientific approach, he terms "effective altruism." Effective altruism necessitates that we consider five questions. MacAskill devotes a full chapter to each of these questions. The questions are as follows:

1 "How many people benefit, and by how much?
2 Is this the most effective thing you can do?
3 Is this area neglected?
4 What would have happened otherwise?
5 What are the chances of success, and how good would success be?"

Ill Effects of Giving and the Need for Creating Boundaries 223

This analysis requires that we do a bit of research and inquire as to how our resource is utilized. It requires that we make logical and not just emotional decisions as to where we put our resources. The outcome to our analysis may be that the most effective way to give is not in our immediate interest area. The "right" decision is the fair decision, based on MacAskill's model putting economics to good use. But this analysis, albeit focusing on essential elements, could result in only a handful of highly effective organizations being supported and less effective or deemed less urgent causes being sorely under-supported. I recommend analyzing these components, as with all other factors mentioned in this book, to make an informed decision. However, allow for some variance and preference which will likely fuel our motivation plus allow for a variety of causes to be supported.

MacAskill covers other topics regarding the economic effects of giving in underdeveloped countries and the effect on local commerce. There are economic considerations for giving to ensure that we are not undermining people's ability to be independent. He also discussed what some term "dead aid" a perspective of anti-aid. These views claim that aid is not working and, in some cases, even detrimental. MacAskill used economic principles and mathematical computations to dispute these claims. Though aid is deemed overall effective, MacAskill's challenge is for us to consider the **best** use of our resources, not just to do some good, but to do the "most good." Using effective altruism, one can assess the best use of their resources before giving. Part of this analysis is to consider the "law of diminishing returns" when comparing causes. Is one cause more supported than the other? The law of diminishing returns would indicate that supporting the lesser-supported cause would be a more potent use of our resource as the value is higher. For example, if you have $100 to spare and are considering donating to an organization. You narrowed your search to two options: one a popular entity known as X who receives millions of dollars in funding, albeit serves many people versus entity Y which is new and less known. They serve many people too, but their funding stream is not as strong. The law of diminishing returns would have it that donating to entity Y gives more value to your $100. Human behavior is not always consistent with this calculation as we fail to research and consider mathematical reasoning when making giving

224   *Ill Effects of Giving and the Need for Creating Boundaries*

decisions. Instead, we tend to be biased toward well-advertised causes and even "jump on the bandwagon" with causes that are already highly supported. Another human tendency that perpetuates the use of sound mathematics is our desire to support causes that are perceived to have low risk; causes that are already well established. The reality is that the first set of donations to any cause are the most critical, getting the process started and theoretically when the most need is evident. Consider this, suppose we are fundraising for a family that needs funds for heating oil for the winter season. They need a total of $2,500. The first three donations total $225. The need is now $2,275; the gap is closing as the earlier donations help reduce the overall current need. Imagine more donations come in totaling $1,000! The need now closes to $1,275. Even if the total goal is not reached, the "dent" in the need has occurred creating a powerful impact. If we wait to donate to see what others are doing or if the cause is popular, to "top off a need," we run the risk of the cause not garnishing support. Plus, we also know from social psychology that being the first to support a cause can create a powerful social learning effect in that others would be more likely to follow suit. Considering the law of diminishing returns; as this fund exceeds the goal of $2,500, the value of further contributions is less potent as the need has already been satisfied.

Funding depends in large part on how well publicized the cause is. This is especially true of natural disasters and explains why there are wide discrepancies in financial support across causes. Racial and economic biases also exist when considering how the world views suffering and its willingness to lend support. Logic would conclude that if we want to make more of an impact, we should donate to the causes less known. It is also true that people tend to respond to isolated events more often than ongoing events. This is why aid for natural disasters is often high, but not so for chronic issues like poverty. Many do not realize that there are daily crises for many that go without food and shelter. Our psychological tendency is to think that singular events are more of a crisis than issues we have perhaps become desensitized to.

Another economical way to be efficient in giving, according to MacAskill, is "earning to give." This occurs when people choose fields that optimize their income, enabling them to give more to charitable causes. Mathematically, this option may yield more annual contributions than donating one's time or working for a nonprofit organization. Of course, the challenge with this plan is to

Ill Effects of Giving and the Need for Creating Boundaries 225

secure a high-income job and to resist temptation to adjust one's lifestyle to live up to their means.

The challenge with determining the effectiveness of giving is that we often do not know the impact. This makes it hard to gauge the outcome, whether it was successful or not, whether it was helpful or not, and to compare between needs. Further, it is difficult to ascertain what would have happened if we did not choose to give.

Be Mindful of Resources

Boundaries need to be set on any resource you give, these can include, but are not limited to time, money, possessions, expertise, and emotional support. Some resources have limited volume and are non-renewable, such as time. Other resources can be renewable such as earning more money. Still other resources are theoretically limitless, such as emotional support and the sharing of one's expertise. Whether the resources are renewable or not, one needs to set boundaries so not to be exploited or have ill effects to their well-being. Developing boundaries around the frequency of giving is also important so not to create dependency.

General points on setting boundaries:

1 Be clear: Vague statements leave expectations open to interpretation.
2 Be consistent: Follow through with boundary, even when it is hard to do. If not, you have shown that your boundaries are pliable and open to influence.
3 Know your resources: Know what you can give and the amount. Create a budget for time and money and stick to it.
4 Ensure your needs are met first: You do not want to run the risk of ill effects from giving too much or too often.
5 Identify expectations: Your expectations and those of the receiver should be identified prior to giving.

Setting Boundaries/Budget for Giving

How to Set Boundaries/Budget for Giving Money

Create a budget for giving by setting a monthly amount devoted to giving. This does not mean that you need to give it all away each month, just that you cannot go over the amount. Any further

226   *Ill Effects of Giving and the Need for Creating Boundaries*

need/amount would need to wait until next month. Determine the interval, such as once a year and month, in which you want to give to the predetermined entities. Some of the organizations I give to send additional solicitations. If I did not keep track to know I already donated, I run the risk of sending another donation putting me outside my designated budget. Having a set time or times in the year for giving will prevent confusion and over-giving by enabling the giver to stick to their own schedule and ignore the rest. In the United States, many people set November as the giving month as they are observing Thanksgiving and reminded of their many blessings. "Giving Tuesday" (https://www.givingtuesday.org/) is observed the Tuesday after Thanksgiving to encourage charitable giving. It was established in 2012 with the motto: "everyone has something to give and every act of generosity counts." This time of the year is close to the end of the calendar year when many people try to get their year-end gifts in for income tax benefits.

Sometimes the best gift is not giving the money directly, instead, the giver can use the budgeted money to buy items in need directly. When considering a monetary gift to someone what may be hurt by it, e.g., addictions, consider instead buying the necessary essentials such as food, or providing a meal. Pay the bill directly instead of handing the individual money. In deciding on monetary gifts, I think about how many hours I need to work to make that gift. Another boundary consideration for monetary giving is imposed on us through the government. In the United States, as of Fall 2023, there is a $17,000 gift limit per individual, anything over that the giver will need to file a federal gift tax form and the recipient may need to pay 18–40% in taxes. Note that this maximum is per year. So, if one would like to give an amount more than $17,000, say $25,000, it would be wise to stick within this maximum the first year ($17,000), then give the remaining ($8,000) the following year. Another way to gift is through life insurance. A donor can take out a life insurance policy for the desired amount and list any beneficiary of their choosing. Multiple beneficiaries and an allotted percentage of the funds can also be determined. Giving to our children by way of a *Last Will in Testament* (Will) can also lead to significant taxation in the United States such as probate, which is state-specific. Do your research and hire an estate attorney and/or financial advisor to help navigate this process and ensure that you are not setting your children up for a financial burden.

Ill Effects of Giving and the Need for Creating Boundaries 227

Before you even consider giving money, you need to have a firm handle on your household budget: "what goes in and what goes out." Even if you know your budget, I encourage you to reassess. Budgets change regularly as income and expenses change. Before making any goal that would cause change to one's budget, it is best to work with the most updated information. A simple method for knowing a budget is to add up total revenue for the month. This would include the total amount of paycheck after taxes have been taken out and any other regular income. Then make a list of monthly expenses such as rent/mortgage, average cost for groceries, utilities, gas/travel expenses, and recreation. You may have other expenses to include such as credit card and car payments. I am not a financial guru, but there is a lot of psychology to how we spend money, so a word of caution on debt: If you have credit card debt or any "revolving debt" (pertains to money that is taken out, repaid, and can be taken out again often with high and variable interest rates), you are not in a good position to donate money. This violates the above item #4 in taking care of yourself first. Explore why you want to give money away when you are being charged high interest rates for the debt you currently have. Consider volunteering your time or other ways of giving until your debt ratio is better. Once your list of income and list of expenses are totaled, subtract the expenses from the income. Ideally, there is an excess that you can use for "wants," savings, or giving. Decide how much of this excess you would like to use for giving. Donations do not need to be made monthly; this is just the amount that is being budgeted. You may decide to donate one time a year, monthly, bi-yearly, etc. or as the need presents itself. The key here is that you know, in total, how much you can afford to give. If one donation consumes three months of giving, then you know you will need to put monetary giving on hold for three months. Table 7.4 provides a sample monthly budget for giving.

From this $1,334.00 excess, you may decide that $300.00 per month will be earmarked for giving. You may decide to donate each month to the same or different cause. You may decide to take the total budgeted giving the year of $3,600.00 ($300 × 12) and divide it into half for two intervals of $1,800.00 of giving twice a year. Notice that you never want to use all your excess money for giving, or for any expenditure for that matter, as you want to have a cushion for yourself and the needs that life throws at you. You

228 *Ill Effects of Giving and the Need for Creating Boundaries*

Table 7.4 Example of a Monthly Budget with Excess for Monetary Donation

Income source	Income (after tax) ($)	Expense	Cost of expense ($)
Paycheck first two weeks	1,800.00	Rent	1,500.00
Paycheck second two weeks	1,800.00	Electric	85.00
Side hustle average earnings	400.00	Water	31.00
		Groceries	450.00
		Gasoline for car	100.00
		Car payment	300.00
		Recreation	200.00
Totals	**$4,000.00**		**$2,666.00**
Income ($4,000) expenses ($2,666) = excess ($1,334.00)			

also want to ensure that you are saving money for your own needs. If there is a negative number with expenses coming in higher than income, you are not in a position right now to give monetary. As noted above, other ways of giving should be explored.

How to Set Boundaries/Budget Giving Time

Budgeting time is like that of money. Like money, if we are not aware of how our time is spent, it is likely to lead to depletion with not much to show for it. Budgeting time is an important life skill. It is essential for anyone interested in volunteering their time in a sustainable and balanced manner. Budgeting time starts with inserting blocks of time on one's schedule for essentials, such as sleep and work. These two items will likely consume half of your hours each week (each week has a total of 168 hours). Assuming you sleep eight hours a day, seven days a week ($8 \times 7 = 56$), and work eight hours a day five days a week ($8 \times 5 = 40$), the total hours per week spent sleeping and working is 96, divided by total number of hours in a week (168)results in 57×100 (to turn into a percent) equals 57% of one's time. Add in time commuting, hygiene, hopefully some exercise, and other wants and needs, there is likely not much time left. Perhaps you are a student, and your available time fluctuates, or are retired and have more time than in previous years. More availability does not mean less budgeting. Be sure to budget

Ill Effects of Giving and the Need for Creating Boundaries **229**

your time so you do not run the risk of overextending. There is always a lot of need, do not use that as the gauge for how many hours you should volunteer. The gauge comes from your budgeted allotment. Once your time is budgeted, is there available time to volunteer? With this potentially available time, determine how much you want to spend volunteering. Let's say you decide two hours a week is feasible. Terrific. Now block out that time in your schedule so other demands do not interfere with it. Offer a specific amount of time on a specific day to volunteer. This should be a day and time that is most convenient for you. Stick to the time allotment by setting an alarm on your phone. A wonderful example was a friend who very much wanted to help with a fundraiser but was out of town on the date of the event. She reached out and asked if she could come for an hour or two to help set up the day before. This was a wonderful balance for her as it resolved the ambiguity she was feeling about wanting to be in two places at the same time. Plus, it turned out to be an incredible asset to have an extra set of hands-on deck the day before the event.

If you are helping someone and giving them your time and they cancel, you are not obligated to reschedule. When you agreed to help, your schedule may have been different than it is now. Ask yourself, if I was being asked to give of this time now, would my current schedule allow for it? Do I still want to offer this time? If the answer is "yes" to both, then proceed with rescheduling. However, the reschedule time must be at your convenience. If you have an opportunity to give of your time and want to, but are currently booked, say "yes" but not until your schedule permits. Be as specific as possible as to when you can give of your time and even schedule for a date in the future. We all know those dates come upon us quicker than expected. This will help keep your time balanced and prevent feeling over-taxed. A colleague I used to work with had a great response when the boss asked him to complete additional tasks. He would honestly say: "I am rather busy this week, but circle back around and ask me next week if you have not found someone else."

A cautionary note for retirees, at-home parents, or anyone that is not working a traditional full-time job. Society can and does send crushing messages regarding the value of their time. Especially in the United States, messages are pervasive assuming the individual "is not busy, they can take care of it." The individual often feels guilted into

230 *Ill Effects of Giving and the Need for Creating Boundaries*

"doing something with their time" and takes on more and more. I am sure you can list people you know that are in this situation who are overextended with volunteering to the point that the hours invested are like those working part-time or full-time hours. This is a quick recipe for burnout. Volunteering has many wonderful social benefits and can even aid longevity, however, it needs to be balanced and rewarding, remember, stress deflects from positive benefits.

How to Set Boundaries/Budget Giving in Kind

Budgeting for giving in kind items may correspond to regularly scheduled clean outs like "spring cleaning" or seasonal change over. It may also be planned in that you anticipate the need and have the items ready for when the opportunity presents itself. An example would be leaving items in your car to hand to the homeless, such as granola bars, socks. When cleaning out to give, it helps to have an idea of a person or organization in mind to give items too. This helps us part with items. Sort items in piles of "keep," "donate," and "think about." For "think about" clothing items, put in a separate dresser drawer or in the closet with a different color hanger. This technique is to separate the items you are not sure you still want from the ones you do. Now, at least once a week, force yourself to put on and wear one of those items for the day to see if you want to keep it or not. In doing this, I am always surprised by the compliments I receive about the colors, pattern, or design, making me fall back in love with the item. If you decide to keep it, put it back into the mix with your other items. If you decide to part with it remembering how itchy it was or perhaps it did not fit right, then put it in a container for donation.

The following caution for donating items in kind is also applicable to volunteering in person. The caution regards your own personal safety. Unfortunately, those most in need are often those that live in unsafe areas. We put our own safety in jeopardy when we go into communities with high rates of violence and crime. This is not to say do not go, just to be cautious and plan. Ensure that you know how to get there and where the parking area is located, relative to the location. Ask about security measures in place. Bring someone with you for added security, ideally someone that has been to the location before. Ask volunteers/workers at the location to assist you with the unloading of the donations.

Ill Effects of Giving and the Need for Creating Boundaries **231**

How to Set Boundaries around Giving Emotional Support

Giving emotional support consists of listening and providing empathy to another. It can be rather time-consuming and emotionally draining on the giver. You must guard against the toll emotional giving takes. Additionally, at times, it may be necessary to create a boundary for the good of the individual who may be "oversharing" or sharing personal information in public. Here are a few ways to state a boundary on emotional giving:

- "This is a heavy topic that I am not ready to manage." You may want to go on and say, "You would be best to seek out support from someone trained to help. Would you like me to help you contact someone?"
- If you decide to give emotional support, set aside time to provide the support. Refrain from distractions such as checking your cellphone. Let the individual know a time parameter, e.g., "I am happy to lend you some support. Let's talk for a bit. I have about 30 minutes before I need to leave. If we need more time after that we can set up another time."
- Ask the person how you can help them best. Do they need a listening ear? Do they want you to help problem solve? Or a mixture of both? Then respond accordingly.

These ideas for budgeting are a starting block. Feel free to adjust for comfort in keeping balance with your own needs. Starting small is a safe way to "pilot" the budget. Budgets are meant to be revisited and adjusted accordingly. Perhaps your plan all along was to start small and increase the amount in sustainable increments. You may opt to increase your financial budget with a portion of a raise received or when you are a recipient of an unexpected windfall.

Mindfulness Theory Analysis

Integrating the Four Rs of mindfulness (covered in Chapter 2), mindfulness giving involves awareness and consideration of the self along with others. It necessitates that good self-care is practiced and that you adhere to your personal boundaries. This is achieved through reflection and intention. Table 7.5 reintroduces the four elements of mindfulness with applications to boundaries.

232 *Ill Effects of Giving and the Need for Creating Boundaries*

Table 7.5 Four Rs of Mindfulness as It Applies to Boundaries

Four Rs of mindfulness	*Defined*	*Application to boundaries*
Reflect	Thinking through one's thoughts and beliefs.	Review your responses to "where" on Worksheets 7.1 to get a sense of interests and themes to "lessons learned" column on Worksheets 7.2
Reenergize	Involves conserving and refueling one's resources.	Take inventory of the resources you have (Worksheet 7.3)
Reconnect	Involves socialization and the benefits we receive from interacting with others.	Consider the settings where you enjoy volunteering or participating in fundraising events (Worksheet 7.3)
Refocus	Occurs when we engage in activities consistent with our life's goals.	Prioritize your goals by identifying your top three areas of interest (Worksheet 7.3)

Now, considering the information presented so far in this and earlier chapters. Use the below worksheet to identify your giving boundaries. Giving needs arise in many ways, at times stretching even the most robust boundaries. Having your main tenets in mind to serve as a boundary for expected and unexpected giving will prove helpful in guiding the manner of your giving. With the material from the first two worksheets and additional thoughts you uncovered, list your lessons learned, then the "counter-pose" of an established boundary in the worksheet in Table 7.6 on personal boundaries to giving.

Creating personal boundaries is a strong start to preventing ill effects of giving. It will preserve you as a giver enabling you to sustain the practice. Sticking to these boundaries is essential. You can always revisit, and revise boundaries as needed. Once boundaries are created and are known to you, decisions about who, what, where, how, and how much become clear. Andi, an interviewee mentioned earlier, noted: "When I give money, I don't feel guilty but not as gratified as when I provide a service. In possible situations where I may be exploited for my good nature, I let my husband manage it." Andi's comment demonstrates her knowledge of her own vulnerability and the need to set limits so not to be exploited. Developing boundaries enables us to not only have a

Ill Effects of Giving and the Need for Creating Boundaries **233**

Table 7.6 Worksheet Personal Boundaries to Giving

Lessons learned	Boundary
Example: It is difficult for me to see the enormity of need firsthand.	I will give to these causes peripherally. I will give monetarily instead of times in person, or I can volunteer time for a task to do outside the setting.
Example: I have donated more money than I should have in the past.	I will stick to the monthly budgeted amount. Anything more will be considered next month.
Example: I have given clothing to someone that did not appreciate it.	I will only give to organizations I have researched and know will put in-kind gifts to good use.
Add your lessons learned:	Add your boundary statement:

guideline to follow but also a "radar" to something that does not seem right. Radar is an intuition, felt in the "gut" or cognitive suspicion. Do not dismiss this, although often difficult to pinpoint. Giving should feel good, if it does not, then your intuition could be telling you to hold off; stop, think, and explore. When Andi was asked about her boundaries in giving, she stated: "I think it is a feeling – I have not thought about it." Reflection helps us get a deeper understanding of our true goals and intentions, ensuring that what we do is aligned with what we want.

Consider your responses from Worksheets 7.1, 7.2, and 7.6. What are the themes that emerged? What are your interest areas? What are the themes to your lessons learned? For the final worksheet on boundaries, use Table 7.7 to pull material previously explored to create boundaries around giving.

The top priorities that you have identified as right for you are the ones you give too. When other solicitations emerge, you remind yourself that you have other giving priorities and will have to say "no" at this time to any other requests. If you have a surplus in resources and would like to give outside of your identified priories, be sure to think it through first to ensure that the resources are disposable.

Ms. Dawkins, mentioned earlier, is a rather astute giver. She noted researching organization prior to giving by reviewing their IRS 990 form, organization webpage describing mission, and the organization's annual report. Although she did not report having

234 *Ill Effects of Giving and the Need for Creating Boundaries*

Table 7.7 Worksheet: Creating Your Boundaries: Resources, Priorities, and Boundaries

Resources	Priorities	Boundaries
What do you have to give after careful consideration of your time, money, and possessions	From Worksheet 7.1 "where" and other interests. Order with the highest interest first	Based on your lessons learned from Worksheet 7.2 and knowing thyself.
Volunteer time	Children	Extra self-care, frequent but short intervals for coping.
Monetary donation	Animals	Stick to budgeted $200.00 in a once-a-year donation. I determined the time of the year to send donation (my birthday). In researching organizations, I have decided to give to my local animal food cupboard.
Clothing donations	Homeless & transitional housing	I will give directly to the individual in need or a trusted pre-researched organization.
Add your resource	**Add your priorities**	**Add your boundaries**

difficulties developing and maintaining boundaries around giving, she did share the experience of a family member who

> … has such a giving heart. I learned so much from her and seeing all humans as God's creation. Since she has retired, she has been bombarded with requests and solicitations, especially if they put a dollar in a mailing, she feels compelled to give. She wants to give to them all. I worked with her and asked her what she knew about the organization. I taught her to research the organization and to not feel guilty throwing away solicitations that she decided not to give too. She has shifted her giving and now wants to see the giving have an impact.

For me, I have established some of my own general rules for giving that allow me to respond quickly and do not require contemplation. For example, I decided to always stop at a child's lemonade

Ill Effects of Giving and the Need for Creating Boundaries 235

stand and make a purchase, regardless of my thirst. I have specific empathy for this as I remember what it was like trying to make a sale when I was little and when my kids had stands as a child. It is not the lemonade I am acquiring that motivates me, often I do not even drink it, but the idea of entrepreneur spirit that I want to reinforce. The child is trying to raise money for a cause I may never know. With this effort, they are learning the value of work, perseverance, and most importantly, hope. Support this effort is worth the small price tag.

Another boundary I have set is to always buy cookies from the Girl Scouts during cookie season. Once a year, for about six weeks, grade schoolgirls and their chaperones set tables up outside grocery stores, post offices, convenience stores, etc. and sell boxes of cookies. In addition to supporting the fundraiser, I always ask the girls what flavors they would recommend. Usually, the child is quick to offer an exuberant response of her favorite. I add these to my order, purchasing a box for each of them. It is my way of further supporting the cause while also giving the girls a treat. My empathy soaring as I imagine them staring at these delicious cookies all day and not being able to enjoy them themselves. As a previous assistant Girl Scout Leader, I know that approximately \$.50–60 per box sold goes directly to the Girl Scout troop, even though the cookie cost approximately \$5–6 per box. Even if I am not in the mood for cookies (when am I not), I will make a small cash donation directly to the troop, equivalent to what they would earn had they sold me several boxes. Another option is to purchase boxes in mass to send to troops, nursing facilities, police department, etc. to share gratitude for their service and compound giving.

Another small, yet consistent tenet I follow is when I need to pick up supplies for an event or project, I grab an extra set when my finances allow. This extra set is for any child/parent that may have forgotten. This small gesture has tremendous gratitude connected with it. Imagine being a busy parent bringing their child(ren) to an afterschool activity only to realize that supplies they needed for the activity were left at home or not purchased. Now, that extra set of supplies is a lifesaver! The same logic applies for school trips and book fairs. I am sure I do not need to state as any reader would know, but there are children who are left back from a school trip

236 *Ill Effects of Giving and the Need for Creating Boundaries*

or can only browse at a book fair because their family cannot afford to send in the money needed to participate. Here again is another opportunity to anticipate a need and give. When my finances allow, I send in double the trip fee or any extra $5 with a note to the teacher to give to the student that forgot their money or did not have it. On this note of school expenses, there are children who are refused lunches at school when their bill has not been paid. Often around the holidays, I read of feel-good stories where some donor pays off the cafeteria bill for a local school.

Now that your analyses are complete for the three worksheets, solidify with a statement that incorporates your giving priorities, respires, and boundaries. For example: my statement is to give to children, animals, and homeless/transitional housing with my resources of money, volunteering, and items in kind, monthly. The entity I researched includes the local homeless shelter, but I also give directly to community members in need.

Construct your statement by finishing the sentence: My giving priority(ies) consist of _____, with my resource(s) of _____, based on _____ (schedule, e.g., once a year) to entities such as _____ (name people or places).

Key Points

- Not all giving experiences are positive, however, we can learn from our negative experiences.
- Insight into our giving experiences can help us create personal boundaries.
- Shame and pride are a few concepts that affect the receiver and thereby their reaction to your giving.
- Cultural and personality aspects also impact the receiver's reaction to your giving.
- There are strategies for preventing ill effects of giving and in preserving the dignity of the receiver.
- If boundaries are not created and adhered to, ill effects of burnout, secondary trauma, compassion fatigue, and giving fatigue can occur.
- Working or volunteering for nonprofit organizations have additional factors to consider.

Ill Effects of Giving and the Need for Creating Boundaries 237

- Reflecting on areas in which you already give, along with lessons learned from your experiences in giving, are a good start to creating personal boundaries around giving.
- Some professions have additional boundaries around giving.
- Identifying boundaries around giving money, time, possessions, and emotional support are important in curtailing ill effects from giving.
- Many professions have professional boundaries around giving.
- When setting boundaries for giving, be selective, be effective, and be mindful of resources.

Action Steps

- Reflect on your experiences as a giver. Have any resulted in ill feelings?
- Thinking about boundaries, do your boundaries come easily to mind? Are there themes that emerge when you think about your attempts to establish and maintain boundaries around giving?
- Utilize the worksheets and question prompts to explore your boundaries for giving.

References

ACA. (2014). *Code of ethics.* https://www.counseling.org/

APA. (2016). *Ethical principles of psychologist and code of conduct.* https://www.apa.org/

Aronson, E., Wilson, T.D., Sommers, S.R., Page-Gould, E., & Lewis, N. (2023). *Social Psychology,* 11th edition. New York: Pearson.

Clay, R. (2022). *Are you experiencing compassion fatigue? As psychologists continue to help those suffering from the impact of COVID-19, they should watch for signs of their own distress or burnout.* https://www.apa.org/topics/covid-19/compassion-fatigue

Davis, E.B., Worthington, E.L. Jr., & Schnitker, S.A. (2023). *Handbook of Positive Psychology, Religion, and Spirituality.* New York: Springer. https://doi.org/10.1007/978-3-031-10274-5_12

Elsey, W. (October 2, 2023). *The reality of donor fatigue and strategies to overcome it.* https://www.nonprofitpro.com

Freudenberger, H. (1974, winter). Staff burn-out. *Social Issues,* 30(1), 159–165. https://doi.org/10.1111/j.1540-4560.1974.tb00706.x

Giving Tuesday. https://www.givingtuesday.org/

238 *Ill Effects of Giving and the Need for Creating Boundaries*

Lee, H.J., Lee, M., & Jang, S.J. (2021). Compassion satisfaction, secondary traumatic stress, and burnout among nurses working in trauma centers: A cross-sectional study. *International Journal of Environmental Research and Public Health*, 18(14), 7228. https://doi.org/10.3390/ijerph18147228

MacAskill, W. (2016). *Doing Good Better: How Effective Altruism Can Help You Help Others Better.* New York: Penguin Random House.

Newport, C. (December 29, 2022). The year in quiet quitting: A new generation discovers that it's hard to balance work with a well-lived life. *New Yorker.* https://www.newyorker.com/culture/2022-in-review/the-year-in-quiet-quitting

Silverstein, S. (1997). *The Giving Tree.* New York: The Harper Collins Publishers.

Sobell, M.G. (2015). *A Practical Guide to Ubuntu Linux.* New Jersey: Pearson Education.

Stellar, J., Feinberg, M., & Keltner, D. (2014). When the selfish suffer: Evidence for selective prosocial emotional and physiological responses to suffering egoists. *Evolution and Human Behavior*, 35(2), 140–147. https://doi.org/10.1016/j.evolhumbehav.2013.12.001

Strazdins, L., & Broom, D.H. (2007). The mental health costs and benefits of giving social support. *International Journal of Stress Management*, 14(4), 370–385. https://doi.org/10.1037/1072-5245.14.4.370

US 2022 Bureau of Labor Statistics. https://www.bls.gov/

8 Developing Your Plan/ Creating a Ripple

What Will Be Your Story?

Introduction

Now that ideas for giving, methods for evaluating organizations, and personal boundaries have been reviewed, the reader is guided through the development of a giving plan. The reader begins by further exploring their interests. A worksheet aids in prioritizing these interests. The scope of the chapter is twofold. It begins with reflection on one's intention in giving, then prompting to generate ideas for who, what, where, and how sections of a giving plan. The second part is to plan for a legacy, making giving sustainable. The focus of this part of the chapter is on sustaining giving and leaving a legacy that will outlast any one individual. A crucial part of this plan is to create a ripple effect. The ripple effect suggests that one act can have many consequences. Even the smallest ripple can reverberate resulting in larger effects elsewhere. The ripple permutates. It also suggests that even small changes can evolve to larger effects. Social science provides some research and theory to aid in the conceptualization of this potential ripple, albeit difficult to fully measure. One can be assured that their giving contributes to positive benefits to the recipient now and in the future. A giving plan involves the who, what, and where of your giving. Establishing a giving plan can help you stay focused and within budgeted giving boundaries. Having a plan makes things happen! The reader will be inspired by stories of interviewees and giving examples throughout.

Exploring and Setting Your Intention

Before you set your goal for giving, it helps to consider your intention for giving. What do you hope to gain by giving? Exploring your

DOI: 10.4324/9781003438359-8

240 *Developing Your Plan/Creating a Ripple*

expectations can give you a sense of what you hope to gain. Is your intent to gain power or prestige? If so, you may be creating a pattern of control and sovereignty over another that results in suppression and/or disparagement. If we only give to feel good or to relieve our sense of guilt, then we run the risk of not considering the effect on the receiver. We may also miss the opportunity to give more efficiently and more specifically to the need. Intent and effort in giving came up in my interview with Lois. She reflected on the ill effects that can be the result of giving with an ulterior motive. In thinking about those that spend excessive time and money, she reflected: "getting the right gift for less personal people – like in the work environment – there is a transaction. There is an agenda there. Makes others perhaps feel less valued" referring to when the giver does not exert the same effort in finding the right gift for more personal individuals. The goal, in this case, is to use giving to earn an advantage, it becomes transactional.

In further contemplation on your intent for giving, refer to Martin Seligman's three elements of authentic happiness: pleasant life, good life, and meaningful life. A pleasant life includes everyday enjoyment. A good life applies strength to challenges to reap positive outcomes and a meaningful life is when we apply those strengths to help others. Being aware of our intentions in giving will ensure that we are on track to authentic happiness. To experience meaning in giving, we would want to apply our skill sets to others, sharing our resiliency and grit, to help them overcome adversity. Making another person's life easier is a powerful motivator. Not all giving needs to be at this level. Indeed, all giving is noble.

Consider: Explore why you give. What specifically about a situation makes you want to give of your time, effort, or money? Explore your expectations. Are your expectations to please others, to be liked? If so, be cautious. Are you expecting a "return on your investment"; be cautious here as well. The returns may not be reciprocated and if not, would you still want to give? Do you feel obligated to give? Giving is good, but that does not mean that you must give all the time. Before you give or commit to giving, ask yourself what are your intentions? What do you hope to accomplish? What do you hope to receive in return? Ask yourself, "Will I feel good about this afterwards?"

Plan for your intention to give by completing the following statement:

My intention to give is _____. Examples: to be kind, to advance my position, etc. Now, let's move onto your goal to give.

Developing Your Plan/Creating a Ripple 241

Who to Give To?

Thinking over the material covered so far, recall your ideas for giving and your previous examples of giving. What new ideas come to mind? What are your top priorities? Explore what resources are needed and assess your own availability of resources. Giving related to your interests will make the experience more enjoyable and sustainable. However, perhaps there is a more pressing need that shifts your priority. Fortunately, we all have our own areas of interest and passions, making the range of giving wide. Additionally, we all have our own circumstances regarding what and how much we can give and when. Consider how well a cause matches your interests. Is it a cause that is neglected or does not get the level of support you deem it should?

In addition to all the examples provided throughout the book, I recommend that you start conversations with others to discuss ideas for giving and to identify needs you may not have known. Acquire the philosophy that no resource is wasted, that there is a home for every unwanted possession. Items like blankets, newspapers, and showboxes are often collected and much appreciated at animal shelters as they use them for bedding for the animals. Shoeboxes are often broken down and recycled at shoe stores. If you are at a shoe store, ask if they have any boxes they are discarding and offer to take them to the animal shelter. Donate clothing and household items to your local shelter, such as Salvation Army. Contact social workers at your local school to see what items students may need. They often have a closet for children in need of clothing, school supplies, even cleaning supplies such as laundry detergent. Some schools also have washing machines and dryers for students to wash their clothes before/after school. Start a project with your church or community organization. Start a giving group within your neighborhood or workplace. Volunteer your time, start small, like once a month to see if you like it. Crochet hats for the homeless and leave in areas where homeless frequent. Crochet hats for pre-mature babies in the neonatal intensive care units. Sew dresses to send globally to girls in impoverished countries. Volunteer to sew angel gowns. Take a budgeted amount of money each month or year and search online donation sites, such as *Fundrazr* and *GoFundMe* to make several small donations. Post an interesting solicitation to your social media to "market" a cause you have found to create awareness and potentially garner

242   *Developing Your Plan/Creating a Ripple*

additional support. Invest in microlending projects, such as those mentioned previously like Kiva. Send Girl Scout cookies to military personnel. Utilize *Amazon* boxes to send clothing, jewelry, household items for donation through their "Give Back Box" program (https://www.aboutamazon.com/news/community/ways-to-give-back-on-amazon) which provides a free shipping label. Amazon receives these items and sends them to different charity sites. Give blood and platelets. In looking for more ideas and following my own advice to create discussions on giving, I asked my social network through *Facebook* to identify places where they give. As expected, the responses did not disappoint. Here are the responses received:

- Animal welfare and kids out on the streets
- Stick to local to see impact
- Young moms-donate time
- Christmas lights and toys through children's hospital – bring a gift and enjoy a light display
- *Livestrong*
- Anonymously to a person that helped me
- To a student that had no funds in their lunch account
- Cat shelter in memory of a former employee
- *Savage Sisters* (in Philadelphia) that help women find a pathway to recovery – I'd love to create care purses/backpacks for them
- Taking a person shopping instead of giving them cash
- Giving food or water to homeless person
- Adopted an elementary school kid through work to fill stockings for holiday
- *Sebastian Riding Association* provides equine services to people with disabilities
- Donated clothes and shoes to *Mitzvah Circle* also accepts unopened personal care items
- Glasses/eyewear to the *Lions Club*
- Books to the public library for their book sales
- Children's books to *YMCAs* with childcare, also to food pantries that have a waiting room
- Gently used athletic equipment to youth organizations

How about that for more ideas on giving! You can pose the same question to your social network. Not only will you get

Developing Your Plan/Creating a Ripple **243**

more ideas, but others reading the responses will become aware of the variety of needs.

Consider: Plan to give to _____.(Identify priority causes.)

What to Give?

Now that you have explored several need areas, think about the types of resources you have available to give. Plan to give at least one of your resources: time, money, expertise, etc. Be sure to contact the agency or recipient to check what specifically they may need. Make sure what you are giving fits the need. An example of a failure to consider the need is when I served on a service board at my previous church. This board had quite the committee of strong powerhouse women. With all those dominant personalities in the room it was hard to be heard. However, I had to speak against the majority and dispute the plan to donate coffee beans to families in impoverished neighborhoods. My opposition was that this was not the most pressing need for them. The counter-argument from the majority was that since they were poor, they likely did not have the opportunity to experience the savoriness of fresh coffee beans. This is an example of privilege, a concept mentioned in the first chapter. We are privileged when we do not have the experience of hardship and, therefore, cannot know another's frame of reference. Instead of assuming, we need to ask. Would the poor even have a coffee bean grinder? Do they even like coffee? Often it is best to ask the individual or group directly what they need most. For example, often food banks get a disproportionate number of pastas, but no sauce or sources of protein. Usually, diapers and baby formula are a high need. I do not know the outcome of this service group's project as I attended another meeting or so but then did not continue in the group.

With an understanding of the need, determine what you have available to give. Review your boundaries which serve as ground rules for giving and not giving. In addition to the boundaries I shared in the previous chapter, I have set boundaries for when I will not give. One such boundary is that I have decided that I do not "round up" at the register to support vocational programs at nonprofit stores whose mission is to provide the very same vocational training programs they are soliciting for in the round-up.

244 *Developing Your Plan/Creating a Ripple*

To this later point, my research of the nonprofit's IRS 990 form shows that a significant portion of their funds goes to executive leadership salaries. So, it is not that I do not support their mission, it is that I know a large part of the revenue is going toward salaries and "perks," and now the organization wants customers to further foot the bill for their mission; I say "pass."

In deciding whether to volunteer your time, research to see that your time will be well utilized. You do not want to be sitting idle, wasting time? You do not want to volunteer and not have a role or tasks to do? Inform the organization of your skill set and ask them what role and tasks you could do to be of service to the organization. Communicate with them the skills and roles you are comfortable doing as this may differ from the skill set that you have. For example, as a psychologist, perhaps I do not want to volunteer my time conducting psychotherapy, but rather as a break for me, complete another task such as working in a food pantry taking inventory. Or it may very well be that you want to volunteer your expertise to a cause and only do that role. Nonprofit organizations need a wide variety of expertise such as accounting, marketing, social media, etc. It could also be that your professional skills do not necessarily match the organization's needs, but you have time to offer which could fill another role needed, such as coverage of the morning shift at a homeless shelter. Offering one's skills and time is noble. But do not be afraid to sign up for a volunteering task that you have never done. Ask for training and empower yourself to learn new skills, gaining valuable expertise along the way.

Maintaining your boundaries is always important in all aspects of giving. If you sense your boundaries are being disturbed or merged, stop and reflect. Sometimes when we become involved in a cause and see the need up close, it becomes overwhelming. This can cause one to give more than they should. Remember, if we all just do a little, a lot can be accomplished. Recruit others to your effort as many hands make for less work.

Nicole Bouchard Boles (2009), author of *How to Be an Everyday Philanthropist: 330 Ways to Make a Difference in Your Home, Community, and World at No Cost*, offers many creative ideas for giving. Her premise to the book is that philanthropy is not just for those with substantial means, instead, it is a mindset of an action done for the betterment of humankind. She offers plenty of simple examples that make a big impact on those in need. She

Developing Your Plan/Creating a Ripple **245**

encourages the reader to make giving a pattern, done daily. Boles (2009) states: "I believe there is a powerful 'giving solution' for each person (pg. ix)." I also agree with her plea to not let a single thing go to waste – that there is always someone who could use it or the item can be recycled or upcycled (upcycling is reusing all or parts of something to make it anew, adorned differently and/ or creatively).

Boles (2009) provides ideas for giving with our bodies, such as participating in fundraising walks, donating organs, and holding babies in a neonatal intensive care unit. You can be an organ donor upon death by electing this option at the Department of Motor Vehicles (DMV) who then identifies it on your driver's license. Some people donate organs while they are still alive. These donations are often given to family members but can also be given to strangers. Other resources given from the body include donating blood. Blood rejuvenates, so this is a gift one can give regularly.

Consider: Will my giving make a difference? How much is needed to make a difference? Do I have the resource to give? Is it within my budget to give?

Plan to give _____ resource. (Identity a resource or two that you have available to give, e.g. blood, time)

Where to Give?

Remember the information in Chapter 4 covering strategies for evaluating organizations, especially nonprofit 501(c)(3). An ideal organization will have their mission and outcomes available for review. These are likely to be posted online or obtained in person. Organizations may be small and under the threshold for reporting or may be affiliated with a religious organization and not required to post their financials. Ask questions if not clear. How receptive an organization is to speak with you is indicative of their respect and accountability for how they utilize your resources.

An organization does not necessarily need to be a nonprofit 501(c)(3) to be worthy of your giving. It may not be an organization at all. It could be a fundraising event to help a neighbor or a friend in need. Similar levels of scrutiny should be utilized. Chapter 7 also provided strategies for making a loan or a gift. Caution should be heeded to ensure that your resources are given in good faith and that they will be utilized appropriately. Ask questions,

246 *Developing Your Plan/Creating a Ripple*

review reports, attend events to see for yourself how resources are utilized. Getting involved in an organization gives an insider's perspective. The donor will also feel more joy in giving if they see and feel the difference they are making. Trust your instincts.

Consider: Does the organization fit your values? You do not need to agree on every point, but the main ideals such as the mission should be congruent. Do you know how they will spend your money? Will they value your effort and time? Do they pass your scrutiny, have you researched the organization/need? Do I know how the resource will being used? Is the organization/person legit?

Plan to give to _____ organization or person. (Identify a few organizations or people you have researched and wish to support.)

When to Give?

Refer to your budgeted schedule discussed in Chapter 7. Stay within your budget. If a need or solicitation is beyond your budget, give what you can and offer more resources the following month when your resources are renewed. This is especially important as organizations tend to send multiple solicitations. It becomes easy to lose track of when you last gave. This can cause you to give more frequently than you budgeted. To avoid over giving, you may decide to select one time a year to give to the cause. This could be the end of the calendar year also corresponding to the end of the tax year in the US, on your birthday, or a date in honor of a loved one. Ask what the organization's funding cycle is – what is their "year end?" Check to see how much you have already donated to them in the current year. How does it compare with previous years? It is amazing how we can lose track of time and thereby money. There have been a few occasions in which I called an organization and asked when my last donation was made, only to find out that I was behind my self-determined goal. At other times, it may very well be that you are on track, but the organization is sending out extra solicitations.

Plan to give _____ intervals or schedule. (Identify a monthly or weekly goal.)

How to Give?

Be as efficient as possible with giving – work smarter, not harder! How you give should be through the method that makes every dollar and minute count. If setting up automatic electronic giving

Developing Your Plan/Creating a Ripple   247

saves the organization postage and letter expenses, then consider doing so. It will also save you on postage in mailing a check and even save on the cost of the check itself. Consider contributing through online platforms, keep in mind that they charge a service fee. This can be bypassed by sending funds directly to the organization through their webpage link. Many banks allow for automatic billing per the parameter you establish (see the example of automatic bank payments when loaning money from Chapter 7).

Find the giving format and method that is right for you. Matching aspects of giving to your lifestyle makes giving more sustainable. Of course, if you are looking to make a significant change in your lifestyle and routine, then adding a commitment may help. For most, it will be more likely for you to continue with your plan if it is realistic and consistent with your existing patterns. If you are not a morning person, do not volunteer to serve breakfast at a shelter. Instead offer to cover the dinner or evening shift. If you are allergic to animals, do not volunteer at an animal shelter. Perhaps you could arrange for a neighborhood collection of food, supplies, blankets, etc. instead.

Another efficient way I like to give is through what I call "compound giving." Compound giving, as mentioned in Chapter 3, is when giving benefits more than one person or entity. I see it as an opportunity to double the benefit of a gift. An example is purchasing items through a fundraiser that can be used as holiday gifts. I am supporting the cause but can also take care of a few gifts on my list. Opportunities for compound giving are all around us, such as food fundraisers around the holidays, purchase a pie for a good cause then gift it to the host of the holiday event. Perhaps the most direct example of compound giving is the dollar for dollar matching by another sponsor. Consider being that sponsor! If you are in the position of making a large donation, you could entice others to give by offering to match their donation up to a predetermined amount. Of course, giving is known to have benefits to the giver, as reviewed in Chapter 5, and to the receiver, so theoretically all giving can be considered compound giving.

Your giving can have an added impact if you plan a large goal and work backward. This may enable you to make an even larger impact than initially thought. Set a goal and pledge an amount, dividing it out by X amount of time. For example, imagine making a pledge of $1,000. Seems like a lot, but when planned out over 12 months ($83.33 per month) or 52 weeks ($19.23 per week), it

248 *Developing Your Plan/Creating a Ripple*

becomes more manageable. The gift can be further impactful by renewing it annually increasing it by x% (perhaps a portion of one's yearly raise or bonus).

Another "how" to giving is to decide whether to give anonymously or not. "Blind donations" (giving anonymously) are considered the highest form of giving across many religions, such as Christians, Muslims, Jewish. Anonymity allows the receiver to maintain their dignity whereas the giver can feel good about the actions, but not hold a position of dominion over another. Many large donors prefer to give anonymously so others do not try to solicit donations from them. A downside to anonymous giving is that the giver's influence and model to others is muted. Having a popular or well-known donor give anonymously, the organization does not have the opportunity to entice others to follow suit. Consider, as an example, the current iconic American singer Taylor Swift. As of the end of 2023, Bloomberg's article "Taylor Swift is in her billionaire era" (Ponsot, October 27, 2023) estimates that her net worth is 1.1 billion dollars. She owns multiple houses and two airplanes – indicators of the wealthiest. Swift is known for her generosity to employees working on her tours and many others. She has donated to organizations fighting cancer and other causes such as those that support music education. Her support for *GoFundMe* and other crowdfunding has evidenced the power of her influence. Her fan base of approximately 54% of the US adults, according to Forbes March 14, 2023 blog (Dellatto, 2023) entitled *More than half of U.S. adults say they're Taylor Swift fans, survey finds*, have followed her lead in making donations to various causes. According to a CNN online report from December 12, 2023, Margaret Richardson, the Chief Corporate Affairs Officer at *GoFundMe* said about Swift: "Her generosity brings people together, creates community and inspires others to pay it forward" (https://www.cnn.com/us/taylor-swift-birthday-charities-donate-iyw/index.html#:~:text=The%2012%2Dtime%20GRAMMY%20Award,Hall%20of%20Fame%20and%20Museum). Taylor Swift's name and influence offers tremendous leverage for other donors. Imagine if her donations were anonymous, few would know of her support and thereby lose the ability for others to join her efforts. Even more modest donors have an amazing influence on other donors. Large donors of major capital projects like to see a strong base of supporters directly involved in the cause before they are

Developing Your Plan/Creating a Ripple **249**

comfortable offering their significant gift. The more modest donors, having their names listed in an annual report, could inspire co-workers and others to do the same.

The "how" of giving also includes modality, such as in person or online. There are community resources online such as *Buy Nothing* groups on *Facebook* where people post items that they are giving away free of charge. Certainly, the oddest things can be found and rehomed in forums like these. I have listed free unusual items that were quickly claimed by appreciative members in the community. One year, we were removing a small evergreen tree and listed it before Christmas time for any family in need of a Christmas tree. Two maturing trees towered over our front windows needing to be removed. Once again, we offered them free on *Marketplace* to anyone that could come and dig out, within a day they were rehomed. Perhaps my favorite example is my listing of beautiful mauve, gray, and tan rock that continuously gets unearthed on my property. Many community members respond to the post to claim their free rocks to build landscape walls. I have met a dear "giving friend" this way. During her rock pick up, she shared with me information about giving group to which I now belong. Talk about a network of giving! We have also listed for free logs from trees that have fallen around the property. People like to collect these resources as they can use them for their own fireplaces or firepits. Some may even split the wood to sell. There is a growing interest in upcycling furniture. Creative people find free or very cheap furniture items to bring back to life with a fresh coat of paint. With some sanding, paint, and finish, old pieces are modernized and given a second life. I have also seen creative train tables crafted from wooden end tables and children's kitchen sets made from old wooden entertainment centers. Similar upcycling is done with clothing. The beauty of these projects is that old quality pieces are restored. It helps commerce and helps to keep materials out of landfills.

Consider: How is the best way for me to give? Can I compound my giving by also helping another cause, e.g. entering a raffle to win a basket that can be used to donate to a women's shelter? Should I donate anonymously?

Plan to give through _____. (Identify the modality most efficient and convenient for you. For example, I will give virtually through my *Venmo* account, or I will give in person gifts in kind when I am near the organization.)

250 *Developing Your Plan/Creating a Ripple*

Goal: Set an Intention

To ensure that your giving is within your boundaries and intentions, establish a goal for the year. Some giving is spontaneous and will fall outside your plan, so perhaps you can include a cushion in your budget of time and money to give throughout the year to unexpected causes. Treat this goal as your very own "giving pledge." Solicitations that do not fit with your goal and below plan will receive a "no" or consideration for next goal. Having this goal and plan will make decision making easier.

Identify a giving goal/pledge: _____
_____
_____

Example: I will donate money to an organization(s) serving people in need of food.

Create a Giving Plan

Here are several steps for thinking through and creating your plan for giving.

1 Identify Interests. A plan starts with your interests. Note that I do not use the word "passion" here as that is perhaps too strong of a word and may cause one to feel overwhelmed or stagnant. Starting with what catches your interest/attention is more realistic and flexible in that our interests may change as we become more aware of needs. If you are not entirely certain of a few areas of need and interest, search online with key terms like "stories of giving," "ways to give," "giving needs," etc. Think about the stories covered in this book. Did you find stories any more compelling than others? Identify one to three causes or needs that you deem priority. Refer to the worksheets in Chapter 7.
2 Start Small. When developing a plan, start small. You can always add more time or money to the cause. It is better to start small than to over-commit or go all in and feel overwhelmed. Starting small will also ensure that giving is sustainable.

Developing Your Plan/Creating a Ripple 251

3 Create a pattern. Creating a routine in a manner that is easy to maintain regularly and consistently will aid sustainability. The frequency should fit with your schedule and be in your time frame. Giving regularly creates a pattern that is easily maintained as it becomes something you do not need to reengineer.
4 Create a tradition. Create a tradition around giving or fold in an aspect of giving into an existing tradition. This can be accomplished by making giving a family affair. This will be discussed in Chapter 9.
5 Capitalize on a crowd. If planning an upcoming event, utilize the masses and pair the event with a solicitation for a donation to a cause. For example, if hosting a holiday dinner, in lieu of guest bringing a side dish, ask them to bring canned goods or toiletries for the local food bank, socks for the shelter, towels for the animal shelter, etc.
6 Prepare in advance. Expect the unexpected by having items ready for giving when the need arises. An example would be to have care bags with water bottle, snacks, etc. to give to the homeless you may see while driving or out in the community. I also carry winter coats in my trunk to give to homeless people I see. Prepare items to give and keep things in your car, office, or home that are easily accessible and replenished.

The following worksheet offers a snapshot of a giving plan. List the top needs you would like to support (the "who"). Then list the resources for giving with your budgeted frequency in mind ("what" and "when"). This column can also include future giving by noting a future date. Typically, there are a variety of entities serving the needs identifies, so the next column serves to identify the "where." Utilize the strategies covered in Chapter 4 to research which organization is the best suited for your resources. The "how" column is an important one as it will lead to better follow through and sustainability in giving. The last column identifies the lessons learned from Chapter 7. This reminder serves to keep one's boundaries at the forefront to ensure mindfulness giving. Incorporating the material explored so far in this book, fill in the sections of the Personal Giving Plan worksheet in Table 8.1.

252 *Developing Your Plan/Creating a Ripple*

Table 8.1 Worksheet: Personal Giving Plan

Who?	*What & when?*	*Where?*	*How?*	*Boundary/lesson learned*
Example: People in need of food	Money: $25 once a month budgeted	Local food pantry	Virtually on an automatic withdraw schedule through the organization's website.	Given my lessons learned Worksheet 7.2, I will donate money virtually instead of going in person to drop off food.
Add your who:	**Add your what & when:**	**Add your where:**	**Add your how:**	**Add your boundary/ lesson learned:**

Restate giving goal/pledge: _____

Ripple Effect

Now that a plan for giving is established, let's focus on creating a ripple. The ripple effect, as stated throughout this book, is the continuation of benefits from giving. It is a metaphor used to describe how one act of giving, like the skimming of a stone across a pond, creates waves of influence, ripples. Pay it forward experiences create a ripple effect. These experiences occur when someone does a kind act and suggests that the recipient "pays it forward" by bestowing kindness onto another. Social psychologist, like Phillip Zimbardo, speak of the ripple effect as a form of heroism as even small acts can have huge implications. Zimbardo, after decades of studying not-so-favorable aspects of human behavior, recently started to focus more on factors that make for heroic behavior. He is interested in determining the variables needed to "dial up" heroisms. He designed a Heroic Imagination Project (www.heroicimagination. org) where people are encouraged to think of themselves as "everyday heroes" in waiting. A series of not-so-favorable human traits are already known in social psychology research to hinder prosocial behavior. These traits mentioned in previous chapters consist of the bystander effect, diffusion of responsibility, desensitization, and learned helplessness. Deindividuation is another social psychology concept that impacts our ability to see others as human,

Developing Your Plan/Creating a Ripple 253

thereby effecting our ability to feel and express empathy. When people are not seen face to face, it is harder to experience empathy.

Additional social psychology factors Zimbardo has identified as antiheroic traits are an egocentric point of view and blind obedience to authority (Aronson et al., 2023). An egocentric point of view is self-serving. It is a perspective that we find ourselves in when we think about our needs first and foremost. This mindset is often what prevents others from helping and giving. The concept of blind obedience Zimbardo knows of firsthand as the researcher of the classic "Prison Experiment" (Zimbardo, 2007). This study is taught in every introduction to psychology and social psychology college course. It is rather controversial by today's research ethics. It involved the use of undergraduate students participating in Zimbardo's research study in 1971. The study was conducted on Stanford University's campus in a converted basement to resemble a prison. Of the pool of candidates, 24 men were selected as they were deemed to be the most physically and mentally stable per diagnostic interviews and personality assessments. Participants were randomly assigned to a role of "prisoner" or "guard."

The experiment was planned to take place over a two-week period. Zimbardo recruited the assistance of the local police department who picked up the participant prisoners at their houses, simulating an arrest. They were taken to the converted basement area known as the prison, fingerprinted, and photographed to mimic the arrest booking process. They were stripped down and given prison clothes, possessions were confiscated, they were given prison numbers to replace their names, and put in rooms with bars on the windows. The guards were dressed in uniforms, complete with a night stick and mirror sunglasses so that their eyes could not be seen. They worked in eight-hour shifts and were given very little restriction on their actions. They were told that they could not physically harm participants/prisoners. However, as time progressed, both the prisoners and the guards began to behave in accordance with their established roles. The guards belittled the prisoners and made them engage in degrading tasks. The prisoners began to adhere to the rules established by the guards without much resistance. The prisoners experienced group conformity to authority and learned helplessness. It was not until one prisoner began to experience an emotional breakdown and another

254 *Developing Your Plan/Creating a Ripple*

participant joined the study that conformity was broken. Prisoners began to rebel against the assumed authority and the experiment had to be stopped on the sixth day.

Zimbardo (1973) was surprised to see the speed and extent to which participants assumed the roles they were told and conformed to authority so intensely. He was surprised to see how those in authority were so quick to exploit their power. These findings were the focus of the experiment, it was just not expected to occur so quickly and potently. Zimbardo himself reported losing his sense of realism in that he was caught up in the study and did not see the blurring of the professional and ethical lines in not stopping the study even sooner. It was not until a colleague of his questioned what he was doing that Zimbardo realized that he too got caught up in the simulation, stating later that he lost sight of being a primary research investigator and instead became a "Stanford prison superintendent." These findings speak to the power of group influence and acquiescing to authority. These findings were not completely new as a decade prior Stanley Milgram (1963) conducted a study to see just how far participants would go in administering what they believed to be electric shocks to other participants, just because someone in authority told them to do so. This study, known as the Milgram Shock Experiment, is also a classic study in the field of psychology/social psychology. It is taught, like the prison experiment, to highlight the ethical concerns by today's standards, but to also highlight the powerful influence the social world has on our behavior. This study documented antiheroic human tendencies that are shaped by social influences. These antiheroic factors hinder the willingness to give. Conformity, being a significant factor to choosing to act or not, was also studied by Milgram.

Milgram was interested in understanding the concept of obedience. He was curious how German military personnel could complete horrendous acts of atrocities during the Holocaust, just because they were told to do so. This 1961 study recruited 40 males from the local community near Yale University's campus. Participants were told that they were "teachers" and that other participants were the "learners." The learners were part of the study, actors playing the role of a learner. Teachers were instructed to administer progressively higher voltage electric shocks to the learner for each word pair they answered incorrectly. The learners

Developing Your Plan/Creating a Ripple 255

did not actually receive the shock, but responded as if they were in pain. The shock voltage ranged from 15 to 450 volts. Would anyone inflict even the mildest shock on another? Not only did subjects administer these shocks, 65% continued to the highest level of 450 volts! Teachers showed distress and opposition, but still conformed to the assumed authority of the researcher. Even when the learner pretended to be unresponsive, the researcher stated to the teacher, "you must continue," and the majority did. Milgram himself went on to repeat this study with different variables to see if he could further dial up obedience.

Many that read about these classic studies believe that they would have acted differently. That they would have spoken out against social influence and authority. But continual social psychology research would say otherwise. Research on conformity and social influence continues, albeit less dramatically than pseudo electric shocks or simulated prisons. A large premise of social psychology research is that what we think is not always consistent with what we do. How we act is influenced by the social environment. Zimbardo has said that one never quite knows how they will act in a new circumstance unless they put themselves in different situations. Indeed, it is important for us all to realize the social influences that dial our actions up or down. When it comes to prosocial actions, it behooves us all to understand the social influences that make our behavior occur and the influences that may restrict our actions. If we are not aware of such influences, we are at the mercy of environmental influences. If one can resist the social dynamics and tendencies to act unheroically, then they can act in a prosocial manner in times of need. Giving is a prosocial act. Social science has identified that the benefit of the act does not stop there, but that there is a continuation, a ripple, that continues in the recipient's life, in the lives of those that witness the act, and in the benefits felt by the giver. Social learning theory is consistent with findings of social psychology in that we are influenced to act by what we witness from others. Human tendencies and social influence can create a barrier to giving. A common social tendency is to think that giving does not matter, that it is a "drop in the bucket." Giving does not need to solve the problem for everyone, just for someone. That small drop in the bucket can create a ripple for others as it serves as a positive social influence for others to give and act pro-socially.

256 *Developing Your Plan/Creating a Ripple*

A compelling example of such a ripple and one that segways into our next topic on creating a legacy is that of Alex's Lemonade Stand Foundation, a 501(c)(3) started by a young girl, Alex Scott (https://www.alexslemonade.org/). She held a lemonade stand to donate all her proceeds to fight childhood cancer. Word spread and others held lemonade stands sending their proceeds to Alex. The ripple continued into a wave resulting in her reaching her one-million-dollar goal. Sadly, she died shortly afterwards at the age of 8½ years. Her parents thought the fundraising would stop, but it just continued and remains active to this day funding research and treatment of childhood cancer. Not only do kids across the United States and Canada register their stands online, but major corporate sponsors also donate to the organization and have donation days where patrons can donate to the organization and write a message or their names on sheets of paper shaped as a lemon. These lemons are hung up on the walls near checkout counters. *Rita's* water ice even sponsors Alex Lemonade–flavored water ice. As noted on their website, more than $250 million has been raised so far, funding over 1,000 research projects and providing programs to families affected by childhood cancer.

Creating a Legacy

Giving to Heal and in Remembrance

No one is immune from hardships and pain. Some of the most painful life experiences are the loss of a loved one and trauma. Adversities can devastate one to the core making coping a challenge. Some people experience a perpetual state of depression, unable to be as they were. Others find healing through "Post-Trauma Growth." Tedeschi et al. (2018) defined Post-Trauma Growth (PTG) as the positive psychological changes that occur due to the struggle of managing a trauma or very difficult situation. PTG can include a deeper appreciation for life, increased self-awareness, enhanced relationships with others, and many more possible positive outcomes. Those that can grow from their adversity find ways to turn negative events into positive outcomes. To do this, one needs to empower themselves to build and even rebuild after the devastation. Lifting others also lifts you up as your mood improves and

Developing Your Plan/Creating a Ripple 257

you feel a sense of purpose. When we rise above hardship, we develop grit and resilience. Grit is a concept of interest in psychology as it defines one's ability to persevere. In the face of adversity, grit is what pushes one through. Resiliency is the capacity for one to recover from setbacks. It describes their elasticity. If one is highly resilient, they tend to use challenges to create growth. Grit and resiliency give us power to endure, to grow, and to contribute. PTG harnesses resiliency and grit to learn and grow from adversity. This power allows us to step outside our own problems to see the need in others.

One interviewee, Gina Marasco Emmons, really stood out as experiencing PTG through her giving. She is the author of *My Compelling Significance* (2022); a true story about her traumatic experiences, starting at the age of three when Gina witnessed her father murder her mother. Her life story covers a series of traumas from years in an abusive foster care placement to being physically and sexually assaulted. All along, Gina struggled for connection, care, and safety. She strove to feel love. Gina writes about these experiences and notes that she is an empath. She understands the pain of others and is sensitive to their needs. Part of healing involved her turning her pain into growth through giving. Gina takes an annual trip, from Florida to Pennsylvania, to help staff at the Children's Home of Easton wrap gifts for the children that live there. Gina describes the experience:

> I get a warm and fuzzy feeling at the Christmas party seeing the kids open the presents. It's more about being in the gymnasium full of kids having fun and being happy. These kids don't get anything and have to go back to their tough lives every day. It makes me want to do more. I love seeing the smiles on their faces…even if it is just one day.

When she described her own early experiences with receiving gifts, she stated:

> The first gift I received from my foster mom was when I was 4 years old. It was a toddler's cleaning kit. It represented the role I knew I had to do (clean). I also noticed the disproportionate number of Christmas gifts her biological son received compared to me and my brother. My brother got more gifts

258 *Developing Your Plan/Creating a Ripple*

than me, but not as much as the biological son who got double that of my brother. My foster mom was biased towards the boys. I noticed this year after year and would be jealous of it. Now, I look for kids that have nothing. They are the ones I want to give too.

The first time my foster mom gave me money was a dollar I earned from cleaning. I knew she did not want to give me the dollar, but her husband insisted because I did such a good job. I could tell she did not want to give me the dollar. I immediately went to the gift store to buy her a figurine. I did not want to, but I did it out of fear.

When I was in placement (Children's Home of Easton), I received a *Polaroid* camera. I loved that gift! It was the only gift I received, and I loved it. You had to have a job to buy the film. We had fun with that one roll. I did not have photos as a kid, so I was finally able to capture moments.

I received a special gift when I was in the hospital as a teen due to an overdose. My staff from the children's home came to visit me and brought me some pistachios from their parents who had just met me the day before. They were so kind to remember what made me happy. They knew this about me, what I liked, after only knowing me for 15 minutes.

When I was assaulted, I had another girl's shoes on as she let me borrow them. I lost one of the shoes during the assault. When I left the children's home, she bought me a pair of the same shoes. It was a nice gesture, but just reminded me of a difficult time. Instead of throwing them out, I gave them to a homeless person. I regifted it to the homeless person turning a misfortune into good.

The examples of gifts Gina shared with me highlighted the power and effect, both positive and negative, giving can have on someone. Gina's earlier examples of giving were scant and conditional. She felt guilty and undeserving of the few gifts she acquired. She saw the inequities in the gifts which sent her a message of insignificance. It is no wonder the title of her book is *My Compelling Significance*! She has worked hard throughout her life to overcome her feelings of insignificance. Later in life, she received gifts, such as pistachios, that made her feel seen. It made her feel special. The *Polaroid* camera allowed her to capture valuable memories with each

Developing Your Plan/Creating a Ripple   **259**

picture yielding an additional gift of memories preserved. Giving became her power and her vehicle for post traumatic growth. Feeling the strength in her journey, I commented to her: "You don't look for the silver lining, you are the silver lining." She has worked through her trauma and has rebuilt herself with layers of grit and resiliency. She did not let her life experiences harden her, just the contrary, she is incredibly empathic. When I asked Gina what her giving priorities are, she stated:

> I prefer to focus on children with no parents, no home base. There are tons of kids now that do not have parents because of Covid. They are so alone. Who is hugging those kids? I would tell the Director at the Children's Home of Easton to "please make sure those kids are getting love." I also focus on causes that help people experiencing domestic violence leave their homes and having to start fresh.

Adding to her resiliency, she described her brother as a positive social influence on her life. Thinking about how she learned about giving, she stated: "My brother was very giving; he had a paper route. One day I noticed him giving a homeless man a dollar. I was around 10 or 11 years old. My brother taught me about giving, that it makes you feel good. He taught me this and said: 'you'll learn.'"

Another example of PTG is that of Barbara's and her husband, John's, decision to start a scholarship program for their daughter Caroline Gallagher Cranston. The scholarship page (https://chescocf.org/fund/caroline-gallagher-cranston/) reads:

> Caroline Gallagher Cranston passed away Saturday, May 8, 2010, at her home with family at her side. Throughout her life Caroline was an inspiration to those around her. She embraced living every day with a positive spirit – most notably in the last 21 months while she courageously battled leukemia. Caroline's compassionate and selfless personality positively impacted each and each person she encountered in her brief life.

As of the Fall of 2023, there have been 12 scholarships awarded, furthering Caroline's ongoing legacy. Many nonprofit organizations and scholarship programs have been initiated due to loss.

260 *Developing Your Plan/Creating a Ripple*

Refer to the angel gowns noted earlier. Founders of these programs never imagined establishing such a program until life circumstances occurred. Like anyone, they had the option to succumb to the grief or to rebuild through post traumatic growth. Fortunately, these founders chose to spearhead these programs that help others. But with that, they have helped themselves and their volunteers to growth and heal. During my interviews, I learned about a nonprofit that was started by parents of a 12-year-old boy who died in a sledding accident during a trip with his Boy Scouts troop. When his snow boots were removed at the hospital, a bible verse, James 1:2–4, was found. The verse read:

> Consider it pure joy, my brother, whenever you face trials of many kinds, because you know that the testing of your faith develops perseverance. Perseverance must finish its work so that you may be mature and complete, not lacking anything.

His parents started a nonprofit 501(c)(3) called Ian's Boots (http://www.iniansboots.org/) where they raise funds and collect shoes to distribute to those in need. *Ian's Boots* ships shoes all over the world.

Chris Hutelmyer, founder of the Arts and Athletic Club (https://www.artsandathleticsclub.com/), is the youngest founder and executive director I have met. Chris started his nonprofit organization shortly after finishing college. The idea originated as a senior year college project that he decided to "give it a try." In 2019, the organization became a nonprofit. The organization provides free theater and reactional activities to the community. All are welcome and have a role, from his 30 volunteers to the 80–100 individuals who participate in the programing each year. Originally, they were meeting at public parks, but they would often get rained out. Now, their main location is in a partially vacant mall, occupying one of the previous retail stores. They produce approximately ten productions a year. The work is hard as he is the only employee. So far, their revenue has been under $50,000, the threshold for reporting earnings. When asked what the organization's main need is at this time, he stated: "Sustainability." He added: "We run the program with the intent of making it free, that is a challenge." Chris used "we" a lot throughout the interview. When asked about this, he emphasized that he sees

Developing Your Plan/Creating a Ripple 261

the organization as collaborative. The community created in this organization was evident. Chris noted that the organization receives an annual grant from the Huston Foundation and that other funds are obtained through

> ...two major fundraisers: 5/11 is our day of giving as it is the anniversary of our first show. August is our annual summer bash, a celebration of our shows for the year. It is our show gala with awards, raffle baskets, food, and celebration. We also have small fundraisers throughout the year. Sometimes families put together a fundraiser for the program, one family member donated proceeds from their light show to the program.

These examples demonstrated that a legacy and ripple can occur through the efforts of one, but that giving does not need to occur in isolation. Part of the ripple is to network with others that could benefit from involvement, that have gifts to share, and passions to fulfill. What is your gift to offer?

Create Your Own Legacy

Planning your legacy starts with what you are already doing and taking a step further to create a ripple. That could be ensuring sustainability through networking and recruiting others' involvement. It could mean creating a nonprofit organization or scholarship program. It could also include influencing others to give. Starting traditions within your family, community, workplace, etc.

Our developmental need to leave a legacy is especially evident during adulthood. But can be empowered at any age. As will be discussed in the next chapter, helping children become effective givers is an effective way of preventing learn helplessness. Your legacy can be enhanced by serving as a positive social role model to others, of all ages! Tell family and friends about your giving behavior and your giving plan. Provide them with updates on your progress toward your goal. This will help you receive the support and encouragement to continue, but also provides some positive contagion. We are powerful social models for one another. Who knows, communicating your giving behaviors may compound results by getting others on board with the cause or sparking interest in them support a cause of their own.

262 *Developing Your Plan/Creating a Ripple*

Our influence on others can create a ripple effect, thereby a legacy. To this point, I think about my interview with Barabra, mentioned above. She is a retired university professor, grandmother, mother, and wife. True to her generous nature, she comes to the interview with a bag of chocolates for me to "help the flow of my writing" as she said and indeed it did! Unsolicited, she mentioned three specific examples of being influenced by my giving. It is amazing to get this kind of feedback and hear how one's actions influenced others, clear evidence of a ripple effect. As noted earlier, we are all influenced by others. Barbara recalled a story that I only vaguely remembered. It was a lunchtime fundraiser we coordinated to raise money for a cafeteria worker that lost everything in a fire. She also commented: "I started collecting a thank-you card basket like yours." I started collecting thank-you cards from students and colleagues a few years ago at my office at the university. The basket is jammed pack with gratitude. Just looking at it makes me feel the abundance of impact I have made. I display the basket above my desk in the office (see the picture of the basket in Figure 8.1). When people ask me about it, I share the benefit of keeping these cards as they are a nice symbolic reminder of my impact of giving.

Figure 8.1 Thank-You Card Basket.

Developing Your Plan/Creating a Ripple **263**

Her third example was the most powerful to me in that she stated:

I always think about people that are less fortunate than I am. You turned me on to the local food pantry. I just gave to them over Christmas. I still remember you told me about that – I remember the first time I walked into the place. I came home thinking that there were people in there that looked just like you and me!

When asked what other cause she donates too, she stated:

We give a lot to the dayroom at the church because I know they will use it and I know where it is going. During Covid we would buy groceries and bring to the day room. The day room is a resource room and provides breakfast and lunch to those in need. I like to give where I know it is going.

Barbara and her husband continue to create ripples in their giving through direct donations to people in need and through the Caroline Gallagher Cranston scholarship mentioned above.

The internet is filled with motivational stories of giving legacies. I came across a story about a farmer, Hody Childress, from Alabama. He gave his local pharmacy $100 a month for ten years to pay for customers that could not afford their medication. Upon his death, the pharmacy kept the tradition by creating a fund in his name (https://sports.yahoo.com/town-discovers-farmer-had-secretly-202013340.html). Another legacy story, perhaps one of the most powerful blood donation stories, is that of an Australian, James Harrison. He was 81 years old when he gave his last donation. James started donating his blood as soon as he was old enough at the age of 18. Years prior, he made the commitment to donate when he survived chest surgery at the age of 14, the success of which depended on donated blood from strangers. It was found that his blood contained a valuable antibody which was deemed to have helped save over two million Australian babies. Over his lifetime, James has donated over 1,100 times! (https://www.life-blood.com.au/news-and-stories/stories/james-harrison).

Another way to leave a legacy is through planned giving, usually in a Will. A Will is a document, typically written by a lawyer that is signed and notarized by the individual then sent to the registry

264 *Developing Your Plan/Creating a Ripple*

of wills in the individual's county office. Items one may leave to an individual or organization in a Will include money, stocks, insurance policies (preferably the beneficiary is named on the insurance policy), jewelry, property, or other possessions. When making these legacy gifts, be aware of individual state requirements for probate or other taxes on such gifts. Wills prepared by a lawyer can cost hundreds to thousands of dollars depending on the level of complexity. *LegalZoom* is an online company that helps the customer create their own Will within the guideline of their state location starting at $89. You can certainly write your own will, be sure that it follows the guidelines of your state, and have it notarized. The more formal, the better. Remember, the Will serves to prove your wishes at a time when you will not be able to clarify. I recommend consulting an expert. Matters can be rather tricky indeed. What may seem like a simple Will can become complicated by wording and logistics at the time of its implementation. For example, perhaps you are planning to leave your estate to your nieces and nephews. You know what and who you mean, but technically what may be considered a niece and a nephew. Is it to include your sibling's ex-wife's adult child from another marriage? To be sure you are bequeathing to whom you desire too, you should list their full name and birthdate in the documents. Be as clear and as specific as possible so that a judge is not left to interpret what you may have meant. Be sure to share with those closest to you where you keep your copy of the Will and what your explicit wishes are so that there is no guessing and no surprises (hence lessening the chances of conflicts between loved ones). In Chapter 1, I wrote about my husband and I being in a Legacy Circle at People's Light Theater. This is a planned giving method for leaving a legacy to a selected organization upon your death. You chose the parameters around this gift. It could be a percentage of your estate, a set amount, possessions, etc.

Your legacy could be the giving tradition. It could be an accumulated list of organizations and their needs. Creating this list on a Google document and sharing it with others enables them to review it and add to it. Remember your list of giving from Chapter 7. Add to this and keep it active. It would be helpful to have as "data" to see if you are fulfilling your plan. With this, I also suggest keeping thank-you cards or notes you may receive. Keep them in one easy-to-find area and watch them accumulate. Review these

Developing Your Plan/Creating a Ripple **265**

notes periodically, especially when you need a mood boast or when you feel like you are not making a difference.

A legacy can be in the ripple you create. Numerous times, I have been told that someone started giving in a particular way after they learned about it from me. Wow, that is the ultimate evidence of a ripple. Ripples are there, but we are not always fortunate to see, hear, or feel them. This is why feedback itself is a gift. I suggest assuming that the ripple is made! In the absence of feedback, what is the harm in thinking positively? If you desire more concrete evidence, then simply ask. Sometimes, as with anonymous donations, it is not quite possible to follow up and ask for feedback. But in incidences in which the recipient is known and it is not deemed to infringe on their dignity, then ask. An example I often encounter is making donations in kind in response to a solicitation on social media or in my personal circle. I work hard to match need with specific clothing sizing and do my best to add a few extra unsolicited items, such as when a mother requests clothing and shoes for her children, I assume she has little for herself and is prioritizing her request to be only for the children. I will do my best to fulfill her request for the children, but will add perfumes, hand cream, or clothing items for her. If contact information is known and I desire feedback, I may send a message and ask if the items fit or if the items worked out. I have learned not to assume an individual does not appreciate generosity if they do not provide the feedback first or if their response to your request for feedback is less than expected. I remind myself that they are struggling with issues larger than communicating with me and that perhaps they feel bad about having to be in the position of needing help. These reasons, and more, make it hard for them to face continued dialogue about the gift. Often, I try to give with the mindset that it is out of my hands how the gift is utilized. I mainly believe the benefit to my giving is in the action – the symbolic message that goes with a gift that someone cares. This message does not get changed by the response to the gift.

Large donors may leave a grand legacy such as a building donated in their name. Many of us are not able to make such a financial gift, but do have the capacity to leave a physical legacy perhaps on a smaller scale, such as a park bench and a brick along a path one's favorite location. Scholarships are also a great way to leave

266 *Developing Your Plan/Creating a Ripple*

an impact and make a difference for generations to come. Legacies can be left through leaving a business to someone, a group of people, or an organization. Donate property for nonprofit use. Many treatment facilities have acquired their property from large donors leaving their homes to the nonprofit organization. On occasion, the property is donated in exchange for care of their dependent for the remainder of their dependent's life.

Another way to leave a legacy is by creating your own nonprofit organization. While this may seem a mammoth feat, many have done so. Like any large task, start small. The first step, once your focus has been determined, would be to articulate that focus with a mission statement. A mission statement identifies the goals of an organization. It is aspirational and serves as a grounding foundation for which decisions are made. It defines what an organization is and what it is not. Take time to develop this, review mission statements from similar organizations. As critical and fundamental as this statement is, it can be modified over time, but I suggest in a limited manner. Otherwise, it is as though the organization is chasing a moving target. It is not necessary or feasible to assume that one organization can do it all. Focus on what aspect can be done exceptionally well and target that as the goal.

The next step is to research the regulations for forming a nonprofit. In the US, there are plenty of good resources. Start with governmental resources provided by the IRS on their website (https://www.irs.gov/charities-and-nonprofits). This information may initially be difficult to decipher, so additional resources such as the popular book written by Anthony Mancuso (2021) *How to Form a Nonprofit Corporation* (15th edition): A Step-by-Step Guide to Forming a 501(c)(3) Nonprofit in Any State will help in the application and interpretation of steps. One does not need to do all this on their own. You can solicit the expertise of professionals in the field that have set up nonprofits. At times, these members may even be or become your board members. A requirement for nonprofit organizations in the US is that they have at least three board members, a president, treasurer, and a secretary. There is plenty of advice on who to select as board members. Know that it is the board that ultimately has final word on the direction of the nonprofit organization, not the founder. The founder often serves on the board, but they are one vote. The purpose of the board is a "check and balance" to the processes and assurance that not one

Developing Your Plan/Creating a Ripple **267**

person is acting in a self-interest manner. Members often represent a variety of disciplines and have expertise in the necessary areas of organizational functioning, such as fiduciary, accounting, and operations. The board is responsible for ensuring the strategic plan of the organization and that it is operating within legal parameters. It is there to ensure that the organization's mission is the focus. Explore other reputable online resources for more ideas and information. An example of a resource for tips for writing grants is provided by the Chester County Library as follows: https://www.ccls.org/224/Grants.

Once an organization is registered as a 501(c)(3), it can offer receipts to donors for their use in reducing their income tax burden. The 501(c)(3) organization is also now eligible for grants. Grants are funds provided from private, nonprofits, and government entities that are given without the need to be repaid. However, there are stipulations and sometimes costs to the nonprofit organization receiving the grant money, such as agreement to establish additional positions within the organization or to assuming fiduciary responsibility for part of the grant-funded project or equipment. How to find these grants and their requirements, one can search online, however, there are exclusive databases, often available through a public entity, such as a local library. These library databases are foundation directories throughout the country. As of now, they are accessible only at a few libraries, in person by using the computers at the library for reserved intervals of time. This is a robust database for nonprofit organizations seeking grants. The Chester County Library (https://www.ccls.org/) is one such location for the *Funding Information Network (FIN)* of the Foundation Center of New York.

In my home state of Pennsylvania, the Pennsylvania Association of Nonprofit Organizations (PANO) (https://pano.org/starting-a-nonprofit-organization-in-pennsylvania/) offers a plethora of resources. The PANO website notes:

When you are ready to start your nonprofit, plan to incorporate and apply for 501(c) status, as these are important steps to fully achieve your goal. As an incorporated nonprofit, you limit the liability of your organization's officers and directors. If you apply for 501(c)(3) status, you will be able to apply for grants, provide tax deduction to your donors for their contributions,

268 *Developing Your Plan/Creating a Ripple*

and be exempt from federal corporate income tax. Most importantly, you will gain credibility and legitimacy for your cause, instilling the public with confidence in your organization.

Other states provide lists of their nonprofit organizations and the grants that support them. There is a slew of companies online that offer databases, but these companies are private and charge for the service.

Secure in one's ideas for giving, strategies to give, researched entities for giving, boundaries and plan, now the reader can compound their giving by spreading the word and otherwise creating a ripple of inspiration to others. Social science provides some research and theory to aid in the conceptualization of this potential ripple, albeit difficult to fully measure. One can be assured that their giving contributes to positive benefits to the recipient now and in the future. Giving creates hope in others. It is always within one's power to choose what to give and how to do so.

A mindfulness plan to giving starts with identifying yourself as a giver and adopting a giving lifestyle. Identify with this role and you will be more inclined to act. Create a "cognitive script" for giving. Cognitive scripts are thoughts and statement we have. We can use these thoughts to define ourselves as a giver. Prepare statements to have at the ready-to-build fluency in asking "what is needed," "how can I help," and "how can I make the situation better." Practice looking at one's environment with the mindset of giving. Give with your hands, your heart, and your words.

Reflect

Now that a giving plan is created and ripples are set in motion, reflect. Review all you do. Reflect further on your giving effectiveness. How do you feel about your giving? Do you feel a positive sense of meaning? You are more likely to experience the positive effects of giving when you are engaged in the process and can see the results. Seeing the outcome can be by simply reviewing your monthly donations, reviewing totals contributed, taking inventory from time to time of your good deeds. This reflective process is likely to amaze as accumulative giving really adds up. Going to organizations to see their work and your outcome of giving is another way to reflect.

Reflection also involves keeping one's eyes open for other needs. Utilize your network of resources you are acquiring to

Developing Your Plan/Creating a Ripple **269**

refer others too. Look in your immediate vicinity at neighbors, co-workers, community members that may be in need. Do they need help completing a task? Do you have a specific skill that could be of service to them? Recently, as I was sitting at the kitchen table with my colleague working on a giving event, I heard her husband packing up tools to go off to the neighbor's house to hang a smoke detector for them. This is a five-minute task for those in the know, something of complete necessity, but also something that an elderly person or person not able-bodied would be able to do independently. Reflect by keeping your eye and ears open to the mindfulness giving all around us. Allow yourself to be inspired by this beauty.

Key Points

- Before setting an intention to giving, explore the intent in our giving.
- All giving is noble.
- A giving plan involves determining who, what, where, and how of giving.
- Research organizations and needs to determine resource needed but also the worthiness of the organization.
- Trust your instincts.
- Once a giving plan is developed, plan to create a ripple.
- One way to make for a ripple effect to giving is to leave a legacy.

Action Steps

- Complete the giving plan worksheet.
- Identify ways to create a ripple and legacy to your giving.

References

Alex's Lemonade Stand Foundation. https://www.alexslemonade.org/
Amazon Give Back Box program. https://www.aboutamazon.com/news/community/ways-to-give-back-on-amazon
Aronson, E., Wilson, T.D., Sommers, S.R., Page-Gould, E., & Lewis, N. (2023). *Social Psychology*, 11th edition. New York: Pearson.
Arts and Athletic Club. https://www.artsandathleticsclub.com/
Boles, N.B. (2009). *How to Be an Everyday Philanthropist: 330 Ways to Make a Difference in Your Home, Community, and World- at No Cost.* New York: Workman Publishing Company.

270 *Developing Your Plan/Creating a Ripple*

Caroline Gallagher Cranston Scholarship Page. https://chescocf.org/fund/caroline-gallagher-cranston/

Chester County Library. https://www.ccls.org/

Chester County Library. Grants: General Resources. https://www.ccls.org/224/Grants

CNN. (December 12, 2023). *Celebrate Taylor Swift Through Her Favorite Charitable Causes. CNN Impact Your World.* https://www.cnn.com/us/taylor-swift-birthday-charities-donate-iyw/index.html#:~:text=The%2012%2Dtime%20GRAMMY%20Award,Hall%20of%20Fame%20and%20Museum

Dellatto, M. (March 14, 2023). More than half of U.S. adults say they're Taylor Swift fans, survey finds. *Forbes.* https://www.forbes.com/sites/marisadellatto/2023/03/14/more-than-half-of-us-adults-say-theyre-taylor-swift-fans-survey-finds/?sh=28ca423b6877

Hody Childress. https://sports.yahoo.com/town-discovers-farmer-had-secretly-202013340.html

Ian's Boots. http://www.iniansboots.org/

IRS on their website. https://www.irs.gov/charities-and-nonprofits

James Harrison. https://www.lifeblood.com.au/news-and-stories/stories/james-harrison

Mancuso, A. (2021). *How to Form a Nonprofit Corporation (15th Edition): A Step-by-Step Guide to Forming a 501(c)(3) Nonprofit in Any State.* California: NOLO

Marasco Emmons, G. (2022). *My Compelling Significance: A True Story of Survival, a Parentless Child, Mental Illness, Childhood Trauma, Domestic Violence, PTSD and Healing.* Seattle: Amazon Publishing.

Milgram, S. (1963). Behavioral study of obedience. *Journal of Abnormal and Social Psychology, 67*, 371–378.

Pennsylvania Association of Nonprofit Organizations (PANO). https://pano.org/starting-a-nonprofit-organization-in-pennsylvania/

Ponsot, E. (October 27, 2023). *Taylor Swift is in her billionaire era.* https://www.bloomberg.com/news/newsletters/2023-10-27/taylor-swift-is-now-in-her-billionaire-era-bloomberg-big-take

Tedeschi, R.G., Shakespeare-Finch, J., Taku, K., & Calhoun, L.G. (2018). *Posttraumatic Growth: Theory, Research, and Applications.* New York: Routledge.

Zimbardo, P.G. (January, 2024). Heroic Imagination Project. www.heroicimagination.org

Zimbardo, P.G. (1973). On the ethics of intervention in human psychological research: With special reference to the Stanford prison experiment. *Cognition, 2*(2), 243–256. https://doi.org/10.1016/0010-0277(72)90014-5

Zimbardo, P.G. (2007). *The Lucifer Effect: Understanding How Good People Turn Evil.* New York: Random House.

9 Empowering Children in Their Giving

Introduction

Within Chapter 9, research on what children understand about giving will be reviewed along with suggestions for empowering them to give. Perhaps the two most beneficial reasons to teach children to give is that it aids in their development of empathy and helps them ward off feelings of learned helplessness as they begin to realize hardships in the world. Empathy is developed through experiences and social models. Learned helplessness can be experienced when exposed to adversities that are outside of one's control. A helpless mindset affects motivation and thereby results in inaction. Empowering children to act in small ways enables them to seize control in situations in which they would otherwise feel overwhelmed. Specific ideas for cultivating a giving mindset in children suitable to their developmental level is offered. Special care is provided in separating child from adolescent strategies to reflect their differences in cognitive functioning and interests.

Brief Overview of Child Development

Developmental theory and research note progressive development throughout childhood into adulthood across all areas of being. In addition to physical changes, children undergo gradual advances in cognitive and emotional development. Where they are in their developmental stages will indicate their ability to take another's perspective and initiate giving. Erickson's psychosocial developmental stages, summarized in Table 2.3 provides application to giving through all stages of development. Teaching children explicitly about giving provides them with a tangible expression of

DOI: 10.4324/9781003438359-9

272 *Empowering Children in Their Giving*

morality. It gives them a point on the moral compass that they can identify making them less suggestible to selfishness.

As children's cognitive development matures, they are better able to see the perspectives of others, making empathy easier to acquire. Since they may not be inclined to think outside their egocentric ability, external motivation may be needed when they are young. Social psychology research on motivation is relevant here, specifically attribution theory's (Aronson et al., 2023) noting two types of motivation, intrinsic and extrinsic. Intrinsic motivation involves the use of one's own thoughts for growth and betterment. The outcome of intrinsic motivation is not always immediate and is usually not tangible. Extrinsic motivation involves more tangible results such as money and other tangible rewards. Typically, intrinsic motivation fuels our actions and leads to higher feelings of well-being compared to extrinsic motivation (Bradshaw et al., 2022). Social psychology research consistently finds that when we are already intrinsically motivated for something and are then given extrinsic motivation for the same action, our internal drive decreases. As noted in Chapter 3, this is known as "over justification effect." Applying this knowledge to teaching children about giving, it is important that we do not try to reinforce something that is already intrinsically motivating to them. External reinforcement should only be offered when intrinsic motivation does not exist or until it develops. Intrinsic motivation can be prompted by asking the child to think about their giving after completing a giving act. Ask them how they feel about what they did. Ask them to think about what the giving act meant to the recipient. Ask them to recall the reaction from the receiver and speculate on how that made them feel.

Research on Children and Giving

Research on children and their ability to give has occurred across a variety of ages. Even as young as infancy, there is indication of the potential for giving behavior. Several brain structures have been found to have an influence on empathy, most recently, the hippocampus (Stern et al., 2019). These structures are present in newborn babies and are noted to develop as the baby grows. The hippocampus is involved in memory, but also appears to have an impact on emotion and social information processing. The researchers found evidence to indicate that the hippocampus may be even more important in the development of empathy in boys.

A few years back, researchers Atance et al. (2010) explored perspective taking on gift choices in preschoolers. The researchers had two objects, one geared toward children, the other toward adults. They asked children to select the item they would most like and then to select an item their mother would like. The results showed that three- and four-year-olds were more likely to choose the child item for their mothers than the five-year-olds. Interestingly, when the researchers changed the design to where the children received their choice, they were much more likely to correctly choose an adult item (magazine) for their mothers. The researchers believed that children were now able to reflect on another's perspective when their desires have been fulfilled.

Since their cognitive functioning is emerging, it is typically believed that children do not have the wherewithal to determine deservingness for giving. Additionally, children tend to be rather vulnerable to exploitation. So, how does their cognitive ability impact their understanding and differentiation between who is deserving and who is not? Children have been found to have some ability to ascertain intention and genuineness. Some research shows that toddlers will help others without differentiating. Other research shows that they will favor giving to those that show prosocial behavior. For example, using puppets, Van De Vondervoort et al. (2017) investigated whether toddlers witnessing a prosocial puppet show would give a toy to the puppet more frequently than those that witnessed an antisocial puppet show. Not only did the prosocial group result in more giving, but the researchers also found that all giving resulted in more happiness after the act, regardless of what puppet show was seen. These results indicate two critical pieces of information: toddlers can be selective in their giving and that toddlers feel happy after they give. Other researchers have explored children's perception of fairness in giving. Young children have been found to determine fairness based on amount as opposed to proportion. For example, Hurst et al. (2020) found consistent with previous research that three-year-olds were more likely to base their fairness on the amount shared as opposed to the percentage shared. So, if someone has eight apples and shares

274 *Empowering Children in Their Giving*

three, they are viewed as more generous than someone who shares two apples when they only have three. Children do not reason in proportions as adults do. In the first case, three out of eight apples are 37.5% of the apples, whereas in the second case, two out of three apples are a much larger percentage of 66.66%. The child believes that more is better, even when it is not proportionately better. Hurst et al. (2020) found that children would use proportional rationalization when the material was presented to them in a manner that showed the proportion.

How proportionality is used in giving was also explored by Olson and Spelke (2008) who conducted an experiment to see how 3.5-year-olds would divide up resources, such as seashells. The researchers read scenarios and even had dolls as props to see who the children would give to. When there was an equal number of resources to people, the children tended to distribute evenly. However, when the amount of resource was less than the number of people, the children directed resources to family and friends over strangers. These researchers also found that children tended to direct more giving to models that were direct givers versus those that were not givers. Children seem to have at a young age a foundation for reciprocity and a bias toward one's own.

Children seem to have a general idea of the intent of others' actions. It has been found that 68% of infants (between the ages of 4–32 months) will reach for or help a helper over a non-helper. Now, you may be asking yourself "how did the researchers measure this in babies?" The researchers (Margoni & Surian, 2018) analyzed 26 studies that included a total of 1,244 participants. These studies measured reciprocal interactions of reaching out, sharing toys, reaching for toys, etc. to indicate helper versus non-helper. How much a child understands is difficult to assess due to communication limitations and cognitive ability when they are young. It may very well be that they are attuned to their environments at a nonverbal level and react based on these observations. I think of the classic work by Dr. Ed Tronick in 1978 known as the "still face experiment" that was conducted on two-month-old babies. Mothers were instructed to face their infant and engage, then stop, look away, then look back with flat affect/no emotional response for two minutes. The baby responds with distress, indicating that the baby receives value from the expression (or lack of expression) in others. This work and that of others adds to what

Empowering Children in Their Giving 275

we understand about a child's attachment to caregivers, dependent on back-and-forth interactions that are mostly nonverbal. These interactions are called reciprocal interactions. Reciprocal interactions are physical manifestations of giving and receiving, creating trust and emotional bonds.

A recent study (Szarek et al., 2023) of 727 European toddlers and preschoolers found that children between the ages of two and four years thought all helping was good and all hindering behavior was bad, regardless of outcome. However, children closer to five years and older used both the intention and the outcome of a behavior to evaluate a behavior and liked those that hindered a negative act over those they helped. A previous study (Baumard et al., 2012) found that very young children, such as three-year-olds, took merit into account when determining rewards. This finding was important as it showed that children, although initially preferring equal distribution for all, were able to distribute rewards according to earned contribution. This shows a level of sophistication not previously noted in research findings. Researchers (Charlesworth et al., 2019) found that children as young as three years of age use facial cues to determine other's worthiness of prosocial action, such as giving. This means that children are more likely to infer positive qualities to those that "look" trustworthy. While the research demonstrated their inclination to use this information, it stands to be noted that impressions are not always accurate.

Children were found to help regardless of the perceived level of control a recipient had in the situation. Bennett and Flores (1998) studied elementary and middle school students involved in a group activity. They were specifically interested in finding factors that influenced students to offer help to another student. These researchers based their study on the notion that the degree to which we believe someone has control over their circumstance impacts their willingness to help. It is further noted that the belief in the cause of a problem, along with the responsibility for the solution factored into whether one was inclined to help another or not. Interestingly, the results of their study did not show a difference in students' willingness to help per reason (in control or outside control). This is different than findings with adults who tend to take into consideration whether one had control over the need and responsibility to take care of the need. The researchers concluded that these children did not differentiate between an individual's

276 *Empowering Children in Their Giving*

"fault" in their need for help. The researchers did find a cultural difference in that Chinese American students were found to attribute responsibility and fault more to the individual than Caucasian students. Other cultural findings impacting children's giving were found by Renno and Shutts (2015) in that a sample of mainly Caucasian five-year-olds, that more resources were given to Caucasian children. Gender was also found to have been correlated with more giving for same gendered peers. Previous research showed that girls tend to engage in more prosocial behaviors than boys (Putnick et al., 2018).

Influences on Children's Giving

How receiving a gift impacts children's willingness to help was also studied. Shoshani et al. (2020) not only tested the effects of giving a gift to the children but also the condition of a gift when it came as a sacrifice from the giver. A total of 126 children in Israel participated in an experiment were all but the control group were given bubbles and a wand. One group had a broken wand. The experimenter offered the child their own wand, making the intent of the gift hypothetically more powerful. They then tested how many tasks each child would help the experimenter complete. The children in this emphasized giving group were found to help the giver more than another group, plus were more inclined to also help a stranger. Researchers conducted that these groups showed the differences between happiness for a gift and gratitude for a gift. The conclusion noted that children, even as young as four years of age, can experience gratitude and that their behavior toward helping can be increased.

The influence of parents on children's giving was explored by Putnick et al. (2018) in a cross-cultural study. The researchers were interested in exploring how parent interactions impacted children's prosocial behavior in a sample of over a thousand families from nine countries. They found consistent results across countries. Positive parenting and encouraging prosocial behaviors were found to increase children's prosocial actions over the years. Of further interest was that children in the nine to ten age group had a positive impact on increasing their parents scores on acceptance as their prosocial behaviors grew. This finding was not the case for children

Empowering Children in Their Giving 277

in the 10–12-year range. These researchers identified a reciprocal interaction between nurturing prosocial social behavior leading to positive changes in children while also increasing parents' degree of acceptance rather than rejection of their child.

Children's Happiness in Giving

A research study published in 2015 (Aknin et al., 2015) conducted an experiment with 20 two-year-olds in small village in Vanuatu. This location, being a series of islands in the South Pacific Ocean region, was selected for its isolation and little Western culture influence. The researchers were interested in measuring children's happiness while sharing candy with a toy monkey puppet. Children shared their own candy, known as "costly giving," or the experimenter's candy, known as "non-costly giving." Research assistants scored videotapes of the children's facial expressions during the experiment. The results showed that they were happiest when they shared their own candy versus when they shared the experimenter's candy. They were happier when the giving came at a cost to them. The implications to this are that children benefit from giving, especially when it comes at a cost. An application to a finding like this is to empower children to donate toys and items they no longer need to others. Having had plenty of success with this, I have noted a few suggestions below on how to help children become cheerful givers:

1 Get them involved in the process.
2 Have them select the destination for the donated items.
3 Have them find, even decorate, a box for "giving," a box for "thinking about it," and a box for "keep."
4 Allow them to go through their items placing them in the boxes of their choosing.
5 The items in the "thinking about it" box will stay there for two weeks to see if the item is being used. After two weeks, then prompt the child to go through the box to place items in the "give" or "keep" box.
6 Have the child join you when dropping off the donations. They may not see who the recipient of the items is, but they will have a full picture of the process to help them concretely comprehend.

278 *Empowering Children in Their Giving*

It is especially important to help them create action steps when they come to you with concern or have witnessed a need. This is a way to empower them, help them experience hope, and generate a difference fueled by energy and compassion. A similar process is recommended for helping children give monetarily:

1 Ask the child what need they would like to support. Offer ideas if needed.
2 Provide a container designated for saving money toward the cause.
3 Have them decorate the container for storing money.
4 Ask them to set a goal for the final amount and within what timeline.
5 Assist them in generating ideas for securing funds such as earning through chores and asking family and friends to contribute. They can practice their writing skills by crafting a letter requesting others to donate.
6 Have the child join you when dropping off the donations!
7 Take a picture of their prideful moment of giving. With the child's permission, share the picture in a neighborhood newsletter, newspaper, and social media to inspire others.

Regarding the sixth step, I remember taking my son, probably around six years old at the time, to drop off clothing donations. It was an icy day. I can still picture him running across the parking lot carrying donations, slipping but not falling, as if his guardian angels were working in tandem pulling him up as he floated along the ice. I reminded him to slow down, but he stated, "I have to give my donations." The pure motivation and pride he conveyed was precious and ranks at the top of my list of proud mom moments.

Prosocial behaviors are not only a good thing for children to learn, but they are also valuable in helping them repair hurt feelings they may have caused. Researchers (Donohue & Tully, 2019) found that children engaged in more prosocial behaviors when they believed they hurt a peer's feeling. Children who were given the opportunity to repair their actions that made them feel guilty were found to have less feelings of guilt overtime, whereas those that did not have the opportunity to offer prosocial gestures like kind words or awarding stickers were found to have high rates of guilt. This research speaks to the importance of enabling children to engage in prosocial actions.

Empowering Children in Their Giving 279

Research on Adolescents and Giving

Regarding adolescents, researchers (van Rijsewijk et al., 2016) explored the question "who helps?" among a large sample of adolescents. They found that girls were more often mentioned as helpers than boys, especially by other girls. Adolescents with depressive symptomology were noted to be less helpful toward peers. Both high and low in popularity teens were noted to help peers less than those with average popularity. These results are likely attributable to status within peer group, more popular teens trying to hold onto their status may be concerned that they appear dependent, while less popular teens not being viewed as ones in a position to help. Teens who were noted to be high academic achievers received help less often than other levels of achievement. Also found was peer rejection was related to receiving help over time, but negatively related to giving help. The authors noted that teens tended to prefer help from similar peers. The researchers concluded that not all teens give and receive help at the same level.

Weisz et al. (2022) found that when middle schoolers were exposed to three classes of either empathy or flexible mindset, they were more motivated to be empathic than those that did not receive the classes. The researchers emphasized that the desire to be empathic needs to be targeted when teaching empathy as skills alone are not deemed enough to influence action. Motivation, it would seem, comes from awareness. Researchers have explored this concept too. Roy et al. (2019) conducted research on hundreds (217 in the first study and 461 in the second study) of primary African American and Latino adolescents from poor neighborhoods. In the first part of the study, they found that the teens were very much aware of societal concerns such as discrimination, violence, and poverty. They referenced their own experiences and made mention of the desire to be involved in social change. The second part of the study explored how many teens reported being involved in "critical action," a term used to describe an act that serves to create social change. This act can be conducted in a variety of ways, such as posting advocacy on social media, working on a political campaign, and participating in a rally. Sixty-five percent of the 461 teens studied reported being involved in at least one critical action. Of particular interest, the researchers also found that higher rates of exposure to violence were related to higher

280 *Empowering Children in Their Giving*

rates of involvement in critical action. An interpretive take-away point of this study is that teens are particularly passionate about acting. They are motivated for change and have the energy and compassion needed for action.

These results are not surprising given the current media attention to teen advocates. Twenty teen activists are listed along with their causes online at https://www.goodgoodgood.co/articles/teen-activists. Among the names are Greta Thunberg, environmental activist; Malala Yousafzai, girls' education activist; and Naomi Wadler, gun reform activist, to name a few. What all these teens have in common is their compelling drive for change. Adolescence is a critical time of growth and identity formation. Fueled with enormous amounts of energy and a new perspective on the world, their cognitive development now enables them to think more abstractly and less egocentrically. They are rightfully angered by significant societal injustices and suffering. When I read of their grassroots efforts, their empowerment, and their demands for change, I feel optimistic about the future. But where does all this energy and passion go after years of slow and even stagnant progress? How does the teen negotiate setbacks and regression to a cause? Do they end up getting consumed by their own future and career paths that time erodes their crusade? Worse yet, do they become "jaded" and their passion stifled? How do we keep ourselves and teens from losing their drive for change and empowerment to make a difference? Here are a few suggestions that are likely to help:

1 Help them recognize that large systematic changes take time.
2 Encourage them to make small steps, which are better than no steps, when progress is slow.
3 Help then create a pattern of involvement that is sustainable throughout their changing life.
4 Recruit others to be involved, there is power in numbers and others serve as strong social motivators.
5 Encourage them to take a break instead of quitting when frustrations ensue.
6 Help them recognize when to and how to modify passions/goal as needed.
7 Remind them of why they are involved in the cause.

Empowering Children in Their Giving   281

Encouraging adolescents to engage in prosocial behavior, such as giving, helps lift their mood and gives them a sense of hope. As noted in Chapter 2, Schacter and Margolin (2019) found that on days adolescents rated themselves more prosocial, they also rated their moods as more positive. It is difficult to determine what came first, the positive mood or the action, however, the effect was strongest in participants that had the most depressive symptoms suggesting that the action lifted the depressive symptoms. Interventions for depressive symptoms, especially in a cognitive behaviors treatment model, typically recommend action steps to help an individual gain internal motivation and energy to improve. These actions typically include following a daily schedule that involves self-care like hygiene tasks. An action step could also include working on a task to help another. This is therapeutic in that it provides the adolescent with a distracting activity to help step outside their own thought processes while empowering them to do for others. As mentioned in Chapter 5, the physiological result of giving behavior will result in a burst of neurochemical benefits improving mood.

Teaching students to engage in prosocial behavior such as giving has been a focus in academics in recent years. Curricula from grade school through college have service-learning requirements. College clubs, sports teams, and Greek charters require philanthropic activities. These projects expose students to the needs of others and empower them to create change. However, does requiring giving hinder the enjoyment of being a giver? There is debate about this, not only in service-learning projects but in any explicit attempt to teach children to give. It seems that the outcome is more contingent on **how** the program is presented, worded, and implemented. Nobody likes to be told what to do or hear that they have another requirement to fulfill. But when the opportunity is worded from the perspective of creating positive change and making a difference in the world, who would resist?

Children's Influence on Parents

The environment is known to have an impact on children's giving, but do children impact parents' inclination to give? Previous research has indicated that parenting a daughter increases prosocial

282 *Empowering Children in Their Giving*

actions in men for corporate social responsibility (Cronqvist & Yu, 2017). This area of research and findings that followed have been referred to as the "daughter effect." However, more recently, Leder and Niszczota (2021) found no differences in giving actions for men that had daughters. Their sample consisted of over 1,400 participants in the German Socio-Economic Panel (SOEP) Innovation Sample Study of 2017. Participants were asked how much money they would allocate to a domestic family in need and how much would they allocate to a foreign family in need. Father of daughters were not found to allocate giving differently than other participants. Additionally, mothers of daughters did not donate more than other participants. There was no evidence in this study for the "daughter effect." However, regarding gender, men did give less overall than women in this study. The next section provides ideas for influencing giving, through stories and activities.

Teaching Giving through Stories

Story telling is a wonderful way to engage children, teach morality, and create life scripts for them to follow. Explicit teaching is needed in young children as developmentally, they are concrete thinkers. They have yet to acquire the ability to think abstractly and independently about abstract concepts like empathy and another's perspective. Piaget identified stages in which children develop their thinking, progressing to more and more abstract through once they are approximately 11 years of age. Prior to that, they are rather concrete and lacking in perspective taking. Story telling can make abstract concepts more concrete as it supplies an application and memorable material.

There are many wonderful children's stories on giving, often tailored to children under the age of ten years. A few are reviewed here.

1 *The Giving Tree* (2014) by Sel Silverstein, as previously mentioned, has endured much popularity and critique. The premise of giving until there is nothing left is seen as a metaphor to one-sided giving, giving too much, and even lack of appreciation. On the other hand, others recognize the theme of the story to parallel parental giving, selflessness and unconditional role. At minimum this story is important as it creates opportunities to discuss gratitude and boundaries in giving.

Empowering Children in Their Giving 283

2 *Give* (2023) by Jen Arena and illustrated by Rachel Jomepour Bell is a book of mostly pictures displaying small acts of kindness. The story builds to show the accumulating effect of giving. This effect, I have been referring to as the "ripple effect."
3 *The Berenstain Bears Think of Those in Need* by Stan and Jan Berenstain (1999) depicts the classic Berenstain Bears family members realizing that they have more than they need. The story shows how good family members feel to donate items and time to those in need.
4 *The More You Give* (2022) by Marcy Campbell and illustrated by Francesa Sanna is marketed as "a great alternative to *The Giving Tree*." The focus is on learned gifts of love and generosity being passed down through the generations.
5 *Give This Book Away!* (2022) by Darren Farrell and illustrated by Maya Tatsukawa centers on how it feels to give and encourages readers to give the book away to someone they have never spoken to before. There is space for readers to note their location and for others to see the journey the book has taken. The beauty of this book is in the direct application and encouragement of the act of giving.
6 *Should I Share My Ice Cream?* (2011) by Mo Willems depicts an elephant contemplating sharing his ice cream with his friend Piggie. As in all of Mo Williams' books, he entertains readers while sending a powerful message. This book is helpful for toddlers to identify the internal struggle one feels when learning to share.
7 *A Chair for My Mother* (2007) by Vera Williams is a story about resiliency as a young girl is driven to raise money to purchase a comfortable chair for her mother after the family lost their home and possessions in a fire. The girl's generosity is evident as she is more concerned about purchasing this chair than replacing her own lost toys. Perhaps the real virtue of this story is the redeeming aspect of growth and strength that comes from the empowerment of being a giver.
8 *14 Cows for America* (2016) by Carmen Agra Deedy is a powerful true story about international giving after 9/11. This inspirational story shows us how we all have something to give and that giving is healing.

Older children will likely find meaning in giving with classics for all ages such as the *A Christmas Carol* by Charles Dickens or stories

284 *Empowering Children in Their Giving*

about young activists such as *Teens with the Courage to Give: Young People Who Triumphed Over Tragedy and Volunteered to Make a Difference* (2000) by Jackie Waldman and *The Power of Kindness for Teens: True Stories Written by Teens for Teens* (2004) by Mary Lou Carney.

Videos offer multi-modal sensory inputs that are especially engaging to children. These brief videos are perfect for a child's short attention span. They are often animated with cartoon characters to engage children with cute depictions of animals and other colorful and fun stimuli. Other videos, especially good for older children, show snapshots of a cause or organization. These online videos are often used to provide a brief overview with just enough information for one to research more if they choose. For older children, this could be a good starting block to exploring their own interests by providing an overview of the types of needs and organizations that exist. There are several videos available online regarding stories on giving, a few are tailored to children under the age of ten and are reviewed below:

1 *A Cheerful Giver* (https://www.youtube.com/watch?v=A9vjg Nt3_Fo) by Latter Day Kids is an animated poem depicting a girl sharing a cookie with the animals around her. After witnessing her daughter share her cookie with a variety of animal, her father asks, "wasn't that cookie for favorite kind?" She responded: "I do like cookies very much you see, but I love those around me even more, that matters the most to me." The video ends with a Bible verse from 2 Corinthians 9:7 "every man according as he purposeth in his heart, so let him give; not grudgingly, or of necessity: for God loveth a cheerful giver."

2 *Giving Is Better: A Little Arrow Story* (https://www.youtube. com/watch?v=UdgALI_UgUg) is about a fox that initially feels jealous about seeing others happy. He comes across a happy rabbit that sings "giving is better," then a chipmunk who always smiles because he is thankful for all he has in his life. The chipmunk then offers his acorns to the fox saying: "I have plenty you see, I've got less than I want, but more than I need." The Fox ponders: "How can giving be better?" "Is less somehow more?" Next, he encounters a Moose who encourages the fox to search within and gives the fox his hat and scarf. The last animal encounter is a beaver who is sad as she is building

Empowering Children in Their Giving **285**

a snowman with nothing but three balls of snow. The fox wondered how he could help when he too was sad. Then he remembers the gifts he received from the other animals and decides to give himself. The fox felt a new feeling of warmth instead and pondered: "Was it the things he had given or the kindness he has shown?" This is a very valuable lesson as the act of giving is the power; often far exceeding the material item in value. The fox's final glimpse of insight occurs when he realizes that "just trying to be happy kept him sad all along."

3 *A Little Spot of Giving* by Diane Alber (also a book) on ideas for giving is animated online (https://www.youtube.com/watch?v=aMvEbOZEdm8). Ideas for giving mentioned include gifts of helping, teaching, friendship, advice, listening, compassion, love, time, empathy, hope, teamwork, gift to nature, gift to earth, appreciation, volunteering, gift of generosity, sharing, and gift of joy. This list of gifts is vast, lending itself to daily opportunities, such as encouraging children to focus on one gift idea each day. This could be a family activity where each member serves as a model for other members.

4 Like so many of Mr. Roger's stories, Season 17 episode 21 (https://www.pbs.org/video/mister-rogers-neighborhood-giving-receiving-eric-carle-visit/) focuses on giving and receiving. Mr. Rogers gives fortune cookies to the delivery man, Mr. McFeely. Mr. Rogers reflects on his good feelings, knowing that the gift made others happy. A puppet show ensues depicting a gift not being appreciated. Later interactions show gratitude.

For adolescents, classic movies like *Pay It Forward* (2000) and *The Pursuit of Happyness* (2006) show inspirational acts of giving.

Ideas to Cultivate Giving in Children and Their Families

As you contemplate ideas for cultivating giving in your child, be sure to collaborate with them and involve them in the process. Be sure to have them involved in all steps along the way, making the "who, what, where, why, and how" explicit. If collecting donations, monetary or otherwise, have them come with you when you deliver them. This shows the child the outcome of their efforts. Plus, often those accepting the collections are overjoyed and

286 *Empowering Children in Their Giving*

appreciative, this too is wonderful for them to experience. Seeing this gratification will likely reinforce the action, making it occur again. Direct contact with the cause fuels passion and enables us to see the benefit of our resources. It allows us to get connected to need and emotionally invested. Allow for choice as it will lead to ownership and investment in the activity. Start with areas in which your child is interested. Perhaps they enjoy animals, sports, theater. Look for causes that need supplies or fundraising to target a giving activity. Exploring other areas is a good idea too as children are still exploring their interest areas. Finding a need area could lead to a new interest for your child. Table 9.1 provides some recommended "dos and don'ts" for cultivating giving in children.

Below are a few giving categories and examples that would appeal to children.

Give Items In-Kind

An easy and often necessary project to do with children is to have "clean-out days." Encourage periodic days to devote a few hours for each family member to go through their possessions to purge what they no longer want, no longer fits, or is in excess. Prior to starting the clean-out, work with your child to identify a source or two for the items to go. Set up separate bins for these places and of course have a trash and recycling receptacle close by. Allow the child to place the items in the bins they think most appropriate. You can (and should) go through the items later to make sure you agree with the categorization. If you or the child is not sure they are ready to part with an item, keep it. It will be reviewed again at the next clean-out. People can get rather emotionally attached to their possessions. The item itself takes on a memory for the individual making it at times difficult to detach. If you or the child no longer wants the item, but wants the memory, I suggest taking a picture of the item to save as a memory. There certainly needs to be a balance with parting with objects that have meaning attached to it. Too much attachment and hoarding can become an issue, too little concern for the item may result in regret when it is given away. Regular, structured clean-out with patient encouragement from an adult will help the child learn a healthy balance and realistic ways to preserve memories. Hoarding, a clinical condition

Empowering Children in Their Giving **287**

Table 9.1 Dos and Don'ts for Cultivating Giving in Children

Do	*Don't*
Engage the child in the process of researching need.	Do not force the child to give.
Model giving for the child.	Do not force them to give up their toys or to have a donation instead of birthday gifts at their party. This can create resentment and send the message that they are not worthy of gifts.
Make giving a family tradition.	Do not deter them from making a difference.
Make giving social by volunteering as a family or with their peers.	Do not take over their roles.
Teach children a method for tracking their progress toward their goal or just a list of their good deeds. This could be a photo list where they take a picture of the resource they collected for donations. Or it could be a visual thermometer where they fill in intervals showing their fundraising progress.	Do not shame or guilt the child to participate.
Capitalize on their energy.	Do not focus on giving as a transaction by focusing on the reward to the child over the reward of feeling good for helping.
Talk with children about their thoughts and feelings to help identify empathy.	Do not cultivate pity.

that is rooted in anxiety, is a serious condition that warrants professional help. Developing healthy habits when young can offset concerns later in life. A child can be coached to consider the following factors when deciding to keep or donate:

- When was the last time I wore/used the item? If it is over a year or so, the chances are far less that it will be used again, especially if there are other similar items. When in doubt, I suggest wearing/having the child wear the "maybe" item one day before deciding.

288 *Empowering Children in Their Giving*

- Will I need it to wear/use in the future? If yes, keep unless you have others.
- Does it still fit me? If not, get rid of it. If you are trying to fit into it, assess the likelihood and how long it would take to do so – will item still be of style for your taste. Perhaps you are saving for the child to grow into, such as the case with "hand-me-downs." This is a terrific way to reduce, reuse, and recycle; just make sure the sizing will be a match with the season, e.g., if your three-month-old is currently in size six months and it is springtime, chances are he will not fit a sweater sized six months six months later in wintertime.
- Do I like it? Feel comfortable in it? If not, get rid of it. You may really like something, but just how it looks on you. Pass it on to someone that could benefit from it.
- Does it make me think of special memories? If so, keep it or take a picture of it for memories.
- Do I already have enough of this/similar item? If so, pick a few of the ones you like best and donate the rest.
- Will it bring me more joy to keep it or give it away? Act accordingly on this, there is always the next clean-out where the item can be evaluated.

Think carefully about donating items that are damaged, missing pieces, or broken. While an individual may not be able to use it, the material may be given a new life. You could give to organizations that recycle, upcycle, or refurbish. When giving damaged items, just make sure it is known to the recipient. Imagine a coat being donated to a shelter that has a broken zipper. It is highly unlikely that they will have the means to fix it. Instead, one could fix it before donating or donating it to a facility that refurbishes the item or uses the material. Call the shelter and ask if they have a use for it or if they have a way of getting these types of things fixed. There could be a seamstress on their volunteer list.

Freecycle.com (https://www.freecycle.org/pages/about) global reach is made up of over 5,000 communities where members post items they are giving away for free or to request an item. Like the "Buy Nothing" communities on Facebook. Also, be mindful of your safety by meeting in a public area and refraining from giving personal information.

Empowering Children in Their Giving   289

Collections

Ask organizations what specific items they need. Post that list on your social media – offer to be the collector. Play matchmaker: You can also privately send links and lists to people you know on social media that may be a good match to service or may have items needed. Religious organizations or community organizations that have free clothing days. If your religious organization or community organization does not have one of these days, work with those in charge to start one. It can be as simple as a few signs and short window for collections, then hosting the giveaway for a few hours one day. This can be done seasonally to offer items for people in need for the upcoming season. Join or start a giving group. These groups typically have an identified purpose and mission. This should be known to all members. They usually involved a dozen or so people that all contribute a set amount of money to each meeting to be pooled and distributed to needs members have identified. Meetings are social, often with food and drink; a time to gather and discuss, a time for fellowship. These social elements add to the incentive of the member and can create lifelong friendships while being a valuable service to the community. The group is usually anonymous.

Collect food or money for the local food bank. *Philabundance* is a large food bank serving nine counties in Southern Pennsylvania and Southern New Jersey. They are a 501(c)(3) nonprofit with a robust amount of information on their website, including transparency in financials. Their November 23, 2023 website positing (https://www.philabundance.org/increaseinfoodinsecurity/) reports on the startling reality of food insecurity in the United States as follows:

> The U.S. Department of Agriculture (USDA) recently released their annual Household Food Security Report, revealing national food insecurity rates for 2022. We learned that **44.2 million people, including over 13 million children, lived in food insecure households** – an increase of over 10 million people from the year prior. The overall food insecurity rate rose drastically from 10.2% (1 in 10 households) in 2021 up to 12.8% (1 in 8 households) in 2022. This is the highest national

290 *Empowering Children in Their Giving*

food insecurity rate since 2014, and the highest one-year increase since the 2008 Great Recession.

The USDA Report found that food insecurity increased in every studied demographic: every household size and composition, every race and ethnicity, every gender, every age. While food insecurity increased across the board from 2021 to 2022, children and people of color face an especially disproportionate burden. Nearly 1 in 5 children live in food insecure households – a sharp 44% increase from the year prior. Black and Hispanic people were food insecure at more than double the rate of White people, with 22.4% of Black households and 20.8% of Hispanic households experiencing food insecurity, compared to 9.3% of White households.

An impromptu activity my family and I did one Friday evening when we had no plans was to purchase food for the local food pantry. We were low on funds with only $26 in cash. Instead of feeling down about our limited resources and lack of plans, we split into two teams (one adult with one child) for a competition to see what team could purchase the most pounds of food all while staying in the allotted budget of $13 each. The food was then donated to the local food pantry. This created a fun and quite competitive activity, getting us out of the house and out of our own heads so to speak. Fifteen years later, we all remember the activity but have conflicting recollections on what team won!

Host a community drive. Flyers in the door is a great way to give a tangible reminder, but electronic announcements are good too (assuming you have all the neighbor's emails or social media). Perhaps your neighbor has a social media group, if not create one. When hosting a drive, make it as simple as possible for people to participate. If collecting items like food or clothing, note in the announcement as specially as possible the items to be collected. Give a date, time, and instructions for drop off. Make the announcement catchy. See the example in Figure 9.1.

Volunteering Time

Your time is very valuable. It is a nonrenewable resource. Be sure to use it wisely. There are many causes that need volunteers. An inspiring example of volunteerism is the former US president, Jimmy

Empowering Children in Their Giving 291

Hi neighbor, the XXX family is collecting socks for the Pennsylvania Thoroughbred Horseman's Association. Socks will be distributed to workers at the racetracks as well as others in need.

Please contribute by donating new or gently used/clean socks to this cause!

If you have socks you can donate, please put in a plastic bag at the bottom of your driveway on March 21st by 12 noon. We will be by to collect and bring to the center that afternoon. Our goal is to collect 100 pairs of socks!

Figure 9.1 Example of a Collection Announcement.

Carter, and his wife, Rosalynn Carter volunteered a week of their time every year since 1984 to build houses for Habitat for Humanity. Their work took them around the world to places like Thailand, Loas, Philippines, and Cambodia, to name a few. Mr. Carter continued this work well into his nineties. Finding opportunities to volunteer can be online, searching with key words for populations and causes of interest. Check with local schools, churches, community centers, and shelters to see if they have a need for volunteers. In the United States, volunteer.gov is a search website for finding opportunities across the country. Also in the United States, AmeriCorps (https://americorps.gov/) is a national association of volunteers that strive to help others in six key areas: disaster relief, education, economic opportunity, environmental stewardship, healthy futures, and veterans and military families. Locally, one can volunteer to prepare and serve a meal to the homeless at a shelter or provide care for animals at the local shelter. Also locally are plenty of schools, religious organizations, and community centers that would benefit from the support of volunteers to assist with their service projects. You can even volunteer your time from home! Some organizations donate money to charities for clicks. When people click on advertisements, small monetary donations are made to various causes. For example, *Freerice* (https://freerice.com/

292 *Empowering Children in Their Giving*

home) mentioned previously is a great way for children to practice academics while earning donations to impoverished communities.

Boles (2009) suggested the online site *Care2.com*, a site housing a variety of petitions that anyone over 16 years of age can sign. In researching this, it seems like an interesting resource and one that would be especially good for children. Anyone can create a petition. This would be an excellent project for children too as it does not cost them money and they can practice on their writing skills. Work with them to put into words their concern and to be persuasive so that others will support their petition by signing. The idea has merits; however, the organization utilized must always be researched and evaluated for its suitability. In researching Care2.com specifically, I found bimodal reviews, reviews on one end or the other. No middle ground was evident which made me speculate further – not about the organization necessarily but about the reviewers. Sure enough, it appears that there are some politics afoot. Politics in the "types" of petitions that are posted and certainly politics in some of the reviews that happen to be of opposing politics. The website proudly displays

> Care2 Stands Against: bigots, racists, bullies, science deniers, misogynists, gun lobbyists, xenophobes, the willfully ignorant, animal abusers, frackers, and other mean people. If you find yourself aligning with any of those folks, you can move along, nothing to see here.

Given that the nature of a petition is grounded in conflict and advocacy, it is not surprising that the reviews are from both sides of the coin. However, this is not helpful and necessarily relevant information to have when evaluating an organization. If one does not agree with the views of the organization, then they should go through another organization. It is helpful to know the mission and philosophy of an organization before deciding to utilize the resource or not.

When working with volunteers or even in your own volunteering, be sure to establish roles and tasks. If people do not know what is needed or expected of them, they will likely not be utilized. Being under-utilized is a quick path to boredom and dissatisfaction, resulting in maturation (loss of employees/volunteers). Under-utilizing someone hinders their sense of purpose and joy

Empowering Children in Their Giving 293

from volunteering. On the other hand, once you start volunteering, it is easy to see how productive your service is – pace yourself and stay within the allotted time you budgeted. Protecting your time will enable you to sustain the pattern and ward off burnout. This is certainly a challenge as you are now witnessing firsthand to the need, it will likely make you want to do more.

Mindful Consumerism

Another way for the family to get involved in giving is through mindful consumerism. By this, I mean, research products that sponsor causes. The research should not just take the product manufacture's word for it but use the tools in this book to research for yourself where the company spends their revenue. Look for indicators such as charitable causes being sponsored and Fair Trade. Keep in mind that this endorsement alone is not enough to ensure that your money is being well spent, but it can be a start.

Give Social Support

Teach children that giving includes social support. When we give our support, we are helping another feel seen and valued. Guide them to look for those alone or in need of a friend. Teach them how to not be a bystander, but to reach out to other children that need a friend. Provide them with safe ways to speak out against bullying, such as reporting what they see to an adult and befriending someone that has been picked on. Helping the child remain empathic and arming them with action steps will empower them, thereby diminishing feelings of learned helplessness.

This chapter served to highlight specific factors related to children and their capacity to give. Ideas for supporting children in developing a plan for giving were mentioned above. It is further noted that discussions with children on elements in Chapters 7 and 8 are important in ensuring that they too are mindful givers.

Key Points

- Children want to help; children want to give to others.
- Research shows that children are biologically primed to give.

294 *Empowering Children in Their Giving*

- Research shows giving-like behaviors such as reciprocal interactions and reaching-out behaviors to occur in infants.
- Children have been shown to differentiate, to some extent, the deservingness of a gift.
- Children as young as toddlers have been shown to distribute giving according to perceived earnings.
- Children as young as three have been shown to use other's facial expression to determine their worthiness for giving.
- Children were found to help regardless of the perceived level of control a recipient had in the situation.
- Children are happy when giving.
- Adolescents vary in their helping behaviors, likely linked to their social status.
- Adolescents are motivated for change and have the energy and compassion needed for prosocial action.
- There are numerous ways for children to give.

Action Steps

- Read stories and show videos on giving.
- Create family experiences and traditions around giving.
- Engage in discussions with your child about their thoughts and feelings about their experiences with giving.
- Assist your child in identifying a cause that is meaningful to them.
- Review material and strategies in Chapters 7 and 8 that may be helpful in helping your child create their own plan.

References

The Cheerful Giver: A Story About Giving. Latter Day Kids. https://www.youtube.com/watch?v=A9vjgNt3_Fo

Aknin, L.B., Broesch, T., Hamlin, K.J., & Van de Vondervoort, J.W. (2015). Prosocial behavior leads to happiness in a small-scale rural society. *Journal of Experimental Psychology: General*, 144(4), 788–795. https://doi.org/10.1037/xge0000082

Alber, D. *A little spot of giving*. Magical Little Minds- Read Along Storytime. https://www.youtube.com/watch?v=aMvEbOZEdm8

AmeriCorps. https://americorps.gov/partner/communities-initiatives/united-we-serve

Arena, J. (2023). *Give*. New York: Penguin Random House.

Empowering Children in Their Giving **295**

Aronson, E., Wilson, T.D., Sommers, S.R., Page-Gould, E., & Lewis, N. (2023). *Social Psychology*, 11th edition. New York: Pearson.

Atance, C.M., Bélanger, M., & Meltzoff, A.N. (2010). Preschoolers' understanding of others' desires: Fulfilling mine enhances my understanding of yours. *Developmental Psychology*, 46(6), 1505–1513. https://doi.org/10.1037/a0020374

Baumard, N., Mascaro, O., & Chevallier, C. (2012). Preschoolers are able to take merit into account when distributing goods. *Developmental Psychology*, 48(2), 492–498. https://doi.org/10.1037/a0026598

Bennett, T.R., & Flores, M.S. (1998). Help giving in achievement contexts: A developmental and cultural analysis of the effects of children's attributions and affects on their willingness to help. *Journal of Educational Psychology*, 90(4), 659–669. https://doi.org/10.1037/0022-0663.90.4.659

Berenstain, S., & Berenstain, J. (1999). *The Berenstain Bears Think of Those in Need*. New York: Random House Children's Books.

Boles, N.B. (2009). *How to Be an Everyday Philanthropist: 330 Ways to Make a Difference in Your Home, Community, and World at No Cost*. New York: Workman Publishing Company.

Bradshaw, E., Conigrave, J., Steward, B., & Ferber, K. (2022). A meta-analysis of the dark size of the American dream: Evidence for the universal wellness costs of prioritizing extrinsic over intrinsic goals. *Journal of Personality and Social Psychology: Personality Processes and Individual Differences*, 124(4), 873–899. https://doi.org/10.1037/pspp0000431

Campbell, M. (2022). *The More You Give*. New York: Random House Children's Books.

Carney, M. (2004). *The Power of Kindness for Teens: True Stories Written by Teens for Teens*. New York: Ideals Publications.

Charlesworth, T.E.S., Hudson, S.T.J., Cogsdill, E.J., Spelke, E.S., & Banaji, M.R. (2019). Children use targets' facial appearance to guide and predict social behavior. *Developmental Psychology*, 55(7), 1400–1413. https://doi.org/10.1037/dev0000734

Cronqvist, H., & Yu, F. (2017). Shaped by their daughters: Executives, female socialization, and corporate social responsibility. *Journal of Financial Economics*, 126(3), 543–562. https://doi.org/10.1016/j.jfineco.2017.09.003

Deedy, C.A. (2016). *14 Cows for America*. Atlanta: Peachtree Atlanta.

Dickens, C. (1999). *Christmas Carol. A.* Tyndale House.

Donohue, M.R., & Tully, E.C. (2019). Reparative prosocial behaviors alleviate children's guilt. *Developmental Psychology*, 55(10), 2012–2113. https://doi.org/10.1037/de0000788

Farrell, D. (2022). *Give This Book Away!* New York: Random House Children's Books.

296 *Empowering Children in Their Giving*

Giving is better: A little arrow story. https://www.youtube.com/watch?v=UdgALI_UgUg

Freecycle.com. https://www.freecycle.org/pages/about

Freerice. https://freerice.com/home

Hurst, M.A., Shaw, A., Chernyak, N., & Levine, S.C. (2020). Giving a larger amount or a larger proportion: Stimulus format impacts children's social evaluations. *Developmental Psychology*, 56(12), 2212–2222. https://doi.org/10.1037/dev0001121

Leder, J., & Niszczota, P. (2021). Parenting daughters does not increase monetary prosocial behavior: Evidence from the Dictator Game. *Social Psychology*, 53(6), 383–389. https://doi.org/10.1027/1864-9335/a000508

Margoni, F., & Surian, L. (2018). Infants' evaluation of prosocial and antisocial agents: A meta-analysis. *Developmental Psychology*, 54(8), 1445–1455. https://doi.org/10.1037/dev0000538

Mr. Roger's stories, Season 17 episode 21. https://www.pbs.org/video/mister-rogers-neighborhood-giving-receiving-eric-carle-visit/

Olson, K.R., & Spelke, E.S. (2008). Foundations of cooperation in young children. *Cognition*, 108, 222–231. https://doi.org/10.1016/j.cognition.2007.12.003

Philabundance. https://www.philabundance.org/increaseinfoodinsecurity/

Putnick, D.L., Bornstein, M.H., Lansford, J.E., Chang, L., Deater-Dechark, K., DiGiunta, L., Dodge, K.A., Malone, P.D.S., Oburu, P., Pastorelli, C., Skinner, A.T., Sorbring, E., Tapanya, S., Tirado, L.M.U., Zelli, A., Alampay, L.P., Al-Hassan, S.M., Bacchini, D., & Bombi, A.S. (2018). Parental acceptance-rejection and child prosocial behavior: Developmental transactions across the transition to adolescence in nine countries, mothers and fathers, and girls and boys. *Developmental Psychology*, 54(10), 1881–1890. https://doi.org/10.1037/dev0000565

Renno, M.P., & Shutts, K. (2015). Children's social category-based giving and its correlates: Expectations and preferences. *Developmental Psychology*, 51(4), 533–543. https://doi/10.1037/a0038819

Roy, A.L., Raver, C.C., Masucci, M.D., & DeJoseph, M. (2019). "If they focus on giving us a chance in life we can actually do something in this world": Poverty, inequality, and youths' critical consciousness. *Developmental Psychology*, 55(3), 550–561. http://doi.org/10.1037/dev0000586

Schacter, H., & Margolin, G. (2019). When it feels good to give: Depressive symptoms, daily prosocial behavior, and adolescent mood. *Emotion*, 19(5), 923–927.

Shoshani, A., Lender, K.D., Nissensohn, A., Lazarovich, G., & Aharon-Dvir, O. (2020). Grateful and kind: The prosocial function of gratitude

Empowering Children in Their Giving **297**

in young children's relationships. *Developmental Psychology*, 56(6), 1135–1148. https://doi.org/10.1037/dev0000922

Silverstein, S. (1997). *The Giving Tree*. New York: The Harper Collins Publishers.

Stern, J.A., Botdorf, M., Cassidy, J., & Riggins, T. (2019). Empathic responding and hippocampal volume in young children. *Developmental Psychology*, 55(9), 1908–1920. https://doi.org/10.1037/dev0000684

Szarek, K., Baryla, W., & Wojciszke, B. (2023). Is helping always morally good? Study with toddlers and preschool children. *Developmental Psychology*, 59(5), 918–927. http://doi.org/10.1037/dev0001521

Tronick, E.Z., Als, H., Adamson, L., Wise, S., & Brazelton, T.B. (1978). The infant's response to entrapment between contradictory messages in face-to-face interaction. *Journal of American Academy of Child Psychiatry*, 17, 1–13. https://doi.org/10.1016/S0002-7138(09)62273-1

Martinez Laurel, A. (December 6, 2022). Twenty Teen Activist. https://www.goodgoodgood.co/articles/teen-activists

Van de Vondervoort, J.W., Aknin, L.B., Kushnir, T., Slevinsky, J., & Hamlin, J.K. (2017). Selectivity in toddlers' behavioral and emotional reactions to prosocial and antisocial others. *Developmental Psychology*, 54(1), 1–14. https://doi.org/10.1037/dev0000404

Van Rijsewijk, L., Dijkstra, J.K., Pattiselanno, K., Steglich, C., & Veenstra, R. (2016). Who helps whom? Investigating the development of adolescent prosocial relationships. *Developmental Psychology*, 52(6), 894–908. https://doi.org/10.1037/dev0000106

Waldman, J. (2000). *Courage to Give: Young People Who Triumphed Over Tragedy and Volunteered to Make a Difference*. Miami: Conari Press.

Weisz, E., Chen, P., Ong, D.C., Carlson, R.W., Clark, M.D., & Zaki, J. (2022). A brief intervention to motivate empathy among middle school students. *Journal of Experimental Psychology: General*, 151(12), 3144–3153. https://doi.org/10/.1037/xge0001249

Williams, V. (2007). *A Chair for My Mother*. New York: Greenwillow Books.

Willems, M. (2011). *Should I Share My Ice Cream?* New York: Hyperion Books for Children.

10 Cultivating Giving

Ideas for Advancement
Personnel and Those
That Fundraise

Introduction

Throughout this chapter, research and theory on factors that affect donors' willingness to donate are reviewed. This information is likely to benefit advancement/development offices or anyone striving to raise funds. As a matter of fact, this information is so sought after that a whole field of science and academic training is devoted to it. This field is known as *philanthropy*. Some universities offer certificate programs and academic programs up to doctorate degrees in philanthropy. It is a science and practice, typically focused on high impact giving. The material in this chapter is in no way an attempt to capture all aspects of this emerging field. Instead, it is a brief overview of some of the social science findings impacting giving. Aspects of the donor such as their age, gender, ethnicity, socioeconomic status, and distance from the need have an impact on their giving. Understanding these factors are important in "dialing up" of giving. The science of the wording of the solicitation and the need for providing feedback to donors are also reviewed. Strategies for preventing donor fatigue and aiding donor retention are discussed. The final part of the chapter is devoted to a brief review of salient aspects from each chapter that are applicable to a fundraising campaign.

Theory and Research on Social Influences Affecting Fundraising

Fundraising is an ever-evolving science involving the study of research findings, theories, and models. Philanthropic professionals work in nonprofit organizations, academic institutions, and even

DOI: 10.4324/9781003438359-10

Cultivating Giving: Ideas for Advancement Personnel **299**

for-profit sectors, competing for funding dollars. Knowing the science to human tendencies on giving can maximize a fundraising campaign's results. Some gentle strokes of social psychology are covered here with the theme of "dialing up" giving, based on what is known about social tendencies. Social psychology studies human tendencies and the many factors that can influence behavior. Imagine a behavior as a dial that can be turned up or down. Social psychologist study not only the behavior (the dial) but also the points on the dial that could change the behavior to be activated or deactivated. For example, when it comes to the "dial" for positive or negative behavior, temperature is a point on that dial. High levels of heat are known to be associated with aggression (Aronson et al., 2023) whereas other studies have found warmer temperatures to be associated with prosocial behavior such as giving (Lynott et al., 2017). Some studies have found that holding something hot versus something cold is enough to dial up prosocial behavior (Kang et al., 2011; Storey & Workman, 2013). Another point on the dial is gratitude. Using the "Give some dilemma game" participants who were placed in a situation in which they felt grateful showed a positive impact on the amount of donation they were willing to make (DeSteno et al., 2010). Other points on this theoretical dial are covered throughout the chapter. Knowing these variables provides an advantage in one's fundraising attempts.

Any advantage to fundraising efforts is prudent as fundraising is timely and costly! Expenses include marketing, consultant fees, and staff salaries to name a few. Time goes into planning and implementing events and in cultivating relationships with donors. Nonprofit organizations likely have an advancement or development department or at least an employee or two whose primary job is to secure funds. These professionals may be involved in writing and securing grants. Universities, especially in the United States, survive in large ways depending on their size of endowment. Endowments are pooled donations of money and/or assets, such as property. Endowments, when invested wisely, provide dividends to the university providing additional revenue. The goal is to keep growing the donations to expand the pool and thereby security in the foundation and in the increasing interest (dividends).

Any development specialist will tell you that it is exciting to receive an enormous gift or two, but these are not frequent nor consistent. Most fundraising professionals recognize that a wide

300 *Cultivating Giving: Ideas for Advancement Personnel*

base of low, but consistent donors, provides foundational stability needed for any campaign. Sustainability comes with consistency and predictably of donations. Large donors often want to see a strong foundation of consistent, yet smaller donors, prior to making a substantial pledge. Often smaller donors are employees themselves in the organization, further indicating their trust and belief in the cause.

As noted throughout this book, social psychology offers valuable insights into human tendencies that persuade behavior. The Elaboration Likelihood Model (Aronson et al., 2023) identifies two routes to persuasion, the "central route" and the "peripheral route." The central route is an appeal that offers facts and figures about the need or product. The peripheral route tries to persuade by appealing to one's senses, such as visual imagery. Combining both strategies is deemed to be a highly effective method of persuasion. Therefore, solicitations should seek to pair facts on the need with pleasurable visual or auditory depictions. But there is more. Understanding how potential donors think about their spending provides another variable worth considering.

Mental Budget

LaBarge and Stinson (2014) interviewed 42 donors to determine if they have a "mental budget" for their giving, if their giving is confined to that budget, and whether their budget was flexible. They found that all 42 interviewees had a mental budget for how much and where their giving would occur. Interestingly, they had various categories to their giving, various "pockets," for which funds were allocated. For example, a golf tournament for a charitable cause, employees were likely to see this as a networking or social opportunity, taking funds from their allotted expenses for recreation. The researchers also found that participants' mental budgets were flexible, predominantly due to factors such as the degree of intrinsic value the donor felt to the cause and the degree to which the donor thought the additional amount or cause would make a difference. Expanding on these findings, giving can be enhanced by helping donors see the gift from other pockets of their budget. For example, fundraisers such as an auction around the holidays can emphasize the win-win benefit of supporting a cause while also shopping for the holidays. The donor, wanting to

Cultivating Giving: Ideas for Advancement Personnel 301

support the cause, finds additional funds in their "need to purchase holiday gifts" pocket.

How a donor gives also offers opportunities for expanding their mental budget. Donations do not need to be with money they currently have available. Donors can be encouraged to leave their gift through a life insurance policy with the organization as the beneficiary. This option provides a large pay out with minimal yearly expense to the donor. The donor may rationalize giving with specific categories in their mind, such as purchasing extra boxes of Girl Scout cookies to support the cause, but to also give to co-workers as a thank-you gift. As noted earlier, I refer to this as compound giving as the benefit serves both the Girl Scouts and the co-worker. Chances are they are picking up a box for themselves – triple the benefit! But notice how the funds can be taken out of other "pockets."

Some successful campaigns target the mental and actual budget with a process called "Pennie-a-day" framing. These solicitations prompt the potential donor to think in small regular increments and to compare the relatively small expense with small purchases, such as a cup of coffee a day. Other research has focused on the framing of the solicitation as either frequent or infrequent. In a series of studies, Sussman et al. (2015) found that participants were significantly more likely to donate and donated higher amounts when they were led to believe that the donation was "exceptional" (infrequent) versus when the donation was "ordinary" (regular). In other words, their findings showed that people were less likely to think about their budget with exceptional donations compared to ordinary. Additionally, the average donation amount was higher in the exceptional (infrequent) versus ordinary (regular) cause. Presenting the solicitation as regular seems to prompt the mental budget through calculating the total expense, whereas infrequent does not appear to trigger the same level of budget accountability. The researchers discussed the practice of organizations highlighting regular opportunities to give, such as in an annual auction and walk-a-thon, but highlighted that altering the messaging to a more infrequent request would likely increase willingness to donate and the amount of the donation. Perhaps a combination of the two would be fruitful. Annual events add to the network and passion around the cause as these social events cultivate a community. They are foundational to many campaigns and should remain a

302 *Cultivating Giving: Ideas for Advancement Personnel*

part of the development portfolio. Regular appeals add to the stability and consistency of the fundraising base. Whereas infrequent appeals can really boost support for unique needs.

Advancement and development personnel should consider their development portfolio to ensure many of the above components. Like a stock portfolio, I refer to a development portfolio as an eclectic plan that includes goals such as large capital campaigns, but also general and ongoing endowments. The portfolio should include goals for donations for not just money but also time, service, and in-kind giving. Therefore, a developmental professional is looking to solicit and utilize all contributions. Some donors may only have time to offer other services. A portfolio would have a role for all. There are some donors that may give more than one resource. A plan soliciting a variety of resources will highlight that for the donor making them aware of the variety of needs and opportunities to give.

What Is Important to the Donor?

Before soliciting donations, it behooves development personnel to understand what aspects are important to a donor. Why do or will they decide to give? Find out what matters to them. Haddad (2000) summarized the *Network for Good*, a 501(c)(3) charity that enables donors to raise and direct funds to their selected charities, survey of 3,000 people as to why they give. The results were reported as follows:

"The top eight reasons from most important to least important in inspiring donors to give were:

1. I know the nonprofit's mission and it does good work.
2. I believe the nonprofit will use my gift to stabilize or expand programming.
3. The nonprofit communicates program outcomes.
4. I know someone that benefited from the nonprofit work.
5. I want to be associated with the organization and its brand.
6. I see the organization online and on social media.
7. I want a tax deduction.
8. I know someone who volunteers or serves on the organization's board."

Cultivating Giving: Ideas for Advancement Personnel **303**

I was fortunate to have the opportunity to interview Michelle Johnson, associate director of Development at People's Light Theater. She agreed to share her experiences and philosophy on fundraising. She noted that with being "kind, honest, and forthright – with rapport," she does not need to ask for a gift, that it is offered. She works to rejuvenate the spirit of giving. She enjoys learning about donors and how they came to be involved with the theater. She likes to learn about each donor. She described there being a bit of art in the process of cultivating gifts. She discussed enjoying educating others about giving and how to be philanthropic.

She noted that an error would be to ask for a gift too soon – before a relationship is established. Michelle offered a story early in her career when she and her supervisor met with a donor. Michelle was to make the pitch and when it came time to solicit a monetary gift, the donor responded quickly with a "yes." While Michelle was ecstatic about the success of their meeting, her supervisor later reflected that given the speed of the response, it was likely that the ask was too low.

Michelle offered a second more recent example of a regular donor of many years, giving $5–10 annually, asked to meet with her. Michelle learned that this donor inherited money and chose to donate a substantial gift to the theater. Michelle reflected that one never knows the gifts another can give and that one's life circumstances can change, creating opportunities for giving. Both stories share a theme of understanding the mindset of the donor. This mindset can change over time but is best to be described by the individual themselves. Development personnel are wise to keep an open mind and resist the urge of having expectations about donors.

Understanding the mindset of the donor regarding the alignment to the cause is valuable information to know. Does the cause align with their moral identity? If so, soliciting volunteers may be the appropriate target whereas donors that are less morally aligned with the cause, soliciting a monetary donation may be more likely. At a deeper level, cultivating moral connectedness to a cause is one way to enhance time giving. This can be done through activating the donor's moral identity through programming and including potential donors' interest and skill sets, e.g., identify for the donor where their time and expertise could be utilized. Match their skill

304 *Cultivating Giving: Ideas for Advancement Personnel*

set and experiences with the need of the organization. For example, a local theater may request from teachers' suggestions on developmentally appropriate educational material for their children's programming. The teachers may or may not be interested in the theater program but are certainly interested in and knowledgeable of developmentally appropriate teaching methods. This creates a volunteering opportunity that is targeted and may potentially lead to more involvement within the organization. Sometimes we just do not know where our passion is until we get involved. How many times have we heard of stories about how someone got started with an organization, quite serendipitously, and ended up staying? Passions come from the outcome of experiences, not something we know to find. One such story of serendipity was shared by one of my interviewees, Dina. Dina noted while on social media she saw a post requesting assistance in helping a hurt deer. Dina noted that no one replied, except for a local horse rescue and sanctuary. She was not familiar with this facility and researched them. She noted: "God used the post about the deer to get my attention...." She now volunteers there cleaning stalls once a week with the goal of working up to riding one day.

Donor Demographics

Social science research has also shown effects on giving across a variety of variables such as age, gender, ethnicity, socioeconomic status, and distance from the need. The possibility of gender differences in giving was studied in 2012 by Jonason, Tost, and Koenig. They asked 235 participants about their reasons for gift giving. Men were statistically more likely to give gifts to build a romantic/sexual relationship and as a way of maintaining a relationship. The two main reasons all participants reported for gift giving was a special occasion and to show affection. Research from 2014 (Dyble, van Leeuwen, and Dunbar) asked 99 participants in an online survey to list the value of gifts in British pounds, relationship to recipient, and frequency of contact with the recipient. Findings showed similar amounts spent by men and women on gifts to family, whereas women spent more on gifts to friends and to people whom they were not in frequent contact.

Cultivating Giving: Ideas for Advancement Personnel **305**

Leslie et al. (2013) looked at workplace giving and the effects of employee gender and ethnicity on giving. They sampled over 17,000 employees on their donations to charitable giving campaigns. Women were found to donate an average of $30.59 more than men. Minorities donated $25.82 less than their Caucasian counterparts. The researchers explained these differences through the lens of social exchange theory and the role society places on factors like gender. There were fewer minorities in this sample of workplace, so results should be viewed with caution. Theoretically, it was speculated that minority individuals felt the effects of being underrepresented, thereby impacting their exchange rate as donors. To this point, it was later found that minority giving increased when the percentage of minorities in the workplace setting increased. The finding that women gave more than men was explained through the cultural expectation that women are expected to be communal in a role of caregiver and thereby are likely to incorporate this stereotype into their own psyche, leading to behavior consistent with this expectation.

The Dictator Game is an experimental tool used by economist and others to explore dynamics in giving. The dictator determines if and how much giving is to occur whereas the receiver represents the charitable organization. Studies have found gender differences in that women are typically noted to give the receiver a higher percentage of the resources compared to what men offer. In one such study, Piff et al. (2010) used this game to see if there were differences in lower or higher income participants in giving. Although they did not find a gender difference, they did find that participants with less income gave **more** than participants with higher income. The researchers noted that this result is consistent with national data showing that lower-income individuals give a higher percentage of their income to charities than upper-income individuals. This finding seems counterintuitive for several reasons. One is that higher income individuals make seemingly large donations, but when factored by how much they earn, the proportion is the more telling factor. Another counterintuitive point is that lower-income individuals have less resources than higher income individuals. The logic is that they need these resources more and have less to spare. However, the psychological explanation is that

306 *Cultivating Giving: Ideas for Advancement Personnel*

the low-income individuals know what it is like to do without and to struggle, therefore, empathy can be easily activated.

Rand et al. (2016) conducted an analysis of 22 studies that used the *Dictator Game*. Altruism was noted to be deemed as expected in women and thereby making giving more intuitive for them. The researchers found that men and women with more masculine traits were less effected when given reduced time for deliberation than women with more feminine traits. The authors reasoned that when given less time to decide, one must rely on internal beliefs that are often developed through stereotypes.

Regarding aging and altruism, Sparrow et al. (2021) also conducted a meta-analysis (review of studies) with over 16 studies and over 1,500 participants. The studies used different measures such as the Dictator Game and self-report altruism scale. They found that older adults were more altruistic than younger adults. This finding fits with what we know from developmental theory and research. As Erickson's psychosocial theory, covered in Chapter 2, indicated, people become more "generative" as they get older, seeking to give back and to leave a legacy. This is an important factor for development personnel to know and to offer donors a variety of options to express their legacy.

Touré-Tillery and Fishbach (2017) studied the impact distance had on peoples' perceptions regarding their impact on giving. They found that people believed the impact to be greater when they gave to causes closer to them in proximity. They also found that the amount of donations was larger for closer causes. To this last point, the researchers looked at data from over 170,000 alumni from a large US university. They found that the amount donated increased as the alumni lived closer to the university. This study, in a series of six studies, measured "perceived impact" as determined by proximity, on one's motivation to give. When people believed the need was far from them, they were less likely to give, thinking their impact was less powerful. For those in the field of fundraising, it would be advantageous to highlight the location of a cause being nearby to activate this belief. For causes abroad or further in distance, making the case for the need on a more humanistic level in that the gift helps not only a specific locale but also humankind, maybe a way to combat the tendency for people to belief less close is less significant.

Cultivating Giving: Ideas for Advancement Personnel **307**

Words Matter!

The wording of a solicitation has been studied for its impact on donor's giving. Koo et al. (2021) summarized the results of their five studies using American and Korean college students. The researchers noted that the path to increasing donors is different than the path to increasing the amount of a donation. They explain that motivation to express commitment to a cause is the deciding factor for donating whereas the amount of the donation is determined by the motivation to make progress in the cause. In their research, they found that messages that noted "express support" increased the number of contributors versus the messaging "make a difference." On the other hand, they found that "make a difference" messaging increased the amount of the donation more than "express support." Giving can be based on both motives. The strategy used depends on the goal. Are they looking to make a substantial difference or to give support to a cause? I recommend the use of both strategies, just not together. But to use the "express support" strategy to solicit new donors and the "make a difference" strategy for existing donors.

Donors decide primarily whether to give and if so, how much. As noted by the authors, the decision to give expresses commitment whereas the decision to give more expresses desire to make progress. Even small donations serve a role as they send a message of support. The gift shows them and others that they care about the cause. Symbolic giving boosts self-esteem and serves the role of increasing awareness to a cause. Making a difference type of giving is often large and serves to make a substantial impact on a goal.

Donor amounts are often increased when donations are matched (Karlan & List, 2007) and when donors believe others will follow suit in donating (Grant, 2007). Social learning theory maintains that people are more likely to engage in an activity if they see others doing it. It is important then that solicitations emphasize that all size donations help and send a message of hope; for who wants to support an unfixable cause?

Lessons inferred from Kumar and Epley's 2023 studies mentioned earlier have implications for fundraisers in that donors should be reminded of the power of their giving. The appeal should focus on the benefit that will come from the donation, such

308 *Cultivating Giving: Ideas for Advancement Personnel*

as what the donation can purchase, but also the "warmth" aspect in the message the donation sends. An example is a solicitation that strive to "show our troops they are thought of by helping us reach 1,000 new donors." The "warmth" factor in the solicitation could offset the tendency a giver may have to underestimate their monetary contribution, thereby increasing the chances that they give, even in small amounts. Further, small amounts accumulate! We have all said, "If I could have a dollar for every time x" realizing the accumulating benefit of many little things. Imagine a financial campaign in which everyone in an organization of 1,000 employees contributed $1 per week to a cause. That would accumulate to $52,000.00 a year! Imagine an even larger audience. In December 2022, Amazon started a program called "tip my driver." Amazon customers, at no cost to them, could tell *Alexia* or the *Echo* device or app to tip their Amazon driver. Amazon then gave the driver $5.00 (see program description online at Amazon https://www.amazon.com/b?ie=UTF8&node=18271648011). Once 1 million "thanks yous" were received within 36 hours and the program ended. A few weeks later, Amazon infused more funds to briefly reopen the program for another 1 million thank yous. This is another example of how small contributions could really add up. If we all do a little, big things happen! Imagine how the Amazon driver felt as their virtual tip jar grew! Cha-ching$. As of the date of writing, it is unknown if Amazon will run the program in 2023 and beyond. Looking closely into this interesting program, it is not without controversary. The program was rolled out the day Amazon was being sued for allegations of previous tip fraud, directing tips to pay for employees' salaries, which led to a settlement in 2021.

Another study on the wording of a solicitation found interesting results. A study by Howe et al. (2021) explored the impact of adding a statement about working together in a solicitation. The two groups consisted of the "normative information appeal" and the "working-together normative appeal." The normative information appeal provided facts about the need for financial support in Haiti whereas the working-together normative appeal provided the same facts but added an appeal to join with others and donate. Sixty-four Stanford University students of varying ethnicities were split into two groups. Upon viewing one of the two flyers, they were asked if they would be inclined to donate to this case and if

Cultivating Giving: Ideas for Advancement Personnel **309**

so, how much. They found that participants were more interested in and had higher giving when the solicitation referenced the idea of working together toward a common goal versus the normative statement. The researchers concluded that focusing on working together increases motivation to give and the amount given. Several variations of this study occurred which demonstrated similar results. In one variation, participants amount of paper towels usage in a public restroom was reduced just by displaying a sign encouraging patrons to "join others" in helping to save the environment. The researchers further explained that creating an appeal focused only on social norm creates pressure from the individual whereas adding a phrase to cue collective efforts reduces the individual pressure and increases motivation to contribute to a group effort. These appeals encourage others to act for the common good. Another study on the effect of the solicitation (Croson & Shang, 2011) found when donors were told the amount of a previous donor, i.e., "we had another donor that gave $X dollars," the amount of the donation increased. Donors not given this "social information" were found to donate a similar amount as their donation a year prior.

A recent study (Zürn et al., 2021) experimented on the concept of "maybe." The researchers were curious if adding the option of "maybe" to an ask for help would increase the number and amount of donations. The premise of this potential factor was rationalized by the authors in that saying "maybe" already provides the giver with the "benefit" aspect of the cost analysis. The giver can be seen as generous in their own view and to that of the receiver. As with most studies, the findings are multifaceted and fascinating. These researchers found that participants were more likely to agree to help their friends when the need increased in certainty, whereas the opposite was true with strangers. When a stranger's need was a possibility, the individual was more likely to endorse helping, than when the need was certain. The authors explained that it may be that when friends add a "maybe" to their need for help it signals a reduced need, whereas when a stranger does so, it signals reduced cost to the giver. How would these results impact donors to a cause as there are varying degrees of involvement as opposed to "friend" and "stranger." The researchers addressed this in another part of their study with 664 US residents who were given the option of donating the small amount of money earned

310 *Cultivating Giving: Ideas for Advancement Personnel*

for participating in the survey to a national charity. The "maybe" donation was mimicked by the researcher's note that there will be a percentage of donations that will be revoked. There was a control group that was not told that a percentage of the donations would be canceled. The findings showed that 74% of the participants in the "maybe" group donated whereas 69% in the control group donated. This difference was statistically significant. The reason for this difference is believed to be that the "maybe" group was able to receive the "warm glow" of giving without the certainty of loss (cost). Whereas the control group had to consider the cost analysis, the loss, when presented with the opportunity to give.

In an online survey of over 5,000 participants, Bruine de Bruin and Ulqinaku (2021) were interested in determining if one's thoughts on their own death would impact their willingness to donate. They conducted a study in which participants were randomly assigned to either a "mortality salience" group in which they were asked questions about their fear of death before given a donation opportunity or a control group in which they completed the survey and donation opportunity, then answered question about fear of death. Donation opportunity consisted of four options. Findings showed that the mortality salience group made higher donations. The control group, seeing the fear of death questions after the donation opportunity, was found to have lower fear of death than the mortality salience group. This finding suggests that giving, being a form of preserving one's legacy, may buffer the fear of death.

Pietraszkiewicz et al. (2017) explored how the factor of language used in a proposal or request for donations can impact the response. They summarized previous literature and found language depicting genuineness, warmth, and prosocial attitudes aid acts of giving. The trustworthiness and sincerity of the communicator is important for the donor when deciding whether to fund a cause or not. Words that focused on human need versus profits were found to have higher support from donors. Feminine language (words of inclusion and affiliation) was also found to lead to more success in fundraising than masculine language (words associated with money and profit). Previous research also showed that nonprofit campaigns reached their goal quicker than for-profit campaigns (as cited in Pietraszkiewicz et al., 2017). Pietraszkiewicz et al.'s (2017) study found that the more prosocial words used the higher the campaign success and the higher the number of donors.

Cultivating Giving: Ideas for Advancement Personnel   311

Jen Shang is the co-founder and co-director of the Institute for Sustainable Philanthropy in the United Kingdom. She is identified as the first and, as of this writing, only philanthropic psychologist who explores donor behavior. Shang et al. (2020) studied the wording of a solicitation as it impacts one's sense of moral identity. They studied various terms and gender as they impacted donations. The researchers noted that solicitations should prompt potential donors to reflect on who they are, their moral identity. Connecting an appeal with an individual's core sense of meaning increases the chances of giving. Gender differences were found in that woman increased giving when solicitations used the words "kind" and "compassionate," whereas men increased their giving to words like "strong," "responsible," and "loyal." Shang offers a powerful reminder that "your 'thank-you' is just as important as your 'please'." Follow-up on a donation aids the relationship and trust. In addition to promptly thanking donors, Shang noted that it is important to let donors know the result of the campaign and how their donations helped. Shang noted that a mistake made in an appeal is to focus on the organization rather than the donor. A "donor-centric" appeal is critical. An example provided is of a hospital soliciting donors from previous patients. The appeal noted that the patient trusted the hospital in their time of need and now the hospital is asking for their help.

Inspiring Donors/Dial Up Giving and Preventing Donor Fatigue

Organizations need to spend time to determine what motivates the donor. What aspects of the cause motivate them? Instead of focusing on "closing the deal" or giving a sales pitch, the development personnel would do well to listen to the interests and motives of the donor. Find out what their reason to donate may be. Donors themselves ask the question, "Why should I donate to this cause?" Recently, I saw a statement on a fundraising appeal that stated: "Need a reason to donate?" It seems that an appeal that imbeds an answer to this question would likely entice more donors. Make the reason explicit, but research to ensure that the messaging is consistent with the targeted audience. Another effective appeal is to know that most people give in some manner or the other. Tailor the appeal to why they should give to your cause. Perhaps one

312 *Cultivating Giving: Ideas for Advancement Personnel*

of the better examples I have come across was years ago, a nonprofit I worked for started their fundraising campaign by asking employees to support the cause. Development personnel made the statement "We all donate somewhere.... why not it be here, where you work?"

In soliciting donations, it would behoove the cause to appeal to one's emotions and social connection, but not to the point of inspiration porn, but just enough to activate empathy and the release of feel-good neurochemical at the thought of giving. Remembering Gaesser and Fowler (2020) work reviewed in Chapter 5, advancement personnel would be wise to capitalize on one's history of giving, evoking such memories in donors. This can be done through pictures, stories, articles, etc. Having the donor recall their experiences and share their ideas on their further involvement can be a powerful way to remind the donor of their connection and identity as a giver. Another concept impacting the donor is that of "psychic numbing," a term identified by Paul Slovic (2007), referring to feeling overwhelmed by the enormity of need. To offset this, focusing on smaller appeals to make a difference helps the donor feel less overwhelmed and view themselves as able to make an impact.

Nonprofit organizations have started to engage in joint ventures with other nonprofits, for-profits, and governmental agencies to pool resources to serve a common goal. A powerful example was mentioned above with JBJ Soul Foundation who works with local government and other nonprofit entities to provide services to food and home insecurities. Another example is a bingo hall, *State Street Bingo Entertainment Hall* (https://www.statestreet-bingo.com/about) located in Pennsylvania. It is owned and operated by Transplant Alliance Foundation, a 501c3 charity raising money for the Transplant Alliance Foundation (TAF). The website declares that 100% of proceeds go to TAF. The bingo hall works with other nonprofits to run fundraising events benefiting both organizations. They devote set nights to community fundraising and other nights to theme-based bingos, creating a "something for everyone" effect. Their story, like many, started from grief and loss. As noted on their webpage:

> In 1998 our foundation's founder was told her husband died and she donated his organs. Six years later she was told she would not survive without a lung transplant. It was during this

Cultivating Giving: Ideas for Advancement Personnel 313

time she met a lot of people that were going through similar medical problems, but they had the added anxiety of having to deal with co-pays and co-insurance. She made it her mission to help people pay their medical expenses. In 2007 she started Transplant Alliance. In 2015, Transplant Alliance became a full public charity. Our Bingo program helps fund our foundation's charitable giving efforts. We are proud of the fact that 100% of the profit from Bingo is donated to help people pay for their organ transplant related medical expenses. We also donate to other charities that work with organ transplant patients.

Most people in the US do not have enough health insurance to pay for all the co-pay's and other out of pocket expenses of a major surgery like an organ transplant. If you have a standard PPO, you have co-insurance. That co-insurance is generally about 20%. It is not out of the norm to have a $1,000,000 medical bill. With the standard 80/20 PPO, you would be responsible for $200,000. Now imagine if you were the breadwinner of the house and no longer getting a paycheck.

Some fundraising campaigns identify monetary levels for donations, such as tiers ($10, $20, etc.). This will increase the amount of a donation when the donor is on the high end of the previous level, encouraging them to round up to get to the next level. However, once at the low end of the next level, they tend to stay there at just enough to be in the range. Other ideas and resources are offered through Greater Good Science Center, University of California, Berkeley (https://ggsc.berkeley.edu/). This research center conducts research and offers resources on a variety of topics for promoting good. Their website description is: "Our programs turn cutting-edge research into practical resources for happiness, compassion, and the meaningful life." Resources for individuals, schools, workplaces, etc. consist of online resources, magazines, podcast, speakers, to name a few.

Balancing Donor Retention with Donor Fatigue

Getting donors to give to an organization is a challenge as well as getting them to return year after year, known as retention. Retention rates are important for an organization to calculate as they impact their planning and achievement of financial goals. QGiv.

314 *Cultivating Giving: Ideas for Advancement Personnel*

com notes that the average retention rate is 40–45% (https://www.qgiv.com/blog/donor-retention/). This means that approximately 55–60% of donors do not give again the following year. It seems to me that these numbers speak to the need to cultivate a relationship with donors, matching meaning, and keeping communication strong.

Balancing communications with donors is more of an art than a science. There needs to be communication to understand a donor's motivation, to welcome them into the community, to solicit donations, to follow-up with a thank you, share impact stories, and information on how their donation was used. Communications should not just be around giving, but also on the community and program functions. Reminders may also be needed to aid retention. All these forms of communication, if not balanced appropriately, can lead to ill effects on the donor, such as donor fatigue, as mentioned in Chapter 7.

Donor fatigue can result in feelings of bombardment and burnout, causing the donor to stop giving. The donor is likely receiving solicitations from a variety of sources creating further fatigue. They may become desensitized to all the needs and appeals for help. Donors become overwhelmed with the enormity of requests. This experience is especially debilitating if one does not see the outcome of their efforts. It makes them believe that the problems cannot be solved. In addition to balancing the frequency and types of communication sent to donors, organizations should show their outcomes and invite donors to see the work being done. Organizations must be prudent in utilizing volunteer time and expertise. Volunteers need a role and specific tasks to feel a sense of purpose. They need to see how their efforts are part of a larger collective. Having this sense of purpose is what fuels volunteers. They will stop volunteering if their role is ambiguous or unvalued.

The NonProfitPRO (https://www.nonprofitpro.com/) article, "The reality of donor fatigue and strategies to overcome it," offers strategies for nonprofit organizations to utilize to prevent donor fatigue. These tips are summarized as follows:

1 Look for other income streams. These may include planned giving and fundraising partnerships.
2 Personalize solicitations.

Cultivating Giving: Ideas for Advancement Personnel **315**

3 Develop a community around the mission.
4 Encourage automatic giving such as monthly or quarterly to prevent the need for continual solicitations.
5 Be transparent regarding the outcome of donations by publishing tax forms (990), reports, and success stories.

Balanced and personalization communication aids a giver's sense of value. Follow-up and giving thanks can go a long way toward preventing donor fatigue and other ill effects.

The Power of a "Thank You"

Follow-up to a donation and a thank you are important. People want to feel appreciated, otherwise, it may affect their motivation to give again. Several interviewees commented on times in which they were not given credit or someone else got the credit for their giving. In describing his feelings on giving, Tom stated:

> At times I was not given credit for giving where others were. When I reflect on these issues, I feel bad, but it does not make me stop giving again. Recently, I have slowed down on outside giving because of the zero return – so I focus on my family and the outside world did not matter so much anymore.

He also recalled a time when he gave of his time and expertise:

> I gave a lot to that effort. After a while, I saw it was not going to mount to anything, but I continued to do it out of commitment. I did it because I hoped someone would do it for my kid someday.

Showing gratitude, as discussed in Chapter 6, is important for the giver to feel good about their efforts. When gratitude is not expressed, the giver can only extrapolate the outcome. Shang offers a powerful reminder that "your 'thank-you' is just as important as your 'please'." Following-up on a donation aids the relationship and trust. In addition to promptly thanking donors, Shang notes that it is important to let donors know the result of the campaign and how their donations helped.

316 *Cultivating Giving: Ideas for Advancement Personnel*

However, like communication, there is a balance to strike with how an organization thanks their donors. Existing literature, such as that by Chao (2017) noted that thank-you gifts for charitable giving undermine giving. However, a study by Huang et al. (2021) found that participants believed that thank-you gifts would promote giving. The emotional gain hypothesis would indicate that a donor would give more when given a thank you that focused on the emotional value of the donation over the monetary value. Other cautionary notes regarding donor recognition were noted by Savary and Goldsmith (2020). These researchers hypothesized that public recognition for a small donation would reduce the potential for a donation. They explained that we tend to use our actions to draw conclusions about ourselves in a process called "self-signaling motivation." When offered recognition, an individual may experience ambiguity, not sure if they are donating for the cause or for the recognition. This phenomenon is consistent with the notion that offering an extrinsic reward negatively affects intrinsic motivation, a phenomenon discussed earlier called "over-justification effect." Savary and Goldsmith did indeed find that when given an opportunity to make a small donation, people who were told that their donation would be private donated more often than those that were told they would be publicly recognized for their donation. The researchers concluded that public recognition may undermine a person's sense of altruism. In application, I think of the shamrock campaign for muscular dystrophy. Grocery store cashiers encourage customers to buy a paper shamrock and put their name on it to be displayed around the store. This is also a familiar campaign for *Alex's Lemonade Stand*, but the slip of paper is a lemon. Many people do not write their full name, sometimes only their first name, other times a witty or inspiring message is written. It is the latter that makes me wonder if the donor was preserving their "self-signaling motivation" as altruistic by remaining anonymous while being publicly displayed. The above findings warrant some balance in that with small donations, it may be that the donor does not want others to know of their amount unless it was of great value. If too high of an amount, donors may prefer anonymity so not to be bombarded by solicitations from others. The best way to balance recognition is to allow the donor to decide.

Cultivating Giving: Ideas for Advancement Personnel 317

Although there are mixed findings as to whether thank-you gifts should be provided or not. It is safe to assume that a letter and small gift would be effective. A larger gift would likely spark a transactional mindset as opposed to preserving the generous intent of the giver. A small memento, such as a t-shirt of the cause maybe also serve to increase others awareness of the cause. These small thank yous are private and essential. Keeping donors abreast of the use of funds donated through annual reports and program updates is respectful and includes the donors in the community as opposed to being a silent partner. Contact donors for reasons other than monetary solicitation. Knowing specifically what an organization is doing with their donation would yield more pleasure in the giving process. Ideally, information on where funds will be used is specified in the solicitation. This is not always the case and will deter potential donors. For example, community donation boxes that do not specify where the items are going are likely to have people pass on donating. Here is an example of a hopeful worded appeal with a follow-up message:

Dear (potential donor's name),

I am delighted to have the opportunity to communicate again with you and hope that you are well. As you know, we are living in critical times regarding saving our environment. The enormity is too much for a small few to bear and needs the collective efforts from us all. Small actions by many can and do make significant changes. We have already seen this to be the case with the current lowering of global emissions by X%, all due to the support of people like you that have donated funds to increasing awareness through education and marketing. Our work is not complete and for that reason, I invite you to give your support once again to (organization's name) efforts to save the earth.

Your gift will go toward cleaning oceans, planting trees, developing alternative energy sources, and educating the world about recycling. Much work remains. All gifts help make a difference, the choice is up to you. Some ways in which your generous donation will be put to work include:

- A donation of $10 pays for 50 Balsam Fir tree seeds.
- Donations of $100 pays for a day of care for ten wildlife effected by oil spills.

318   *Cultivating Giving: Ideas for Advancement Personnel*

- Any size donations can also go toward the $70,000 cost for an autonomous underwater vehicle (AUV) used to clean up the ocean.

Thank you for your support and commitment to ensuring our environment continues to thrive. Please follow our website to see your efforts making a difference!
Sincerely,
(organization representative name and contact)

Follow-up message:

Dear (donor's name),
Thank you for your recent donation of $XX! This generous donation is being used to buy seeds for our upcoming panting season. With your kind gift, we can purchase enough seeds to plant 100 trees! Thanks to the many donors like you and the many hands that will take part in the planting, 300 acres of reforestation can occur. What an impact this will make on the environment. Be sure to follow our website to see pictures of the progress we are making during the planting season.
Together, we will continue to make a difference.
Sincerely,
(organization representative name and contact)

Considering the above factors and research findings. Table 10.1 is provided to organize some strategies for fundraising.

Organizations should ensure that they are providing regular notifications of impact to donors. Let them know how their time and money were utilized and the difference that it made. Make it tangible to the giver so they know how the resources were utilized. The American Red Cross tallies the number of lives a blood donor saved with each donation. Make sure appeals are hopeful and not constantly about the dire need, as this can make the donor feel as though their efforts would not matter. Be sure to build a relationship with donors and involve them in the community, inviting them to the facility to show the work being done. Without opportunities, it can feel to the donor very one-sided in that the organization is only wanting their money/time. If this one-sided relationship was occurring with a friend and it continued, it is likely

Cultivating Giving: Ideas for Advancement Personnel 319

Table 10.1 Areas of Fundraising Focus and Strategies

Before event	*During event*	*After event*
Planning the campaign/event	**Collecting funds**	**Thank you and follow-up**
Set monetary goal.	Provide link or QR code for electronic donations.	Send personalized thank-you letter.
Brainstorm ideas.	Offer donor challenges.	Let donor know the outcome of fundraiser.
Recruit volunteers and assign specific roles.	Offer small donor incentives.	Continue regular communication for more than solicitations.
Solicit donations for goods and services (have a letter ready).	Seek out matching funds or workplace matches.	The donor decides if the gift is anonymous or not.
Take time to know donor's motivation.	Ask for a commitment, pledge or a "maybe."	Award small prize or reward.
Marketing the campaign/event	Help donor see any compounding benefit to gift.	Invite donor for a tour or other ways of getting involved.
Advertisement: low fee or free social media sites.	Highlight models of other givers.	Send out solicitations sparingly throughout the year. Ideally during set intervals.
Those involved in the cause, recipients, employees, and volunteers are the best marketers. They are testament to the mission.	Help donor see other budget pockets for giving, e.g., "Enjoy a fun night out while support a valuable cause."	
Prepare props that tell the story/mission.	Remind donor that all levels of giving help.	
Request free airtime on the radio/podcasts to make public service announcement of fundraising campaign.	Make explicit why one should give to this specific cause.	
Use warm, hopeful, and collaborative language in solicitations and announcements.		

(Continued)

320 *Cultivating Giving: Ideas for Advancement Personnel*

Table 10.1 (Continued)

Before event	During event	After event
Make a donor-centric appeal.		
Plan for comfortable and sensory pleasing ambiance.		
Identify the cause as local. If not local, make connection to humanity clear.		
Spark empathy without exploiting.		

that we would eventually not tolerate it. This is true in our relationships with organizations which explains some of what happens with donor fatigue.

Strategies for advancement summarized from previous chapters:

- Chapter 1: People have a variety of experiences that have shaped their empathy. The first step in creating empathy is to create awareness of the need.
- Chapter 2: Fundraisers that offer an opportunity to win a prize, a small gift, or a tangible incentive may increase the behavior of giving.
- Chapter 3: Be sure to promote a variety of methods for giving such as time and resources, not just monetary. Offer education around the option of making a legacy commitment through an insurance policy or a Will.
- Chapter 4: Being a nonprofit is not enough to earn donor trust. Be sure to be transparent about financials and programming.
- Chapter 5: When we think about our good fortune or think about our future in favorable ways, we are more likely to help others. There are many physical and psychological benefits to giving, be sure to maximize these good feelings for donors. Fundraising should elicit effects or mirror neurons by sharing stories and visuals of the cause.
- Chapter 6: Expressing gratitude is healthy and leads to more prosocial behaviors.

Cultivating Giving: Ideas for Advancement Personnel **321**

- Chapter 7: Pace solicitations so not to create giving fatigue. Be sure to help doors see the positive outcome to their giving.
- Chapter 8: Encourage compound giving, provide examples, and offer strategies for compound giving.
- Chapter 9: Harness the energy and eagerness of children in causes. Present needs concretely with visuals depicting percentages so that younger givers do not need to infer.
- Chapter 10: See the key points below.

Key Points

- An effective method of persuasion is to use facts and pleasurable sensory materials in solicitations.
- Capitalize on a variety of mental budgets donors have in their minds.
- Infrequent or exceptional solicitations tend to garner more support than regularly needed solicitations.
- Data continually shows that lower-income individuals give a higher percentage of their income to charities than upper-income individuals.
- Women are consistently found to give more than men, a finding explained by cultural expectations.
- People tend to prefer to give locally over far away.
- Research finds that wording a solicitation with the phrase "make a difference" yielded more support whereas "express support" impacts new donors.
- There is empirical evidence that the path to increasing donors is different than the path to increasing the amount of a donation.
- The donation appeal should focus on the good that will come from the donation along with acknowledgment of the message of support being sent by donating.
- Focusing on "working together" in an appeal increases donor motivation to give and the amount given.
- Giving, being a form of preserving one's legacy, may buffer the fear of death.
- Language that is genuine, warm, and prosocial increases giving.
- Solicitations should prompt potential donors to reflect on who they are by strategically using words pertaining to morality.
- Tailor the appeal to why they should give to your cause.

322   *Cultivating Giving: Ideas for Advancement Personnel*

- Appeal to one's emotions and social connection, but not to the point of "inspiration porn."
- Build relationships with donors at all levels.

Action Steps

- Consider the working of an appeal; making it hopeful that one can make an impact.
- In fundraising efforts, ensure a role for all that want to be involved.
- Express gratitude for support and communicate for other reasons outside fundraising.

References

Aronson, E., Wilson, T.D., Sommers, S.R., Page-Gould, E., & Lewis, N. (2023). *Social Psychology*, 11th edition. New York: Pearson.

Bruine de Bruin, W., & Ulqinaku, A. (2021). Effect of mortality salience on charitable donations: Evidence from a national sample. *Psychology and Aging*, 36(4), 415–420. https://doi.org/10.1037/pag0000478

Chao, M. (2017). Demotivating incentives and motivation crowding out in charitable giving. *Proceedings of the National Academy of Sciences of the United States of America*, 114(28), 7301–7306. https://doi.org/10.1073/pnas.1616921114

Croson, R., & Shang, J.Y. (2011). Social influences in giving: Field experiments in public radio. In: Oppenheimer, D. M., Olivola, C. Y. (eds) *The Science of Giving: Experimental Approaches to the Study of Charity*, 65–80. New York: Taylor and Francis. https://doi.org/10.4324/9780203865972

DeSteno, D., Baumann, J., Bartlett, M.Y., & Williams, L.A. (2010). Gratitude as moral sentiment: Emotion-guided cooperation in economic exchange. *Emotion*, 10(2), 289–293. https://doi.org/10.1037/a0017883

Dyble, M., van Leeuwen, A.J., & Dunbar, R.I.M. (2014). Gender differences in Christmas gift-giving. *Evolutionary Behavioral Sciences*, 9(2), 140–144. https://doi.org/10.1037/ebs0000022

Gaesser, B., & Fowler, Z. (2020). Episodic simulation of prosocial interaction: Investigating the roles of memory and imagination in facilitating a willingness to help others. *Psychology of the Consciousness: Theory, Research, and Practice*, 7(4), 376–387. https://doi.org/10.1037/cns0000232

Cultivating Giving: Ideas for Advancement Personnel **323**

Grant, A.M. (2007). Relational job design and the motivation to make a prosocial difference. *Academy of Management Review*, 32(2), 393–417. https://doi.org/10.5465/amr.2007.24351328

Greater Good Science Center, University of California, Berkeley. https://ggsc.berkeley.edu/

Haddad, D. (September 11, 2000). Giving and the psychological reasons behind it. *NonProfit PRO*. https://www.nonprofitpro.com/post/giving-and-the-psychological-reasons-behind-it/

Howe, L.C., Carr, P.B., & Walton, G.M. (2021). Normative appeals motivate people to contribute to collective action problems more when they invite people to work together toward a common goal. *Journal of Personality and Social Psychology: Attitude and Social Cognition*, 121(2), 215–238. https://doi.org/10.1037/pspa0000278

Huang, H., Zhang, Y., Lv, J., Jiang, T., Zhang, X., Chen, X., & Luo, Y. (2021). Laypeople's belief of the influence of thank-you gifts on charitable giving. *Social Psychology*, 52(6), 331–342. https://doi.org/10.1027/1864-9335/a000461

Jonason, P.K., Tost, J., & Koenig, B.L. (20012). Sex differences and personality correlates of spontaneously generated reasons to give gifts. *Journal of Social, Evolutionary, and Cultural Psychology*, 6(2), 181–192. https://doi.org/10.1037/h0099216

Kang, Y., Williams, L.E., Clark, M.S., Gray, J.R., & Bargh, J.A. (2011). Physical temperature effects on trust behavior: The role of insula. *Social Cognitive and Affective Neuroscience*, 6, 507–515. https://doi.org/10.1093/scan/nsq077

Karlan, D., & List, J.A. (2007). Does price matter in charitable giving? Evidence from a large-scale natural field experiment. *The American Economic Review*, 97(5), 1774–1793. https://doi.org/10.1257/aer.97.5.1774

Koo, M., Fishbach, A., & Park, H.K. (2021). What to say to round up more donors, or bigger donations. *Motivation Science*, 7(3), 291–305. https://doi.org/10.1037/mot0000228

Kumar, A., & Epley, N. (2023). A little goes a long way: Underestimating the positive impact of kindness on recipients. *Journal of Experimental Psychology: General*, 152(1), 236–252. https://doi.org/10.1037/xge0001271

LaBarge, M.C., & Stinson, J.L. (2014). The role of mental budgeting in philanthropic decision-making. *Nonprofit and Voluntary Sector Quarterly*, 43, 993–1013. https://doi.org/0899764013489776

Leslie, L.M., Snyder, M., & Glomb, T.M. (2013). Who gives? Multilevel effects of gender and ethnicity on workplace charitable giving. *Journal of Applied Psychology*, 98(1), 49–62. https://doi.org/10.1037/a0029943

324 *Cultivating Giving: Ideas for Advancement Personnel*

Lynott, D., Corker, K., Connell, L., & O'Brien, K. (2017). The effect of haptic and ambient temperature experience on prosocial behavior. *Archives of Scientific Psychology*, 5, 10–18. https://doi.org/10.1037/arc0000031

NonProfitPRO. https://www.nonprofitpro.com/

Pietraszkiewicz, A., Soppe, B., & Formanowicz, M. (2017). Go pro bono: Prosocial language as a success factor in crowdfunding. *Social Psychology*, 48(5), 265–278. https://doi.org/10.1027/1864-9335/a000319

Piff, P.K., Kraus, M.K., Cote, S., Cheng, B.H., & Keltner, D. (2010). Having less, giving more: The influence of social class on prosocial behavior. *Journal of Personality and Social Psychology*, 99(5), 771–784. https://doi.org/10.1037/a0020092

QGiv.com. *Donor retention: The essential guide for fundraisers.* https://www.qgiv.com/blog/donor-retention/

Rand, D.G., Brescoll, V.L., Everett, J.A., Capraro, V., & Barcelo, H. (2016). Social heuristics and social roles: Intuition favors altruism for women but not for men. *Journal of Experimental Psychology: General*, 145(4), 389–396. https://doi.org/10.1037/xge0000154

Savary, J., & Goldsmith, K. (2020). Unobserved altruism: How Self-signaling motivations and social benefits shape willingness to donate. *Journal of Experimental Psychology: Applied*, 26(3), 538–550. https://doi.org/10.1037/xap0000261

Shang, J., Reed, A., Sargeant, A., & Carpenter, K. (2020). Marketplace donation: The role of moral discrepancy and gender. *Journal of Marketing Research*, 57(2), 375–393. https://doi.org/10.1177/0022243719892592

Slovic, P. (2007). "If I look at the mass I will never act": Psychic numbing and genocide. *Judgment and Decisions Making*, 2(2), 79–95. https://doi.org/10.1017/S1930297500000061

Sparrow, E.P., Swirsky, L.T., Kudus, F., & Spaniol, J. (2021). Aging and altruism: A meta-analysis. *Psychology and Aging*, 30(1), 49–56. https://doi.org/10.1037/pag0000447

Storey, S., & Workman, L. (2013). The effects of temperature priming on cooperation in the iterated prisoner's dilemma. *Evolutionary Psychology*, 11, 52–67. https://doi.org/10.1177/147470491301100106

Sussman, A., Sharma, E., & Alter, A. (2015). Framing charitable donations as exceptional expenses increases giving. *Journal of Experimental Psychology: Applied*, 21(2), 130–139. https://doi.org/10.1037/xap0000047

Touré-Tillery, M., & Fishbach, A. (2017). Too far to help: The effect of perceived distance on the expected impact and likelihood of charitable action. *Journal of Personality and Social Psychology*, 112(6), 860–876. https://doi.org/10.1037/psp000089

Zürn, M., Gerten, J., & Topolinski, S. (2021). Maybe favors: How to get more good deeds done. *Journal of Experimental Psychology: Applied*, 27(3), 503–507. https://doi.org/10.1037/xap0000357

Index

Note: **Bold** page numbers refer to tables; *italic* page numbers refer to figures.

Alex's Lemonade Stand Foundation 256; *Alex's Lemonade Stand* 316
altruism 10, 24, 32, 58, 83, 125, 147, 222–3, 306, 316
altruistic giving 46
Altruistic punishment 24
Amazon Smiles 124
American Red Cross 84–5, 87, *114–15*, 318
American Society for the Prevention of Cruelty to Animals 119; ASPCA 119–21
aneconomic 50
Authentic Happiness 29, **30**, 240

Bandura, A. 7, **23**, 42–4; Bandura's Social Learning Theory **23**, 42–5
benefits of giving 19, 34, 138–9, 141, 221
Better Business Bureau 111; BBB 111–14
blind donation 248
blood donation 85, 263
Box Tops for Education 75
burnout 114, 180, 195–8, 200, 202–3, 205, 207, 210, 214, 219, 230, 236, 293, 314
bystander effect 9, 46, 252

Campbells Labels for Education 75
charity 5, 6, 32, 56, 61, 64, 91, 112–13, 124–5, 147, 191, 242, 302, 310, 312–13
Charity Navigator 70, 82, 88, 112, 116, 119–23, 125, **127**, 130
Charity Watch 71, 112, 116, 120, 122, **127**, 130
cognitive dissonance 47, 50, 59, 153, 201
compassion 6–7, 31, 58, 81, 88–9, 94, 97, 133, 200, 220, 222, 278, 280, 285, 294, 313
compassion fatigue 180, 195, 196, 200–201, 203, 207, 214, 219, 236
Compliment Squad 76
compound giving 97, 135, 235, 247, 301, 321
contagion effect 11, 61, 133
corporate co-ops 93–94
cost-reward ratio 46
COVID-19 2, 32, 52, 57, 80, 95, 135, 196, 259, 263
crowdfunding 103, 248

Darwin, C. 22–3
Day, D. 44
desensitization 44–6, 200, 203, 252

326 *Index*

Dictator Game 165, 305–6
diffusion of responsibility 46, 252
donor fatigue 201–2, 209, 298, 311, 313–15, 320
donors choose 91, 95–96
dopamine 51, 145–7, 149, 158
double blind donation 62

earn to give 205, 224
egoistic giving 46
Elaboration Likelihood Model 300
Emma and Evan Foundation 76–7
empathy 5–9, 19, 27, 32, 37, 43, 46, 56, 89, 112, 133, 135, 148, **158**, 159, 162, 181, 193, 195–6, **218**, 219, 231, 235, 253, 271–3, 279, 282, 285, 287, 306, 312, 320
empathy-altruism hypothesis 7
Empowering Cuts 107
Erickson, E. 13, 15, **23**, 27, **28–9**, 88, 271, 306
evolution theory 22–4, 46

Fairtrade 126
501(c)3 77–8, 87, 96, 108–10, 113, 119, 245, 256, 260, 266–7
flow 31, 36, 198, 206, 262
41 Days 71
Four Rs of mindfulness 35, 231
Frankl, V. 156
fundamental attribution error 45, 65
Fundrazr 91, 241

generativity 13, 15, 27, **29**, 51, 88
generosity 9–10, 16, 18, 37, 43, 45, 48, 102, 143, 147, 161, 165–6, 172–3, 176, 189, 222, 226, 248, 265
generous favor giving 66
Give Back Box 242
GiveDirectly 91
giving defined 5
giving fatigue 180, 195–6, 201–3, 214–16, 219, 236, 321

GoFundMe 101, 103–105, 107, 241, 248
goodwill 19, 85
Goodwill Industries 117–19
Grameen Bank 91
gratitude 3, 11, 14, 34–5, 40, 66, 105, 107, 132, 134, 137, 141, 153–66, 168–77, 209, 235, 262, 276, 282, 285, 299, 315, 320, 322
GuideStar 122, **127**

Happiness Trifecta 147
health psychology i, **23**, 33–4
Help No Kid Go Hungry 71
helper's high 147
Heroic Imagination Project 252
Homeless Jesus 44
Humanistic theories 24, 29, 51

Indirect reciprocity 24-5
Influencer 81–2, 102
in-kind 55, 91, 108, 117, 182, 212, 230, 236, 249, 265, 286
inspiration porn 103, 312, 322
IRS 990 form 70–1, 76, 82, 87, 111, 116–17, 233, 244

Jon Bon Jovi (JBJ) Soul Foundation 70, 312
Just World Hypothesis 17

Karma 47, 96–7, 140, 193
Kin Selection 23–4
Kiva 72, 89–90, 103, 242

learned helplessness 144, 198, 252–3, 271, 293
legacy 3, 13–15, 17, 20, 24, 80, 92, 239, 256, 259, 261–6, 269, 306, 310, 320–1

Maimonides Ladder of Tzedakah 61, 64, 98, 157, 207
Maslow, A. 23–5, 27; Maslow's Hierarchy of needs **23**, 25, 27, 69, 159, 189, 219
matched favor giving 66

Index 327

mental budget 300–1, 321
micro-lending 89
mindful consumerism 293
mindfulness theory **23**, 33, 38, 89, 231
Ministry Watch 129
Mother Theresa 6
MrBeast 82, 102

New Jersey Anti-Hunger Coalition (NJAHC) 70
NICU Helping Hands Angel Gown®Program 76–7
nonprofit *see* 501(c)3
norm of reciprocity **23**, 46–8, 165

organ donation 83–4
Over Justification Effect 59, 146, 272, 316
oxytocin 33–4, 145, 147–9, 154, 157

Pausch, R. 88, 171
Pavlov, I. **23**
Pavlov's Classical Conditioning 41
pay it forward 60–1, 66, 70, 161–2, 165–6, 248, 252, 285
PERMAs 30, 32
philanthropy 6, 10, 56, 93, 201, 244, 298, 311
positive psychology i, 2, 3, 5, **23**, 24–5, 27, 29, 32–3, 88, 132, 138, 154, 158, 168, 180, 211, 217, 221
poverty 16, 18, 46, 55, 68–70, 98, 207, 224, 279
privilege 7–9, 17, 19, 72, 243
prosocial behavior 23–4, 45–6, 92, 222, 252, 273, 276, 278, 281, 299, 320

random acts of kindness 81, 134
reciprocal altruism 23–4
ripple effect i, 5, 19, 81, 94, 105, 132, 144, 239, 252, 262, 269, 283

Salvation Army 105, 118–19, 241
Save the Children 69, 71
secondary trauma 180, 195–6, 198–201, 203, 214, 219, 236
Seligman, M. 29–30, 32–3, 240
serotonin 145, 147, 149, 158
Shang, J. 309, 311, 315
Skinner, B.F. **23**
Skinner's Operant Conditioning **23**, 39
social exchange theory **23**, 48–9, 65–6, 162, 305
social learning theory 5, 7, 10, 12, **23**, 42, 92, 105, 173, 255, 307
social psychology 17–18, **23**, 45–7, 52, 59–60, 65, 67, 86, 104, 153, 176, 199, 224, 252–5, 272, 299, 300
Soles4Souls 82
stingy favor giving 66
survival of the fittest 22, **23**
Sweet Grace Ministries 76, 78–80
Swift, T. 16–17, 248
sympathy 6

Thank you 175, 184, 308, 314–18
The Giving Pledge 94
tithing 184
Transplant Alliance Foundation (TAF) 312–13

Urban Overload Hypothesis 46

vicarious reinforcement 43
voluntold 191

warm glow 138, 146, 310
Will 92
World Food Programme (WFP) 92
World Giving Index (WGI) 56, 98
World Happiness Report 31–2, 133, 138

Zakat 191

Printed in the United States
by Baker & Taylor Publisher Services